PERSONALITY

a cognitive view

PERSONALITY
a cognitive view

RONALD FORGUS
Professor of Psychology
Lake Forest College

BERNARD H. SHULMAN
Chairman, Dept. of Psychiatry
St. Joseph's Hospital, Chicago

PRENTICE-HALL, INC., ENGLEWOOD CLIFFS, N.J. 07632

Library of Congress Cataloging in Publication Data

Forgus, Ronald H (date).
   Personality.

   Bibliography: p.
   Includes index.
   1. Personality. 2. Cognition. I. Shulman,
Bernard H., joint author. II. Title.
BF698.F64   155.2   78-23529
ISBN 0-13-657882-9

© 1979 by Prentice-Hall, Inc., Englewood Cliffs, N.J. 07632

Printed in the United States of America

10 9 8 7 6 5 4 3 2 1

*Editorial/production supervision and interior design by Marina Harrison
Cover design by Saiki and Sprung
Manufacturing buyers: Phil Galea and Ray Keating*

Prentice-Hall International, Inc., *London*
Prentice-Hall of Australia Pty. Limited, *Sydney*
Prentice-Hall of Canada, Ltd., *Toronto*
Prentice-Hall of India Private Limited, *New Delhi*
Prentice-Hall of Japan, Inc., *Tokyo*
Prentice-Hall of Southeast Asia Pte. Ltd., *Singapore*
Whitehall Books Limited, *Wellington, New Zealand*

To our parents

MARIE AND WILLIAM FORGUS
HARRY AND YETTA SHULMAN

contents

Preface   **xiii**

1

A Context for the Study of Personality   **1**

Overview 2
Some Guiding Postulates for a Theory of Personality 4
Empirical Evidence for the Seven Postulates 6
Definition of Personality 9
Conventional Constructs Used to Describe Personality 11
Nomothetic and Idiographic Laws 18
Plan of the Book 19
A Note on the Sequence of Chapters 19

2

Theoretical Conceptions of Personality I:
Freud and the Behaviorists   **21**

Overview 22
Psychoanalysis: Sigmund Freud (1856–1939) 25
Erik H. Erikson (1902–   ) 36
Behavoristic Theories 39

3

Theoretical Conceptions of Personality II: Becoming the Active Organism   53

Overview 54
Analytic Psychology: Carl G. Jung (1875–1961) 55
Karen Horney (1885–1952) 61
Interpersonal Psychiatry: Harry Stack Sullivan (1892–1949) 65
Personology: Henry Murray (1893–   ) 71
Self Theory: Carl Rogers (1902–   ) 77
A Personalistic View: Gordon Allport (1897–1967) 80
Existential Theories 83
The Self-Theorists and the Seven Postulates 88

4

Theoretical Conceptions III: Field and Cognitive Theories   90

Overview 91
Holistic-Field Theory: Goldstein, Lewin, Angyal 92
Kurt Goldstein: Organismic Psychology (1878–1965) 92
Kurt Lewin (1890–1947) 94
Andras Angyal (1907–1960) 98
Individual Psychology: Alfred Adler (1870–1937) 101
Personal Constructs: George Kelly (1905–1966) 111

5

Personality and Adaptive Behavior   116

Overview 117
An Outline of the Perceptual System 119
Innate Physiological Needs 120
The Four Motive Systems 121
Murray's Classification of Needs 143

6

How the Perceptual System Organizes Personality Structure   144

Overview 145
Structure of Personality 147
Perception Organizes Motives 148
Cognitive Styles 155
Cognitive Information in Emotional Arousal 158

7

Personality Development I:
Conception to Preadolescence   **162**

Overview   163
Prenatal Foundations   164
The Essence of Personality Development is the Articulation
  of the Perceptual Program   170
The Perceptual (Information-Seeking) System   172
The Cognitive Motive: From Ignorance to Knowledge   180
The Attachment Motive: From Dependence to Affiliation   181
The Security Motive: From Fear to Courage   184
The Competence Motive: From Inadequacy to Competence   187
Social Influences on the Motive Systems   191

8

Personality Development II: Preadolescence
to Old Age   **194**

Overview   195
Self as an Organizer of Development   196
Preadolescence   201
Adolescence   208
Adulthood   215
Old Age   223

9

Psychodynamics I: Goal Behavior   **228**

Overview   229
The Person and the Situation   230
The Organization of Motivated Behavior   237
Emotions in Motivated Behavior   252

10

Psychodynamics II: Nature of Interpersonal
Behavior   **264**

Overview   265
Dependency   266
Affiliation   268
Aggression   273
Communication   281

11   **Personality Assessment   291**

Overview   292
Measuring the Person and the Situation   293
What Do We Assess: A Cognitive Perspective   294
Behavioral Methods   295
A Transition: Cognitive Social Learning Theory   297
Objective Tests: The Assessment of Traits   300
Projective Techniques   304
Cognitive Assessment Techniques   308
Interview and Life History Methods   314

12   **Maladaptive Personality: Psychopathology   321**

Overview   322
A Cognitive Explanation of Maladaptive Behavior   323
The Motive Systems and Pathology   323
Personality Disorders   327
Cognitive Style and Psychopathology   340
The Motive Systems in the Personality Disorders   340

13   **Changing Behavior and Personality   344**

Overview   345
The Cognitive Model of Personality Change   347
Ways of Changing Personality and Behavior   349
Cognitive Style and Behavior Change   369

Bibliography   375

Index   417

preface

The purpose of this book is to fill a gap that exists among the currently available textbooks on personality. Existing books either analyze representative personality theories or describe various aspects of personality. The latter are either eclectic in their approach or organize their presentation of personality around a particular point of view. These organizing perspectives have been either psychoanalysis, behaviorism, or social learning theory. While cognitive theory has been discussed in some texts, no book has as yet organized its presentation of personality around a cognitive viewpoint.

As the field of psychology has developed, it has become apparent to students of personality that cognitive structure is an important director of human behavior. Therefore, an adequate understanding of personality requires that we understand the role of cognitive structure in personality.

While the present text has a cognitive perspective, it covers a wide range of concerns to the student of personality. It discusses a representative selection of personality theories, personality structure, development, dynamics, assessment, maladaptive behavior and personality change. While we describe other interpretations of these phenomena, our integrating theme is a cognitive explanation.

We want to show that the scientific study of personality (often called personology) is not remote from the personal experiences of the student who may use this text or the concerns of the person who applies psychology in daily work—such as the clinical psychologist, industrial psychologist, counseling psychologist, or educator. Therefore we have included some pertinent material not found in other personality texts—such as the relationship between personality and adaptive behavior.

The book starts with an attempt to explain why a knowledge of personality enables a more accurate understanding and prediction of human behavior. Seven postulates are presented that state that personality is adaptive, learned, influenced by culture, unique to the individual and directs selective behavior. In our approach we try to show that a normative science of personality can still predict individual uniqueness.

The next section of the book surveys representative theoretical explanations of personality in order to provide a broader base against which the cognitive point of view can stand out in relief. In our order of presentation we move from the less cognitive to the more cognitive. These earlier chapters are intended to prepare the reader for a more balanced presentation of a cognitive treatment of personality—the subject matter of the rest of the book.

As in all books, we have had to make some choices. One of our choices was, whenever possible, to illustrate scientific principles with everyday examples, in order to help the student assimilate the scientific principle in the context of his experience (itself a cognitive teaching technique). Another choice came in our selection of research to discuss. We probably include less of the research in social learning and social psychology than some other texts, in order to include more research generated by cognitive theory. We originally had a chapter on the neurophysiological concomitants of personality structure and dynamics, but had to delete it because an adequate treatment of this subject made the book too long for the usual course in personality.

The research data to support our position comes from a wide range of sources—biology, ethology, anthropology, general experimental psychology, experimental personality research, and clinical personality research.

Our ideas have been influenced by all the psychologists who have contributed to cognitive and organismic psychology. The influence of the following scholars, who are mentioned in alphabetical order, can be particularly noted throughout the book: Alfred Adler, Gordon Allport, Albert Bandura, Rudolf Dreikurs, Donald Hebb, Jerome Kagan, George Kelly, Richard Lazarus, Kurt Lewin and the Gestalt psychologists, David McClelland, Henry Murray, Jean Piaget, Julian Rotter and Herman Witkin. To all these and many others we owe an intellectual debt.

All books require patient and competent clerical and secretarial help. Our special thanks to Mrs. Patricia Harlan, Mrs. Harriet Weichman, Miss Ann Rimland and Miss Lynne Williams. Their dedicated and conscientious service made the book possible. We also were fortunate in having as reviewers Norman Sundberg and others whose criticisms helped immeasurably to improve the book. Our gratitude goes also to Neale Sweet, the publisher's editor, who believed in and encouraged this book from the beginning.

On a more personal note, we are fondly and lovingly grateful to Phyllis Shulman who gave us spiritual and bodily sustenance during the long hours of composing this book.

R.F.

B.H.S.

1

a context
for the study
of
personality

OVERVIEW

Personality is not just the study of human behavior. It is the study of persons and personhood. Theories about personality do not focus on mental functions or separate acts of behavior; they focus on why a particular individual behaves the way he/she does. Different people react in different ways to the same objective stimulus. These diverse reactions presumably result from differences in each personality organization. If we know the nature of the personality organization, we can make a prediction about the influence it will exert on a response to a stimulus.

Seven postulates are offered to guide us in understanding the nature of personality organization. They emphasize that personality is adaptive, learned, influenced by culture, and unique to the individual. It determines the choice of response and the motivation; that is, it permits us to predict not only the response but also the functional utility of the response to the person. Some empirical evidence is evaluated which supports the postulates. The data lead us to the conclusion that the perceptual process is the mediator of all motivations.

Various definitions of personality can be grouped into six categories. Four of these categories are consistent with the hypothesis that perception directs selective response and they represent the departure point for our theory of personality. They emphasize that personality is a pattern, is hierarchically organized, leads to adaptive behavior, and is distinctively unique for each person.

A number of constructs have been used to describe the domain of personality: trait, role, type, temperament, character, and style. After reviewing how each of these constructs contributes to our understanding of personality, we conclude that the construct of "style" is the most congenial to the theory we espouse in this book.

Knowing "style" permits us to predict the individual case and thus to develop nomothetic or general laws about idiographic individual differences.

This chapter ends with a brief description of the plan of the book.

Scientists differ in the priorities they assign to various fields of scientific knowledge. While not all psychologists stress the importance of personality study, we consider it one of the most important areas in the science of psychology. Indeed, whatever we learn about human behavior can only be fully understood when we understand the person who does the behaving. Since different people respond differently to the same situation, a multiplicity of theories has been advanced to explain the organization of the person's behavior. Some representative personality theories will be discussed in Chapters 2 through 4. Personality theories do not focus on mental functions or separate acts of behavior; they focus on the individual and why that person behaves the way he/she does. Personality theories must therefore cut across the whole gamut of human life. They must explain who the person is, his motives, why his behavior sometimes seems unusual or inappropriate, why there are such vast differences between people, how the person became what he is, and how he can change.

If all this is true, personality would seem a most important field of study. All of the social sciences and the humanities—anthropology, sociology, political science, economics, history, art, linguistics, philosophy, perhaps even theology—would require some familiarity with personality

---

Box 1-1   Three different reactions to the same stimulus situation and what this implies about persons and the study of personality

Let us imagine that three college students are faced with the same stimulus situation—whether or not to accept the invitation of a dating acquaintance to go steady and have an exclusive relationship. Each considers the offer and each chooses a different path of action. The first chooses to go steady because of the security of having someone who will always be available even though there are doubts about really wanting this person. The second chooses to go steady because of the belief that this will be a sign of status and personal competence. The third person declines the offer, preferring the excitement of exploring a variety of interpersonal relationships at this relatively young age.

What issues about the personalities of these three people are raised by these different choices? What implications do these have for the study of personality?

We cannot explain behavior solely as a function of the stimulus condition. Individual behavior consists of making *adaptive* responses to environmental stimuli. Each person adapts in a characteristically *unique* way, which is influenced by *learning* and socialization experiences within a *culture*. This unique organization of personality gives rise to *selectivity* of responses which is directed by the person's perceptual makeup, and psychologists can *predict* behavior only if they understand the directed response in the context of the underlying personality *patterns*.

The seven key words in italic form the basis for the seven postulates that will guide our study of personality.

study. Every study that purports to discuss the human being has to know something about who this human being is. First and foremost, personality is not just the study of human behavior, it is the study of persons and personhood.

As we can deduce from the analysis in Box 1-1, personality study includes the following aspects: (1) the underlying motives and strategy of human behavior; (2) the organization of behavior into an overall system; (3) the relationship of the parts of the system to the whole; (4) the process of selection by which the person chooses particular ways of perceiving, evaluating, and responding to life situations; (5) the prediction of behavior; and (6) maladaptive behavior and how to remediate it. To this end, our presentation espouses certain postulates which form a philosophic ground for our own theory of personality.

SOME GUIDING POSTULATES FOR A THEORY OF PERSONALITY

Postulate 1: All behavior is adaptive. Life itself is a continuous process of adaptation. Behavior which seems maladaptive on the surface will, on close study, reveal that it is a selected response to a stimulus and has some form of adaptation as a motive. Even suicide is a misguided form of adaptive behavior.

Postulate 2: Personality is a learned pattern of behavior. In observing any human being, proper training will allow us to see certain consistent ways of responding, which we term style or pattern. Patterns result when innate adaptive mechanisms are modified by learning into set ways of responding. Modification is generally brought about by the process of *socialization,* the development and growth of personality through experience.

Postulate 3: The culture influences the method and type of conditions of socialization. Thus, the Zulu mother carries her infant with her everywhere, even to work in the fields. Some modern child development theorists believe this practice produces a greater feeling of inner security than the more limited mother-child contact provided in most Western cultures. Therefore, the *culture influences the patterning of personality.*

Postulate 4: Each personality has its own intrinsic and unique organization. Individuals are likely to behave in different ways in the same situation. To illustrate, let us refer to one of Aesop's fables.

> Two frogs fell into a milk pail. One frog, thinking that there was no salvation, drowned (he gave in to the inevitable). The other frog, because of some inner quality, decided to keep trying to swim in the milk. He kept beating and beating his legs until eventually he found himself floating on a pad of butter.

The same principle applies to human behavior. What two different individuals will do in the same situation will depend on the inner nature of each—in a word, on personality.

Postulate 5: Personality determines the selection of response (selectivity). Each individual selects what he will notice and respond to; this is the perceptual aspect of selectivity and attention. For example;

> Two girls walk into a room. All the men look at them. The student of personality, however, looks at the other men, studying their reactions.

What we look at depends on our interests and attitudes. To illustrate how the behaving organism evaluates the external stimulus, consider the following situation:

> It is the first day of class. The professor describes his requirements for the course and specifies very clearly all the criteria. One student rates the professor as quite "tough," while another sees him as very thorough and looks forward to a learning experience.

How the behaving organism selects a response and evaluates the consequence(s) of that response can be inferred from another classroom situation.

> A professor of economics makes a provocative statement about Marxism. One student responds by being disturbed and offended. He angrily questions the statement. He is then worried that the professor will give him a bad grade—his evaluation of the consequences of his response.

Postulate 6: Understanding the pattern permits the prediction of behavior. If behavior follows a pattern, then knowing the main trends of the pattern will allow us to predict how the behaving organism will perceive and respond to a situation.

> In the situation described in the previous section, the professor guesses that the student is motivated by a desire to share the limelight. The professor thus permits and encourages the student to express his point of view, expecting that this will satisfy the student. If she has predicted correctly, the student's behavior will match the professor's expectancy. If, on the other hand, the interpretation of the student's behavior is inaccurate, the student's anger is likely to persist.

Postulate 7: Understanding the underlying personality pattern permits us to understand the specific functions of a given behavioral act. This is related to the principle of *idiography* described later in the chapter. Behavior cannot be understood except in terms of the individual personality and the life situation with which the person interacts. To understand any behavioral act we must ask three questions: Who is the person who acts? What else do we know about him/her? and In what situation does this act occur and what possible purpose can it serve?

> Even our understanding of mental symptoms depends to a great extent upon our understanding of how the individual's personality pattern functions. For example, compulsive people tend to be anxious when not in control of the situation (letting someone else drive the car). *When* and *for which purpose* anxiety occurs is influenced by personality.

EMPIRICAL EVIDENCE FOR THE SEVEN POSTULATES

While these postulates fit into the common experience of the reader, the studies we describe briefly in this section provide some evidence in support of the postulates. Other studies are found in abundance in later chapters.

Postulate 1 is supported by the studies on attachment in Chapter 5. Postulates 2 and 3 are supported by various socialization experiences that reveal certain definite effects between culture membership and personality pattern (see Chapters 7 and 10). Evidence for the rest of the postulates will be discussed in more detail in this chapter. This evidence comes from the field of experimental psychology, especially perception.

Postulates 4, 5, and 7 imply that units of behavior can only be understood in the context of the *whole*. This viewpoint became the dictum of the influential Gestalt school of psychology. Examples of this principle, which was first presented by Max Wertheimer, the founder of the Gestalt school, are presented in Figure 1-1.

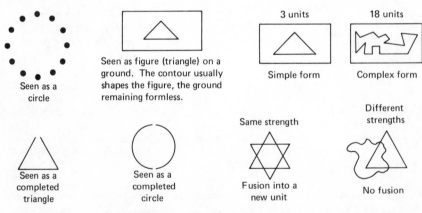

Figure 1-1   Examples of the Gestalt law of perceptual organization. The tendency to organize parts into a whole is seen in the tendency to see a ring of dots as a circle. This tendency operates not only in perception but in all human behavior. Source: Forgus, 1966, p. 113.

Applying the technical insights of modern communication and information theory, Attneave (1954) offered an explanation of why stimuli are organized into wholes and why this organization follows Gestalt laws. Attneave starts by noting that our capacity for processing separate units of information is limited. However, assimilating all information presented is unnecessary and would just lead to overload and error. Therefore much of what is presented in the stimulus is ignored. But points of maximum information, such as sharp intensity differences and changes in the direction of contour are emphasized. Elements of similar color, shape, size, and texture are grouped together and figures are constructed (in perception) so as to minimize the number of changes in contour direction.

Postulate 7 implies that context is an important part of every experience. This is illustrated in Figure 1-2 in the perceptual principle of inclusiveness. Not only is what we see limited by how much we can process, but what we see *and* feel are also affected by daily fluctuations in environmental conditions, and our habitual ways of reacting to such environmental effects.

> Have you, for example, ever noticed (I caught myself doing it the other evening) how different the same kind of weather may appear to your senses on a Saturday night and a Sunday night? It was late autumn, on a dusky Sunday afternoon. As evening came on, I felt a little melancholy, looking out on the dreary scene through the living room window. Then all of a sudden, it occurred to me. If I were looking at the same scene on a Saturday night, it would seem far less sad and my mood would be elated, not gloomy, because Saturday night is a night for excitement. The experience was like perceiving darkness as depressing when you are alone and friendly when you are with your lover. (Forgus, 1975, p. 1)

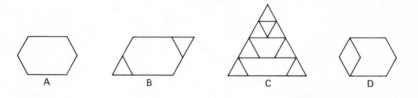

Figure 1-2   Illustration of inclusiveness. Form A is included in Forms B, C, and D. The contexts provided in Forms B, C, and D mask the appearance of A, making it harder to recognize. Source: After Gottschaldt, 1926. (Reprinted from Forgus and Melamed, 1976).

The last three postulates are part of a larger postulate which states that the choice of a person to move in one direction rather than another is determined by selective perception. This point has been a matter of controversy among psychologists. The basic issue at conflict is whether a "need" determines perception or whether perception determines "need." In this sense, the term *need* is used to mean a psychophysiological requirement, such as a need for nourishment. Need-oriented theorists assert that what we perceive is influenced by our attempts to satisfy unfulfilled needs. For example, a hungry person is more likely to notice food; a starving person dreams about food; a thirsty traveller in the desert sees mirages of water.

The term *perception* refers to the extraction of information from the environment. Perception theorists assert that the true cause-effect sequence is from perception to need. For example, a young woman who perceives herself as deprived of love may feel less deprived when she is the object of sexual attention. She may therefore feel a "need" for continuous sexual activity. One of the early proponents of the need perception selectivity hypothesis (Bruner, 1951) early anticipated a counter-theory that would propose a "perceptual selectivity → need arousal" direction.

Support for the primacy of perceptual selectivity comes from a penetrating analysis of so-called perceptual defense—that is, behavior in which certain information is blocked out of conscious perception. Most of us are familiar with Freud's famous allegation that people defend themselves from thoughts or memories that would upset them. Erdelyi (1974), however, has theorized that what looks like defensive behavior is really the result of underlying memory storage programs which operate either to facilitate or inhibit the recall of information. One such stage where information can be either stopped or gated (let through) is at the retrieval of information from long-term to short-term memory. An experiment by Erdelyi and Appelbaum (1973) illustrates the selective and blocking effects of what Erdelyi has termed "chronic sets" of perception. In this experiment, subjects who were members of a Jewish organization were asked to look at a circular array of neutral pictures for 200 msec under three different conditions. In two of them either the Star of David or the swastika was at the center of the array. In the third array a picture of a window was at the center. It was found that there was a *lower rate of processing* in the first two emotionally charged arrays—that is, when viewing these arrays, subjects recognized fewer pictures than when viewing the third array. Interestingly enough, reactions to the two emotional arrays (with the Star of David or the swastika) did not differ from one another. Thus, the presence of an emotional stimulus can disrupt (that is, selectively inhibit) the processing of other information.

Perhaps the attention-capturing effect of the emotional stimuli detracts from the coding of the other pictures. That this may be so receives support from two other research reports. In the first one, Forgus and DeWolfe (1969) tried to find out whether perceptual defense is in fact a special case of perceptual accentuation (selectivity). In this study, actively hallucinating male and female hospitalized schizophrenic patients were interviewed. The interviews were tape-recorded verbatim so that they could be analyzed for thematic content. A reliable scoring manual for categorizing hallucinatory themes was constructed using the hallucinations of a representative sample of ten males and seven females.

Now a second group of patients was asked to listen to a short recording which contained a composite of the four themes present in the hallucinations of the entire sample. In 18 of 23 subjects, the major hallucinatory theme category of each patient predicted the dominant recall themes.

The study showed that at least in some cases we can measure the dominant perceptual sets (or schemata) of subjects and that these sets, in fact, direct perceptual selectivity. Thus selectivity is apparently a result of active processing or sensitization rather than repression or defense. New stimulus material is categorized according to schemata already existing in long-term memory. Forgus and DeWolfe (1974) cross-validated their findings with delusional patients, whose perceptions could also be predicted on the basis of their diagnosed delusions.

Support for the notion that one can predict behavior from knowing the personality style comes from a study by Hedvig (1965). Hedvig asked three clinicians to examine the early childhood recollections of 51 children between the ages of 5 and 16 who had been referred to a child guidance clinic. In each case, the clinicians were asked to decide if the child had been diagnosed by the clinic as having either a psychoneurotic disorder or a behavioral disturbance. The combined ratings of the three judges were correct at a statistically significant level (.001). One clinician correctly predicted the diagnosis in 42 out of the 51 cases. Even from such a limited amount of information, and with no other knowledge at all about the child, a behavioral pattern could be predicted from subjects' perceptions.

Our own review of the data leads us to prefer the perception need hypothesis over its counterpart as a way of explaining choice of direction of behavior. However, the jury is still out and a future theory may well combine these two apparently contradictory hypotheses into a more holistic theory.

DEFINITION OF PERSONALITY

In everyday speech, the word *personality* takes on any number of different meanings. Hall and Lindzey (1957) point to the difficulty of trying to define personality. They do not believe that any definition of personality can be generally applied.

> Personality consists concretely of a set of values or descriptive terms which are used to describe the individual being studied according to the variables or dimensions which occupy a central position within the particular theory utilised. (1957, p. 9)

However, several definitions of personality do offer a representative outlook on the subject. Nevitt Sanford (1963) gives a list of definitions in a paper devoted to this subject. The italicized words in Box 1-2 reveal how different theories of personality still center around a common, unifying theme. Personality is always viewed as organized, enduring, and character-

---

Box 1-2   Definitions of personality: Unity within variety

Allport: "the dynamic *organization* within the individual of those psychophysical systems that determine his *'unique adjustment'* to his environment." (Sanford,* pp. 494–495).

Newcomb: "personality is known only as we observe individual behavior. By observing John Doe in such capacity as husband, host, employee and employer, we can discover those kinds of *order and regularity* in his behavior which are the goals of the student of personality." (Sanford, p. 496).

Eysenck: "the *enduring organization* of a person's character, temperament, intellect and physique which determines his unique adjustment to his environment." (Sanford, p. 496)

Sullivan: "the relatively *enduring pattern* of recurrent interpersonal situations which characterizes a human life." (Sullivan, 1953, pp. 110–111)

Maddi: "Personality is the *stable set of characteristics and tendencies* that determine those commonalities and differences in the psychological behavior (thoughts, feelings and actions) of people that have continuity in time and that may or may not be easily understood in terms of the social and biological pressures of the immediate situation alone." (Maddi, 1976, p. 9)

Angyal: Using general systems theory, Angyal defines personality as a "hierarchy of systems, an *organized whole*, each personality having its own particular system principle." (Angyal, 1965, p. 50)

Jaspers: The German existentialist, similarly conceptualizes personality as "the individual's differing and *characteristic totality* of meaningful connections in any one psychic life." (Jaspers, 1963, p. 428)

* All references to Sanford are from the 1963 work.

istic. Arndt (1974, p. 7), following Allport (1937), classifies definitions of personality into six varieties:

1. external appearance definitions—personality is overt behavior (the *persona*)
2. omnibus definitions—personality is a "sum total" of qualities
3. integrative definitions—personality is a "pattern"
4. hierarchical definitions—the pattern is organized with a unifying principle at the top
5. adjustive definitions—personality is the style of coping in the world
6. distinctiveness definitions—personality is the attribute which makes a person unique

Our own theory of personality will have characteristics that will permit it to be classified under the last four of these six varieties. It will not be a theory of external appearance nor of a "sum total" of attributes.

Some students of personality, however, have used a narrower focus in describing personality, emphasizing a particular aspect such as trait, type, temperament, or character as a central construct.

CONVENTIONAL CONSTRUCTS USED TO DESCRIBE PERSONALITY

Trait

Trait is a conceptual construct inferred from observable behavior. Constructs of the various traits provide a conceptual system individuals can use to classify the overt behavior of people they meet. Thus, people may be aggressive or passive, spontaneous or inhibited, may move quickly or slowly, may be impulsive or cautious, outgoing or reserved. A study by Passini and Norman (1966) investigated the notion that individuals classify each other according to a preconceived set of trait categories. The essential features of their study are outlined in Box 1-3.

Experimental personality research such as Passini and Norman's not only uncovers data which is important in its own right but also helps us to be skeptical of everyday beliefs about our abilities to understand each other.

We may like, dislike, or be puzzled by a certain trait that we observe in another person. The trait itself is simply one aspect of the total personality that reveals itself in characteristic ways in specific situations according to an overall pattern. One may say that a trait is something a person possesses; however, knowing the trait does not necessarily tell us how or when that person will display it. It is important not to mistake one or two traits for a more complete understanding of an individual's personality. Among the theories of personality we will discuss, Gordon Allport's might be described as a sophisticated trait theory.

Raymond Cattell (1965) distinguishes between a *surface* trait, which is a set of behaviors that are observed together, and a *source* trait, an underlying influence that can be discovered by factor analysis. Cattell has devised methods for discovering such source traits. Our general use of the term *trait* will be restricted to surface traits, such as those identified by the subjects in the study by Passini and Norman.

It is important also to remember that a particular pattern of behavior observed at any given time may represent a temporary state rather than an enduring trait. The distinction of trait from state is still in its conceptual infancy (Cattell, 1975). A recent study by Barker and his colleagues (1977) has indicated, however, that it is possible to distinguish between temporary anxiety (situationally determined), and anxiety which is a more enduring trait (personally determined).

Role

The concept of role was introduced into personality theory by sociology and social psychology. The term is borrowed from the theater—a part played by an actor according to a rehearsed script. The continued enactment of a role produces characteristic personality dispositions and personality is the sum total of the played roles (Wiggins, et al., 1971). For Goffman (1959), however, the apparent personality is only a dramatic effect arising from the manner in which the role is played, the setting and the audience response. Role can be defined as the organized set of behavior that belongs to an identifiable position in the social structure. Argyle, the British social psychologist, defines role more broadly. For him personality has no structure other than what one person reveals to another in an interpersonal situation (Argyle, 1967). For example, when two friends meet, and one looks at the other, the second person tends to look back and maintain the eye contact. When strangers meet, intimacy is less likely to be encouraged—one person will look away if the other "accidentally" makes eye contact. In this, however, Argyle may be mistaking conventional cultural behavior for the consistency of unique individual patterns. Sociologists and cultural anthropologists have constructed elaborate role theories of personality.

Type

A broader category than trait, type may be thought of as including a collection of traits and allowing for changes in the way traits manifest themselves. Allport (1937) points out that a person can possess a trait, but cannot possess a type. Instead individuals fit into one or another type.

Rudolf Dreikurs described how a trait such as competitiveness could manifest itself in seemingly opposite ways. He described a 6-year-old in the first grade who always strove to attain the highest grades in the class. He was at that time the best student in the class and the hardest worker. In the middle of the school year, another boy was put into the class and he consistently out-performed the first child, getting higher grades and being the first to know the answers to the teacher's questions. The first boy now did an about-face and became the *worst* student in the class, seemingly losing all interest in his studies. Dreikurs pointed out that the trait of competitiveness still existed, that only its manifestation had changed. Other observations on the child showed that he always wanted to be first among his peers in everything he did. However, if he couldn't be the *first best,* he would be the *first worst,* but at all costs, he would be *first.*

It would be difficult for a personality theory based on traits alone to account for the varying manifestations of any given trait. However, a type theory can do this. One could say, of the example above, that this was a child of the *type* who always "wanted to be first" and that this motive would manifest itself in many different traits. Type theories commonly classify individuals according to their dominant motives rather than their changeable traits.

Raymond Cattell (1965) and H. J. Eysenck (1947) have both used factor analysis to study how traits combine to form *molar* types, and how knowledge of these types can be used to predict behavior in a variety of situations. Clearly, personality typing is a useful device, yet we must not forget that all such systems are of necessity incomplete: each individual, no matter how neatly he or she fits into a type, is never completely that pure type.

A classical theory using the type construct is that of Carl Jung, which is discussed in Chapter 3. One severe limitation of type theory is the lack of consensus on what constitutes a type. Jung's types, for example, might be considered traits by Allport or Eysenck. In any case, there would probably be more consensus among raters about traits that people manifest than about the types into which they fit. The latter requires more data and more interpretation and is probably subject to more error.

Temperament

Temperament refers to a biologically based disposition that determines a person's mood. The early Greeks attempted to categorize people and even to give reasons for their behavior based on emotional mood or temperament. The Greek physician, Hippocrates (c. 460–c. 370 B.C.), taught that the temperament of an individual was associated with the presence of increased or decreased amounts of the *four humors* or body fluids, which the Greeks held responsible for four separate personality types. They were the *sanguine* type, the aggressive, outgoing, active individual who had a plentiful supply of blood (sang); the *phlegmatic,* easy-going, slow, perhaps somewhat lazy individual, whose passions were not easily aroused (associated with an excess supply of lymph); the *choleric* type, irritable and quick to anger because of an excess supply of white bile; and the *melancholic* type—sad, unhappy, and depressed on account of too much black bile. In common parlance we still speak of an angry person as one who has his *choler* up. The cheerful, active person is described as *sanguine,* while the word *phlegmatic* is still used today to describe the type of person who is not easily aroused.

The German psychiatrist, Ernst Kretschmer, proposed a theory based upon the relationship between physique and temperament. He devised a checklist of descriptive terms for various physical aspects of the body and also measured various body dimensions. He concluded that there were three main body types, *asthenic, athletic,* and *pyknic.* He then studied and classified a list of 260 patients diagnosed as psychotic according to body type. Kretschmer found an "affinity" between manic-depressive psychosis and the pyknic body type and another correlation between schizophrenia and the asthenic body type. However, not only was the type of psychosis related to body build, it was also related to temperament. For example,

Kretschmer ascribed to asthenics a schizothymic temperament—shy, seclusive, introverted, and tending to avoid much closeness with people. Pyknic types he characterized as having a cyclothymic temperament—gregarious, desiring to be close to people, and rather outgoing except during the low phase of the mood swings to which they were subject.

Kretschmer's work has not been supported by other investigators on the ground that many other variables were involved. Body build, for example, tends to change with age and eating habits and Kretschmer's study did not allow for these.

The American, William H. Sheldon, trained both as psychologist and psychiatrist, has developed a much more reliable and sophisticated theory of the relationship between physique and temperament. Sheldon tried to identify the main body types and to relate them to varieties of temperament. After he had identified three "primary" components of physique—endomorphy, mesomorphy, and ectomorphy—he tried to identify the primary components of temperament. He eventually found three major groups of traits which seemed to correlate with the physique types—*viscerotonia, somatotonia* and *cerebrotonia.* The three physique types of Sheldon correspond roughly to those of Kretschmer, as do the three temperament types (Sheldon & Stevens, 1942).

In the course of his work Sheldon photographed thousands of dimensions. He made measurements before and after weight gain and weight loss

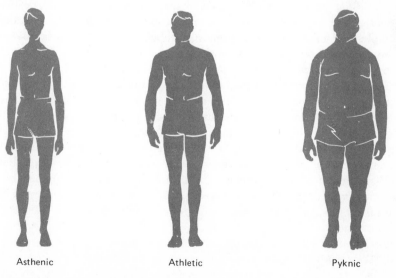

Asthenic   Athletic   Pyknic

Figure 1-3   Kretschmer's Body Types

and claimed that the basic body type does not change (as long as nutrition and health remain constant). Sheldon developed his concepts of temperament by rating his different types for 50 different traits. He found a close correspondence between traits assigned by observing persons and the expected traits derived from measuring physique in photographs.

Correlations between physique and temperament are broad generalizations about the biological underpinnings of personality. Sheldon's work dealt with statistical correlations of certain general tendencies in behavior. He admits that socialization and other factors also influence behavior. Knowing a relationship between physique and behavior is useful, but does not yet reveal the unique person to us.

Thomas and Chess (1977) performed longitudinal studies on large numbers of children, from early infancy on, and concluded that newborns display differences which are unique, characteristic, and enduring—differences they termed temperaments. These temperaments act as independent variables and can be used to predict future behavior, including the susceptibility to becoming a problem child. Since these temperamental characteristics are observable in early infancy, Thomas and Chess believe they are constitutional. Additional research is needed to rule out other factors such as prenatal influence and early childhood training, environmental variables that are also capable of producing enduring traits in a person.

Although traits, temperaments, and types are useful devices for helping us to classify individuals, each is of limited usefulness. For example, the statement that someone is "energetic and courageous" is a statement about a characteristic of temperament. To a student of personality the above statement would have limited meaning, since it offers no significant information about the actual behavior of the individual in a specific circumstance.

Character

The word *character* is sometimes used as a synonym for personality; it is also used to describe acquired traits, in contrast to those inborn traits that comprise a person's temperament. Another usage is as a value judgment about personality; here such labels as good or bad, desirable or undesirable, and honest or dishonest come into play. Early studies on character were essentially moral judgments and, therefore, belong more properly in the history of theology and philosophy. Although Freud and others have used the term *character* to refer to personality, we prefer to use the word *personality* as the parent construct.

Style

If personality is a pattern of behavior, we should expect that a personality can be recognized by its style (a recognizable theme), just as the trained ear can recognize and remember a musical composition by hearing the melodic theme. Pattern is a repetitive design with a recurring theme or *motif.* One need not personally observe every aspect of personality in order to recognize its theme. For example, sometimes we can tell by a person's behavior that it is important for her always to be good and to win approval from others. She constantly tries to please, and is distressed when she does not; she avoids situations in which she does not feel able to please. If she has displeased, she will feel guilty and anxious until she can atone. It is as if the person's life is ruled by a motto that says, "Above all, I must always make sure to be good and please people." Another kind of person acts as if everyone were his enemy or potential enemy. He does not trust others. He hesitates to enter into any kind of close relationship with others. He may be cautious and reserved, or he may be quick to anger and irritable. The recurring theme that one sees in his behavior is a distrust of other human beings that results in movements to protect himself against possible harm from others. This sort of behavior has also been labeled clinically as paranoid. In each case, the individual demonstrates a particular style of behavior that might be summed up in a motto—in the one case, "I must be good," in the other, "You can't trust anybody"—to which the person closely adheres.

Because style or theme seems to be unique to each individual, Alfred Adler (1969) has termed it a person's "life style." This use of the term *life style* should not be confused with the sociologist's effort to define a group characteristic such as "middle-class suburban life style" or "inner-city ghetto life style."

Contemporary studies in psychology tend more and more toward the concept of pattern, style, or theme in personality research. This particular way of studying personality, with its focus on the unique, individual style, is also most congenial with the approach of the present authors.

Some theorists consider style such an important construct that they have conceptualized a number of dimensions along which differences in style can be measured. Since these dimensions are usually concerned with the way an individual construes knowledge about him- or herself and the world, they are called cognitive styles. We will have occasion to utilize this concept of cognitive style repeatedly in our explanation of personality. (See Chapter 7 for a discussion of cognitive styles.)

NOMOTHETIC AND IDIOGRAPHIC LAWS

The statement that human beings have individual styles cannot be understood without realizing that an individual deviation must somehow be related to a general or normative condition. This is as true of psychology and the study of personality as it is of any other field of knowledge. All science is concerned with discovering and understanding universal laws—in this case the laws of human behavior. For example, the existence of attraction between the sexes permits us to study the attraction as a phenomenon and come to general conclusions about sexual attraction as a form of human behavior. Such general laws are called *nomothetic* laws.

In personality study, however, the scientist is interested in studying the individual's unique style of behavior; for example, how a particular person deals with the issue of sexual attraction. The idiosyncratic rule that the particular individual follows is, in a sense, also a law, but it is a law that applies only to him/her. This type of law is called an *idiographic* law by H. L. and Rowena Ansbacher. It acts as a law for one individual alone rather than for all humans (Ansbacher & Ansbacher, 1956). George Kelly described the idiosyncratic rules that the specific individual follows as *personal constructs* which each of us uses to order our own behavior in highly personal and unique ways. Joseph Rychlak, a student of Kelly, says, "We behave in relation to these [the core constructs] as if our very life depended on them . . ." (1973, p. 480). Personality study deals with these idiographic laws: how to recognize and understand them and how to influence them.

There are, of course, general rules (nomothetic laws) for recognizing and classifying idiographic phenomena, and the personologist uses these nomothetic laws as a general frame of reference in studying the individual. An example of a nomothetic law in personology would be Kelly's statement that each person forms a unique set of personal constructs. Applying this law, the investigator would set out to understand one individual's specific and unique personal constructs.

The statement, "Anger is an emotional response to a variety of stimulations," is a nomothetic statement. The statement, "John typically becomes angry at his girl friend if she is out when he phones," is an idiographic statement. It is as if there is a nomothetic scale about, in this case, anger—and the individual can be seen at one or another point on the scale. Without the nomothetic, the idiographic statement has no context. Without the idiographic, the nomothetic remains a general abstraction which tells us nothing about the individual. Some thinkers, such as Gordon Allport (1962), have expressed their disbelief that the individual case can be predicted in terms of a general law. We argue that we cannot predict the idiographic without the context of the nomothetic.

PLAN OF THE BOOK

The considerations in Box 1-1 and the postulates and the analyses in this chapter express our conviction that personality consists of an enduring, characteristic, unique pattern or organization of behavior. Different theories have been advanced to explain the nature of these stable organizations or personality dispositions, and they form the basis of Chapters 2 through 4, at which point we introduce our own theoretical departure.

Chapter 5 concentrates on adaptive behavior—how it is regulated and why it is necessary for survival and effective living. We also show how built-in genetic physiological needs are modified through socialization experiences into four major motive systems which constitute the structure of personality organization, with a perceptual system as its core integrator. Since the core integrator of the motive systems is the perceptual system, which deals with the processing of information and the acquisition of and utilization of knowledge (cognition), Chapter 6 provides a cognitive model of personality organization.

Since two of our postulates assert that personality is learned and influenced by cultural experience, Chapters 7 and 8 describe the development of personality.

Chapter 9 introduces the reader to psychodynamics through a study of goal-directed behavior, while Chapter 10 analyzes how this behavior becomes functionally operative in interpersonal relationships.

Chapter 11 provides an overview of some representative ways of measuring or assessing personality structure, while Chapter 12 presents representative accounts of some maladaptive personality patterns. Chapter 13 discusses behavior change both as a normal adaptive process and as a method for remediating maladaptive deviation.

A NOTE ON THE SEQUENCE OF CHAPTERS

At this point, the reader may skip to Chapters 5 and 6 which present the foundations of a cognitive theory of personality. This theory deals with the structure, dynamics and origin of human motivation (goal behavior), postulating that behavior is connected to the way people perceive events. The authors, however, feel it is good pedagogy to precede a cognitive interpretation of personality by reviewing representative personality theories which are in current vogue. These theories could all have been studied in other sources. We have included them here because it gives us the opportunity to appraise how well they fit into a cognitive interpretation of personality.

2

**theoretical
conceptions
of personality I:
Freud and the
behaviorists**

OVERVIEW

This chapter launches our review of personality theorists. After a brief historical background of the philosophic forerunners of personality theory, we conclude that the Leibnizian-Kantian versus Lockean perspectives of the human being apply to modern personality theories as well. Personality theories can be classified as to whether they are more Lockean or more Leibnizian. The theorists in Chapter 2 are more Lockean.

Sigmund Freud's psychoanalysis offers the first complete and systematic theory of personality. It is a hedonistic theory. The fundamental motivators of behavior are libidinal and aggressive drives. Personality is the consequence of the individual's struggle to satisfy his/her drives in the face of social constraints. Reinforcement theory is also hedonistic. It emphasizes how responses are shaped by environmental contingencies, either because the response reduces drive (Dollard and Miller) or the contingency rewards response (Skinner). There is no central construct of person or personality in reinforcement theory. The learned response, which is under environmental control, is the unit of study rather than the person. Social learning theorists are a blend of Lockean and Leibnizian views. While emphasizing the importance of learning, they include central mediating constructs. As such, they are a bridge to the theorists discussed in Chapter 3.

The formal study of personality did not begin until the twentieth century. Henry Murray (1938) coined the word *personology* to designate the systematic, scientific study of personality. However, it is possible to trace the historical development of modern philosophic conceptions which underlie personality study to the classical Greek philosophers Plato (c. 427–c. 347 B.C.) and Aristotle (384–322 B.C.). For our purposes, however, the main distinction between modern personality theories can be traced back to the disagreement between the systems of Gottfried Wilhelm Leibniz (1646–1716) and John Locke (1632–1704). This disagreement, and its influence on our own views of personality, has been thoroughly explored by Allport:

> John Locke, we all recall, assumed the mind of the individual to be a *tabula rasa* at birth. And the intellect itself was a passive thing acquiring content and structure only through the impact of sensation and the crisscross of associations, much as a pan of sweet dough acquired tracings through the impress of a cookie cutter. . . . To Leibniz the intellect was perpetually active in its own right, addicted to rational problem solving and bent on manipulating sensory data according to its own inherent nature. For Locke, the organism was reactive when stimulated; for Leibniz it was self-propelled. (1955, pp. 7–8)

According to Allport, the Lockean view of man as "reactor" became dominant in British and American psychology and formed the ground for the tradition of behaviorism. From this point of view motives are *drives*, which are *responses* to stimuli and which can become *conditioned* so that they respond to external *cues* of many types. What Leibniz called the "intellect" pales before the all-importance of conditioning. Furthermore, since in Locke's terms "simple ideas" are more basic than "complex ideas," the basic unit of behavior is small (such as a habit) and the complex everyday behavior of human beings is a summation of small parts. What is experienced earlier is more important than what is experienced later, because the early sensory impressions lead to those simple ideas which remain important in later life.

> The Leibnizian tradition, by contrast, maintains that the person is not a collection of acts . . . the person is the *source* of acts. And activity is not conceived as agitation resulting from pushes by internal and external stimulation. It is purposive . . . Aristotle's doctrine of *ouxis* and *entelechy* anticipated the spirit of Leibniz, as did the doctrine of intention in St. Thomas Aquinas. Spinoza insisted that *conatus,* the striving toward self-preservation and self-affirmation, is the secret of all becoming. (Allport, 1955, pp. 12–13)

David Hume (1711–1776), for whom the self was merely a bundle of sensations, continued the Lockean approach. Its subsequent disciples in-

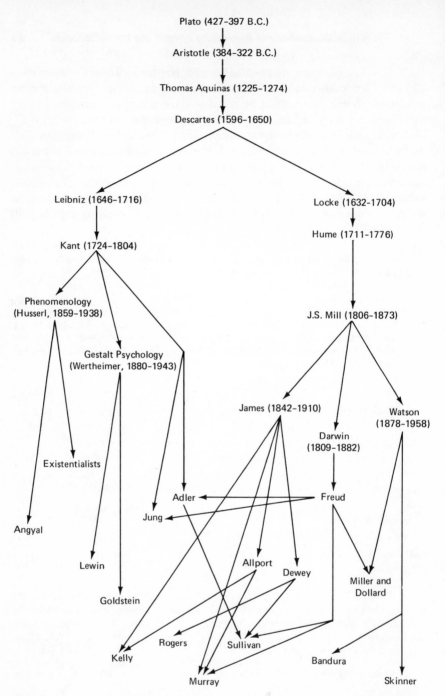

Figure 2-1   Philosophical Line of Descent of Twentieth-Century Personality Theorists

cluded the nineteenth-century utilitarians Jeremy Bentham (1748–1832) and John Stuart Mill (1806–1873). This school of philosophy, the British empiricist school, forms one major line of approach to modern personality theory.

Like Allport, Arndt (1974) also distinguishes between the Lockean and the Leibnizian traditions. Rychlak makes a similar distinction, using the terms "Lockean" and "Kantian." He points out correctly that most theories are mixtures of both models and distinguishes (1) the mixed models of Freud, Jung, and Adler, (2) the Lockean model in Sullivan and the behaviorists, and (3) Kantian models in the phenomenology of Rogers, Boss, and Kelly (Rychlak, 1973). See Figure 2-1.

The personality theories we will discuss in this chapter are descended, more or less, from the philosophical world view of Locke, while the ones discussed in Chapters 3 and 4 are variations of the Kantian and Leibnizian traditions.

PSYCHOANALYSIS: SIGMUND FREUD (1856–1939)

Philosophic Background

Freud, the founder of psychoanalysis, based his theoretical conclusions upon careful and systematic observation. The subjects of his observations were usually his patients, but he also observed the everyday behavior of the people around him and conducted a famous self-analysis.

The scientific atmosphere of Freud's day was imbued with the notion that all phenomena could be understood if they could be analyzed and reduced to their bare elements. Darwin's theory had labeled man as another animal with instincts and survival mechanisms, and it was against this background that Freud developed his theory. Behavior is the result of sexual and aggressive drives, and since the drives create conflict with civilized society, the human beings must find ways of satisfying their drives while preserving themselves within an antagonistic society. Freud considered observable behavior as an effect, caused by the pressure of drives, modified by the "mental apparatus." His theory is thus grounded in his view of biological structure, with the primacy of drives being the main and ultimate source of behavior. Later psychoanalysts have modified some of these views, and modern psychoanalytic theory recognizes some functional autonomy in certain mental structures.

After presenting traditional Freudian theory, we will consider some of its mechanisms in cognitive terms.

Personality Structure and Its Foundations

The newborn infant has not yet formed attachments to objects in his external environment. His mental life is chaotic—and is propelled by a set of psychophysiological drives. When he is hungry, he cries. His behavior, therefore, is strictly driven and he is making no choices. The principle that the aim of behavior is drive reduction is called the *primary* or *pleasure principle* and the infant's psychological state, *primary narcissism*. As the infant grows older and becomes aware of stimuli from his environment, he recognizes that unless he comes to terms with the environment he sometimes suffers pain rather than pleasure. He therefore begins to pay attention to the environment so that he can cope with it effectively. At this point he begins to operate according to the *secondary* or *reality principle* which is the principle of social limitations. It may be a simplification, but it would not be wrong to say that the ensuing personality structure is the result of the dynamic interplay between the two principles, pleasure and reality.

In the newborn infant, the personality structure consists of only one mental system which Freud called the *id*. The id, the source of most mental drives, operates solely on the pleasure principle. It is mainly unconscious and seeks only tension reduction. That part of the personality which operates according to the reality principle is called the *ego*.

The ego, developing somewhat later than the id, is a regulating structure that controls behavioral response to the id drives by operating on the reality principle. It is partly inborn and partly "split off" from the id. The ego has the task of self-preservation. It performs this task by becoming aware of stimuli, by storing them in memory, by avoiding excessively strong stimuli (through flight), by adapting to moderate stimuli and by learning to take action to change the external world. It asserts control over the instinctual drives of the id and regulates them by directing how and where they are satisfied or denied satisfaction (Freud, 1953–66). The ego is thus partly autonomous (Hartmann, 1964) and exerts its control by inhibiting id drives. Freud drew a distinction between that part of the mental life which is conscious and which is unconscious. *Primary processes* (unrealistic wishes for immediate gratification and disregard of realities and logic) are the type of mental operations found in the id, whereas secondary processes (more rational) are the operations of the ego. The third structure of personality, the superego, does not develop until sometime later, and we will postpone our discussion of it. The three parts of Freud's personality are schematized in Figure 2-2.

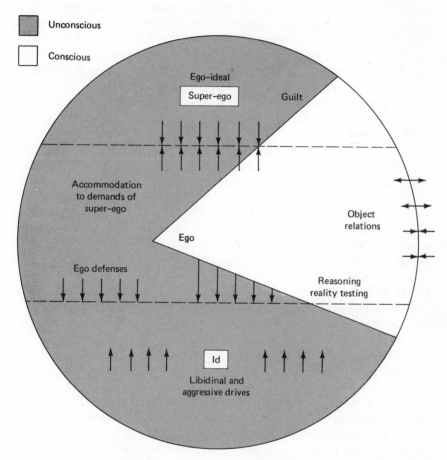

Figure 2-2 Schematic diagram of Freud's personality structure. The arrows represent transactions between the different areas of personality. Where arrows oppose each other, conflict takes place.

Psychosexual Stages of Development

Personality development takes place through psychosexual stages. Since the main purpose of the id is to seek pleasure and since some parts of the body—erogenous zones—are more pleasurable than others, Freudians view the development of personality as directly related to the individual's experiences with these parts of the body. According to psychoanalytic theory, the mouth, anus, and genitalia are more liberally endowed with sensitive nerve endings. At different times during maturation—that is, at specific psychosexual stages—different openings become important (maximally erotic). Libidinal drive (desire for love) is the force basic to personality development.

Oral Stage. The first psychosexual stage is called the *oral stage.* The important erogenous zone in this stage is the mouth. In the first few months of life, the oral stage is further defined as the passive-receptive phase. The *aim* (activity through which pleasure is attained) of the passive-receptive phase is sucking and taking in food, and the *object* is that person or item which provides the gratification of the libidinal drives. Typical objects in the passive-receptive phase would be the maternal breast, the thumb which is being sucked, the nipple of the nursing bottle, and other objects that can be placed in the mouth.

At about the time the teeth develop, the oral stage changes from a passive-receptive to an active-aggressive phase. The mouth not only becomes an organ for receiving the object of pleasure, but also for actively seeking it out and even biting it. It is associated with the teething activity of the infant. The objects remain largely the same as in the receptive phase, but occur in greater variety.

It is a tenet of psychoanalytic theory that the libidinal drives require a certain amount of appropriate gratification. Overindulgence, such as excessive feeding, and deprivation—as when the child is prevented from introducing his thumb into his mouth—both lead to inappropriate development. Such individuals commonly manifest character traits that reflect the effects of their arrested development or *fixation.* Fixation in the oral stage leads to oral traits. Freud considered common oral traits in the adult to include overeating, excessive smoking, excessive drinking (passive-receptive traits); or aggression, sadism, compulsive devouring, excessive talking, and "having a biting tongue" (active-aggressive traits). Excessively dependent people who rely upon others for decision making and problem-solving are considered by the psychoanalyst to have had an inappropriate development of the oral stage. The person who is distinguished by excessive oral traits is called an *oral character.* Some research supports the hypothesis that there is a personality type who behaves like an oral character (Fisher & Greenberg, 1977).

Anal Stage. The second stage of psychosexual development, the *anal*, concerns itself with the expulsion and retention of fecal material, both of which can be sources of libidinal gratification (pleasure). Since the fecal material is itself the object of pleasure, it is not surprising to find that the child at this age may enjoy smearing his feces on himself, his crib or the walls of his room. The disapproving reaction of the parental figure then becomes a *frustration* for the child. The parent has an interest in encouraging the child to deposit his fecal products in the socially acceptable receptacle, while the child may neither want to nor see the necessity of doing so—nor indeed be able to exercise that much control over the products of his body. At any rate, if the child experiences the parental reaction as an attempt to thwart his pleasure, conflict can easily occur. Retaining feces and refusing to move one's bowels may then be a way of defeating and frustrating the parent. Conversely, if the child moves his bowels when requested by mother, he may feel that he is giving her a gift. This stage seems to be characterized by a power struggle in the context of development of conscious control over bladder and bowel. Fixation in the anal stage leads to the formation of an *anal character*, of which there are two kinds, anal-retentive and anal-expulsive.

Anal traits that occur in the adult personality structure include hoarding, stinginess, and stubbornness (retentive traits) and/or destructiveness, soiling, disorderliness, and messiness (expulsive traits). Anal traits such as parsimony, neatness and obstinacy (retentive traits) have been found to cluster, providing some empirical evidence for the existence of an anal character (Fisher and Greenberg, 1977).

Freud further believed that since the child receives his primary discipline of ego energy during the anal stage, the extremes of discipline forecast the kinds of *work habits* the adult will have. Thus, anal retentives prefer precise work, such as accounting and physical chemistry, whereas anal expulsives are more likely to go into "expansive" professions such as art. Moreover, the anal-retentive tends to be a methodological thinker while the anal-expulsive person is more likely to be the "grand" creator.

Phallic stage. As maturation continues, the libidinal interests of the child turn gradually away from his anus to his sexual organs which now become the most highly sensitive erogenous zone. This occurs at about the age of 3 to 5, and the aim is genital stimulation. The object is the person to whom the child feels the closest attachment, generally the mother. In the usual case, the little boy is attracted to his mother, wants her as a love object, and feels in competition with his father for mother's love. However, being afraid of the father, he fantasizes that either the father will do away with him, or he with the father—in either case a frightening prospect. This may sometimes lead to a fear of castration by the father (*castration anxiety*). Freud compared this situation to the Greek drama of *Oedipus;* thus the triangle between father, mother and child is called the Oedipal situation. A corresponding situation (the Electra complex) occurs in females.

At this point, it would be important to return for a moment to the different structures in the personality. We have previously discussed the id and the ego, and now we may conveniently discuss the *superego*. Superego is the internalization of parental rules and prohibitions which continue to influence the individual's later life, to a great degree unconsciously. Superego rules pertain to what is good or bad, right or wrong in a particular culture, not to the everyday realities of existence. Since violation of superego codes generates anxiety about losing parental love, it can be thought of as a moral censor. From this point of view, *conscience* develops largely as the result of threat of punishment, either loss of love or physical punishment. The violation of an internalized parental rule, or even the impulse to violate such, leads to *guilt,* a superego mechanism for enforcing obedience. The guilt-ridden person becomes inhibited and avoids aggressive and sexual be-

Box 2-1	Summary of psychosexual stages and personality structures			
Psychosexual Stage	*Erogenous Zone*	*Object*	*Aim*	*Major Consequence for Personality*
Oral	Mouth	Nipple	Sucking Biting	Interpersonal attachment
Anal	Anus	Feces	Retention Defecation	Work and competence
Phallic	Genitalia	Opposite sex parent	Genital stimulation	Conscience and guilt
Latent	None	None	Reducing troublesome sex impulses	Ability to learn to work; to be with others without sexual or aggressive feelings
Genital	Genitalia	Opposite sex lover	Satisfactory heterosexuality	Ability to sustain a loving heterosexual relationship

havior. On the other hand, if there is not enough guilt, and not enough rules have been learned from the parents, there is little conscience and the individual feels little or no constraint to keep him from behaving as he pleases. He may, therefore, be too aggressive, too free, or too licentious. A person who behaves in criminal or excessively self-indulgent ways, is considered to have a weak or inadequate superego.

The latency stage. The development of the superego, with its moral censor function, ushers in a stage in which the sexual drive is relatively quiet. Libidinal drives are now sublimated (see Box 2-1) into various other activities, such as learning and play. Gender identity becomes more certain and impulse control increases. This period lasts until puberty.

The genital stage. With the onset of puberty, the sexual drives are again awakened and previous fixations renew old infantile sexual conflicts. Excessive guilt or unresolved castration fears interfere with normal heterosexual adjustment and all the reemerging conflicts must now be resolved anew.

The Dynamics of Behavior

In psychoanalytic theory, the motivation of behavior is largely unconscious (people are not aware of the underlying reasons for their behavior). In addition, behavior is strictly determined by the interplay between id, ego and superego. Every act can in theory be traced back to an instinctual drive. This principle is called *psychic determinism.*

Freud's basic motivators of behavior are two constructs: *libido* and *aggression.* The concept of libido plays a far more important role in his theory and the concept of aggression was added by him when he felt that libido did not serve to explain destructive human behavior to his satisfaction. Freud also called these two dynamic forces *eros* (life instinct) and *thanatos* (death instinct). At death, these forces become united since there is no longer any tension in the system.

Libido is a drive, a compelling impulse to action which is instinctive and inborn. Freud compared it to a quantity of energy which literally presses for expression, either as pleasure, relief of discomfort, or sexual expression. This energy can be invested (cathected) in any part of the body or in an external object. Because the newborn can experience pleasure in any part of the body, Freud described the infant as "polymorphous perverse." This polymorphy later recedes as the psychosexual stages bring first the mouth, then the anus and finally the genitalia into focus.

The aggressive drive, also inborn, is a destructive urge and was used by Freud to account for destructive human behavior that could not be explained by libido theory.

Because the inborn drives press for satisfaction, their thwarting leads to frustration. A thwarted drive seeks to express itself in any way possible. The energy attached to one drive may be released and attached to another. Thus, thwarted love may turn to hate.

Defense mechanisms.   Because drives *compel* (pleasure principle) and the ego *mediates* (reality principle), the notion of conflict plays a dominant role in the theory. The methods by which the ego mediates and censors the id drives are called *defense mechanisms.* Box 2-2 shows some of the common defense mechanisms of the ego.

Ego and id are in constant tension with each other and this balance may be upset at any time. A smoothly functioning ego in Freud's system is one which is strong enough to keep id drives under control at any time, yet permits a sufficient amount of drive gratification. When ego defenses fail,

---

Box 2-2   Defense mechanisms of the ego

Denial: An attempt to deny external reality by refusing to admit to oneself what is happening.

Projection: Attributing one's own feelings or behavior to others. Delusions are examples of projections, as are hallucinations.

Displacement: Unconscious, but purposeful shifting of feelings or interest from one object to another in order to avoid a conflict.

Rationalization: Self-justification of behavior that is otherwise unacceptable by using logic to obscure the true facts.

Reversal of affect (reaction formation): Controlling unacceptable impulses or feelings by turning them into their opposites.

Withdrawal: Removing oneself from a dangerous situation.

Isolation: Splitting away of the emotion associated with an idea.

Regression: Changing behavior to that type used at an earlier age in order to avoid the conflicts and challenges of one's present state of development.

Somatization: Focusing on body symptoms as a defense against unacceptable wishes.

Identification: Imitation of another.

Repression: Pushing dangerous ideas and impulses out of consciousness.

Doing and undoing: Behavior which symbolically carries out the desired act and then cancels it.

Sublimation: Symbolic expression of the forbidden act by using socially acceptable behavior.

anxiety and other symptoms result. This is spoken of as a conflict between ego and id.

Conflict between ego and superego is also possible. Although ideally the superego functions as a sort of overseer to help the ego control libidinal drives, it also imposes on the ego its own "higher" rules—those internalized, largely unconscious dictates of conscience—and punishes the ego with disapproval (*guilt*). There is no psychopathology in Freudian theory without some kind of intrapsychic conflict.

Anxiety.   Freud makes anxiety another central construct in his theory. Basically, anxiety is a form of displeasure and thus something to be avoided. But it also has a signal function. When a repressed and forbidden wish threatens to erupt, the ego receives a signal that trouble is on the way—in the form of anxiety. One of the main motivators of behavior is the desire to avoid or deflect such unpleasant anxiety. Id drives may be activated by external stimuli; for example, the sight of a beautiful girl may activate lustful feelings. The ego must then repress more strongly, withdraw from the activating stimulus, gratify the drive in a partial way, or use any other available defense mechanism. In sum, Freud accounted for the dynamics of behavior by using four constructs: libidinal cathexis (investment of sexual energy in an object), hostility generated by frustration and by the existence of aggressive id drives, the various intrapsychic conflicts, and the genesis and management of anxiety (defense mechanisms).

Psychopathology

Psychoanalytic theory was originally designed to explain neurotic symptoms. In his early work with hysterical patients, Freud concluded that most human mental activity was unconscious. The drives themselves were kept out of consciousness in order to avoid anxiety. Even unacceptable ideas and feelings were unconscious. For any symptom, one could, by the psychoanalytic method, discover which drive and which defense were interacting. A symptom was thus either the modified expression of a drive or a defense against it. The hysterical paralysis of an arm could be a defense against using the arm to do something forbidden—such as masturbation. Meanwhile, the paralyzed arm may flop loosely in the lap and rest against the genital area (a partial satisfaction of the desire to masturbate). Each of the neuroses has its own explanation in terms of psychic conflict. A phobia is an example of displaced anxiety, and depression is an act of mourning for a lost love object or hostility turned inwards. Schizophrenia, a psychosis, is the consequence of regression to a narcissistic stage in which ego defenses break down and are overcome by id impulses. The schizophrenic stops acting according to the reality principle, and gives more complete expression to the id drives.

Behavior Change

Freud developed psychoanalysis not only as an explanation of behavior, but also as a form of treatment. The chief method of psychoanalysis is interpretation. The patient reclines on a couch in a quiet room and says whatever comes into his mind (free association). Since all behavior ultimately stems from basic drives (the principle of psychic determinism), the associations eventually touch upon the patient's underlying concerns, even though he is unconscious of them. The analyst helps the patient become aware of the drives and the defense mechanisms and to accept them if they are not really dangerous or give them up if they are harmful. This entire process is called *abreacting* and *working through*. The chief ally of the analyst is the conscious, rational ego of the patient. In essence, the patient comes to terms with his drives, accepts social reality, and permits himself to seek pleasure that is not forbidden by society. When id drives are satisfied or consciously controlled and when ego defenses are mature rather than immature, the patient becomes symptom free.

Evaluation

Sigmund Freud deserves the credit for being the first to develop a theory of personality which approaches in its fullness what we would like a personality theory to tell us. Beginning with his study of mental symptoms, he was able to explain deviant and normal behavior with the same set of principles. His global generalizations: libido, pleasure principle, unconscious mental processes, the ability of drives to be transformed, the ability of psychic energy to be invested first in one place, then in another; all permitted him to construct a dynamic theory of behavior based on how drives are expressed or hindered. The concept of psychosexual stages led to a theory of personality development, and the three constructs, id, ego, and superego, lent a structure to personality. A theory of how to modify mental processes and behavior (through psychoanalysis) completed the picture of the human being.

Freud based his theory upon his understanding of the biological nature of human beings. However, biological science at the turn of the century was far less advanced than it is today. Psychoanalytic theory shows its age. One example is the status of women in the theory. Since the main drama of childhood is the Oedipal desire of the child for mother's love and the fear that father will take revenge, what place is there for the little girl who loves her daddy? Freud explains this as follows: When the little girl discovers she has no penis, she turns her love from mother to father, hoping that father will provide her with the use of his penis. This tendency to view all dyadic relations in Oedipal terms is a serious defect in the theory. It keeps the theory *past-oriented*. Adult behavior is still involved with "unresolved" infantile problems. The meaning of behavior must be sought somewhere in the past and the present can only be understood by understanding the past. This salutary reminder of the importance of a person's history is not balanced by the equally important observation that one cannot understand a person unless one knows him in his present context.

Although Freud's propositions have been modified by his followers, the theory as a whole has not withstood the rigorous tests of modern science and theory construction. It fails on two counts: (1) Freud's scientific language, that of his constructs, does not lend itself to the public verifiability that science requires; and (2) the theory lacks cultural universality. What was a suitable explanation for hysteria in Victorian society does not explain behavior in cultures at different times and with different sociological institutions.

It has generally been believed that it is difficult to collect empirical data on psychoanalysis because its constructs do not lend themselves easily to testable hypotheses; moreover, existing data has seemed non-supportive of Freud's theories (Sears, 1943, 1944). There are, however, more recent reviews of research relevant to Freudian theory (Kline, 1972). Fisher and Greenberg (1977), in a thorough review of research, conclude that there is empirical support for some of Freud's constructs. Such support comes from statistical analysis of direct behavior, such as self-report elicited by questionnaires. The previously mentioned clustering of anal traits was found through factor analysis of the responses to such questionnaires. Masling, et al. (1974, 1967) demonstrated that one could use indices of oral character derived from projective techniques to predict the existence of phenomena such as obesity and relative inaccuracy of interpersonal perception.

A cognitive neurological model in Freud's theory. It is generally believed that Freud did not specify a central neurological structure for the organization of the ego. Actually, Freud postulated an attentional mechanism as early as 1895, but his ideas on the subject were not published until long after his death and his other writings do not show any reference to or explicit use of this idea. Pribram and Gill (1976) have reviewed Freud's early work and interpreted it in the light of modern cognitive neuropsychology. They point out that Freud postulated a "memory motive" structure which is actully an attentional mechanism which channels energy. At birth, energy is located in subcortical structures which Freud called "psychic neurons." At first it is diffuse. As memory grows, the energy becomes regulated and directed and gives rise to the motives that guide behavior. The mechanism works by inhibiting the direction and flow of energy—by telling us what, when and how much to pay attention. Without this memory, the ego could not become the director of the motives.

Modern cognitive and neuropsychological theory distinguishes between executive routines and sub-routines. Sub-routines are programs which regulate automatic behaviors which do not require conscious monitoring. Executive routines are conscious decision-making processes which are alerted when necessary to exert conscious control over sub-routines. In psychoanalytic theory, the ego is the core of the executive routines.

Freud's memory-motive mechanism is in fact a cognitive structure. Consistent with the theory of perception we discussed in Chapter 1, it describes an outflow model in which the extraction of information is directed from within rather than from without. However, Freud specifies that information is managed by inhibiting its admission into consciousness. Other theories, including our own, propose that information is managed by having a wide enough range of differentiation in perceptual structure to extract the information required for effective adaptive behavior.

The postulates and psychoanalysis.   Freud's theory speaks about adaptive behavior and thus fulfills Postulate 1. However, the uniqueness of personality (Postulate 4) is not an important issue in his theory; all males, for example, can be expected to go through an Oedipal situation. The development of personality is a maturational process, since the psychosexual stages are biologically determined. To the extent that the ego uses experience to regulate behavior, we may say that personality is learned. Cultural experience is important in that it provides the social realities which lead to selective inhibition of id drives. While Freud had a theory of perception (the memory-motive hypothesis), it never became an important aspect of his theory. In traditional psychoanalytic theory, what we perceive is always in service of needs.

The theory, like all others, does permit prediction (Postulate 6)—in fact, it is highly consistent and easy to predict from. Freud does talk about patterns in his discussion of various character types (Postulate 7); yet psychoanalytic theory offers so many explanations, that it is difficult to challenge on empirical grounds. All in all, psychoanalytic theory ignores only one of the seven postulates.

ERIK H. ERIKSON (1902–   )

Erikson modified Freud's theory by incorporating into personality theory the importance of culture and social history. This broadened the narrow focus on psychosexual development to include important psychosocial factors. A review of Table 2-1 reveals, however, that both theorists contended that a successful resolution of the critical issues in an ongoing stage is necessary for proper development in the next stages.

Table 2-1   A comparison of Freud's first three psychosexual stages and Erikson's psychosocial stages

Freud's Psychosexual Stages	Erikson's Psychosocial Stages	The Psychosocial Behaviors According to Erikson	Developmental Issues According to Erikson
Oral	Incorporative	Getting and taking	Trust versus mistrust
Anal	Retentive	Holding on versus letting go	Autonomy versus shame and doubt
	Eliminative		
Phallic	Intrusive	Exploring	Initiative versus guilt

Structure and Development

The primary modification that Erikson makes in Freud's theory is to change the stages from psychosexual to psychosocial and to extend the number of stages to eight. Each stage represents a critical juncture at which the person is faced with a new psychosocial developmental task. Normal development consists of the successful resolution of each crisis. Erikson has taken Freud's concept of "resolution of the Oedipal conflict" and has applied it to each of his eight stages. The first three stages are identical with Freud's psychosexual stages, though described in psychosocial language (see Table 2-1). The remaining stages carry his theory of personality development far beyond Freud's, well into advanced adult life. Sex is definitely not central to Erikson's theory—development through critical phases is his main issue.

Each of the stages has an *immature,* a *critical,* and a *resolution* phase. Thus the search for identity has its critical phase in adolescence, but even the young child seeks to identify himself and the mature normal adult has a fairly clear recognition of who he is. Erikson's psychosocial stages along with the task appropriate to each are listed in Table 2-2. To summarize briefly, the first psychosocial task the infant faces is learning whether or not he can trust himself and the world around him. His second task is to learn whether or not he can exert some control over events. Third, he learns whether or not he can make decisions for himself; fourth, if he can accomplish something; fifth, who he is and what he will try to become; sixth, how

Table 2-2   Erikson's eight developmental stages

Stage	Developmental Task (Resolution versus Failure)
1. Early infancy	Trust versus doubt
2. Later infancy	Autonomy versus mistrust
3. Preschool	Initiative versus guilt
4. School	Industry versus inferiority
5. Adolescence	Identity versus role diffusion
6. Young adult	Intimacy versus isolation
7. Middle adult	Generativity versus stagnation
8. Maturity	Integrity versus despair

much he can let himself be deeply committed to others. The seventh stage issue is what that commitment to life and others shall be and how it will be carried out. The eighth stage seems somewhat retrospective—it looks back at how well the other stages have been resolved. Its main issue is determining the meaning of one's life. How has each problem-solving effort contributed to one's personality? Was it worthwhile or not? Successful resolution of the earlier stages as part of a consistent progression leads to self-integration and harmony.

The Dynamics of Behavior

In Erikson's theory, attempts to resolve the major psychosocial problems of life *are* the basic conflicts. Successful resolution depends on cultural influences, social values, child-rearing practices, changing life conditions, and parental models. Erikson has discussed the problems in meeting each of the developmental crises and the results of various kinds of resolution on the basic behavior patterns of the individual. For example, in adolescence, the individual becomes concerned with how he looks, because personal appearance helps him define himself. He likes to discuss his inner feelings with selected peers, to feel accepted and understood. He searches for some area of success with which to identify himself. He thinks about who and what he will become. If previous task resolutions have left him with mistrust, doubt, and guilt, he will have more trouble finding a satisfactory identity for himself.

Evaluation

Through his emphasis on the psychosocial, Erikson exercised an important corrective influence on psychoanalytic theory. He amplified Freud's theory of personality development by taking into account the influences of the entire social field rather than just those of the nuclear family. The concept of psychosocial stages is itself a parsimonious construct which explains a wide range of phenomena. Erikson's theory permits us to compare cultures and social situations to a much greater degree than Freud's theory.

The postulates and Erikson's theory.   Erikson's modified theory includes, of course, those six postulates incorporated in Freud's theory. However, he extends the influence of culture or personality development and he includes the importance of learning. Still, selective perception and uniqueness are not characteristic of his theory.

BEHAVIORISTIC THEORIES

> The practice of looking inside the organism for an explanation of behavior has tended to obscure the variables which are immediately available for scientific analysis. These variables lie outside the organism, in its immediate environment and in its environmental history. (Skinner, 1953, p. 31.)

Locke's vision of experience writing on the *tabula rasa* to shape behavior (empiricism) reached its logical conclusion in the scientific blossoming of learning theory during the first half of the twentieth century. It also received a technological catalyst from the reflexology of the Russian physiologist, Pavlov (1927). A major branch of learning theory today is called reinforcement theory.

Although reinforcement theory, which has emerged as the dominant theory of learning among the behaviorists, has its evolutionary origins in E. L. Thorndike's *law of effect* (1905) and Clark L. Hull's *principle of reinforcement* (1943), we will focus on the representative presentation of more recent theorists, such as Dollard and Miller (1950) and Skinner (1959, 1974). While Freud saw humans as pushed from within, these theorists see humans shaped from without. Within the behaviorist school, however, Dollard and Miller still retain a strong interest in psychoanalysis and the social sciences, whereas Skinner seems singularly committed to reinforcement learning theory. We will close this chapter with a consideration of Bandura (1969b, 1971a & b, 1976) and Rotter (1954), whose theories are an offshoot of behaviorism but also take social interaction and internal mediation into consideration. As such they represent a transition from behaviorist to cognitively oriented theories.

Reinforcement Theory

John Dollard's (1900–   ) commitment to the unification of the social sciences is reflected in the remarkable diversity of his career at Yale, where he held positions in psychology, sociology, and anthropology. Neal E.

Miller (1909–   ) underwent a training analysis at the Vienna Institute of Psychology. Miller and Dollard have written jointly on social learning and imitation (1941) and on personality and psychotherapy (1950); each has also written separately on other topics.

Burrhus Frederic Skinner (1904–   ), unlike Dollard and Miller, does not have a theory of personality. We include him in this section because his views on response-reinforcement have some important applications to behavior control and change. He explains his abortive career as a writer in the following manner: "A writer might portray human behavior accurately, *but he did not therefore understand it.* I was to remain interested in human behavior, but *the literary method had failed me: I would turn to the scientific"* (1967, p. 394, italics ours).

Skinner's conception of the scientific method was probably antedated by his childhood interest in engineering and a tinkering aptitude which he shares in common with other leading behaviorists. When Skinner read Pavlov's *Conditioned Reflexes,* he believed he had found a key to understanding behavior: *"Control your conditions [the environment] and you will see order"* (Pavlov, 1927). He has written widely on the theme of response-reinforcement (1938, 1971, 1974, 1976).

Philosophy

After John B. Watson established behaviorism as a dominant force in American psychology, E. L. Thorndike's work with cats in a puzzle box led him to formulate the law of effect, which states that responses which are rewarded tend to be repeated (that is, have an effect), whereas responses which are not rewarded tend to be eliminated. Following the extension of Thorndike's work by Clark Hull (1943), the principle of reinforcement became an important concept for explaining the development of all kinds of behavior. The main applications to personality were made by Miller and Dollard (1941) and the followers of Skinner.

In a manner similar to Freud, Dollard and Miller (1950) began with the primary assumption that human beings are by nature hedonistic—that is to say, their primary motivation is the attainment of pleasure. However, unlike Freud, they did not limit their definition of pleasure to the release of sexual energy, but rather postulated that pleasure is the emotional component of fulfillment of any tissue need, for example, the emotional components which accompany the biological process of food and water intake, temperature regulation, and the elimination of any noxious stimuli, such as electric shock.

The behaviorist tradition finds a current champion in Skinner who still tenaciously holds that the exploration of the emotional and motivational life of the mind has been described as one of the great achievements in the history of human thought, but it is possible that it harbors one of the great disasters. In its search of initial explanation, supported by the false sense of cause associated with feelings and introspective observations, mentalism has obscured the *environmental antecedents* which would have led to a much more effective analysis (Skinner, 1974, p. 165, italics ours).

Thus the three broad philosophical trends of reinforcement behavior theory still persist. They are:

1. Behavior is learned by the building up of *associations* of response-reward contingencies.
2. Man is basically *hedonistic,* seeking to gain pleasure and avoid pain.
3. Behavior is determined by *environmental* causes.

Structure and Development of Personality

Reinforcement theorists pay almost no attention to internal events and instead concentrate almost exclusively on the developmental process and principles of learning. The structural units of reinforcement learning theory are *response* and *drive.* The essential processes in learning are *stimulus* and *reinforcement.*

For Miller and Dollard, learning is the major psychological process determining the development of personality. You are what you learn! According to these investigators, no learning can take place without the presence of a *drive.* A drive is defined as the energy which is created any time a fundamental physiological need is frustrated or deprived. All of us have drives. What makes us different and creates our unique personalities is the kinds of responses we make to reduce our drives. Drives are always reduced by *instrumental behavior*—that is to say, any behavioral response seeks some *drive reduction.* These instrumental acts, elicited by *stimuli,* begin as trial-and-error responses. Only some of these responses succeed in obtaining the reward which will reduce the drive and satisfy the need. These are the responses that become reinforced.

A stimulus that elicits a response which in turn receives reinforcement is no longer a neutral stimulus. Instead it becomes a *cue* for the repetition of the successful or reinforced response. The response to a cue is always that response which was reinforced in the past.

Since organisms are complex—that is to say, they are capable of producing more than one response in the presence of a cue—it became necessary to explain how responses are organized. Hull (1943) developed the concept *habit-strength* to describe the potency of the particular response which results from the contingency of past reinforcement. The more reinforcements a response has received, the greater its habit-strength.

Given the complexity and uncertainty of environmental reinforcement, it does not always turn out that the most dominant response is rewarded. Consequently, the response which is next dominant will be tried, and so on down the line, until one response meets with success. To describe this ordinal set, Hull coined the term *habit family hierarchy* (of responses). Thus, whenever an organism is placed in a particular cue situation, the response hierarchy becomes operant. If it succeeds and consummation produces a sufficient level of satisfaction, then behavior with respect to that drive will cease. One may wonder why learning does not simply produce extremely fixed and rigid behavior cycles. It is because responses do not always meet success, a situation termed the *learning dilemma.* If the hierarchy of responses is exhausted without satisfaction, a new response will be tried which might be successful, and the cycle can then repeat itself. That is how change takes place. *The only time one has to learn new tricks is when the old ones don't work.*

It quickly becomes apparent to the observant reader that not all adult behavior is guided by those incentives which directly gratify tissue needs. Adults do not act only to get food, water, air, and sex—physiological incentives which reinforcement theorists have called *primary reinforcers.* Money, prestige, and status, among other things, can also be powerful reinforcers. To show how these *secondary reinforcers* operate, behaviorists have performed *token reward* experiments, in which animals learn to hoard chips if the chips can be exchanged for such food gratifiers as peanuts and bananas. These experimental data have been used to explain why such symbols as money become powerful reinforcers in human society. Given the imagination of the human species, the range of secondary reinforcers is virtually unlimited. It is quite clear, particularly in societies that are economically above the subsistence level, that most of our behavior is geared toward secondary rather than primary reinforcement.

In addition to the concepts of response hierarchy and secondary reinforcers, reinforcement theorists introduced a third concept to account for the complexity and variability of behavior. This concept is *generalization,* and there are two kinds: (a) stimulus generalization and (b) response generalization. *Stimulus* generalization occurs when a new and different stimulus evokes the same response, as when, having been frightened by an auto accident, the person is now afraid to ride in a car. *Response* generalization occurs when different responses are made to the same stimulus. Thus, a person may respond to a danger with fearful thoughts, verbal complaints, running away and various physiological changes.

Dollard and Miller account for the major Freudian personality types, for example, the oral, anal, and genital characters, on the basis of those habit responses which received maximum reinforcement during the early stages of socialization. For example, the anal-retentive character is someone who received approval (secondary reinforcement) for being neat and orderly rather than for being spontaneous and impulsive.

Skinner's operant conditioning. Skinner dispensed with the stimulus and spoke only of response reinforcement. He distinguishes between responses which are *elicited* by a stimulus (as when the eye blinks in response to an approaching object) and responses which are *emitted* by the organism without any external stimulus being required; he calls these emitted responses *operants,* responses such as walking, running, pulling, and vocalizing. Dispensing with the construct of personality, Skinner reasons that complex behavior is shaped through the patterning of reinforcement. Anything that strengthens the probability of an operant is a reinforcer. There are two ways of shaping operants through reinforcement—namely, when the operant attains a desired reward (positive reinforcement) and when it removes a noxious stimulus (aversive training). Positive reinforcers are food, water, praise, and attention. Examples of aversive operants are escape and avoidance. Thus, the probability of a particular operant's occurring can be reinforced through following that response with food or water; operants can also be strengthened if they lead to avoidance or escape from painful situations. In addition, punishment, which is the presentation of a noxious stimulus (such as a shock) after the response is made, will decrease the probability that the response will occur again. However, since the Skinnerians have empirically demonstrated that the response decrement following punishment is temporary, it has little value in the elimination of responses in behavior. Thus, Skinner has stressed the use of positive reinforcement in the shaping of behavior.

An effective way to shape more permanent behavior is to vary the *schedule of reinforcement.* Rather than reinforcing the subject each time he makes a correct response, Skinner and his associates have developed the technique of partial reinforcement, which results in behavior that is more resistant to extinction. Either a *variable interval* schedule (one that presents reinforcement at varying times) or a *variable ratio* (one that reinforces the desired response almost at random) is likely to produce the most permanent shaping. Operants shaped under these schedules can hardly be extinguished. A cartoon that depicts Skinner's fascination with control through reinforcement is shown in Figure 2-3.

The Dynamics of Behavior

Since the laws of reinforcement learning are already principles of a dynamic process, some aspects of dynamics have necessarily been discussed above. Suffice it to say that the key to dynamics is the *drive stimulus.* The

Figure 2-3   "Boy, have I got this guy conditioned! Every time I press the bar down he drops in a piece of food." Source: B. F. Skinner. A case history in the scientific method. *American Psychologist*, 1956, *11*, 221-233.

basic foundations for arousing behavior are the primary drives of hunger, thirst, and sex. However, in societies where these primary needs are well taken care of, the drive stimuli associated with them are not the motivators for most social behavior. Consequently, *secondary drive stimuli,* such as those associated with some *place, verbal description,* or *symbolic* aspect of the primary drive become the actual instigators of behavior. Consider all the secondary drive-stimulating effects connected with eating and sexual behavior in our society.

When the responses available to the individual are neither drive reducing nor reinforcing, a *learning dilemma* occurs. This dilemma necessitates the initiation of new responses more distant in the habit family hierarchy.

Conflict can occur between responses to drive stimuli. The most prevalent conflict is approach-avoidance. An analysis of this kind of conflict as seen by Miller is depicted in Figure 2-4.

Notice that whether the actual behavior or response is executed depends on factors such as the following: (1) the strength of approach, (2) the strength of avoidance, (3) the gradient of approach, and (4) the distance from the goal. Whenever the avoidance gradient begins to cross the approach gradient, fear is elicited and vacillation occurs. The maladaptive consequences of such indecision and its relationship to neurotic behavior have been discussed by Dollard and Miller, who recast the Freudian notion of conflict in behaviorist terminology. They suggest that the response of "not thinking" (repression) is used to reduce anxiety, and therefore becomes a reinforced response. For example, if a thought produces anxiety, the latter becomes a drive stimulus, a cue to behave in such a way as to call up a response which can reduce the anxiety drive (this happens in approach-avoidance conflict). In this and other ways, reinforcement theory is offered by its authors as a parallel to psychoanalytic theory, but in concepts which are easier to validate by experimental methods.

Psychopathology

All behaviorally oriented learning theorists view behavioral pathology as a response pattern learned according to the same principles of behavior as are all response patterns. Two leading proponents of this approach have reasoned more specifically that, since all behavior can be seen as an adjustment resulting from a particular history of reinforcement, "the specific behavior termed abnormal is learned, maintained and altered in the same manner as normal behavior" (Ullman & Krasner, 1969, p. 105). Furthermore, these adjustment response patterns are defined as situation specific, that is, they result from causes in the external environment rather than from personality factors within the individual. Thus, behavioral theorists eschew the use of symbolism or any other kind of hypothetical construct or central intervening variables or process such as self or ego.

Behavior modifiers limit themselves to the assessment of specific *inappropriate responses* and the *current reinforcement conditions* which are maintaining the responses. Thus, Ullman and Krasner argue further that the other forms of assessment concern themselves with "why" questions, whereas behavior therapists concern themselves with "what" questions. This prefer-

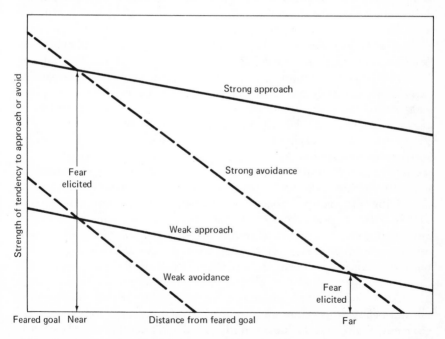

Figure 2-4   Graphic representation of conflict situations. Source: Adapted from Miller, 1951.

ence is explained by their belief that "the answers to 'why' questions are frequently beyond behavioral specification, testing, and direct modification. . . . 'What' questions are much more likely to lead to behavioral answers than 'why' questions" (Ullman & Krasner, 1969, p. 241). This general view that psychopathology is the result of the maladaptive effects of learning is exemplified by the views of Dollard and Miller on anxiety and conflict.

Dollard and Miller on anxiety and conflict.   Anxiety is a drive stimulus, with energizing power comparable to hunger and sex drives. Abnormal symptoms are learned and reinforced because they reduce the anxiety drive. These anxieties originate in the first instance because they are stimuli associated with punishment experienced in connection with the expression of the primary drives of hunger, sex, elimination, and hostility.

The fact that the same stimulus—for example, a sexual incentive—can produce both an approach (anticipation of pleasure) as well as an avoidance (anxiety) response gives rise to the approach-avoidance conflict situation. It is the vacillation produced by these competing drive stimuli—namely the *drive conflict,* which produces the neurotic behavior. Abnormal symptoms are developed and reinforced because they reduce the anxiety drive connected with the conflict.

Dollard and Miller (1950) give the example of a 23-year-old married woman who developed a chain of symptoms related to sex-conflict anxiety. The temporal sequence started when she felt faint in a store. This was followed by becoming afraid of going out alone because she might develop heart trouble. She began to count her heartbeats—an obsessional symptom! All of the early symptoms, namely feeling faint and fear of heart trouble which, in turn, kept her home, protected her from the anxiety and guilt aroused by fantasies of sexual seduction. The counting of heartbeats further reduced her anxiety by preventing thoughts and fantasies of sexual seduction: thus all of these links in the symptom chain were reinforced because they reduced the (guilt) anxiety drive and relieved the conflicts.

Other classical psychoanalytic phenomena are similarly interpreted in drive-reducing, reinforcement terms. Thus, fixation is the residue of previous strong reinforcements, while displacement is a case of stimulus generalization. The dynamics of displacement as generalization was demonstrated in an experiment, the outcome of which is illustrated in Box 2-3.

Skinnerian interpretation of abnormal responses.   Skinnerians interpret abnormal behavior as the result of a history of faulty conditioning—that is, the consequence of unfortunate contingencies of reinforcement with respect to environmental adjustment. The faulty conditioning can come about in three ways.

1. Certain responses which are required for adequate social behavior did not receive the necessary reinforcement and thus did not become part of the organism's response repertoire.

2. The person developed normal responses but the social environment is providing inappropriate reinforcement. Ullman and Krasner (1969) give many examples of such maladjusted phenomena. They include the so-called blandness, flattened affect, delusions and hallucinations that are characteristic of psychotic behavior. They reason that subjects who display such a lack of responsiveness do so because normal emotional behavior failed to achieve the desired effects and was therefore not reinforced. The patient develops delusions and hallucinations because attention to more usual information is not reinforced. Depression has also been interpreted as a withdrawal of responsiveness because of the lack of appropriate stimulation (Ferster, 1973). Furthermore, Skinner (1948) has demonstrated experi-

mentally how ritualistic behavior can result from noncontingent reinforcement. When reinforcement is given periodically, irrespective of the behavior emitted, pigeons will display counterclockwise turning and dancing behavior because this behavior has become coincidentally associated with the reinforcement contingency, even though the reinforcement was not contingent on the turning response. Onlookers may exclaim in dismay, "Dig that crazy pigeon!"

3. Responses which have certain reinforcing effects may be labeled abnormal by society. For example, obsessive-compulsive behavior is explained as a response pattern which became reinforced because it led to the termination of an aversive stimulus. Similarly, so-called masochistic behavior may be seen as self-inflicted punishment which prevents a stronger punishment from following. It will thus have reinforcement value because it again prevents a more aversive stimulus from occurring.

Bandura (1968) has also noted cases where behavioral maladjustment, for example, sexual fetishism or homosexual aberration, conceivably resulted from reinforcement associated with the development of the symptom or with modeling after a culturally inappropriate model.

Behavior Change

Since all behaviorally oriented learning theorists believe that both adjustment and maladjustment result from learned response patterns, it follows that change in behavior is also effected by applying the laws of learning. The social learning theorist, Bandura (1969b), in writing about how behavior can be modified, has listed five learning techniques which are applicable: (1) *Discrimination training.* Through discrimination training the organism learns to distinguish between behavior which is being reinforced and that which is not. Dollard and Miller (1950) had in fact reasoned that much of therapy consists of discrimination learning through which the person comes to distinguish between past conditions of reinforcement and present realities. (2) *Extinction.* During extinction procedure the undesirable response is eventually eradicated through the permanent withholding of reinforcement. In counseling the parents of children with behavior problems, behavior therapists instruct the parents to ignore the undesirable behavior and to pay attention to socially appropriate behavior. It has been demonstrated that hospital staffs can do the same thing to shift psychotic verbalization to more appropriate forms of communication (Ayllon & Azrin, 1965). These are all examples of changing behavior through extinction and discrimination training. (3) *Counter-conditioning.* In counter-conditioning a more adaptive response, which is simultaneously inhibiting of the maladjusted response, is conditioned to the same stimulus. For example, in *reciprocal inhibition,* the behavior modifier might train the client to relax in the presence of successively more realistic encounters with the anxiety-producing stimulus; for example, if a snake is the feared object, the therapist would first expose the client to pictures of snakes, then perhaps to motion pictures, a tank of live snakes at the far corner of the room, and so on, until the client is actually able to handle a snake. (4) *Positive reinforcement.* Behavior modifiers make wide use of operant conditioning to shape more appropriate behavior in maladjusted clients. This has been demonstrated in severe behavior pathology where schizophrenic children have learned more effective speech patterns (Lovass and associates, 1966). (5) *Imitation.* If, as Bandura has noted, maladaptive behavior can be learned through modeling an inappropriate model, then it also follows that more adaptive behavior can be learned by imitating a model who displays effective and mastery behavior. This principle belongs more properly in social learning theory and will be discussed more fully there.

All of the above techniques in one way or another have been used to develop an extensive array of specific behavior modification techniques, including *systematic desensitization* (Wolpe, 1961) and *implosion therapy* (Stampfl, 1970). In systematic desensitization, behavior is gradually changed by successive counter-conditioning of anxiety responses, beginning with the least anxiety-provoking stimulus and progressing to the most fearful. For example, a client who displays a sexual dysfunction will go through a program of gradual desensitization of sexual anxieties that aims to help the person become more comfortable with the sex partner and the sexual act. In implosive therapy, on the other hand, there is massive overstimulation, or flooding, with anxiety-provoking stimuli. Insect phobias, for instance, are eliminated by flooding the client with prolonged and intense stimulation with the feared object—perhaps motion pictures of crawling, flying, and swarming insects.

Social Learning Theory: Bandura and Rotter

While Bandura and Rotter do not have completely developed theories of personality, they have introduced some important constructs that help bridge the gap between behavioral and cognitive conceptions of behavior. The social learning theorists (especially Bandura, 1965a; Bandura & Walters, 1968; Walters, 1968) have emphasized the general importance of imitation to learning. This kind of shaping has been called *modeling, observational learning,* or *imitation.* Observational learning occurs when the learner acquires a response after watching a model perform the response. Bandura (1976) has even made reinforcement a subset of observational learning. Moreover, Bandura shares Piaget's view that imitation is part of the cognitive disposition of the child.

In an analysis of modeling behavior, Bandura (1971a, b) has concluded that the process of observational learning actually depends on four other subsystems or processes. That is to say, the extent to which a child will imitate a model depends on his processes of attention, retention, and motor reproduction. These perceptual, cognitive, and motor processes are necessary for learning acquisition. The fourth process is reinforcement and motivation, which is not essential for the acquisition of behavior but for the overt performance of learned responses. The model can be a person (real or fictional) or a theme, such as aggression in a movie or on television. Human models will be more effective in inducing modeling behavior if they are depicted as having more power or prestige.

Not only does Bandura explain the development of personality structure by invoking the principle of observational learning, he also accounts for psychopathology and change by this principle:

> When the actual social learning history of maladaptive behavior is known, the basic principles of learning provide a completely adequate interpretation of many psychopathological phenomena, and explanations in terms of symptoms of underlying disorders become superfluous. (1968, p. 298)

The principle of observational learning and Bandura's innovative influence will be discussed at greater length in subsequent chapters.

Cognitive aspects of social learning.   As *social learning theory* has developed, it has moved away from the behaviorist's aversion to theorizing about internal processes. Bandura (1974) has asserted that the key to observational learning is the human capacity to represent observed behavior symbolically, not just literally. Thus, the individual generalizes from observations to categorizations. In this way abstract modeling induces rule-governed *cognitive* behavior.

Another social learning theorist concerned with *cognitive* and *internal control* variables is Julian Rotter (1954). The concepts Rotter uses to describe the dynamics of behavior are: *behavior potential, situation, expectancy, reinforcement value, need potential,* and *freedom of movement* (Rotter, Chance & Phares, 1972).

Essentially, Rotter is concerned with action. He wants to predict the likelihood that a particular behavioral act will occur (behavior potential). *Behavior potential* is a joint function of *expectancy* and *reinforcement value* and is also affected by the *situation.* Thus, the behavior potential that behavior A will occur in situation A depends on the expectancy that behavior A will have significant reinforcement value. Reinforcement and situation are environmental variables. It is his inclusion of expectancy, an organismic variable, that places Rotter in the cognitive camp as well.

Need potential (motivators such as love, achievement, and recognition) provide a deeper understanding of behavior potential and reinforcement value. Need potentials vary between individuals and within the same individual. *Freedom of movement* literally refers to the freedom of action a person has in a specific situation where he is affected by a particular need potential. This freedom depends on how many different ways the individual believes he can go about satisfying the need; thus, freedom of movement is related to expectancy.

Box 2-4   An example of dynamics of behavior according to Rotter

A person finds himself in a love-invoking *situation.* If his *need potential* for love is high, he makes moves toward love-attainment, depending on his set of *expectancies.* His positive movement toward love will depend on his assessment of his chances (expectancy), which in turn depends on his *freedom of movement* (his range of cognitive categories for attaining love). However, if need potential is very low, there is no movement irrespective of the person's expectancy and its associated aspects.

Rotter's important integration of *person* and *environmental* (situational) *variables* has led him to construct concepts such as *locus of control* (see Chapter 6). This cognitive style construct will be examined for its influence on our understanding of personality development, structure, dynamics, psychopathology, and change.

Evaluation

Few would deny that behavior theory is not only parsimonious and well organized but also that it has generated much relevant research. Certainly, the behaviorists' stance, that if we know the reinforcement history of a person, we know all there is to know about that person's behavior, could not be much more succinctly stated!

The major reason for the success of behavior theory on these counts is that it is clear and singularly explicit about its stated aims and intentions. All behavior theorists agree that patterns of behavior are the result of response patterning. Therefore, whether our focus is behavior adjustment, behavior modification, or behavior change, all one needs to do is understand and apply the laws of learning. Considering the relatively short life of behavior theory—especially that it was first applied to behavior modification only around 1960—the volume of research it has generated is truly impressive. Moreover, its propositions are stated in ways which readily lend themselves to experimental analysis.

While one is pleased with the objectivity and compactness of behavior theory, one may well wonder about its comprehensiveness and adequacy. The behaviorists have demonstrated that one can develop a body of knowledge about behavior without constructs about brain, mind, or personality.

In the early days of psychology, when knowledge about the brain and thought processes was so meager, hypotheses about neurological and mental events were little more than speculative. The behavioristic rejection of mental structuralism and the study of consciousness, and the methodological revolution to which it gave rise, was thus a positive advance in the science of psychology. But to spend so much time in the last quarter of the twentieth century on elaborate differentiation or response mechanisms, at the expense of studying and theorizing about brain and cognition, seems anachronistic. We have developed considerably more knowledge and technical sophistication about neurological and cognitive functioning. Not only can we theorize with more empirical support but we can also measure the effects of brain and cognitive functioning with acceptable reliability and validity. Some behavior modifiers have even expressed the view that behavior therapy and theory should move from its oversimplified position to a broader perspective. Arnold Lazarus (1971, 1977), a well-known behavior therapist, has extended behavior therapy to include cognitive dimensions. Others have reinterpreted and subsumed behavior theory under cognitive theory (Weiner, 1972).

These limitations apply to reinforcement theory. Many of them have been remedied by social learning theory. Bandura (1976) has broadened the base of behavior theory to include organismic mediating factors—that is, cognitive constructs—between stimulus and response. Thus, observational learning is possible because the child has innate cognitive capacities. Moreover, Bandura believes that reinforcement is a subordinate subset of observational learning.

Rotter, who also calls himself a social learning theorist, employs even more cognitive constructs in his theory. He conceptualizes expectancy as a cognitive variable and his locus of control hypothesis is actually a cognitive style variable, as we will discuss in later chapters.

All of these theorists would agree with our postulates that personality is adaptive, unique, learned, influenced by culture, and can be predicted. Reinforcement theorists, however, would not agree that personality determines the selection of response (Postulate 5) nor that there is a central personality pattern which permits the understanding of the function of a response (Postulate 7). For Rotter, and possibly for Bandura, Postulates 5 and 7 are also valid.

3

**theoretical
conceptions
of personality II:
becoming the active
organism**

OVERVIEW

Unlike psychoanalytic and behaviorist based theories of personality, the theories discussed in this chapter pay more attention to the person as an active, seeking, self-fulfilling organism. This is far more in keeping with the Leibnizian and Kantian traditions rather than the Lockean point of view. A composite view that emerges from these theories depicts a *self* which is creative, future-oriented, continually developing, goal-seeking, integrated, and self-actualizing. These theorists include Jung, Horney, Sullivan, Murray, Rogers, Allport, and the existentialists. All these theories fulfill the seven postulates.

Where possible, we will discuss each theory under the headings of philosophy, personality structure, development, dynamics, psychopathology, and behavior change. Sometimes these headings are combined. Just as it was more convenient in our discussion of psychoanalysis to treat structure and development under one heading, so is it convenient in discussing Jung to combine structure and dynamics. Where a theory is lacking or sparse in its explanations of any of these topics, that heading has been omitted.

ANALYTIC PSYCHOLOGY: CARL G. JUNG (1875–1961)

Philosophy

Born and raised in Switzerland, the son of a clergyman, Jung early showed an interest in religion, philology, and archeology. A physician, he was drawn to psychiatry because it gave him the most opportunity to combine his humanistic interests with his medical training. He broke an eight-year association with Freud in 1914. Jung eventually went on to develop his own system, which he called analytic psychology. A tireless writer and scholarly thinker, he made field trips to various parts of the world to study other cultures. It is thus not surprising that he wove into his system gleanings from Eastern religions and philosophies as well as Western history and religious practice.

It is logical that the son of a Swiss pastor who was interested in philology and archeology should construct a system in which symbols, religion, and racial history have a special meaning. Jung is a teleologist (from Greek *telos*—goal or end point), for whom each human being passes through a life cycle, from birth to death, with a somewhat biologically preordained development of personality. By nature, human beings tend to react to the major issues of life in ways that are determined by their inherited potential. These major issues include birth, death, sex, the problem of good and evil, the issue of power and helplessness, the problem of social relatedness, and so on. However, some inherited characteristics may differ from race to race, what Jung termed a racial or *collective unconscious* (Jung, 1960).

Jung's overall view of personality structure and development accounts for social change and social factors in a special way. For Jung, society and history themselves are continuous developments in some grand unfolding scheme. Societies flourish and decay as they live out their life cycles. Jung is primarily a student of the inner development of the human being. The foundations of personality are archaic, innate, and probably universal.

Personality Structure and Dynamics

Jung's theory of personality structure is in many ways more complex than that of any of the other theorists. He divides personality into four main aspects: *constituent parts,* or the structure proper, *contents, dynamic forces,* and their *interrelationship* (1960).

Constituent parts. The structure of the human personality is comprised of four elements: ego, personal unconscious, collective unconscious, and persona.

1. *Ego.* This is the conscious, self-aware part of the personality. It is that which the person defines as himself. Jung's ego is a phenomenal self, unlike Freud's which is only partly conscious and functions as the mediator between id and external world.

2. *Personal unconscious.* This is material accessible to consciousness, but which exists subliminally in a repressed, suppressed, or a forgotten state. It is similar to Freud's unconscious repressed. It is here that complexes exist.

3. *Collective unconscious.* This is the most influential system in the personality, a set of memory traces left over from our common evolutionary development. It is not the memories themselves which are inherited but the potential for having the same experiences as ancestors. For example, the mother's tendency to cherish and protect her child is the realization of an inherited potential. All humans face the same universe and go through a number of similar experiences. Each infant supposedly has a mother who nurtures and cherishes. The collective unconscious contains a primordial image (archetype) of the mother which can appear in various symbolic forms. *Archetypes* are thus universal ideas about important life issues: they will be discussed further under the section on contents of personality.

4. *Persona.* This is the "public personality," the outer role or mask the person assumes in response to social convention, tradition, and the demands of the archetypes. If the ego identifies only with the persona (the only aspect of himself of which the person is aware), the person becomes a "role player," a "reflection of society," not an autonomous human being and does not experience genuine feelings.

Contents of personality.   Within these regions of the personality certain active factors are at work. These are the contents of personality. They are complexes, archetypes, attitudes, and functions.

1. *Complexes.* These are groups of feelings, thoughts, percepts and memories organized around some nucleus and influencing the rest of the personality (Jung, 1960). If the complex is "strong" it may dominate the rest of the personality; for example, it may be expressed as an exaggerated concern such as a lust for power or a fear of taking action. In Chapter 1 we discussed the reactions of Jewish subjects to both the Star of David and the swastika. In the presence of the emotion-provoking stimuli, the subjects perceived fewer pictures than in the presence of neutral stimuli. Such a tendency would be an example of a complex. Freud also used the term Oedipus complex to describe the situation in which the young boy's desire for his mother's love influences the rest of his personality. He borrowed the term *complex* from Jung before their mutual disagreement.

2. *Archetypes.* As we have stated earlier, archetypes are mental images, found in the minds of all humans. Jung gave several of these names. The *anima* is the feminine archetype in man, the *animus* is the masculine archetype in woman. The archetype of personal power and success is the *wise man* or *magician.* The *hero* is the archetype of struggle against odds. The *shadow* is the symbol for the hidden aspects of oneself. One important archetype is the *self.* It represents the constant striving for harmony within the personality which is part of the inherited developmental process. It holds the parts together and produces unity, equilibrium, and stability.

   Symbols of the archetypes can be seen in dreams, fantasies, myths, artistic productions, and delusions. In Greek mythology, Hercules is the archetypal symbol of the hero who struggles against odds. The Statue of Liberty is a symbol of the earth-mother archetype, which is the image of the nurturing and protecting maternal figure. At different times in life, different archetypes come to the surface, signaling that personality development is entering a new phase.

3. *Fundamental attitudes.* There are two fundamental attitudes, introversion and extraversion. The introvert lives more within himself, like Kretschmer's schizothyme. The extravert reacts more to social influences. The latter is more apt to want to please the people around him or to want their attention. The former is more likely to pay attention to his own values and priorities. The healthy person has a harmonious balance between these attitudes. Generally, however, one attitude is dominant (in the ego) while the other is in the personal unconscious. These fundamental attitudes are actually basic ways of living in the world.

4. *Fundamental functions.* The fundamental attitudes are *modi vivendi*. The functions are *modi operandi*, techniques for orienting oneself in life. They are four in number: *thinking* (analyzing), *feeling* (emotional evaluations), *sensing* (perceiving stimuli), and *intuiting* (unconscious perception and analogic experiencing). To understand what Jung means, let us take the example of four people listening to a concert. The *thinker* follows the music, perhaps with a score, notices how well the orchestra plays and compares this performance with others. The *feeler* is carried away by the music, experiencing joy, sadness, or whatever emotion the music conveys. The *senser* listens, hears the theme and its variations, and hears the different instruments. He has a sensory experience. The *intuiter* may do none of these. His mind indeed may wander away from the music, but at the end of the concert he may be unusually pensive without understanding why. He may find himself humming the theme without even recognizing that he is doing so. The connections between his behavior and the concert experience may remain largely unconscious.

Jung (1960) claimed that in most people one function, which he called the *superior* function, was dominant. In this same person another function would be *inferior* (little used) but would appear as a *modus operandi* in the individual's dreams. If the superior function, for some reason, cannot be used, one of the other functions, called the *auxiliary* would automatically become the *modus operandi*.

The two attitudes and four functions offer the possibility for eight personality types. (See Table 3-1.)

Table 3-1 Jung's eight personality types. They are the result of combinations of the two fundamental attitudes and the four fundamental functions.

		Attitudes	
		Extravert	Introvert
Functions	Thinker	Extravert–thinker	Introvert–thinker
	Feeler	Extravert–feeler	Introvert–feeler
	Senser	Extravert–senser	Introvert–senser
	Intuiter	Extravert–intuiter	Introvert–intuiter

Dynamic forces. Dynamic forces are the underlying motivators of personality structure and style (Jung, 1967). Jung integrates these forces into the continuing process of harmonization and unification so that in the end he focuses on the person's self-actualization. He discusses the dynamic forces under four headings:

1. *Libido.* While libido was largely sexual energy for Freud, Jung saw it in a much larger context. It is the innate striving life force. Psychic energy always moves in the direction of further personality development (the teleological point of view).
2. *Psychic values.* Psychic value represents the amount of energy invested in an item or issue. The more important a psychic value, the more dominant it is in directing behavior. A complex can give rise to psychic values. Anything strongly valued by a person is a psychic value. The extravert values the opinions of others while the introvert values his own internal concerns.
3. *Equivalence.* The law of conservation of energy operates in the psyche. Energy removed from one system appears in another. Thus, if one fundamental function becomes dominant, another tends to become inferior. The analytical person uses thought to keep his emotions under control. Feeling is his inferior function.
4. *Equilibrium.* The major growth movement inside the personality structure is toward psychic equilibrium. This is accomplished by balancing the fundamental functions and fundamental attitudes and accepting and integrating some of the dictates of the collective unconscious. The process by which this harmonization occurs is called *self-actualization.* Its symbolic representative, as mentioned previously, is the archetype of the self.

Other dynamic forces originate outside the personality. Two of these, *life situations* (life experiences) and *conflict,* are interwoven into the basic fabric of life. The process of growth is visualized as the continuing union or integration of oppositional tendencies. Thus any conflict situation becomes an opportunity for growth since it offers the possibility for integration. This is a most important notion, since conflict, from this point of view, is not pathological but necessary for growth. Also necessary are the life experiences which stimulate the continuing development of personality.

Personality Development

Jung distinguishes stages of development according to the *psychic values* of each. In childhood, *survival* values are uppermost, while the adolescent lays greater stress on *sexual* and *self-assertive* values. Adult values become more *culturally* oriented, less impulsive and more introspective. The older adult puts emphasis on *spiritual* values. In development there is a shift in energy from one issue to another.

Life's journey is like an arc ascending to a peak and then descending into senescence and death. The changing phases are milestones in the journey and the process of change is recognized by changing archetypes in the person's dream and other productions. There are some symbols which in themselves signify change (crossing over water, death and rebirth) and these are called *symbols of transformation* (change). Development is a continuous unfolding and, for Jung, it is much more ruled by the collective unconscious than man likes to admit.

Psychopathology

Psychopathology results from interference with personality development. Since the reconciliation of opposite tendencies is the important part of the process of self-actualization, the *one-sided person* is showing maladaptive behavior. Furthermore, by interfering with the functioning of the conscious mind, the *complexes* are also maladaptive. The symptoms of pathological behavior are expressions of the collective unconscious not yet harmonized into the psyche. Consequently a neurosis is an abortive attempt by which the individual tries to resolve conflicting tendencies and to continue growth. Schizophrenia, on the other hand, is a fragmentation of the personality, a failure of the process of reconciliation and integration. Sometimes the excessive demands of society, or of one's life situation, interfere with the person's growth. Jung felt that in our society cultural demands are more likely to rule the ego (the conscious region of the personality only), whereas for wholeness the individuation process (self-actualization) should be the ruler. Jung's concept of maladaptive behavior is thus based on the interference with self-actualization of cultural factors and life experiences.

Behavior Change

Psychotherapy, is a dialectic which leads to a new synthesis. It is an intensely individual process and cannot be stereotyped. As a fellow participant in a grand process of self-exploration, the therapist also experiences growth. For this reason, it is most important for the analyst him- or herself to undergo analysis. The purpose of therapy is for the patient to explore and become aware of his own nature and to experiment with it. Therapy deals with the personal myths of the client, in effect his/her private religion.

Jung wrote quite a bit about the techniques of psychotherapy. A Jungian analysis does not properly begin until certain other problems are resolved. Some problems are better handled by a preliminary approach whose methods help educate the patient to be an effective social being. Thus, Jungian therapy with its emphasis on the inner self is recommended for older rather than younger persons, preferably for those over 35 years of age. Therapy takes a long time, with many stops and starts, because development itself takes a long time. Jungian therapy focuses on understanding one's own internal tendencies, recognizing archetypal contents as they appear in dreams and paintings. Dream analysis and painting are important projective techniques to recognize the effects of the collective unconscious and to appreciate them.

A Jungian studies a person by examining his life experiences and how the individual has reacted to them, by discovering his personal mythology (private beliefs), and examining his dreams and other works for archetypal symbols. He looks for evidence of one-sidedness and efforts of the collective unconscious toward *integration of opposites* and *harmony*. Psychic disharmony can take many forms: archetypal imbalance, as when a man represses his *anima* (tender feelings); attitudinal imbalance—an extreme extravert, for example, may pay no attention to her inner self; functional imbalance, for instance, an extreme thinker ignoring feelings; and complexes, which occur when an overvalued set of ideas and emotions interferes with development.

"Cure" or improvement in functioning is always a movement toward self-actualization by balancing opposites. Such a movement permits dispensing with symptoms. As one-sidedness decreases, subjective improvement increases.

Evaluation

Jung's complicated theory gives us a more thorough look at development in later adult life than any other theory. His notion that myths and symbols are universally used products of an unconscious mind parallels Freud's notion. However, while Freud explains these unconscious products in terms of sexual libido or aggressive drive, Jung sees sex as only one issue among many, and the universal myths and symbols as indicative of inherited tendencies. The notion that we inherit the tendency to have the same experiences as our ancestors is not always congenial to Western civilization, where conscious direction has been predominant and heredity has been discounted. Jung's culture, however, was in some ways special. Switzerland has been a remarkably stable society for centuries. In such an atmosphere it becomes easier to recognize inherited influences than in a fluctuating pluralistic society.

Jung seems most interested in showing us how the collective unconscious influences us and in this endeavor he constructs an interesting and consistent theory which deserves further research. While Jung himself did empirical research, subsequent Jungians have been more inclined to be therapists rather than researchers.

Jung probably never intended his theory to be so complete that it would account for everything. He willingly ignores child development and adolescence because he is focusing on aspects that others neglect: *later life with its spiritual concerns* and the *collective unconscious*. He was the first to point out that the therapist grows along with the patient, that the analyst should be analyzed, and that therapy is a growth experience, not only a treatment for the maladapted psyche.

Cognitive aspects of Jungian constructs. All of the contents of personality, located in the various regions, are cognitive structures. Complexes are groups of percepts, memories and thoughts. The fundamental attitudes and functions direct selective perception. Archetypes are mental images that contain directions for behavior and personality development. Although Jung does not really specify any consistent relationship between these three kinds of cognitive content, one would assume that the archetypes of the collective unconscious are the primary cognitive foundations of personality because they are inborn and guide the development of personality.

KAREN HORNEY (1885–1952)

Philosophy

Born in Germany and trained as a psychoanalyst in Berlin, Karen Horney moved to the United States in 1932 and eventually, with co-workers, founded the American Institute of Psychoanalysis in New York. Although she became increasingly dissatisfied with Freudian concepts, she continued to think of herself as a psychoanalyst who was correcting some of the fallacies in Freud's thinking. Her disagreements with Freud centered around her belief that social and economic forces, rather than biological and sexual, were more important in influencing behavior.

For example, Oedipal problems are not sexual/aggressive but the result of faulty child-parent relationships such as rejection, overprotection, or abuse (see also Adler's comments about pampering and rejection in the next chapter). What Horney retained of Freud's theory was the notion of unconscious motives and psychic determinism.

Structure, Development and Dynamics

A key concept of Horney's personality theory is the concept of self, which she subdivides into real, actual, and ideal. In every human being there is a core of health and growth, which Horney calls the *real self.* The actual self fails to fulfill the potential of the real self because of the social environment. The social customs and reinforcers of society as well as the errors made by parents, primarily because of ignorance or preoccupation with self, frequently lead to inhibited growth of the real self.

The real self is a biological potential which actualizes itself through certain socialization practices, termed the six *social needs* of the real self. They are *emotional warmth, security, freedom, good will, guidance,* and *healthy friction.* When these six social needs are not met, the child experiences a subjective feeling of anxiety which Horney calls *basic anxiety,* a feeling of being isolated and helpless in a potentially hostile world, a feeling of "not belonging." The parental mistakes that induce such a state in the child include excessive domination, indifference, erratic and unpredictable behavior, disrespect for the child's needs, lack of guidance, disparagement, too much or too little responsibility, overprotection, isolation from peers, injustice, and a hostile atmosphere. Significantly, the parents are also considered victims of the culture (Horney, 1937).

In order to combat basic anxiety, the child is forced to develop compensatory strategies. For example, if he feels unloved, he tries to get love by submitting, bribing, or making others feel guilty. If he cannot get love at all he may decide to seek domination and power over others, and if he cannot get that, he may seek revenge. In order to realize himself and attain the satisfaction of his needs, the child develops another compensation, an *idealized image (ideal self),* a picture of what he should be in order to be acceptable to others and avoid basic anxiety. The idealized image is a rigid system of inner dictates by which the person makes demands upon himself. These rigid inner dictates are irrational, inappropriate and, to the extent they are desired to an extreme degree, are impossible (Horney, 1951).

The individual now seeks to *realize* himself by pursuing the idealized image and in so doing becomes further *alienated* from the real self. For example, a male may strive to be a dominant, aggressive, and outgoing person because he believes that is what he should be. Actually, he may prefer to be soft-spoken, gentle, and affectionate. His striving is not in the direction he would really prefer; the idealized image is a *should,* not a *want.* Thus, the dictates of the shoulds, which perpetuate self-alienation, are motivated by the desire to avoid basic anxiety.

The growth of the individual is a juxtaposition between the real and idealized selves. To talk about this in viable ways, Horney used the term, *actual self,* which consists of the overlapping parts of the real and idealized selves (see Figure 3-1).

For Horney, all behavior can be seen as movement in a social context—movement *toward, away from,* or *against* people.

Psychopathology

The previous discussion of structure, development, and dynamics also explains much of Horney's theory of psychopathology. Horney used the word *neurosis* as a generic term for all maladaptive behavior. Neurosis is a matter of degree; all of us have some neurotic tendencies. The neurotic is a person *alienated* from his real self, trying to be like his ideal image (*neurotic claims*). Horney terms this abandonment of the real self and pursuit of the ideal the *search for glory*. Neurosis is thus by definition a character disorder, a disorder of personality. Box 3-1 describes the sequence by which neurosis develops.

Box 3-1   Developmental sequence in neurosis according to Horney

UNFAVORABLE ENVIRONMENT
(rejection, overprotection, punishment—
failure to satisfy the six social needs)
↓
BASIC ANXIETY
(feeling alone and helpless in a hostile world)
↓
COMPENSATORY STRATEGIES
(methods for getting love, power, revenge)
↓
NEUROTIC CHARACTER STRUCTURES
(neurotic pride, neurotic claims, shoulds)
↓
IDEALIZED IMAGE
(the perceived answer to the problem)
↓
SEARCH FOR GLORY
(the pursuit of the idealized image
and abandonment of the real self)
↓
ALIENATION (NEUROSIS)
(neurotic character structures become fixed)

In Western culture there are commonly three major solutions to neurotic conflicts (Horney, 1951). The first of these Horney calls the *expansive solution,* or the appeal of mastery. The person who chooses this way of trying to realize his idealized self-image pursues success, perfection, self-glorification, and can even develop an arrogant vindictiveness and a concern with personal superiority. The expansive person essentially moves against people. On the other hand, while the second most common solution, the *self-effacing,* or the appeal of love, is itself a movement toward people, it is a dependent pattern. Horney calls it *morbid dependency.* In our society, this behavior is more commonly seen among females because of the way females are socialized in the culture (Horney, 1937). It is true that love is a powerful emotion which overcomes many hesitations and, therefore, some people feel that if only they can love and be loved enough, it will solve all other problems.

The third common solution is *resignation* or the appeal of freedom.

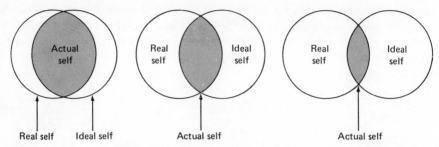

Figure 3-1 Diagramatic representation of relative congruence between real and ideal selves. The diagram on the left represents a healthy adaptive personality, while the one on the right shows the most alienation and greatest degree of psychopathology. The actual self is the area of congruence between real and ideal selves. The greater the overlap between real and ideal selves, the more functional is the person's actual self.

This is essentially a way of moving away from people. It includes the avoidance of responsibility and the pursuit of time-wasting activity, hedonistic excitement, or easy success. Horney is essentially moralistic in her approach to social behavior, and *la dolce vita* is, for her, a form of shallow living which implies resignation from the responsibility to realize the self. The normal person integrates all three types of movement, all the major solutions, and is not alienated.

Horney also explains many other traits seen in adult life as the effects of neurotic claims, as defenses against threats to the idealized image, and/or consequences of unresolved conflicts. These include fearfulness, lack of motivation, hopelessness, sadistic behavior, a diffuse sense of frustration and discontent, insensibility to others, and an uncertainty about what is right (Horney, 1951).

For Horney, the culture is the basic cause of emotional difficulty, and the neurotic is "the stepchild of the culture." Cultural defects in socialization interfere with the actualization of the real self and lead to the compensatory development of an ideal self. The greater the incongruity between real and ideal self, the greater the alienation, the more severe the neurosis. This process is illustrated in Figure 3-1.

Behavior Change

Horney was primarily an analyst and her theory of behavior change is a theory of psychotherapy (Horney, 1939). In her actual work she used a slightly modified version of psychoanalysis. However, her aims and interpretations were different. She explored the childhood situation in order to discover the factors that had interfered and were still interfering with growth. She interpreted the conflict, confronted the patient with his real feelings and values, exposed the neurotic claims, the search for glory, and the tyrannical shoulds as well as all other self-defeating and alienating behaviors. She encouraged the emergence of spontaneous behaviors, considering them growth movements on the part of the real self. The eventual aim of psychotherapy was the same as the aim of any healthy personality development—*self-realization*. Self-realization included four healthy factors: spontaneity, self-responsibility, inner independence, and wholeheartedness.

Evaluation

Horney has a sophisticated theory of structure in her notions of real *self* and ideal *self*, although exactly what the real self is, is not so clear. Her theory of development is a clear statement of how the socialization process affects, for good or ill, the developing child and more than the other theorists, she describes the different kinds of conflict and their consequences. One strength of the theory is in its view of neurotic behavior as simply an unfortunate extreme of normal behavior—it is what you and I would also do if we had been raised the same way and developed the same values. She does not explain fully why failure to satisfy the basic needs should lead to anxiety. Perhaps it is not that faulty socialization leads to basic anxiety, but that it fails to help the growing person effectively deal with the environment that he confronts. The chief cognitive structure for dealing with basic anxiety is the ideal self (idealized image) which essentially consists of messages to the self about how to avoid basic anxiety.

INTERPERSONAL PSYCHIATRY: HARRY STACK SULLIVAN (1892–1949)

Philosophy

Sullivan called his school of thought "interpersonal psychiatry" to stress the focus of his interest. He is the first American-born of the self-theorists we have discussed. A psychiatrist, he made a name for himself through his ability successfully to understand and treat schizophrenic patients during an era of therapeutic pessimism about this condition. There are rumors that Sullivan himself suffered from a psychotic break during his own adolescence and that this personal difficulty made him better able to understand schizophrenia.

Sullivan underwent a classical Freudian analysis early in his career. While his early writings reveal the effects of this experience, he later renounced psychoanalysis as an explanation of human behavior. Since he was strongly influenced by some social scientists, notably Charles R.

Cooley and George H. Mead, he stressed the importance of culture as an influence on personality and believed that the study of cultural processes could lead to an effective preventive psychiatry.

It should not be overlooked that Sullivan's American background was probably important in giving him a pragamtic approach to personality theory. His concepts sometimes seem directly descended from William James, the father of American psychology. His operational approach is also American rather than European. He gave his journal, *Psychiatry,* the subtitle "The Operational Study of Interpersonal Processes."

Personality Structure, Development, and Dynamics

Sullivan begins with the assumption that human beings are primarily social animals who become acculturated through the socialization process by means of *empathy.* The purpose of any behavior is the pursuit of satisfaction and security, items obtained through interpersonal relationships. The proper way to study behavior, then, is to study the interpersonal situation. The therapist is a student of behavior who is both an observer of and a participant in the interpersonal situation he is studying. This participant-observer must study his own responses as well as those of the patient in order to understand what is happening between them (Sullivan, 1954).

Personality is the relatively enduring pattern of recurrent interpersonal relationships (Sullivan, 1953). These interpersonal relationships develop out of *dynamisms,* the relatively enduring patterns of energy transformation. A dynamism can be any habit system that the individual has developed, whether feeling, attitude, or action. For example, a male who is motivated by strong desires repetitively to seek out sexual relationships with females is displaying the lust dynamism. A person who has a strong and enduring pattern of seeking close friendships is expressing the affinitive dynamism. Similarly, an individual who continually likes to take care of other people is expressing a nurturing dynamism.

Dynamisms have developed because of their ability to satisfy the basic needs of security and satisfaction. They are primarily *modi operandi,* ways of relating to the world. For example, the sublimation dynamism consists of learning to use language for what it accomplishes, not for communicating how one really feels. *Selective inattention* (the dissociation dynamism) leads to more effective concentration of attention.

The dominant or focal dynamism is the *self-system,* which directs the individual's perception toward seeking information that is consistent with self-protection and maintaining self-esteem. It will not gate information which is incongruent with security and preserving self-esteem. In effect, selective inattention transforms any information of a threatening or self-deflating nature into messages more congruent with the individual's self-system. Sullivan called this *inflating the self-system* and, in the extreme, this takes on the form of delusions of grandeur. Furthermore, the self-system is self-perpetuating: through filtering of messages, it reinforces itself. This is Sullivan's explanation of why all human beings have "blind spots" and why one of the primary functions of therapy is to help overcome them. The self-system sets into motion a continuing process of selective perception.

Some dynamisms are dissociated (kept out of consciousness) by the selective inattention process because consciously recognizing them would lead to unpleasant anxiety. For example, most of us do not think about our own deaths or the deaths of loved ones. If we do think about death, it is in an abstract, offhand way. To think specifically and thoroughly about it would be upsetting. We all have an awareness of mortality and expect some day to die. Meanwhile, concern with this or that specific problem allows us to push the idea of death into the back of our mind and to ignore it.

In addition to dynamisms, the personality contains *personifications*. A personification is an habitual attitude, a group of feelings and concepts that grow out of past experience as dynamisms are being expressed. For example, a nurturing person is a personification of a "good mother." Frightening and demanding (dictatorial) male figures may be personifications of a "frightening father." The way we coped with one frightening person serves as a general rule for coping with all similar people. A personification gives us a rule for dealing with a certain class of situations.

A third constituent of personality structure is *modes of thought* and *experience*. Dynamisms and personifications require a cognitive mechanism. Since perception is selectively gated, it was necessary for Sullivan to develop a theory of perceptual or cognitive development. He did this by describing a three-stage development of cognitive processes. The three stages are called *prototaxic, parataxic,* and *syntaxic* thought. All children begin cognitive development in the prototaxic mode, with such preverbal and alogical experiences as pleasure at sucking the nipple. Prototaxic experiences are not entirely devoid of thought, however, since each such experience yields some information about the environment.

As the child develops, his natural cognitive abilities lead him to start asking questions about cause-and-effect relationships and thus to construct a world of reality. In these first feeble attempts to create order and reliability, the young child uses the parataxic mode—as when a four-year-old states that the movement of clouds causes the wind to blow. While parataxic thinking makes sense to the individual, it is not necessarily logical to others. Parataxic distortion can be seen in paranoid ideas of reference, as when one observes two people talking to each other and assumes that they are talking about him. By contrast, syntaxic thought derives from causal or logical explanations that have been commonly agreed to by a group of people and therefore have consensual validation.

Sullivan divided the development of personality into six different stages, which he considered typical for our own culture, not necessarily for others. These stages are described in Table 3-2. Sullivan carries personality development later into life than does Freud, but does not consider its application to the older person as do Jung and Erikson.

Table 3-2   Sullivan's Six Developmental Stages

Stage	Age	Developmental Task	Outcomes
Infancy	0–2 years	Identifying oneself Satisfying primitive needs	Primary communica is through empathy
Childhood	2–6 years	Learning appropriate social communication	Language skills develop
Juvenile	6–9 years	Functioning outside the home Learning to interact with peers	Independence begin
Preadolescence	9–11 years	Chum relationships (close friends with same sex)	Affinitive dynamism activated
Early adolescence	11–17 years	Developing heterosexual relationships	Lust dynamism activated
Late adolescence	17–	Mature social relationships Effectively coping with anxiety	Responsibility Security

From birth on, the infant is able to "feel" the emotions of his mother by means of *empathy*. When she is tense, the infant, as if by contagion, can himself become tense. The mother's attitude, her ways of handling the infant and caring for his needs all have an emotional tone and affect the infant's own state of feeling. Empathy is thus an early preverbal process of communication between mother and child that strongly influences later acculturation. For example, if the mother displays intense displeasure, the child may be overwhelmed by *anxiety*—a sense that something is wrong between himself and his world—and find his security and satisfaction in jeopardy. A moderate amount of anxiety, however, is useful in motivating the child to develop effective coping behavior. The child learns to try to please the mother, to be loved and accepted by her, so that her emotional signals to him will be pleasant and agreeable. A rejecting mother may influence the child to avoid close relationships with her and, through personification, with all others like her, in order to avoid the unpleasant threat to security and satisfaction. Later feelings of rejection by peers can lead to avoidance of peer relationships. One's self-esteem depends on how one experiences the reactions of others, and a threat to self-esteem is equivalent to a threat to security and satisfaction.

The experience of severe anxiety, perhaps in relation to a mother's rejecting behavior, leads to a feeling of paralysis so that effective coping becomes impossible. The first priority then becomes to avoid this over-whelming experience. The chief tool in this endeavor is the self-system. This system defines those aspects of the self which are acceptable as the "good me" and reinforces these aspects. Impulses and actions which led to the experience of severe anxiety are denied and dissociated from conscious-ness and experienced as "not me." Such impulses can still be expressed in the unconscious, however.

By contrast, the warm, approving behavior of the mother can be de-fined as aspects of the "good mother," a personification that can extend to adult life. In a similar manner, any number of dynamisms become incor-porated into the personality. The psychodynamics of personality thus in-volves the activation of these dynamisms. Other dynamic processes are empathy, strivings for satisfaction and security, syntaxic thought, and parataxic distortion and self-inflation.

Psychopathology

Human beings must depend upon each other for mutual satisfaction and security. Thus, healthy interpersonal relationships make healthy peo-ple. Maladaptive deviation results from inadequate relationships. Lack of security, for instance, leads to dynamisms such as *fear, envy,* and *avarice,* which in turn further distort relationships and lead to greater insecurity. Examples of how Sullivan applied this theory to specific maladaptive syn-dromes can be seen in his discussion of four personality disorders: hysteri-cal, obsessional, paranoid, and schizophrenic.

The *hysterical* character has a feeling of inferiority and tries to find his security and satisfaction through dependent relations to others (a dyna-mism). Social acceptability is extremely important to him and he tends to conformity in his behavior. Having learned that people will be more friendly to him if he displays distress, he has learned to use symptoms of distress to gain attention, and thus concern and control. The *obsessional* is wary of close personal relationships and tries to stay "in control" of them. Thus he represses his own feelings and prefers an intellectual approach to life (obsessional dynamism). The *paranoid* feels that people are inimical and he protects his self-esteem by being critical of others. He looks for faults in others so that he can excuse himself (paranoid dynamism). The *schizophrenic* has trained himself against human closeness (a dynamism). He feels unable to satisfy others—in effect, "infra-human." If he can become successfully paranoid, he no longer needs to feel "infra-human," he can place blame elsewhere.

Sullivan believed that all paranoids had probably been schizophrenic at one time. The schizophrenic psychosis itself occurs when selective inattention fails and the self-system breaks down. At this point parataxic distortion and prototaxic modes of experience are no longer selectively filtered out by the self-system and the person has lost his main control over severe experiences of anxiety (Sullivan, 1956).

Behavior Change

Sullivan wrote extensively on the process of psychotherapy and on interviewing techniques. The interview is a special interpersonal situation between an expert and a client. The purpose of therapy is to clarify the mistaken patterns of living which disrupt effective relationships (inappropriate dynamisms). Cure occurs when the client understands the unrealistic nature of his parataxic distortions and learns to relate effectively. Because the process of inquiry in therapy threatens the self-system (with its selective inattention), anxiety occurs and the self-system opposes the inquiry (resists looking clearly at its own operations). The therapist respects the client and does not confront him with more anxiety-provoking clarification than he can face at the time. The therapist also avoids behaving like personifications from the client's past. However, by respecting and accepting the client he provides a positive attitude which helps the client to feel self-esteem (Sullivan, 1953, 1956).

Evaluation

Sullivan's most significant contribution to personality theory is his concept of empathy as a form of communication. The strong point of the theory lies in its clinical application. He gives excellent descriptions of patterns of living and how they are manifestations of the dynamisms at work.

It would be fair to say that Sullivan's point of view is not completely Leibnizian. He speaks about drives and energy transformations in somewhat mechanistic terms. He describes satisfaction—a basic motivation—as something that results from need reduction rather than from goal attainment. His concepts of security and satisfaction are themselves not completely worked out; he focuses rather on how they are influenced by interpersonal relationships. However, the self-system is a completely organismic concept. While it is not all of the personality, it is the most important system in it and its integrator.

Like Horney, Sullivan stresses the importance of adequate parental behavior in the socialization of the infant and of the ways in which culture, by being distorted itself, distorts personality development into maladaptive paths. For these theorists, human ethics becomes a necessity for proper growth and survival.

Cognitive aspects of Sullivan's theory. Of all the personality theorists so far discussed, Sullivan is the most consistently and explicitly cognitive. The constructs of dynamisms, personifications and modes of thought are all part of the cognitive process. Dynamisms are patterns of energy transformation which focus behavior responses by directing attention. Personifications are labels which carry a set of instructions for behavior. In describing modes of thought, Sullivan actually described the stages of development in cognition, with syntaxic being the most highly developed form. In this regard Sullivan has something in common with influential cognitive theorists such as Werner and Piaget who will be discussed later.

PERSONOLOGY: HENRY MURRAY (1893-   )

Philosophy

Henry Murray, historian, literary critic, biologist, chemist, physician, and psychologist, is an important American personality theorist. He has had wide influence and is the creator of the Thematic Apperception Test, the most widely used of the projective tests of personality. His approach is to classify personality into component elements which he then interrelates and integrates.

Murray has strong humanistic concerns, pointing out that too many personality theories "make no provision for creativity . . . no fitting recognition of the power of ideals . . . no grounds at all for any hope that the human race can save itself from the fatality that now confronts us" (Murray, 1962, p. 53).

Personality Structure and Development

Murray's unique contributions to structural concepts are *establishments, proceedings,* and *serial programs.* Personality is described as certain consistent *establishments* (existing structures) which the individual manipulates over and over again in the internal and external *proceedings* (events) of his life (Murray & Kluckhohn, 1956, p. 30). Among the establishments of the personality Murray (1938) includes Freud's id, ego, and superego, but modifies and extends their meanings with respect to how the individual transacts proceedings. He rejects the disease model of diagnosis and concentrates instead on the series of consistent *themes* and methods for approaching the world that each individual has developed. It is the job of the personologist (the student of personality) to discover these consistencies as he studies the way the individual transacts proceedings. When the personologist explains the oddities of human proceedings—that is, how the themes in the establishments are invoked in directing specific responses— he is not diagnosing, but *formulating* the consistencies within personality. Proceedings may be *external* (interaction with the environment) or *internal* (daydreaming, problem solving, planning, and fantasy). In fact, Murray effectively used the thematic content of fantasy to arrive at reliable formulations of the individual's personality in his Thematic Apperception Test (TAT).

In the formulation of personality, the personologist is less interested in static structure and more interested in the *serial programs* which guide and organize behavior. Serial programs are *life plans* (containing the consistent themes and methods), orderly arrangements of subgoals integrated into a system, which project into the future and eventually lead to the desired end. Subgoals may vary, but the final end remains the same. Murray believes that this final end is never reached, so that subjectively it is experienced by the individual as a deficiency in the self. The individual thus formulates an ideal self, the *ego ideal,* which represents the unreached aspiration. Murray's notion of ego ideal is similar to Horney's ideal self.

Murray's approach to personality development follows the Freudian model. However, he specifies that personality is formed by the interaction of four determinants: *constitution* (innate endowment), *group membership, role definition,* and *situation.*

Dynamics

Of far greater importance than the structure of personality is its dynamics. Although Murray acknowledged a biological base for energy, he postulated four additional concepts to account for the dynamic forces (direction and energy behind behavior) of personality: *need, press, need-integrate,* and *thema.* The dynamics of personality involve the interaction between a need and a press in the execution of proceedings. Murray uses the term *need* to mean a force which directs the individual's movement in regard to the important incentives of life and lists some 20 or more needs (see Box 3-2).

Those needs which have been satisfied during socialization will become positive incentives; they give rise to approach behavior. Conversely, if attempts to satisfy needs result in failure, those needs are avoided. For example, a bright child whose need for achievement is not being satisfied in the classroom, becomes discouraged, fears failure and avoids the achievement stimulus.

In the pursuit of need satisfaction, the individual has generally learned to anticipate either support or frustration from the environment.

Box 3-2   Illustrative List of Murray's Needs

Need	*Brief Definition*
Abasement	To submit passively to external force. To accept injury, blame, criticism, punishment. To surrender. To become resigned to fate. To admit inferiority, error, wrongdoing, or defeat. To confess and atone. To blame, belittle, or mutilate the self. To seek and enjoy pain, punishment, illness, and misfortune.
Achievement	To accomplish something difficult. To master, manipulate, or organize physical objects, human beings, or ideas. To do this as rapidly and as independently as possible. To overcome obstacles and attain a high standard. To excel oneself. To rival and surpass others. To increase self-regard by the successful exercise of talent.
Affiliation	To draw near and enjoyably cooperate or reciprocate with an allied other (an other who resembles the subject or who likes the subject). To please and win affection of a cathected object. To adhere and remain loyal to a friend.
Aggression	To overcome opposition forcefully. To fight. To revenge an injury. To attack, injure, or kill another. To oppose forcefully or punish another.
Autonomy	To get free, shake off restraint, break out of confinement. To resist coercion and restriction. To avoid or quit activities prescribed by domineering authorities. To be independent and free to act according to impulse. To be unattached, irresponsible. To defy convention.
Counteraction	To master or make up for a failure by restriving. To obliterate a humiliation by resumed action. To overcome weaknesses, to repress fear. To efface a dishonor by action. To search for obstacles and difficulties to overcome. To maintain self-respect and pride on a high level.
Defendance	To defend the self against assault, criticism, and blame. To conceal or justify a misdeed, failure, or humiliation. To vindicate the ego.
Deference	To admire and support a superior. To praise, honor, or eulogize. To yield eagerly to the influence of an allied other. To emulate an exemplar. To conform to custom.
Dominance	To control one's human environment. To influence or direct the behavior of others by suggestion, seduction, persuasion, or command. To dissuade, restrain, or prohibit.
Exhibition	To make an impression. To be seen and heard. To excite, amaze, fascinate, entertain, shock, intrigue, amuse, or entice others.
Harmavoidance	To avoid pain, physical injury, illness, and death. To escape from a dangerous situation. To take precautionary measures.
Infavoidance	To avoid humiliation. To quit embarrassing situations or to avoid conditions which may lead to belittlement: the scorn, derision, or indifference of others. To refrain from action because of the fear of failure.
Nurturance	To give sympathy and gratify the needs of a helpless object: an infant or any object that is weak, disabled, tired, inexperienced, infirm, defeated, humiliated, lonely, dejected, sick, mentally confused. To assist an object in

Box 3-2   Illustrative List of Murray's Needs (*continued*)

Need	Brief Definition
	danger. To feed, help, support, console, protect, comfort, nurse, heal.
Order	To put things in order. To achieve cleanliness, arrangement, organization, balance, neatness, tidiness, and precision.
Play	To act for "fun" without further purpose. To like to laugh and make jokes. To seek enjoyable relaxation of stress. To participate in games, sports, dancing, drinking parties, cards.
Rejection	To separate oneself from a negatively cathected object. To exclude, abandon, expel, or remain indifferent to an inferior object. To snub or jilt an object.
Sentience	To seek and enjoy sensuous impressions.
Sex	To form and further an erotic relationship. To have sexual intercourse.
Succorance	To have one's needs gratified by the sympathetic aid of an allied object. To be nursed, supported, sustained, surrounded, protected, loved, advised, guided, indulged, forgiven, consoled. To remain close to a devoted protector. To always have a supporter.
Understanding	To ask or answer general questions. To be interested in theory. To speculate, formulate, analyze, and generalize.

Source: C. Hall and G. Lindzey, *Theories of Personality*, 2nd ed. (New York: Wiley, 1970), p. 176. Adapted from Murray, 1938, pp. 152–226.

Murray calls the perception of this environmental stimulus a *press,* and, like a need, it influences behavior. Press can be positive, negative or ambivalent depending on whether the individual expects support, frustration or uncertainty. Murray distinguishes between alpha press, which is objective reality and beta press, which is the ideographic subjective interpretation of reality.

An important dynamic transaction occurs when the individual has a positive need and perceives a negative press. For example, "I like people but they are not friendly toward me" creates an approach-avoidance conflict, a kind of conflict common in a variety of behavior patterns.

In addition to cataloging needs and presses and their interplay, Murray also saw the necessity of dealing with the interrelationship and integration of these determiners of behavior. Three concepts serve this integrating function in his theory: *thema, need-integrate,* and *vector-value schema.*

Need-integrate.   The need-integrate consists of the arousal of a need, the image of the goal object, and the instrumental activity required to attain the goal. For example, the succorant person described earlier will perceive his classroom teacher as a potential nurturer (arousing his succorant need). Thus he engages in behavior designed to attain succorance—which is not necessarily appropriate in the classroom.

Thema. A thema is a molar pattern of behavior. It includes the need-integrate, the perceived press, and the anticipation of the outcome and thus constitutes a comprehensive unit of adaptive (or maladaptive) behavior. Themas direct such coping behaviors as problem solving and conflict resolution. The complete plot of a TAT story may be thought of as a thema.

Vector-value schema. Needs, located in the establishment, exist in order to serve important human ends which Murray called *values.* These

---

Box 3-3   Schematic Representation of Murray's Structural and Dynamic Concepts

Structure consists of:

ESTABLISHMENTS (All needs and values flow from establishments)	Id: The unsocialized self containing both socially acceptable and unacceptable impulses.
	Ego: The executor which directs the impulses of the id.
	Superego: Internalized aspects of the culture which directs values.
PROCEEDINGS (includes vectors)	Transactions between the person and the environment.
SERIAL PROGRAMS	Consistent patterns of pursuing goals as directed by needs.

Dynamics consist of:

NEED	An internal force toward movement.
PRESS	A perceived external force toward movement. A perception that the environment supports or blocks satisfaction of the need.
NEED-INTEGRATE	An aroused need, an image of the goal object and knowledge of the activity required to attain the goal object (incentive).
THEMA	The integration of need, press, and need-integrate plus anticipation of outcome and knowledge of coping strategies.
VALUES	The objects of need satisfaction, partly innate, partly learned (e.g. body, property, affiliation, aesthetics).
VECTORS	Forms of movement (proceedings) directed by values, toward goal objects (e.g. dependence, rejection, construction).

values give rise to need satisfying movements (vectors). For example, the value, *body integrity*, can be expressed by the vectors self-defense or retreat from danger. Self-defense and retreat from danger are served by the needs of defendance and harmavoidance listed in Box 3-2. Box 3-3 contains a summary scheme of Murray's theory of structure and dynamics.

Psychopathology

Murray's concept of thema and his invention of the Thematic Apperception Test to measure these molar units of adaptive (and maladaptive) behavior is probably his most influential contribution to the understanding of psychopathology. The TAT is a projective technique for measuring and evaluating personality. In the hands of a skilled clinician it is a powerful tool and thus has gained great popularity among clinical psychologists. In the test, the client is asked to write imaginative stories. From the content of the stories the themas are analyzed and determined.

Psychopathology is the result of maladaptive themas, need-integrates which discourage approach behavior, and vectors which are ineffffective to solve problems. Maladaptive themas, for example, are permeated by themes of failure: The maladaptive need-integrate contains expectations of rejection and danger; the environmental press is likely to be perceived as nonsupportive or hostile; and the maladaptive vectors probably encourage avoidance behavior. Maladaptive vectors are commonly serviced by needs which interfere with satisfying human relationships, such as aggression or abasement. Thus the maladapted person either avoids or attacks the ordinary tasks of life. Another source of pathology can be seen in the individual who has a strong need but a negative press. For example, the paranoid feels a strong need for people but he expects them to dislike him.

Evaluation

While Murray began by imaginatively expanding Freud's theory, in the long run his theory did not seem to need the psychoanalytic substructure. His theoretical constructs and the system he developed around them are complete by themselves.

Although Murray's language seems unfamiliar and involved, it is well suited to his concern with describing the constant interaction of the person with the environment. Concepts such as themas, need-integrates, and serial programs describe the interaction of internal structures, such as themas and establishments, with the environment through proceedings and vectors. Such an outlook naturally fosters concentration on the adaptive aspects of behavior—on growth and health rather than illness—and thus on total personality function rather than just malfunction, in contrast to Jung,

Horney, and Sullivan. Another strength of Murray's theory is that the dynamic formulation of his constructs and their relationship to the social world lend themselves more readily to the formulation and empirical testing of hypotheses. Until the emergence of Rogers and recent behavior research, Murray was the major stimulant to research on personality.

Murray's theory perhaps lacks parsimony—his list of needs may be longer than necessary and fewer categories would adequately cover the range of goal behavior we describe in Chapter 5 (1938). Our own approach singles out as needs only those clearly perceived as physiological, not the mixture of physiological and social incentives that Murray calls needs. We will also use a smaller number of categories to classify human motivation, subsuming a number of Murray's needs into molar classes which we will call motives.

Cognitive aspects of Murray's theory. In certain ways, Murray's theory is antecedent to the theory we will present in later chapters, since Murray sees goal oriented behavior as directed by a perceived need and these perceived needs are directed by perception. His main cognitive construct is the thema, which consists of a hierarchical integration of need, press and need-integrate, all of them cognitive structures in their own right.

SELF THEORY: CARL ROGERS (1902–   )

Philosophy

Carl Rogers is another theorist who began his career as a therapist, which perhaps accounts for the emphasis he places on counseling in his theory. Rogers' point of view is phenomenological, holistic, and teleological. He is an optimist about human nature, agreeing with Horney, Jung, and Murray that there are factors within the organism that make for self-fulfillment, provided there are no blocks to continuing growth. The basic ethical nature of man is good; misbehavior is maladaptive (Rogers, 1961).

Personality Structure, Development and Dynamics

There are three structural aspects to Rogers' theory. The first is the *organism* itself, which has as its basic motive to actualize, maintain, and enhance itself. The second is the *phenomenal field*, which unites the mind and body into a subjective world of experience. Third, the *self* or *self-concept* is a differentiated part of the phenomenal field which brings consistency and direction to the movement of the organism (Rogers, 1951).

The organism reacts as a totality to the phenomenal field as it strives to fulfill its goals. The organism has needs, originating in its physical structure and in cultural factors, the satisfaction of which serves to maintain and enhance the organism.

The phenomenal field is the person's total world of experience. Aspects within the phenomenal field may be conscious or unconscious. The organism may create conscious awareness of experience by *symbolizing* it or may choose to ignore and/or deny symbolization to an experience, so that the experience remains outside awareness.

The self-concept develops from the phenomenal field out of interaction with the environment. It can change by maturation or learning. It strives for consistency and, in its striving, it may ignore the actual needs of the organism because it has introjected distorted values, usually from other people, during its interaction with the environment. When the self-concept is *congruent* with the needs of the organism, a state of psychological adjustment exists and the person is free from tension. In this state, the person views himself as being generally the way he would like to be. During the course of development, *incongruence* may occur, because of difficulties in maturation, because one has introjected distorted parental values, or because one has been trying to live according to a certain role and ignoring the fact that this role does not attend to the organism's needs. In this state, tension and internal confusion exist.

Whether or not the organism will symbolize an experience depends to a great extent on the demand of the self-concept for consistency. An experience which is incongruent with the self-concept is ignored or distorted so that consistency is achieved. The ultimate incongruence is when the organismic experience is so strongly out of line with the self-concept that the latter does not retain its consistency.

Rogers does not really have a theory of development, but rather a theory of growth. Growth consists of the fulfillment of organismic needs by becoming a "fully functioning" and "fully valuing" person. Dynamics for Rogers consists essentially of the consistency seeking of the self and the congruence or incongruence between the self-concept and the needs of the organism.

Psychopathology

Maladaptive behavior is either poor functioning consistent with the self-concept (the child who thinks he is "bad" behaves according to image) or the tension and confusion that result from incongruence. Awareness of incongruence is experienced as anxiety. Essentially, maladaptive behavior is a conflict between the needs of the organism for self-actualization and the direction of action chosen by the self-concept with its distorted symbolizations. At this point the person no longer feels good about himself and the incongruence within himself leads to difficulties in his relation to others.

Rogers is opposed to diagnosis which pigeonholes individuals; thus his theory does not address itself to the different varieties of diagnostic categories. Partly, this is because Rogers uses a *growth model* rather than a disease model of deviant behavior; partly it is because Rogers feels that treatment should be the same for all types of deviance, no matter what their nature.

Behavior Change

The counseling relationship is a special situation in which the client can grow (Rogers, 1951). In order to grow, the client has to look into himself and clearly perceive his feelings, his organismic needs, and his distorted self-concept. When these are adequately symbolized (brought into full conscious awareness), the client can learn to pay attention to the promptings of the organism toward self-fulfillment and can learn to trust them and act upon them (removing incongruence). The key to promoting behavior change is in the counselor's behavior. The latter tries to understand the client's internal frame of reference and accepts the client completely, responding to him with *unconditional positive regard.* The counselor does not probe or interpret, but accepts the self-report of the client. Such positive regard helps the client to regard himself more positively. His self-concept becomes more precise, he learns to know his own feelings, and reduces the defensive operations of ignoring his organismic needs. At the end of counseling the client is "in touch" with himself and has accepted himself. He has also become more spontaneous and more open to experience. He does not need to put on a facade. With the removal of impediments to growth, he becomes a fully functioning person. Table 3-3 shows characteristics of the fully functioning person.

For Rogers, a good friend can be a good therapist (Rogers, 1951). The good friend is empathic, accepting, non-judgmental, prizing, and treats his friends with unconditional positive regard. The good friend, like the therapist, also grows in the friendship experience. His own self-image becomes enhanced because as he accepts the friend he also accepts himself.

Evaluation

Rogers' humanistic orientation, his emphasis on growth rather than disease (he is a clinical psychologist who practices in non-medical settings) and his egalitarian theory of the counseling relationships have made his theory popular among psychologists. Rogers spent as much time studying methods of therapy as he did treating clients. Much of his theory grew out of his research on methods.

Table 3-3 Negative and Positive Directions Characteristic of the Fully Functioning Person (largely derived from statements of clients)

Negative Directions (Moving Away From)	Positive Directions (Moving Toward)
Away from shells, facades, and fronts	Being in a continual process of change and action
Away from a self that one is not	
Away from "oughts" (being less submissive, less compliant in meeting standards set by others)	Trusting intuitions, feelings, emotions, and motives
	Being a participant in experience rather than being its boss or controlling it
Away from disliking and being ashamed of self	Letting experience carry one on, floating with a complex stream of experience, moving toward ill-defined goals
Away from doing what is expected, just for that reason alone	
Away from doing things for the sake of pleasing others at the expense of self	Moving toward goals behaviorally, not compulsively planning and choosing them
Away from "musts" and "shoulds" as motives for behavior	Following paths which feel good
	Living in the moment (existential living); letting experience carry one on
	Possessing greater openness to experience
	Being more authentic, real, genuine
	Moving closer to feelings and self (more willingness to yield to feelings and not to place a screen between feelings and self); journey to the center of self
	Accepting and appreciating the "realness" of self
	Increasing positive self-regard (a genuine liking and sympathy for self)

Source: After Dicaprio, 1974, p. 371.

The theory is not complete. While Rogers recognizes organismic needs, he does not show how they operate. As a matter of fact, the construct of the phenomenal field, a cognitive construct, permits him to avoid this area and to deal mainly with the subjective world of the person. He does not really explain the many individual differences we encounter in people in everyday life. Nevertheless, he was able to make the self concept, also a cognitive construct, an object of empirical investigations and by examining changes in the self-concept, he was able to evaluate through systematic research the process and effectiveness of psychotherapy. No other group has exposed its own behavior as therapists so much to scrutiny, and for this we all owe him and his associates a debt of gratitude.

A PERSONALISTIC VIEW: GORDON ALLPORT (1897–1967)

Philosophy

For many years, while behaviorists were trying to quantify behavior and psychoanalysts were searching for hidden motives, Gordon Allport went against the common trend. He insisted that the study of individuals and their conscious motives were proper subjects of psychological investigation. Allport was not a therapist but an academician and researcher who was much more interested in normal than in abnormal behavior. He claimed with some justification that behaviorists had tried to eliminate the notion of self from psychology because it smacked of an earlier concept, *soul,* and because they did not wish to accept what they could not measure (Allport, 1955). Allport's dissidence foreshadowed the humanistic or "third-force" movement in contemporary psychology, of which he is an acknowledged inspirer.

Allport did not try to construct a complete system of personality, believing that the field was not yet ready for such audacity. He was eclectic to the extent that he was willing to accept any learning model for infant development. He insisted that although such models may serve well for infant learning—and although a psychoanalytic model may serve well for abnormal behavior—such theories are not suitable for the adult normal human. Mechanistic models from physics or animal models from experimental psychology are also misleading. Each human being is unique and so requires individual study. Furthermore, a person lives in the present, not the past, and while he may evidence some leftover effects of his childhood acculturation, he is not a victim of history but is acting in accord with conscious aspirations. In his rejection of the mechanistic model of human behavior, Allport shows signs of having been influenced by the Gestalt psychologists, and his concept of self owes a good deal to William James. Along with Rogers, he is a strong believer in the individual's capacity for self-determination.

Personality Structure and Dynamics

The main feature of Allport's personality structure centers around the concept of *traits,* "a generalized and focalized neuropsychic system" that guides adaptive and expressive behavior (Allport, 1937, p. 295). Allport (1962) later distinguished between common traits, which may be found in all members of a class and personality dispositions. The later are dispositions to behavior, unique to the individual. Three types of traits can be found: cardinal, central and secondary.

Cardinal traits: the ruling passion or master sentiment, the overall guideline for a person's life. Not every person has such a ruling passion. The desire of St. Francis to imitate Christ was such a ruling passion.

Central traits: highly characteristic tendencies that can be seen to occur repeatedly in the person. Former President Nixon's tendency to cover up is an example.

Secondary traits: less important, more limited in focus, and seen only in specific situations. A congenial, affable, mild mannered person may become angry only when rejected by others. This is a secondary trait.

Also within the personality are *intentions,* which reflect the person's orientation toward the future, his hopes, wishes, and aspirations. Each of us is trying to become or accomplish something.

The third structural component of personality is the *proprium* (Allport, 1955). This is Allport's term for all the organizing tendencies which give personality its congruence and uniqueness. By preferring the term *proprium* to self, Allport tried to show that he did not necessarily consider it an agent of organization, but as a set of experiences. Nevertheless, the consistency of personality depends upon the propriate functions. These functions include the *bodily sense* (what is me), *self-identity* (who am I), *self-image* (what am I like), *ego-enhancement* (how can I be more), *ego-extension* (what is mine), *rational agent* (how can I solve problems), *propriate striving* (what is important to me), and *self-knowing* (how shall I value and measure my actions and myself).

It can easily be seen that the propriate functions are concerned with all that is central and important to the person and therefore will influence the development of the important traits. Along with intentions, the proprium and its functions are all cognitive constructs.

The proprium is not innate: it develops over time. Until the child is about three years old, it has only a bodily sense, a self-identity, and an ego-enhancement function. The other functions develop later.

While traits, intentions, and propriate functions give rise to dynamics, Allport has one more important statement to make about personality dynamics—the principle of *functional autonomy* (Allport, 1955). Instrumental acts which are used to satisfy needs can become needs themselves and function autonomously. Since the person lives in the present and is guided by his intentions, motives are contemporaneous. A person acts according to today's intention, not some childhood intent. While archaisms and infantilisms may be left over from the past, the main determinants of behavior are current motives. There need be no relationship between today's behavior and its past roots.

A person who once hunted game because he wanted food, may continue to hunt today because he has learned to enjoy the activity, not because he needs food. This contemporaneity of motive has been recognized by the Rabbis of the Talmud, who argued that continued practice of performing God's commandments was important even if one started such a practice only out of fear, because the motive of fear could eventually turn into the motive of love as one began to enjoy the practice.

Personality Development

Allport is willing to accept either a learning or a biological model for early development. He considers heredity important and accepts the existence of drives but points out that these do not yet constitute personality. During infancy and early childhood, development takes place through differentiation, integration, maturation, learning, imitation, and self-extension. Propriate learning, however, operates according to Gestalt principles—identification, closure, and cognitive insight. Propriate learning begins sometime during childhood and continues all of one's life. Through the principle of functional autonomy, adult motives supplant infantile motives. The developed personality is post-instinctive, it is something other than the interplay of heredity and environment. Adult behavior is determined by a set of organized and congruent traits. The mature personality has three additional characteristics: It has many self-extensions (a wide range of interests and satisfactions), it can view itself objectively (with humor and insight), and it has a philosophy of life (life has a meaning).

Evaluation

Allport's theory adds two new dimensions to the theories we have been discussing. The principle of *functional autonomy* is a welcome change from the concept that a person is nothing more than a product of his past. In this respect, Allport resembles Jung. The other dimension, the *proprium,* seems to be a successful effort to describe the person as an active agent who determines his own values.

Allport is probably best known as one of the few academic (nonclinical) psychologists who has emphasized the study of the individual as a whole, rather than as a conglomerate of responses. Not a clinician, he advanced no theory about psychopathology or behavior change. Yet his conception of the ego as an existence in its own right (propriate self) rather than in the service of some biological function is an important theoretical departure.

EXISTENTIAL THEORIES

Philosophy

During the first half of the twentieth century the dominant school of philosophy in the Anglo-Saxon countries was logical positivism. On the European continent, meanwhile, a few voices spoke out against philosophies which reduced humanity to a collection of atoms, against political systems which declared the state more important than the individual, and against the dehumanizing tendencies of industrialized mass society. Some of these voices spoke out of their own personal despair, for example, Kierkegaard (1813–1855) and Nietzsche (1844–1900). Others tried to construct different approaches to understanding the human condition from more fruitful points of view (Husserl, 1859–1938; Heidegger, 1889–1976;

Jaspers, 1883-1976). The writings of these philosophers had a profound effect on a number of psychiatrists and psychologists who began to use their insights in understanding and treating the complaints of their patients.

In some respects, existential theory is as old as Heraclitus (c. 535-c. 475 B.C.). In others, it represents an entirely new departure from our accustomed scientific point of view. The effect of two disastrous wars led to a rebellion against the view that political systems or advances in technology alone could improve the human condition. This rebellion included a rejection of the physical science model for psychology. A new psychology where the proper object of study seemed to be human existence itself, in all its complexity and confusion, took two paths. One is the study of human experience, *phenomenology*, originated by Husserl. Each individual lives subjectively in a world composed of his own meanings. The existence of the person is best understood by studying the meanings he gives his experiences. The other path is through *Dasein* (being-in-the-world) analysis, the study of the person's mode of existence in response to certain universal "givens."

The single individual who seems to have contributed most to a philosophy of *Dasein* is Martin Heidegger. Heidegger tried to apply phenomenology to derive a philosophy of existence. He posits that *existence* or being is a given. But being means being-in-the-world (*Dasein*). The world is the life space which is the indispensable condition of being. *Action* is another condition of being. In Heidegger's language, the human being is thrown into the world (he didn't ask to be born) and left there to engage himself with the world (to act in it) and concern himself (to care about what happens), using his own devices and acting under his own responsibility. Thus, all of life assumes the character of a task. How the human meets the task is identical with his ontogeny (personal development). The human being is thus compelled to create his own values (Heidegger, 1949).

Two Swiss psychiatrists, Ludwig Binswanger (1881-1966) and Medard Boss (1903-   ), have been among the leaders who applied Heidegger's comments about the human condition to their work with patients.

Personality Structure

Most of the theories about structure have been developed by Binswanger (1963). The two important structural components are *Dasein* and *meaning.* Binswanger postulates the existence of an *a priori* tendency to assign meanings to various loci. There is no formal designation of a "self" in existential theory except as an identity construct. Identity is one locus of meaning in *Dasein,* which emerges from it as a figure emerges from ground. It results from the person's interaction with the world and depends upon the person's ability to struggle against being assimilated and submerged into the world around him. The personality structure, which he calls *onto-*

logical structure, is a matrix of meanings that starts to form in infancy. Experience, another locus, is endowed with meanings by cognition. Such language is quite different from that of traditional psychology and it is this very difference which permits existential theory to present a different way of looking at personality.

There are three worlds in which the human exists: the *Eigenwelt*—his inner experiential world, the *Umwelt*—the physical world in which he exists and the *Mitwelt*—the social world (Binswanger, 1963).

Another descriptive aspect of the human person is his *authenticity.* A person alienated from genuine human purposes and possibilities is engaged in unauthentic *Dasein.* Authentic humans do not give in to the thrownness of *Dasein* but take responsibility. They transcend the "givens" of today and move toward realizing the possibilities of tomorrow. This is how the authentic person avoids assimilation into the world and struggles to maintain his own identity.

Each person lives in a subjective world which is a *world design,* constructed by the person himself. This world design resembles the cognitive aspects of Allport's proprium. The person defines to himself what the world is and conducts his life according to that definition. Binswanger would try to discover the world design of each of his patients by studying their life histories. Any life history or case history was properly an investigation of the person's unique world design.

Personality Development

Existential theories offer no theory of development. Birth takes place into the state of thrownness. The initial meanings given to life usually depend upon the relationship with the mother (or other cherishing adult). If the mother restricts the child's meanings (by preventing him from learning to act, by inhibiting his active engagement) the child will become a person who has a constricted world view.

Dynamics

The motivational constructs of existential theory include the conditions of *Dasein,* the *pitch* (direction) of *Dasein,* the task of giving meaning, and *existential anxiety.*

1. *Dasein* begins as "thrownness" (the human does not ask to be born. It is as if he has just been thrown into the midst of the world). It ends in death and thus eventual *nothingness* is one of its conditions. It continues over time and thus has a past and a future. It takes place in a world of others. All these aspects of *Dasein* influence behavior.
2. *Dasein* is *pitched* or inclined. Its normal pitch is toward the future, toward others, and toward authenticity.

3. Giving meaning is the chief aim of personal existence. Without meaning there is nothingness.
4. The vision of nothingness creates dread (*existential anxiety*). It is a constant fear of the loss of meaning. Therefore, each person tries to enrich his *Dasein* (expand its meanings).

The psychodynamics of human existence consists essentially of the struggle to maintain one's meaning and identity, given the thrownness of *Dasein*. The following quote from Rollo May depicts this.

> Thus, being in the human sense is not given once and for all. It does not unfold automatically as the oak tree does from the acorn. For an intrinsic and inseparable element in being human is self-consciousness. Man . . . is the particular being who has to be aware of himself, be responsible for himself, if he is to become himself. He also is that particular being who knows that at some future moment he will not be; he is the being who is always in a dialectical relation with non-being, death. And he not only knows he will sometime not be, but he can, in his own choices, slough off and forfeit his being. (May, as quoted in Maddi, 1976, p. 127)

Psychopathology

Maladaptive deviation is essentially the result of the person's *constricted* world design, which is related to the constricted meaning the person finds in his world. The more constricted the design, the greater the threat of losing meaning, which is the only thing that stands between the person and the chaotic state of thrownness. Constricted designs block growth into the future and alienate the person from fulfilling his potentialities. This concept is, of course, similar to Horney's alienation from the self and Rogers' notion of blocked growth. It leads to the unauthentic existence of "self-chosen unfreedom." A symptom announces that a person is trapped in an existential problem, but a symptom itself can be a "way out" of the trap. It can permit the continued existence of an unauthentic *Dasein* by giving it an additional meaning, as in hypochondriasis, where the person focuses his anxiety on a body symptom instead of on his true problem. Boss (1963) understands the symptom as a disturbed relationship with the *Mitwelt* (social world) since he considers the *Mitwelt* the main arena of life in which meaning can be extended. The person with a neurosis has surrendered autonomy and independence, without which he cannot make authentic choices. He would like to be secure against the world and against himself but only succeeds in estranging himself. Pathology is thus the result of wrong choices based on a constricted world design. In order to make authentic choices, the person must take the responsibility for creating his own value system, must actively pursue good human relations and new possibilities, and make genuine choices.

Behavior Change

Existential therapy seems to vary among its practitioners. All, however, agree that health and wholeness require a freedom to choose a broad world design and responsibility. Awareness of one's own value system and one's personal set of meanings are aids to self change. The person who recovers from a neurosis regains awareness of his own goals and takes command of his life. He transcends the contingencies of existence. With awareness he can expand his own world design, give additional meanings to his life, and fulfill his possibilities.

Existential theories of behavior change are thus concerned with personality restructuring rather than symptom removal. One does not try to remove existential anxiety entirely because anxiety is one of the conditions of *Dasein.* Change takes place through an act of resolve to choose differently, to transcend the contingencies and create satisfying values. In order to do so, the human must *care,* must *decide,* must *commit* himself to *Dasein* instead of trying to escape from it, and must actively *engage* in self-fulfillment. Rollo May (1973), the leading exponent of existentialism in the English-speaking world, has stated that in order to change, the person must *assimilate* the complexities and contradictions of his existence.

Evaluation

The existentialists offer us no complete theory of personality. We included them because they offer, in unique language, a theory of the human condition. Without an understanding of *Dasein,* how can one understand the existent? More than other theorists, they have stressed the relationship between ethical behavior and personal satisfaction and by doing this they have returned the ancient concern with moral character to the science of personality, defying the attempts of science to remain objectively unconcerned with the question of right and wrong. They have placed the locus of control squarely within the individual himself, denying any significant influence to heredity or environment other than the influence the person himself permits these givens to have. Freud taught that human beings do not have conscious control of their own behavior; the existentialists put each of us back in the driver's seat by making us aware of our power to transcend contingency and reach authentic decisions. Like Jung and Allport, they are more concerned with the future, than with the past, but they are most concerned with the present—the here and now which challenges each existent to transcend and be authentic.

Table 3-4   The Self-Theorists, Their Key Concepts, and the Final Aim of Personality Development

	Self Construct	Some Key Concepts	Final Aim of Development
Jung	An archetype which represents the striving for individuation	Collective unconscious Personal unconscious Psychic harmony by union of opposites	Self-actualization in the union of opposites (individuation)
Horney	Real self versus ideal self; the actual self is where they overlap	Basic anxiety Compensatory strategies Cultural influences	Self-realization
Sullivan	Self-system, a dynamism which protects against overwhelming anxiety	Empathy Dynamisms Parataxic distortion versus syntaxic thought	Successful interpersonal relationships to achieve security and satisfaction
Murray	Serial programs containing life plan	Serial programs guide behavior, establishments, need-integrates, values, vectors	Achieving ego-ideal
Rogers	Self-concept brings consistency and direction to the organism	Organism and its needs Phenomenal field Functional autonomy	Fully functioning and fully valuing organism
Allport	Proprium: various experiences of the self		Becoming
Existentialists	Self: an identity construct	Dasein Subjective world design Existential anxiety	Expansion and elaboration of meanings of the individual's life

Table 3-4 summarizes and compares the self-constructs of the theorists in Chapter 3, some of their key concepts and how each views the final aim in the process of becoming. In each case, the theorist postulates a final aim to development. Each proposes that humans are perfectible: that perfection can be approached through the modification of personality structures and by social experiences.

All of the theorists in this chapter see personality as adaptive. Not all stress the uniqueness of personality. Jung, Horney and Murray do not have a uniqueness construct, although nothing in their theories would contradict such a notion. All except Jung and the existentialists offer explicit propositions that personality is learned, while all grant the importance of cultural influence and state that personality determines the selection of response; that understanding the pattern permits the prediction of response and that response can only be understood in the context of pattern.

4

**theoretical
conceptions
of
personality III:
field
and cognitive
theorists**

OVERVIEW

In this chapter we discuss two groups of personality theorists. The first group are direct historical descendants of Kant and the school of classical Gestalt psychology. Lewin was an actual member of the school. Kurt Goldstein, a physician, collaborated with Gelb, a student of the Gestalt school. Andras Angyal, not a direct student or co-worker, acknowledges the influence of the Gestalt principles in his own holistic theory of personality. Goldstein, Lewin, and Angyal are all examples of a field or holistic theory of personality and will be discussed first.

The other two theorists are Alfred Adler and George Kelly. They are both examples of a constructionist viewpoint which emphasizes that the person is an active, creative agent in the construction of his own personality, not merely a passive reactor shaped by his environment.

HOLISTIC-FIELD THEORY:
GOLDSTEIN, LEWIN, ANGYAL

While the associationist philosophy of Locke and British empiricism, as well as the classification method of Aristotle, were flourishing in nineteenth-century physics, biology, and early psychology (Wundt in 1879), another approach was steadily gaining ground in psychology. It was the Gestalt approach, which asserted that systems have intrinsic organization, and therefore events or parts within them can be understood only in the context of the *organization of the whole*. Goldstein, the oldest of the three individuals who applied Gestalt principles to the study of personality, was born in 1878. He applied Gestalt theory to the behavioral organization of the organism, calling his position *organismic theory*. Angyal called his approach *holistic systems theory*. Lewin conceived of the individual as always behaving within an *environmental field*. His approach to personality is called *topological field theory*. While we will discuss them separately, we will evaluate them together in order to avoid redundancy.

KURT GOLDSTEIN: ORGANISMIC PSYCHOLOGY (1878–1965)

Kurt Goldstein, a German psychiatrist, collected data on brain-injured soldiers from which he developed his organismic theory of behavior (Goldstein, 1939, 1940). He came to the United States in 1935, and became clinical professor of neurology at Columbia University and Tufts Medical School.

Philosophy

In his studies of brain-injured soldiers, Goldstein concluded, consistent with the organismic thesis, that, when a part of a brain is so damaged that it cannot perform its functions, other parts of the brain seem to fulfill the missing functions. This is a neurological example of the Gestalt principle of closure.

Such observations and additional research (Goldstein, 1939, 1940) led him to the following principles of organismic functioning of the nervous system and personality: (1) The brain (and nervous system) functions as a whole so that disruption of function in one area instigates compensatory or vicarious activity in other parts. It is as if there is an inherent (teleological) force directing the whole system to fulfill its destiny. (2) This tendency toward fulfillment is true of the entire personality as well as the brain. Thus, the organism, and its personality, seek self-actualization. (3) Personality must be studied as an organism interacting in a given environment. (4)

With Gelb (1920), Goldstein extended the Gestalt perceptual principle of figure/ground to general behavior. He believed that organismic functioning is also organized into an area of *central concentration* (figure) and its *surround* (ground). Friendly to the movement, but critical of some of their tenets, Goldstein did not consider himself a Gestalt psychologist.

Personality Structure

Organism is a central construct in Goldstein's theory of personality. The organism consists of differentiated parts which are articulated into a unifying system. The primary organization within this whole is into figure and ground. The parts usually work together and only become detached and isolated from one another under abnormal or artificial conditions (for example, brain damage). What makes one part of the organism emerge as figure depends on the situational task. Thus, if one is engaged in the pursuit of achievement, then perception, memories, and skill will be directed toward achievement concerns, and other aspects of behavior will recede into the background. Similarly, if the stimulating conditions from the environment invoke an "anxiety" task, then organismic resources relevant to the management and reduction of anxiety will come into figural concentration. Organismic processes which are brought into figural focus may be flexible (as when personality systems are integrated) or rigid (as when personality is disordered), depending on whether the situation is favorable or traumatic.

Psychodynamics

The three dynamic processes of importance for Goldstein are *equalization, self-actualization,* and *coming to terms with the environment.* The organism creates a balance of energy within the entire system. If one area in the system is disrupted or stimulated, other areas will attempt to absorb the energy in order to equalize the system. Regions spatially or functionally closer will be more influenced than distant regions. Self-actualization is a teleological concept. It is the term used to denote the organism's continuing development toward some ideal end point. The pursuit of self-actualizers requires accommodation with the environment. A favorable environment facilitates self-actualization.

Psychopathology and Change

Consistent with organismic principles, pathology is interpreted as a form of maladjustment. Goldstein distinguishes between direct and indirect symptoms. A *direct symptom* occurs when there is direct damage to the organism. Scattered concentration, a typical result of brain injury, is seen as a reactive adjustment of the entire brain to the injured part. This deterioration of the functional organization is called *dedifferentiation.* Injury can also result in isolation (an *indirect symptom*) of an uninjured part of the brain that is normally closely associated with the injured part. This isolation then manifests itself as an impaired function of the nondamaged part. For example, damage to the auditory cortex of the brain will normally result in some loss of hearing; however, associated problems such as a loss of word comprehension may develop even though the speech area is not damaged. For Goldstein, development consists of the reorganization of old patterns into new and more effective ones, and the acquisition of preferred ways of behaving. Similarly, corrective therapy (change) should be aimed at counteracting dedifferentiation and isolation.

KURT LEWIN (1890–1947)

Kurt Lewin was a professor of philosophy and psychology at Berlin University. When Hitler came to power, Lewin came to the United States, where he eventually became professor and director of the Research Center for Group Dynamics at the University of Michigan in 1945. Lewin applied field theory to a wide range of psychosocial phenomena such as developmental behavior, feeble-mindedness, national character, minority group problems, and group dynamics. Being deeply democratic and humanistic, he also initiated action research which has the objective of changing social conditions for the betterment of society.

Philosophy

Kurt Lewin, the only one of the three who was an actual member of the Gestalt school, emphasized the Gestalt properties of the person within the environment. He believed that the Aristotelian classificatory approach to psychological inquiry was unnecessarily limited and inadequate. He therefore chose *dynamic* formulation (as Galileo did in physics). A dynamic conception always views the person as part of a total field. The person's behavior will be determined by the distribution of forces within the field. Personality characteristics such as *need, tension,* and *communication* do not function independently, but are always functions of the environment. What a person desires (need), what causes conflict (tension), and what he communicates is always influenced by the environment (his perceived behavioral world). A person who perceives a need for love will feel such a need. Love then becomes a positive valence (desired object) which gives rise to a positive vector (movement toward the object). If the environment inhibits the movement, tension exists in the field.

Personality Structure and Its Developmental Origins

As the foregoing example implies, Lewin (1935) put little stock in constants of personality such as fixed traits, rigid habits, or a mediating ego. Rather, he saw personality structure as always interacting within an environmental field, unless tension acts to subvert such a flux. Personality structure consists of two ordinal subdivisions called regions as diagrammed in Figure 4-1. The innermost region *C* is central, while the *P* regions are peripheral. The more distant or outer regions of personality are perceptual and motor. The environment also consists of various regions. Moreover, the regions of both person and environment can have *rigid* or *fluid* boundaries, the latter permitting easier flow between boundaries. Some regions are more easily influenced (fluid boundaries) while others are impermeable to change (rigid boundaries). The field which constitutes the person in the environment is called the person's *life space,* his behavioral world. Two different life spaces, depicting the same individual in two different situations, are diagrammed in Figure 4-1.

Two important aspects of the field articulation of the life space are differentiation and fluidity. Persons with more differentiated and more permeable boundaries have more effective interaction and communication.

Low–stress situation

High–stress situation

1. Fluid boundaries between environment and areas of the person. Influence occurs. C, P and E are differentiated into regions, as indicated by the dividing lines within them.

2. Rigid boundaries within the person and between the person and environment. Influence is blocked. There is little differentiation and boundaries are rigid.

C = central region of the person;
P = peripheral regions;
E = environment

Figure 4-1   A diagram of the life space in low-stress and high-stress situations

Let us for a moment apply Lewinian concepts of differentiation and boundaries to the concept of security. If a person is provoked to fear by a fear-producing stimulus, his coping response depends upon perceived options. The more differentiation, the more alternatives the person will see. The more fluidity, the easier it will be for the person to move from one alternative to another. The environment must also be differentiated; that is, it must admit a variety of responses. An inmate in a correctional institution has fewer environmental options than the citizen of a democratic nation.

If a receptivity to alternative actions is not developed, behavior will be rigid and undifferentiated (stereotyped). Developmental experience or growth thus involves the kind of perceptual training that gives rise to differentiation in cognitive structure. If dedifferentiation (reduction in the number of regions) occurs as a result of psychological stress, corrective therapy should be aimed at reestablishing effective differentiation. While boundaries are necessary, they should be relatively permeable so that sufficient communication between regions can take place to allow for integrated functioning.

Psychodynamics

In addition to the organization and complexities of the life space, Lewin also used such concepts as valence, vector (force) satiation, co-satiation, task-orientation, and levels of aspiration (LA) to describe the dynamics of behavior and personality functioning. All action in the life space results from perception. The individual perceives a positive or negative *valence* (the field is supportive or hindering) in the field as a function of perceived *needs*. The valence gives rise to a positive or negative *vector* (action or movement). A vector is valence in action. Action is more likely to take place if the individual is task-oriented. Completion of a task leads to *satiation* whereas an incomplete task produces *tensions*. When given an opportunity to resume tasks, incomplete or interrupted tasks are more likely to be resumed or remembered—that is, the tasks we haven't completed tend to prey on our minds. Tasks which are similar in nature will co-satiate; that is, during task resumption, tasks similar in nature to satiated tasks will not be chosen. Action takes place because personality regions are attracted by perceived valences in the field giving rise to task-orientation. Change in action results from such processes as satiation and task incompletion. More effort and achievement is evidenced when the individual has a realistic *level of aspiration,* and *conflict* (or indecisive action) results from the perception of competing valences. The person who is realistic will have a level of aspiration slightly higher than his last performance. The unrealistic person will have an inappropriate level of aspiration.

Psychopathology

Lewin used primarily the concepts of dedifferentiation and rigid boundaries to explain a breakdown of psychological functioning. Under optimal conditions the regions within the personality are well articulated and function in integrated fashion. When the person is under tension, is anxious or stressed, articulation between the various regions is generally *diffused*. This is a cognitive explanation of what Freud called regression. Lewin calls extreme dedifferentiation *primitivation*. Chronic maladjustment exists when there are either too few regions and/or rigid boundaries between them so that behavior and thought are encapsulated, such as in obsessions, compulsions and delusions.

Behavior Change and its Relation to Development

For Lewin, the key concept in all behavior change, including development, is *reorganization* of the field. If a physicist wants to change the energy field between two poles, he changes the relationship between them. Lewin's field theory concepts can be used to understand the redistribution of direction of the force between two persons interacting in a field. Since the force (vector) is the resultant of the two valences (positive or negative intent), the relationships between the valences must be changed. There is only one way that this can be done in human beings, and that is by effect-

---

Box 4-1   Application of Field Theory to Marriage Counseling

A married couple sought counseling. In the first session with the counselor, they argued bitterly, each accusing the other:

"You never appreciate what I do for you!"

"How can I appreciate when you're always bitching?"

"If you would think about someone beside yourself, I might not be so bitchy. Anyway, you always start it!"

"I have to think about myself, you never think about me!"

The counselor noted that the couple spoke in terms of "you" and "I" as separate and not as part of a union. He asked them to repeat the argument substituting "we" for "I" and "you."

The ensuing conversation went:

"We never appreciate what we do for each other."

"How can we appreciate each other when we're always bitching?"

"If we would think about each other, we might not be so bitchy. Anyway we always start it."

"We have to think about each other, we never think about each other."

This new conversation permitted the couple to recognize how they had failed to recognize their *relationship as a unity* and had focused on separate parts. The previous negative vector was changed to positive.

ing a change in the *perceptions* of the persons involved, since all valences are perceived values. Lewin's theory of motivation is an expectancy theory and expectancies are matters of perception. Two individuals can alter their conflictual interaction if they focus their attention on their *relationship as unity* rather than on their separate parts.

In field theory, change is intrinsically linked with development. It is easy to alter one's perception if one has more informational categories available. For Lewin that means the possession of more regions in the personality. The personality develops greater differentiation through the creation of boundaries between regions. Since dedifferentiation involves essentially the reduction of boundaries, changing maladjustment to more adaptive functioning involves the establishment of appropriate boundaries between personality regions.

ANDRAS ANGYAL (1907-1960)

Philosophy

Born in Hungary, trained in medicine and psychology in Europe, Andras Angyal came to the United States where he was director of research at Worcester State Hospital from 1937 to 1945. The holistic theory and writings of Angyal reflect his long standing and catholic interest in both academic and clinical issues.

Angyal used a hierarchical principle. The organized whole of personality is a hierarchy of systems whose meaning is synonymous with the individual's philosophy of life (Angyal, 1965). This philosophy, in turn, results from the *symbol-producing* and *symbol-interpreting* nature of the human organism. It is symbolization which primarily distinguishes the human organism from other animals. All psychological functions are to be understood as processes of symbolization.

Personality Structure

Angyal emphasized the interaction of the organism with the environment. The inner structure of personality consists of a duality—homonomy and autonomy. *Autonomy* refers to the need for individuality, self-assertiveness, independence, and a sense of a private identity. *Homonomy* refers to the fact that the individual is always part of a social group. Survival dictates adherence, at least in part, to the customs of this group. In keeping with this formulation, Angyal postulated that the person and environment form a unitary organization, which he called the biosphere. The duality of personality functioning is shown in the bipolar organization of the biosphere diagrammed in Figure 4-2.

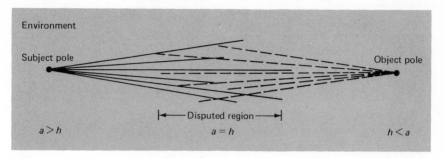

Environment

Subject pole

Object pole

|◄——Disputed region——►|

$a > h$ $a = h$ $h < a$

Figure 4-2   Bipolar organization of biosphere. Solid lines indicate region of biosphere under autonomous control which emanates from subject pole; broken lines represent heteronomous (part of homonomy) control from object pole. Source: Arndt, 1974, p. 295.

Angyal viewed personality as a superstructure composed of subsystems in a hierarchy. The significance of a particular behavioral act depends not only on the subsystem of which it is a part, but also on its meaning within the total context of the entire hierarchy.

Dynamics

The dynamics of personality are directed by the duality of autonomy and homonomy. Angyal believed that the human being from the very beginning of his life is faced with the problem of integrating his desire to be an individual with the necessity to be cared for by other agents—that is, to make autonomy and homonomy compatible. In fact, the unique symbols that an individual develops are bred of the interaction between the tendencies toward autonomy and homonomy.

Psychopathology, Development and Behavior Change

Angyal (1965) asserts that a healthy person has a belief in himself. Conversely, the disturbed individual feels small and weak and sees the world as a big, unmanageable place. This concept is similar to Horney's concept of basic anxiety.

The unhealthy person who perceives the outside world as a threat experiences grave difficulty in meeting the needs of the self and the demands of the outside world at the same time (homonomy and autonomy are not balanced). The individual who thus experiences himself as inadequate can compensate in two major ways, which result in the two dominant forms of neuroses: the *hysterical* and the *obsessive-compulsive*. The hysterical person is an individual who uses a pattern of vicarious living to satisfy his psychological motives. He lives through fantasy, seeks excessive attention, symbiotic attachment, and dependence, frequently denies his own feelings, and is prone to hero worship. He basically abrogates his autonomy, living mainly through others. On the other hand, the obsessive-compulsive person is prone to non-commitment. Unlike the hysteric, who becomes attached to others, the obsessive-compulsive gives a false impression of being extremely independent and has a tendency to keep distance from others, finding it difficult to give or receive love. These are contradictory ways of compensating for the feeling of having a weak self, and yet these patterns of behavior are vicious cycles, which increase the feeling of weakness rather than ameliorating it.

Angyal saw development as consisting of increasing differentiation, like Goldstein and Lewin. Personality develops from the phase concerned with more simple functions of eating and sleeping to the phase concerned with more complicated symbolic functions. In effective human beings these symbolic functions are connected with instrumental psychological processes—that is, with goal-seeking behavior. The obsessive-compulsive *asserts* too much while the hysteric *depends* too much. What is required is a shift in their balance between autonomy and homonomy—and that requires a shift in thinking.

Evaluation

These field-holistic psychologists have contributed to the belief that any behavioral act should be understood in the context of the organization of the whole, and have established the importance of studying the person as a unit. The Lewinian emphasis on field has had a dominant influence on social psychology. In fact, the current interest in group, family, and marriage therapy and the entire group dynamics movement owes its impetus to his original work.

Angyal's concept of the balance between homonomy and autonomy recalls Jung's doctrine of the reconciliation of opposites; although this is a duality, the two parts are not inevitably in conflict. What makes Angyal holistic is his stress on the system principle. What makes him a field theorist is his concept of the biosphere.

Goldstein, Lewin, and Angyal all see the personality functioning as a unit—a *Gestalt* which is different from the sum of its parts. The growth of a healthy person requires the differentiation of cognitive structure; by contrast, pathology stems from its dedifferentiation. These concepts form a bridge to a cognitive theory of personality.

The field-holistic theorists and the postulates. All these theorists view personality as the adaptive functioning of the organism and as a unified structure. Their theories of development are theories of cognitive differentiation, which stress neither learning nor culture. For Angyal, each person operates according to his unique system principle in his unique biosphere. Goldstein and Lewin do not concern themselves much with uniqueness, however. For all of them, personality determines the selection of response, and understanding the organization permits the prediction of response. Thus, the specific response can be understood only within the context of the total organization. The contents of all our seven postulates are encompassed in one or another way by the field-holistic theorists.

INDIVIDUAL PSYCHOLOGY: ALFRED ADLER (1870–1937)

Philosophy

Alfred Adler, raised in Vienna and trained in medicine, broke away from the psychoanalytic movement, starting his own system which he called *Individual Psychology.* When one compares Adler to Freud, one sees a good example of how two theorists can examine the same data and come to very different conclusions.

Like Freud, Adler was influenced by Darwin's theory of evolution, but did not conclude that humans were therefore prey to animal (sexual) instincts. Instead, he felt that humans were primarily social beings who had *created* their societies and that social evolution was a continuing process. He believed that humans could better themselves and their relationships with each other and that each person could contribute to the whole. Adler shared Kant's outlook that humans acted according to their perceptions of the world and that this process was active and creative. Since objective truth is sometimes impossible to discern, people act according to *fictions.* A fiction is a mental construct, which may or may not be actually true, but is useful in directing behavior. The small child might act according to the construct, "Mother knows best." A competitive adult might act according to the construct, "I have to win out over others." Some fictions are useful, that is, they promote efficient adaptive behavior. Others are useless—they lead to maladaptive behavior.

Adler seems also to have been influenced by Nietzsche's concept of the *will to power.* In his early theory, this was a primary motive for behavior. Later, Adler generalized this to say that the specific "will to power" was a neurotic form of the *striving for significance* that he found in all humans. The appropriate and healthy way to strive for significance was with *Gemeinschaftsgefühl.* This term, commonly translated into English as "social interest" means a *feeling of oneness with mankind.* It exists as a potential in the newborn and requires appropriate socialization for its unfolding. The person with social interest is far less likely to suffer from feelings of inferiority or unworth. While alienation from the reference group leads to destructive behavior or difficulties in living, the presence of social interest is health giving (Adler, 1964, p. 273).

Adler did not construct the kind of technical vocabulary we find in Freud, believing that one of the strong points of his theory was indeed its simplicity. A few parsimonious concepts could explain all the important issues in the psychic life of the person. Adler is also a social psychologist. Behavior had to be understood in a social context. Finally he was holistic and teleological. The human was not driven by drives in conflict with each other. Personality is a *unity,* an organized and integrated whole, which moves by any available path toward its own conscious or unconscious goal—that which would provide it with the subjective feeling of significance. Adler's holism led him to avoid the mind-body dichotomy. There is a constant interchange of influence between psychic and physical factors.

Personality Structure

Adler did not envision a map of the mind as did Freud, nor did he find reason to divide the mental apparatus into id, ego, and superego. Mind is simply mind, and he accepted it as a given fact. However, the mental life has an organization and follows the same basic law of life: continual growth and development. It is not at war with itself, but is integrated with the body, forming an organism that is an operating unit. The unitary operation of the organism requires a master plan, which Adler calls the *life style.* Life style is a superordinate pattern of behavior into which all other elements of behavior are integrated. It is a *guiding ideal,* which has the character of a *goal* for individual striving, comparable to Murray's ego ideal. The basic goal of human striving is for growth and significance, away from a feeling of inferiority or lack toward a feeling of worthwhileness or sufficiency. Freud's pleasure principle is only one example of a possible goal that might be selected by an individual. The life style is also an organizing principle. All drives, impulses, tendencies, and traits are subsumed under the life style. Whatever drives a person is born with are simply woven into a pattern and are used to accomplish the dominant purpose of attaining that which is subjectively felt to be the desired salvation.

Adler's personality structure is actually a *pattern of striving.* While the pattern differs for each individual, all such patterns have certain things in common. All contain a theme around which the pattern is organized and by which the pattern can be recognized. The theme can be expressed in words—like a motto.

By observing behavior carefully, one can pick out the theme which is the person's guiding ideal. Students of Adler have pointed out that there is

Box 4-2 Themes expressed in common mottos around which behavior is organized according to Adlerian formulations

Common Mottos

"I must be a superior individual."
"I must hide my deficiencies from others."
"I must always please."
"I must strive to be a good person."
"I can't let anybody get ahead of me."
"I can't let myself lose control."

an implicit structure in Adler's concept of life style. This structure consists of certain key perceptual constructs which differ from person to person but are found in all people. These key constructs are few in number, but are basic to the organization of the personality. They include a self-concept (an assessment of the self and what is crucial to it), a world-image (a view of the world, of human relationships, and of the self interacting with the world), and a set of conclusions which contain the goal of behavior (the guiding self-ideal) and the basic decisions about *modi operandi* (the methods for coping with the world). The last leads to the theme of behavior, or its style, hence the term *life style* (Mosak & Shulman, 1961). Each life style is unique to the individual.

Personality Development

For Adler, life itself is a process of growth and continuing development, a construct he termed the *hypothesis of biological expansion*. The modes of expansion include physical growth, social growth, and intellectual growth. Since growth takes place in the psychic life as well as in the physical organism, it may be thought of as the ultimate goal of all striving or the continuation of the process of living itself. It is from this point of view that Adler's theory would explain common human behavior like acquisitiveness, competitiveness, aspirations, and ambitions.

At birth, the infant is in an inferior position and as soon as he can make comparative evaluation, he recognizes his inferiority. This subjective feeling of inferiority brings into play an important biological law which affects the process of growth and behavior, the *law of compensation* (Adler, 1927). When one kidney is improperly developed, the second kidney hypertrophies and performs the function of two. In some cases when one part of the brain is injured, another part can vicariously take over its function. Even in the psychological and behavioral world one sees examples of the law of compensation—the physically weak boy who is not a good athlete may become a good student. Thus from the point of view of Adler, many

forms of behavior, both constructive and destructive, are compensations. In
the physical organism, the compensations are a response to inferiority in
the body (body demand for increased competence). In the psychic world,
compensation is a response to a subjective perception of inferiority. One
does not have actually to be inferior, only to think that one is. If, for instance, a red-haired child felt that red hair was inferior, that person would
simultaneously experience an urge to compensate for it in some way.

The formation of the life style begins as soon as the individual is able
to formulate concepts in his mind, and as soon as he begins to develop patterned forms of behavior; namely, within the first six months of life. The
development of the life style, in its broad outlines, is usually complete by
the age of five or six.

It is influenced by three main factors: constitution, socialization experiences, and the individual's own *creative self.* Adler saw no necessity to de-
lineate stages of development. Personality development is a constant
process that takes place in the social arena and is motivated by the child's
own striving. Constitutional factors are facts of life which require accommodation. They include gender, body build, personal appearance, and
body defects. The socialization experiences are extremely important. They
include both the cultural ideals of the child's society and his early experiences with the family.

The child's first experiences within the family represent for Adler his
most important socializing experiences. Adler used the term *family constellation* for the operative influences in family structure and dynamics (Shulman, 1973).

One important aspect of the family constellation was the child's *birth
order.* There are five basic birth order positions (see Box 4-4).

Birth order is not an absolute determiner. A firstborn may be overrun
by the second, who then plays a firstborn role. The actual social role is
more important than the individual's ordinal position. Birth order is also

Box 4-4   Birth Order and Its Characteristics According to Adler

The firstborn child is in an exposed position. Since he is the first child that the parents experience, it is likely that he will be valued highly. The firstborn shows certain character traits in adult life, including a desire to remain in a dominant position in relation to his peers and some scars of having been dethroned by a younger (perhaps more favored) child.

    The second born shows a characteristic desire to "get ahead" or "catch up." Parents know that the second born often walks, talks, rides a bicycle, and engages in other activities at an earlier age than the firstborn. The second born is also able to watch the successes and failures of the firstborn, to avoid the failures, and to carve out for himself his own territory of success.

    The middle child, having neither the advantages of the first nor the youngest, sometimes gets lost in the shuffle unless he succeeds in making a place for himself. He tends to feel squeezed out of place, a percept often accompanied by a concern with fairness and unfairness.

    The youngest child is never dethroned and consequently often retains a special position in the family. On the other hand, the youngest also has the longest way to travel in order to catch up, and it is a common characteristic of the youngest that he either becomes the most successful member of the family or remains in the dependent position of the baby.

    The only child never has to struggle with other siblings for a place of importance in the family and thus shows far less tendency to be threatened by peer rivalries and indeed tends to see peers as objects of curiosity rather than as competitors. On the other hand, the only child sometimes does not have the opportunity to learn to share with others and thus may have a peculiar dependent relationship to the parents, or an insensitivity to the needs of others.

influenced by age and sex difference. A family with two children more than seven years apart has, in effect, two only children.

    The family constellation contains other salient features. One of these is the sex of the child in relation to the sex of its siblings, cultural sex roles, and family biases. In addition, parents present *models* for their children who tend to imitate their behavior. A child may imitate a parent for two reasons: (1) the model is viewed as negative, or (2) the model is viewed as positive but impossible to attain. This is why a successful father sometimes has unsuccessful sons. Furthermore, the parents provide a set of *values* from which the child can choose. Rules about the good life, the proper life, ethical conduct, and social ideals are learned at an early age from parents.

    Parental reactions to the child's behavior are also important since they essentially extinguish or reinforce the behavior, and inform the child of his status. There are constructive and destructive parental behaviors. Constructive parental behavior socializes the child in such a way that the child becomes a self-reliant cooperator who feels at home in his social world, feels a sense of self-worth, and contributes to the welfare of the community. In addition he meets the developmental tasks in a courageous and responsible way.

    The destructive parental behaviors consist of *pampering* and *rejection*.

The pampered child becomes dependent rather than self-reliant and is not well prepared for the tasks of life. The rejected child does not feel fully accepted into the human community, has trouble developing a positive image of himself, and anticipates rejection in the future.

Last, *family atmosphere* plays an important part in the development of personality. A family atmosphere may be harmonious and pleasant, or discordant and unpleasant; it may be warm and close, or cold and distant; it may be optimistic or pessimistic, and these elements of the atmosphere all influence the child's development.

The *creative self* is a construct used by Adler to account for the part that each individual plays in his own personality development. Constitution and environment provide only the skeletal framework of personality structure, the life style is the flesh and blood on the bones. Life style evolves through the individual's own perceptions into a unique perceptual framework for coping with the world. Thus the individual is not simply a reactor, but an actor with his own values and choices. This choice-making ability means that personality is not simply a product of constitution and environment. In essence, the person forms himself, heredity and socialization experience only providing influences. Adler used the term *self-training* to describe this creative personality-forming process.

Psychodynamics

Life is expansion; expansion is a form of movement. The organism grows physically and psychically as long as it can. This movement is directed toward an end point, a final goal of self-fulfillment, perfection, self-actualization. The final goal is the ultimate subjective value for the organism. Since each individual has his own private set of perceptions about the world, his own subjective views, the nature of the final goal will differ from person to person. One person will want to make a contribution, another will want to be a winner over others. The goals are largely unconscious, that is, they are either unadmitted or are not the recipients of conscious attention. A person usually recognizes his final goal when it is disclosed to him. A goal may be *distorted;* that is, it is a value antithetical to healthy social living. Distorted (or mistaken) goals lead to distorted forms of striving. Psychopathology is a distorted form of striving, examples of which are enumerated in Table 4-1.

Adler described three social tasks which every human being has to solve: *work* (being productive), the *social task* (having cooperative and satisfying human relationships), and the *sexual task* (developing an intimate and sexually satisfying relationship with a member of the opposite sex).

All forms of behavior (thinking, feeling, acting, physical responses) are thought of by Adler as *movement* of the individual in his field of action.

Table 4-1   Distorted Goals

To be without flaw
To be more impressive than anyone else
To be the center of attention
To be "first" (no. 1)
To be protected by others
To be always loved
To "get" more than others
To be perfectly secure
To never submit
To take revenge on life
To avoid any unpleasantness
To master everything

Source: Modified after a list by Shulman (1973, p. 40).

The direction is provided by the master plan of the life style and its final goal which operates through selective perception. Nonetheless, while the final goal provides an ideal end point, each item of behavior has more immediate goals. In order to understand behavior one has to understand its purpose, its "what for?". Most purposes of behavior are social in nature: they are intended to influence human relationships in some way.

Because each person acts according to his own private perception of the world, Adler spoke of *private logic* (analogous to Sullivan's parataxic thought), which is often opposed to *common sense* (Adler's term for consensually accepted perception). The private logic is a system of percepts which is usually determined by the life style.

> A young woman may feel fat and ugly and try to lose weight until she can fit into a size 5 dress. At that point she feels attractive. All the other people in her life may then consider her too thin. When she gains weight and becomes a size 12, everyone may consider her "just right," but she herself feels fat and ugly again. Her perception is not the same as everyone else's.

Because all behavior is purposive, emotions, mediated by perception, are seen as motivating forces which facilitate movement toward the goal. Selective perception chooses what will be seen as threat and what will be seen as support. One feels fear in the face of a threat because evasive behavior (generated by perception) is the chosen response, and fear is the emotion that facilitates the evasion. On the other hand, if attack is the chosen response to threat, the evoked emotion will be anger.

In Adler's theory, conflict is interpersonal, between the individual and his environment, not between an ego and an id. The individual's relation to life is normally always a questing, forward pushing movement. The desire to master, to give meaning to life, is a ceaseless striving. Much of what other schools of thought call conflict is explained by Adler, according to his understanding of movement and goal, in a different way. An example is ambivalence.

A young woman could not make up her mind about which of two men to marry. One suitor was reliable, industrious, and had a good job. The other was exciting. He had no job and therefore had more time for her. He owned a boat and lived a more romantic life. She could not make up her mind which to marry and thought about it most of the day. Last week she was sure she had decided, this week she was more inclined to the other one. She felt love for both of them but questioned if she knew what love really was.

This young woman experiences her situation subjectively as a dilemma. Her conscious feeling is indecision. Adlerian theory would look at her *movement* and ask what is its purpose. The clues to purpose lie in (1) What emotion is produced? and (2) What is the consequence? The emotional feeling of indecision leads to delay, to marking time. The consequence is congruent with the emotion—the young lady remains poised to choose, but does not do so. The consequence produced is, in Adler's theory, exactly what the young woman wants to bring about and the emotional state of indecision is used to bring about the consequence. The next question that must be answered is, Why would anyone want to do this? Adler's answer would be that something must be gained from such behavior. What is gained? The answer is time. She gains time to enjoy both men and for the moment has the best of both worlds and does not have to give up either. This whole process usually takes place outside conscious awareness. Again, Why? One would probably find that she had a conscious ideal, a woman *should* get married and *should* choose the right man. A desire to have the best of both worlds would not be consciously acceptable to her. However, her real intention is to play out the game as long as she can, rather than submit to the dictates of her *should*. By hiding her real intention from herself she can better pursue it. She preserves the image of herself as a responsible person and has her fun at the same time. Note how differently Freud or Miller and Dollard would explain "ambivalence."

Some notion of Adler's theory of unconscious processes can also be gleaned from this example. One arranges to avoid looking at what one is really doing when awareness would interfere with the plan. The basic process preserves and reinforces the continuing movement toward the final goal of the life style.

Psychopathology

Adler considered psychopathology to be mistaken forms of behavior brought about by *mistaken attitudes* in life. One person may conclude that he is inadequate to meet the social tasks in life and may look for excuses. Another person may feel essentially that life is precarious and may thus spend a good deal of time ordering and controlling his life. A third person may believe that others will never accept him so he withdraws from social participation and lives in a fantasy world. A fourth may consider himself unfairly wronged by others and spend his time and effort taking revenge on his family, the establishment, capitalist society, or whatever he feels is the source of his torment. All forms of maladaptive behavior are failures in meeting the tasks of life, and all such abortive attempts result from lack of social interest, discouragement, and feelings of inferiority. In a vicious cycle, these feelings of inferiority lead to more exaggerated forms of compensation—unless effective social identification can be developed.

A "neurosis" itself occurs when the individual meets a crisis situation which threatens to thwart movement toward the perceived final goal. The neurosis permits the individual to avoid the feared consequence by claiming an excuse, such as "I would if I could, but I can't" (The "yes—but" attitude to life).

A symptom always has a purpose—a payoff. Some common purposes of symptoms are to get love, attention, or service from others; to safeguard one's own position by insuring against failure; to control someone else's behavior; to demonstrate one's heroism or martyrdom; to demonstrate that one is abnormal and therefore entitled to be excused (Shulman & Mosak, 1967).

Others are always involved in a person's neurosis. A symptom is directed against someone or some aspect of life and therefore has an offensive component.

> A wife's headaches can have the unconscious purpose of keeping her husband kind to her while refusing his sexual demands.

Neurotic behavior thus allows the person to put distance between himself and the specific life task at hand.

Some maladaptive behavior is endemic in the culture which, for Adler, espouses faulty values—excessive competition and status inequality. Adler especially spoke of the inferior status assigned to women and children as an injurious factor in our culture. He drew a distinction between *equal rights* (*Gleichberechtigkeit*) and *equal worth* (*Gleichwertigkeit*). He recognized that those with responsibility needed the authority to carry out their responsibilities. However, even the person with the least responsibility is entitled to the same respect as a human being.

Behavior Change

Adler's theory of psychotherapy embodies three main ideas. It is the job of the therapist to be a friend to the patient, to help the patient become aware of his mistaken outlook on the world, and to help him develop healthy mental attitudes. Since the patient feels like a victim of his condition, it is important to show him that he brought it about himself, is unconsciously maintaining it, and has the power to change it. Like Freud, Adler thus wanted to extend the patient's awareness. Unlike Freud, Adler wanted the patient to become aware not of repressed drives, but of his own master plan for behavior and of his immediate goals in any situation. Instead of unconsciously choosing behavior, the patient can choose it consciously. Since maladaptive behavior was chosen because of lack of courage and/or social interest, the therapist must encourage the patient and must foster the development of social interest. The therapist uses friendliness, humor, logic, and other forms of encouragement to win the patient over and show him how his life could be better if he changed. Because Adler recognized the powerful resistance to change that most patients demonstrate, he recommended that the therapist become a sort of model for the patient, interpreting to him what he is doing and why. In this way, the patient can be taught how to interpret and modify his own behavior.

Evaluation

Adler and Kelly, who will be discussed next, are the most cognitively oriented of all the theorists we have described. Adler's key construct, life style, is defined as a cognitive blueprint for behavior. Furthermore, Adler is a constructionist, for whom the individual plays a creative role in the formation of his own personality. Biosocial agents are clearly operative but in no way determinative.

In addition to focusing our attention on the creative aspect of personality growth, Adler also stressed three other factors worthy of mention: (1) Cooperation was more important than competition in human welfare and progress. Consistent with this value, he believed that social equality was the *sine qua non* of a healthy society (Dreikurs, 1971). (2) The human individual is capable of greater control over his own behavior and motives than the mechanistic theories would have us believe, or than we ourselves may realize. The concept of the unified personality implies that perceptions, emotions, and other part processes are all under the influence of the final end point. Thus all behavior is under cognitive direction. (3) Given the premise of self-determination, Adler eschews the conflict model of personality and persuades us to the view that humans do pretty much what they want. Conflict arises from the fact that one choice may preclude another. It is not so much that we fear to eat the cake as that we want to have it and eat it too. Adler's theory contains concepts which contain all seven of the postulates which we believe are necessary for an adequate theory of personality.

PERSONAL CONSTRUCTS: GEORGE KELLY (1905–1966)

Philosophy

George Kelly, a clinical psychologist, was working with children and teachers in a traveling psychological clinic when he began the development of his *personal construct* theory. Later he was director of the clinical psychology program at Ohio State University. These diverse experiences provided much of the data upon which he based his theory.

Kelly (1955) admonished psychologists not to proceed as if their subjects were passive "reactors." He reminded them that their subjects also act as scientists, inferring from the past and formulating hypotheses about the future. Kelly believed that any human being has the potential to be adventurous, seeking new ideas and knowledge. His own theorizing is highly original and differs from the dominant forms of psychological thinking prevalent in America during his day. His open and exploratory attitude, which is probably related to his diversity of experience and background (Sechrest, 1963), is also revealed in his construct theory of personality. Rather than categorize a human being's personality into some preconceived slot, he believes that each individual behaves according to his own *system of construing*. In studying a teacher's reaction to a student's behavior, he would try to understand both the behavior of the student and how the construct system of the teacher elicited the latter's reaction. This approach led him to conclude that all dyadic interactions are determined by the construct systems of the individuals involved.

Personality Structure and Development

Kelly's unit of structure is the *personal construct*. A construct is the way a person interprets or construes the world. All the mottos in Box 4-2 are examples of personal constructs. There are four things we need to know about an individual's personal construct system: (1) the nature and range of constructs he uses; (2) the events subsumed under those constructs; (3) how these constructs tend to function; and (4) how they are organized in relation to one another to form a system. Box 4-5 illustrates how a personal construct system functions.

In order to measure personal construct systems Kelly devised the *Role Repertory Construct Test.* A number of role figures, for example, father, sister, good teacher, bad teacher, are compared, three at a time. The subject is asked to choose the two most similar. He is then asked to tell the central way in which these two are similar, as well as the main way in which the third person differs from the other two. These descriptions (usually adjectives) provide a similarity-contrast dimension. For example, the two similar persons may be described as "fair" and the third as "arbitrary." Fair-arbitrary then become two poles on a *construct scale* for this individual. A large number (about 14 to 21) of such scales constitute the person's *role repertory.*

By inspecting and analyzing the list of obtained constructs one can deduce the nature of a person's construct system. One can assess its relative versatility and integration by looking at the range and variety of constructs and the relationships between them. One can determine the dominant constructs that the person uses to code information about self, threat, support, competence, love, friendliness, and the intentions of others.

Bieri (1961) proposed a way of scaling the relative *complexity-simplicity* of the construct sample. Cognitively more complex persons are more likely to code the full range of the nuances and subtleties of another's personality, including their inevitable contradictions. Cognitively more simple persons, on the other hand, are likely to ignore information which denies or contradicts the univalent impression they are likely to have. They oversimplify. However, people may be complex in some ways and simple in others (Bannister & Mair, 1968).

Kelly speculated that constructs are formed as a result of how the person construes cause and effect in repeated events (what happens over and over again). Salmon (1967) used the Role Repertory Construct Test to explore how a child's construct system develops vertically into a construct hierarchy and finally into a superordinate system. Construct systems tend both to validate themselves and to become increasingly refined.

Dynamics

Guided by personal constructs, action is channeled by the way a person anticipates events. This anticipation, based on present perspectives, directs the individual to reach out into the future. In deciding on a direction, the person chooses that alternative in a dichotomized (similarity-contrast poles) construct from which he anticipates the greater possibility for extension and definition of his system. Having chosen, he makes his prediction about the best way to move and then acts.

However, rational consideration is necessarily complicated by anxiety, fear, and threat. One is *anxious* when one is caught up in an event that lies outside the range of one's constructs. One is *afraid* when a new construct is about to enter one's construct system. All of us have experienced fear of the new and unknown. One is *threatened* by an invalidation of any construct central to one's personal construct system. According to Kelly, a person acts to fulfill the life philosophy contained in the personal construct system. Impediments to action come from anxiety about conceptual adequacy, fear of the unknown, and threat of a major conceptual revision. Action is facilitated when events allow available options to lead to anticipation of construct system confirmation.

The young woman described in Box 4-5 has a construct of being a victim in the center of her construct system (the victim construct is high in the system hierarchy). Her movement (suffering and depression) is also consistent with this construct. Another person, equally preoccupied with rejection, may have a different central construct—for example, offended majesty—and will display different movement (may attack in anger and outrage).

Psychopathology

In addition to the affective terms—anxiety, fear, threat, aggression, hostility, and guilt—Kelly uses the concepts *constriction, dilation,* and *impermeability* to explain the genesis of psychopathology.

Anxiety, fear, and threat have already been defined. *Aggression* is activity aimed at elaborating one's perceptual field, with *initiative* and *inertia* at the two action poles. The aggressive person takes initiative whereas the nonaggressive person is inactive. *Hostility* is an attempt to extort validation for a prediction which has already been recognized as invalid. The hostile expression is an attempt to protect the construct system from invalidation. *Guilt* is experienced when one is behaving contrary to one's core role construct. Thus, the person who defines himself as loving and giving experiences guilt when he behaves in a hostile manner. The guilt feeling permits the person to confirm that he is loving and giving even while he is not behaving that way.

Anxiety, fear, and guilt can give rise to the constriction, dilation, and/or impermeability of the construct system. *Constriction* is a narrowing of the perceptual field (and thus of the construct system) in the face of fear. It is seen in the rigid behavior that is typical of the compulsive person. *Dilation* is the excessive broadening of the perceptual field, as seen in the manic. An *impermeable* construct does not allow new information into its context. It is seen in the encapsulated thought of certain schizophrenics.

The tightening and loosening of thought are not pathological in their own right, for there are times when a person needs to tighten his ideas and other times when he needs to expand them. When a person functions out of anxiety or fear, however, he is not likely to tighten and loosen in appropriate ways or at appropriate times. Maladaptive behavior occurs when emotions produce inappropriate constriction and dilation.

Behavior Change

In the process of personality growth, constructs are tested for their predictive efficiency. As the person successively construes the replication of events, he modifies his constructs so that they will be more accurate and predict the environment more efficiently. This constitutes constructive change. Kelly has noted that people change in an atmosphere of experimentation; that is, when given new information and validating data, people do change. He devised a method to induce change, called *fixed-role therapy*, which assumes that a person is what he represents himself to be. In fixed-role therapy the client is encouraged to represent himself in new ways, behave in new ways and construe himself in new ways. In this way he modifies his behavior and his construct system. Harrison (1966) has found that there is indeed a progressive change in concept usage following increased awareness of one's construct system (Bannister & Mair, 1968). Both the Role Repertory Construct Test and fixed-role therapy have been found useful in assessing and changing personality (Landfield, 1971).

Evaluation

Kelly deserves credit and gratitude from psychologists for directing them to the cognitive aspects of personality. Bruner (1956), commending Kelly's theory as the single greatest contribution of that decade to the theory of personality functioning, nevertheless wonders whether it is too rational an explanation of human behavior, particularly of its affective component, and questions recent psychological thought to the effect that feeling has no context independent of reason. This is too broad an issue to be dealt with here, so that we reserve later chapters for a discussion of the way cognition determines emotion. George Kelly has played a large part in the advance of cognitive theory. He has given an example of a theory with organismic mediators which is still capable of withstanding the rigors of empirical investigation (Mancuso, 1976).

Of the seven postulates, Kelly's theory adequately encompasses five of them. Personality is adaptive and unique. It determines selection of response and permits prediction of response, even the specific function of the response in the overall context. He does not offer explicit hypotheses about the influence of learning and culture, although he certainly recognizes that they are important in the growth, development, and refinement of the personal construct system.

5

personality
and
adaptive
behavior

OVERVIEW

All behavior is adaptive. The newborn human is limited in his ability to adapt to the environment and requires a social caretaker for his physiological needs. The basic needs of the human infant are for nourishment and contact, safety or protection, mastery, and sensory variation. The infant has certain innate perceptual programs which process need-related stimuli. The processing leads to responses. The responses feed back to the innate perceptual programs, modifying them into a perceptual system. Subsequent need satisfaction now becomes processed through the modified perceptual system so that the needs become transformed into motives. The motives which correspond to basic needs are, respectively, attachment, security, competence, and cognition. Each motive becomes further differentiated. Thus, for example, attachment becomes differentiated into love, affiliation, sexuality, and aggression; security, into anxiety and ability to cope with stress; competence, into achievement, industry, and play; and cognition, into curiosity, the search for novelty, and aesthetic preferences. Murray's "needs" can be classified into one or more of these four motives.

From the moment of birth a baby seeks to connect himself with his mother. This is the purpose of his movements. She is his first bridge to social life; and a baby who could make no connection at all with his mother, or with some other human being who took her place, would inevitably perish.

The connection is so intimate and far-reaching that we are never able, in later years, to point to any characteristic as the effect of heredity. Every tendency which might have been inherited has been *adapted*, trained, educated and made over again by the mother. (Adler, 1937, pp. 120)

As Postulate 1 states, all behavior is adaptive. Adaptive behavior is behavior which maintains the organism and helps it to survive in its environment. In human beings, personality contributes to adaptive behavior. In lower animals adaptive behavior is preprogrammed by instincts which are regulated by built-in programs. Human beings do not have such fixed patterns of behavior. The human starts life with certain built-in responses to physiological changes. These responses indicate that the organism has certain physiological needs. The human infant is not capable of satisfying these needs by himself. A social caretaker is required, who inevitably provides certain experiences for the infant and developing child. These socialization experiences feed back to whatever built-in programs the young child has and modify them accordingly.

For example, the infant requires skin contact for survival. We can speak of this as a need for contact which is regulated by a built-in program. The program directs the search for contact, but socialization modifies the program so that the infant seeks specific kinds of contact—for example, with the mother— and later on, certain kinds of social interaction, such as exchanging social smiles with the mother. What was originally a need for contact has now become a motive for attachment to the mother. It is this motive, rather than the need, which now directs the search for the desired goal (goal behavior). There are other physiological needs which similarly become transformed into motives through social experiences.

A motive can thus be defined as the social transformation of a need. Personality consists of the integration of these motives into an organized structure.

This way of conceptualizing personality, in the context of adaptive behavior, requires us to specify a number of factors. First, we must enumerate a necessary and sufficient set of needs with which the infant starts life. Our set of needs must be wide enough to cover the range of responses the infant displays, yet parsimonious enough so that they are not redundant. Second, we need to postulate that one of the built-in programs is an information-processing mechanism, which we call a perceptual program. This perceptual program becomes constantly modified through continuing experience. We will call these modified perceptual programs the *perceptual system.* The perceptual system mediates the motive-directed search for the desired goals. Third, the theory must specify a necessary and sufficient set of motives which will account for the range of human goal behavior. Fourth, the theory needs to explain how the motives are integrated into a personality structure.

AN OUTLINE OF THE PERCEPTUAL SYSTEM

In the newborn, inborn mechanisms signal to the caretaker that the infant is in a state of need. The caretaker usually responds. Stimulus information from the caretaker and the rest of the environment is filtered through innate perceptual programs which process this information and lead to a response. The response in turn acts as a stimulus which feeds back to the innate perceptual programs, producing modified perceptual programs. This cycle is shown in Figure 5-1.

The general information-processing model diagrammed in Figure 5-1 can also be used to explain how physiological needs become transformed into social motives. Figure 5-2 diagrams the stages involved in this transformation.

Basic physiological needs are filtered through the innate perceptual program. Feedback from the innate program to itself produces the pro-

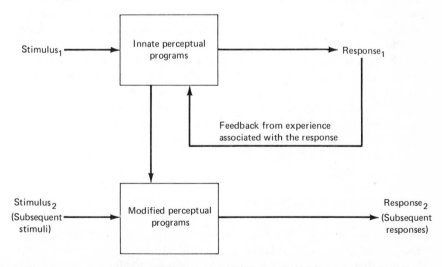

Figure 5-1　A diagram of the modification of innate perceptual programs through experience. Subsequent stimuli are processed by the modified perceptual program.

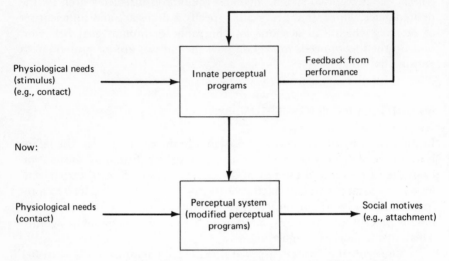

Figure 5-2   Information from internal needs is processed by the sensory system in such a way that the latter is modified into a perceptual system, which in turn modifies the need system into a motive system. This diagram depicts how the infant's contact need becomes transformed into an attachment motive.

grams which we call the perceptual system. All information about needs is now filtered through this perceptual system which modifies them into social motives. From this point of view, personality organization is hierarchical. The perceptual system is a superset subsuming other motive systems as subsets. This theory proposes to describe a minimum set of motive systems adequate to explain the domain of human motives. It also should be noted that from such a perspective individual needs and social requirements will not be in conflict with each other. Rather the socialization process itself provides the medium through which needs become motives. Henceforth motives are the directing force of behavior and, therefore, the proper object of psychological study.

INNATE PHYSIOLOGICAL NEEDS

At birth, the individual's sensory, muscular, glandular, and nervous systems are all functional (Mussen, Conger, & Kagan, 1974), although the neuromuscular system still has some years to grow before it is fully developed anatomically. The organism is capable of receiving and decoding gross information through the sensory receptors and responding through the motor-glandular effectors. The sensorimotor apparatus permits the innate perceptual programs to function. Needs act as stimuli for the arousal of innate programs.

We define needs as physiological requirements which must be satisfied in order for the organism to survive. The word *need* implies a lack, a deficiency in what is available to the person. The concept has been used in various ways both in psychological literature and in everyday speech. The statement "I need . . ." may really mean "I want . . ." That is to say, the person is talking about a desire, not necessarily a biological need. The concept of need has been further confused on three counts: (1) Individuals are not always aware of real needs, such as needs for rest, sleep, a better diet, more information about a situation, and so forth. (2) When individuals come to value something very highly, they are convinced that they need it, and acquiring it becomes a goal of their behavior. Such goals include money, prestige, a new automobile, someone to take care of them, and so on. (3) Many theorists in psychology and related fields have used the word *need* not only in the specific physiological sense, as we have, but have also generalized it to include a variety of learned "wants." For example, constructs such as "need for achievement" and "need for power" have become widely used in the psychology of motivation.

In our judgment, these different ways of using the concept have simply confounded our understanding of what a need is and what human motivation is all about. In this book we use the term *need* only for the personal survival and species survival requirements of the organism.

As our discussion in the following section suggests, all the needs described by psychologists can fit into four categories. They are nourishment and contact, protection or safety, mastery, and sensory variation. Nourishment, contact, and protection are concerned with bodily growth and survival. Mastery is concerned with effective manipulation of the environment. Sensory variation is necessary for innate programs to be aroused and perceptual systems to develop. It is our view that the whole range of human motives can be traced to these four basic need systems.

THE FOUR MOTIVE SYSTEMS

The socialization of the needs gives rise to a spectrum of learned "wants," for which we reserve the term *motive*. In our theoretical model we present parallel sets of categories for corresponding physiological need systems and psychosocial motive systems: Nourishment and contact needs result in the attachment motive; safety needs, in the security motive; mastery need, in the competence motive; and sensory variation needs, in the cognitive motive.

The Need for Nourishment-Contact
and the Attachment Motive

The attachment motive grows out of the socialization of nourishment and contact needs. The relative helplessness of the human infant makes it necessary that the satisfaction of these needs be mediated by a social caretaker. If food intake and contact are accompanied by a physiological state of well-being, the infant feels secure and therefore learns to *trust* the caretaker. However, the feeding and contact situations can also be accompanied by distress and discomfort. In such cases the infant can develop negative withdrawing attitudes toward the nurturing situation.

Thus, some fundamental conditioning of emotions takes place during the nurturing situation in early infancy; moreover, the foundations of security/insecurity and trust/mistrust are established. These emotional reactions to social stimulation are the foundation for later differentiation of social behavior patterns. Such social motives as dependence, succorance, nurturance, and affiliation—and such aberrations as affect hunger (emotional starvation), withdrawal, and severe separation anxiety—have their roots in the socialization of this primary social relationship.

A Conditioning Model

As Figure 5-3 indicates, the mother is initially a neutral object to the infant, since he has no experience associated with her. During the nurturing situation, however, the mother usually provides two kinds of sensory stimulation that have important emotional effects—nourishment and contact. The nourishment and contact stimuli are unconditioned stimuli (US) while the two reactions to them, the feeding and emotional response, are unconditioned responses (UR).

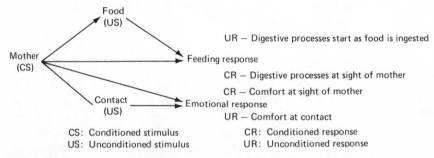

Figure 5-3   The double conditioning model, conceptualizing the nurturing experience of the infant, diagrams the growth of attachment to the mother.

In order for healthy psychological development to take place, there must be compatibility between the information contained in the two responses. If the mother feeds her baby while holding it gently and closely without excessive, unpleasant stimulation, the emotional reaction from the infant will be one of calm. On the other hand, if the baby is fed either without bodily comfort or in the presence of excessive stimulation, the emotional reaction (fright, tension, startle, anguish) will inhibit proper food intake. A wide spectrum of undesirable consequences, ranging from relatively mild to serious, can result from this inhibiting emotional reaction. The mildest ill effects are curdling of the milk or spitting up of food. More serious effects are digestive problems such as colic.

If the mother's contact stimulation is erratic, the baby may develop an approach-avoidance attitude to the mother. The classical studies of Spitz (1946) and Ribble (1943) describe the effects of severe contact deprivation in infants—a state of apathy which is accompanied by loss of weight, tissue changes, and loss of the feeding response. In less severe cases, when the infant's experience with the mother has been unpleasant, the infant may avoid her or even display antipathy. More recent and carefully controlled research on both humans and animals has verified these findings (Bowlby, 1969; Harlow, 1971; Ainsworth, 1972).

As the mother becomes associated with both feeding and emotional responses, she becomes a conditioned stimulus (CS) for both conditioned responses (CR). Socialization conditions the infant's behavior toward the mother and in this way the attachment motive is formed.

Ainsworth (1973) points out that the amount of contact is less important than its quality in forming attachment. She describes three different attachment types and their antecedents (see Box 5-1).

Bell and Ainsworth (1972) found that mothers who responded

Box 5-1	Attachment Types and Their Antecedents	
Type of Attachment	*Characterized by*	*Antecedent Maternal Behavior*
Secure	Child greets mother happily, seeks proximity to mother	Mother is sensitive, cooperative, accessible, accepting (Stayton et al., 1973)
Ambivalent	Child resists contact, wants to maintain contact and seeks security	Mother is ignoring, sensitive, interfering
Avoidant	Child avoids proximity to mother	Mother is ignoring and rejecting
Source: After Ainsworth, 1973; Stayton et al., 1973.		

promptly to an infant's cry, socialized infants who subsequently cried less. This is contrary to the prediction of reinforcement theory that such maternal response increased crying. One of the signals of frustrated attachment is crying.

While clinicians have long realized the importance of good mothering and nurturing during infancy, a more precise specification of the factors involved had been inadequate and controversial. In the 1940s René Spitz (1946) recorded serious retardation of emotional and physical development in infants who had been hospitalized or institutionalized for long periods of time without the usual intimacy of the mother-child relationship. Their susceptibility to other diseases was much higher than among controls. Some of these infants even wasted away and died. Spitz concluded that these infants died from a vague kind of malady which he called "hospitalism," and believed that the major contributor to this syndrome was the lack of intimate contact with a mothering social agent.

Montagu (1950), in reviewing a number of comparative studies, concluded that the contact aspect of mothering is necessary for survival. Goldfarb (1943) reported not only serious deleterious effects on physical and emotional development, but on intellectual growth as well. Ribble (1943) believed that the nature of the deprivation was not only lack of contact with the mother's body, but also the absence of kinesthetic stimulation (as when babies are rocked). She believed that the infant needs a variety of sensory stimulation. She grouped all these sensory stimulations under the acronym *TLC*—tender, loving care!

These clinical observations of the first half of the twentieth century culminated in the extensive work of John Bowlby on British infants deprived of their mothers for a variety of reasons during the Second World War. Bowlby (1969) concluded that the child's ability to form an attachment, or to love, was retarded by deprivation. The experimental research of Harry Harlow (1971) further clarified Bowlby's observations on the importance of these nurturing variables (especially contact) in the growth of attachment and security.

In order to test the effect of feeding and other nurturing variables on attachment and security, infant rhesus monkeys were separated from their mothers and reared by surrogate mothers. These inanimate surrogate models, who bore little resemblance to the live monkey mothers, were constructed either of wire or of bulky material which was covered with soft terrycloth. Diagrams of the wire and the terrycloth mothers are presented in Figure 5-4. The infant monkey was raised either with a wire or a terrycloth mother, by whom he would be fed or not.

Harlow found that contact was more important than feeding in the development of the attachment motive. Although infants, presumably when hungry, would go to the wire mother if she contained the milking ap-

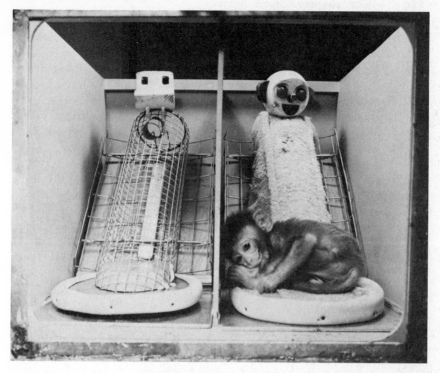

Figure 5-4   Wire and cloth mother surrogates. Source: University of Wisconsin Primate Laboratory.

paratus, they would return at the earliest opportunity to the terrycloth mother for contact and hugging. Whether the terrycloth mother fed them or not, the infants, over time, developed a clear tendency to spend long periods playing on and around her, and in cuddling her, but not the wire mother.

When the infants were subsequently placed in an open field situation, all of them exhibited the characteristic fear reaction (crouching, holding hands over the head, rigidity, freezing posture, and the cataleptic, turmoil-like "shivering"). If the surrogate terrycloth mother was present, the frightened infants quickly ran to her and held on "for dear life." However, the presence of the wire mother produced no such security-seeking reaction. In fact, if the infant was put in the open field situation with a piece of terrycloth and the wire mother, it preferred the piece of cloth over the wire mother, although the fear reaction remained.

Over time, the infant came to rely on the terrycloth mother for a secure home base. In the presence of frightening objects the infant gradually began to wander away from the terrycloth mother, only to return quickly and consistently repeat this back and forth movement. Eventually, the infant would approach the fearful object, explore it, returning at intervals to the mother, and in the end touch, play with, and manipulate the object. It is as if he had learned to cope with this environmental intrusion, and through this coping, mastered his fear. It is like learning courage!

The infant's preference for the terrycloth over the wire mother is pictured in Figure 5-5. According to Harlow (1971), the deleterious effects of maternal separation can be partially reversed by exposure to peers or by intense, prolonged, and enriched mothering (Rheingold, 1956).

Other studies on bonding behavior have corroborated the clinical findings of Bowlby and Spitz and the experimental studies of Harlow. Bonding behavior is common to all mammals. In primates, where there are variations from species to species, there is a general order in the pattern of attachment behavior (Eibl-Eibesfeldt, 1971). At birth and during the first few months of life infant chimps cling to the underside of the mother, grasping her hair and sucking on her nipples even when not feeding. Later,

Figure 5-5 Rhesus infant, raised with a cloth surrogate mother, displaying security and exploratory behavior in a strange situation in the mother's presence. Source: University of Wisconsin Primate Laboratory.

they jump on her back and ride with her whenever the mother moves away. In later development the infant begins to move further and further away from the mother, still using her as home base, however. Approximately coincident with weaning, the young animal spends more and more time in peer play, returning to the mother when danger threatens or to sleep with her. Jane Lawick-Goodall (1968, 1971) observing the behavior of chimpanzees in a natural habitat has documented that attachment behavior persists to a later age in chimpanzees (probably the closest relative to humans) than in other primates. The young chimpanzee does not conclude his attachment with the mother until adolescence and young adulthood. At this time both sexes spend most of their interaction time in the company of dominant mature males. Even then, a mature chimp of either sex may return and spend time with mother.

Eibl-Eibesfeldt (1971) also points out that contact is the primal basis for the development of personal bonds. Even in the first days of its life, a child calms down when it is caressed, picked up, or spoken to and the mother is equally bound to the child by means of a number of signals that release cherishing behavior. Infants will initiate social contact even when the mother does not. During sucking, the human infant shows the grasp reflex. Since the mother has positive responses to the infant who clings to her, looks at her, and smiles at her, the affectional bond grows. The attachment motive retains its importance in adult life, but is now mediated by different patterns of contact, for example, sexual contact, handshaking, "rapping," engaging in a common task, going to a party, or even playing tennis. All affectional and affiliative motives are variations of the attachment motive.

The differentiation of the attachment motive. The attachment motive is the foundation for many other interpersonal motives. While the original attachment bond is to the cherishing mother, during the course of development bonding becomes generalized to other love objects—other humans and beloved toys or pets. The attachment motive itself becomes differentiated into a variety of interpersonal movements. Thus several of Murray's "interpersonal needs," such as nurturance, succorance, affiliation, sex, and aggression, can properly be subsumed under the attachment motive.

Love, affiliation, and sexuality. Breger (1974) pointed out that love is the central force in bonding primate groups, as we have just indicated. Non-emergence of the attachment motive produces a general withdrawal from and warding off of stimuli (Harlow, 1971; Bowlby, 1969; Stayton, Ainsworth, & Main, 1973), which then precludes exploratory behavior and peer relationships. The establishment of the attachment motive enables exploration and peer play to proceed and thus prepares the way for friendship and affiliation to develop.

The pleasures of contact-comfort—holding, touching, cuddling, rocking, cooing—with the mother provide a model for expecting similar emotional consequences from peer relationships. Of all these sensory components, Breger (1974) believes that touch is the most important (compare this with Harlow's finding about the monkey's preference for the terrycloth rag).

Sexuality seems much more important for attachment and love in adult human beings than in animals. Lawick-Goodall (1971) observed that unless the female chimpanzee was in the proper phase of the estrous cycle, neither she nor the available males showed any interest in sex. The human estrous cycle is not so definitely connected with a period of heightened receptivity. Humans can be interested in sex at any time. Easy sexual arousal is not a part of our "bestial" nature, but peculiarly human. Morris (1964) considered humans to be far more sexually active than any other animal. Even in our closest "cousin" (chimpanzee), sexual behavior is limited to a smaller range of functions. Humans, with their increased capacity to modify built-in programs, have greatly extended the range and function of sexual behavior, so that it can be used to obtain love or contact-comfort or for domination, aggression, status, and competence-negotiation (Shulman, 1973).

Klein (1969) prefers using the term *sensuality* rather than *sexuality* to describe the love-contact-comfort and other forms of pleasure-seeking behavior in humans. The pursuit of sensual experience in peer groups is a necessary prerequisite to appropriate adult sexual behavior (Harlow, 1971; Sackett, 1970). Harlow's monkeys, deprived in infancy of the opportunity to develop attachment to a mother, exhibited grossly inadequate peer play behavior; they were socially reticent and did not participate in grooming behavior. As adults, they experienced sexual arousal but did not know how to engage in sexual relationships.

Aggression. This adverse effect of maternal deprivation could be overcome if the young monkey received extensive and enriched peer group experience. While one outcome of peer play is adequate adult sexual behavior, a second is learning to express and experience aggression in socially acceptable and effective ways. Aggression seems to run counter to the attachment motive. However, our subjective experience informs us that the opposite of attachment is apathy, not hostility. Anger at a loved one is usually expressive of a desire to reestablish the attachment more firmly.

Aggression is an affective intensification of behavior. An examination of the functions of aggression will help us to understand the general role of emotions in behavior. Some functions of aggression that have been listed in the literature (Washburn & Hamburg, 1966; Lorenz, 1966) include predation, territorial behavior, dominance behavior, social order, protecting young, competition and mating behavior. Through its affective intensity, aggression is a forceful way to influence the behavior of the others. Since aggression functions in the service of a number of motive systems, e.g. security, it must be understood in terms of the intention of the agent. Aggressive play between males also leads to bonding, and in the absence of destructive intent, it also increases the skills of the protagonists (one enjoys a close contest and develops attachment to the rival who provided the test). Eibl-Eibesfeldt (1971) provides another view of the close relationship between love and aggression. We will examine aggression as an interpersonal movement more fully in Chapter 10. Suffice it to say here that the term aggression is sometimes associated with hostility or the absence of friendliness, at other times it is associated with dominance, rather than hostility; e.g., the person who aggressively tries to take charge of a situation or tries to control another person.

The expression of *all* motives and emotions depends on socialization experiences. In a classic study, Kuo (1931) reared a group of kittens with their own mothers, who killed rats in their presence. Of these kittens, 85 percent killed rats. Another group of kittens was reared with rats as companions. None of these kittens ever molested any of their rat companions, or any similar rat; in fact, only 16 percent of these kittens grew up to become cats who killed other varieties of rats. Like sex, aggression can be used for constructive or destructive purposes. Just as human sexuality is peculiarly human, so is human aggression uniquely human. Conspecific aggression (directed toward members of the same species) that results in killing is rare except among rats and humans (Lorenz, 1966).

The Need for Safety and the Security Motive

Contact not only serves as the basis of bonding but also the original stimulus of the protection motive. The protection provided through attachment eventually results in the child's developing his own ability to cope. If hurt during play or environmental exploration, the infant runs to its mother for contact-comfort. This security effect is so powerful that a mother's kiss will often ease the young child's distress even though the physical pain remains. Conversely, the anxiety produced by separation from the mother makes all other injuries seem more painful. Half-grown baboons, when frightened, run to an older high-status baboon who apparently confers a feeling of being protected. The more we trust, the less protection we require.

Feelings of danger or safety are the emotional experiences surrounding the protection needs. A schizophrenic psychosis may be considered an extreme form of self-protective behavior; the schizophrenic human withdraws from most human contact in order to protect himself against expected unpleasantness from others.

Stress adaptation. In addition to finding security through reliance on a social agent, the organism also becomes secure through learning to rely on its own physiological resources. Psychologists have found that a system for adapting to stress is one component of the protection need, and in order for this system to function, the infant must be exposed to a certain amount of stress stimulation.

A revealing study on stress adaptation was conducted by Seymour Levine (1960), whose primary interest was in investigating the differential effects of bodily contact and trauma. To this end, Levine raised three groups of infant rats under different conditions of bodily stimulation, from the time they were born until they were tested in various stressful environments from day 5 on. During the first few days after birth, the animals would be taken from their home cages for a certain period, usually 1 hour each day, and given one of three kinds of stimulation. The handled animals were gently stroked and played with by the experimenter; the shocked group was placed in a cage and given an electric shock; and the control group was simply separated from the home cage for an hour without additional stimulation. Following these different experiences, the three groups were submitted to a variety of physiological, physical, and psychological stress tests. The results were startling and unexpected!

Physical stress was provided by exposure to cold. Correspondingly, psychological stress was created by placing the infant rat in an open field situation. Levine was interested in assessing the appropriateness and timing of physiological reactions to stress. Figure 5-6 shows the magnitude and temporal sequence of this autonomic stress reaction for two of the groups, the shocked and the non-stimulated group.

Contrary to what one might presuppose, there were no differences between the handled group and the shocked group. It would seem that both handling and mild electric shock produce similar effects—namely, facilitating appropriate protective hormonal reactions to trauma in later life. What seems important is not so much the kind of stimulation but the fact that the animal is stimulated at all. Presumably, early sensory stimulation of the infant is indispensable for adequate coping with stress in later life. It is as if the animal must be exposed to mild degrees of stressful stimulation in order for the autonomic nervous system to be adequately tuned for later coping. We may refer to this effect of early stimulation as *stress adaptation.* In the stimulated groups, there is a sharp rise in autonomic reaction immediately after the stress stimulus is introduced, which quickly reaches a maximum level of arousal. Conversely, the maladaptive autonomic reaction of

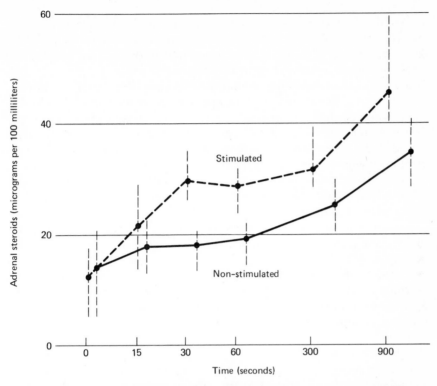

Figure 5-6 Sluggish response to an electric shock is indicated by the rather slow rise in the concentration of circulating steroi hormones in previously non-stimulated animals (dark curve). In stimulated animals the level increases more rapidly for about 30 seconds. The points on the curve indicate the average level and the broken lines the range of values. Source: S. Levine, Stimulation in infancy. *Scientific American*, May 1960, p. 86.

the non-handled, control group is not only sluggish, rising very slowly after the introduction of the stress stimulus, but also does not reach the same level of activity. The net effect is that the non-stimulated animals do not produce enough hormonal activity to fight the stress effectively. There is too little activity too late!

Related research was conducted in a worldwide anthropological survey coordinated and reported by Landauer and Whiting (1964). Over 30 cultures spanning five continents were surveyed to obtain information about the relative prevalence of stressful physical practices during infancy. Such practices as inoculation in Western society, tribal marking on the face in African societies, binding of limbs in Oriental societies, and circumcision in Middle Eastern societies were among the kinds of stressful physical practices that were catalogued. These various practices were weighted to arrive at a cumulative stress index, whose reliability was established. This stress index was correlated with two dependent variables, and care was taken to control for any other variables—including climate, soil conditions, and diet—that could confound the two dependent measures. The dependent measures were average height of the adult male and age of menarche. It was found that the most stressful societies (the upper 25 percent) produced males whose average height was two inches taller than the least stressful (the lower 25 percent). Similarly, the age of menarche in the most stressful society was less than 11 years compared to almost 13 years of age for the least stressful society. Early stress produces physiological mechanisms which lead to earlier maturation and stronger bodies. Levine's rats also showed increased body weight and increased somatotropic (growth-producing) hormones. Physiological growth and stress adaptation go together.

It is really not surprising that the growth of security requires not only learning to rely on the social agent, but also on one's own body. Exposure to minimal degrees of stress facilitates the development of a nervous system which can cope effectively with stressful, fear-provoking stimulation in later life.

Differentiation of the security motive.   The security motive becomes differentiated into a variety of security-seeking movements, including Murray's "needs" of aggression, defendance, and harmavoidance (flight). Most of the defensive behaviors seen in humans such as withdrawal, suspicion, seclusiveness, and avoidance of risk as well as aggressive behaviors, such as attacking when one is frightened, are differentiations of the security motive. Some attachments between people also have security, rather than the love bond, as their primary motive.

Attachment, Security and Anxiety

While anxiety, like all the other emotions, is involved in the functioning of all the motive systems, it is of direct and crucial importance in the attachment and security systems. After reviewing a number of studies, Breger concluded that "the basic prototype of anxiety is abandonment; its earlier state is the helplessness of the separated infant" (1974, p. 89). Bowlby (1960, 1961) felt that attachment was a primary goal in human behavior. Disruption/separation of the primary bond between mother and infant becomes occasion for anxiety in both mother and infant (*separation anxiety*). From birth on, the attachment becomes increasingly more directed toward the mother, and other adults become less satisfactory attachment objects. This perceptual differentiation underlies the emergence of the anxiety response to strangers and unfamiliar objects (Wolfensberger-Hässig, 1974). Hebb (1946) observed that chimpanzees exhibit a strong fear reaction when other conspecifics were presented to them in *unfamiliar* ways; for example, an anesthetized chimpanzee aroused fear, while a sleeping one did not. Hebb (1949) elaborated further that when the chimpanzee is exposed to information he does not recognize, he becomes more excited—a general alarm reaction occurs. Hebb thus gives us an operational definition of one kind of perceived danger—danger of the unknown. Unfamiliar adults elicit negative reactions in infants, while unfamiliar children elicit interest and smiling; a midget elicits prolonged staring. There are also contextual effects. A mask in one situation may lead to a wariness; in another (as on a clown), laughter (Sroufe, Walters, & Matas, 1974). Rafman (1974) showed that if the stranger is trained to behave like the mother, the infant's negative reaction decreases. If, however, an infant does not show fear in the absence of the attached person, it may mean that attachment is not well developed and this bodes ill for later psychological well-being (Bronson, 1972). One final fact: The alarm mechanism and its physiological concomitants is the same in the presence of actual physical danger as it is in unfamiliar situations and in separation anxiety (Campos, 1976; Campos, Emde, Gaensbauer, & Henderson, 1975).

Researchers have also investigated the relationship between fear and curiosity. Infants have been shown to detect novelty and discrepancy long before they become wary of unfamiliar stimuli (Mussen, Conger & Kagan, 1974). Small discrepancies from the familiar produce curiosity; large discrepancies produce fear. Using the mother as a secure base, the infant progressively explores and expands his area of the familiar. With this increased breadth of perceptual categories, the security system (which began with reliance on the mother) moves toward self-reliance. Thus, Erikson's movement from trust to autonomy can be explained in perceptual terms, as can Kelly's idea that anxiety occurs when we do not have a personal construct adequate to the particular situation. There are two ways of feeling secure: relying on trustworthy others or on a trustworthy self. The security system grows out of the attachment system and out of early and gradual stress adaptation.

"As the person progresses beyond infancy, anxiety becomes symbolized in more complex ways and eventually is internalized" (Breger, 1974, p. 89). Just as the base of security expands from the mother to others, so does the base of separation anxiety. Eventually this reaches the point where anxiety is felt when one faces the prospect of losing group membership or of group disapproval. The fear of rejection by others thus comes to supplant the fear of abandonment by the mother, and public opinion becomes a major force in inducing conformity in behavior. Ultimately, the conditions provoking anxiety become so internalized that the individual develops his own standards for acceptable behavior. When external obstacles prevent us from living up to our standards, anxiety appears. When we have failed to meet our own standards, a particular variety of anxiety—guilt—is experienced.

The Mastery Need and the Competence Motive

Adequate contact and nurturing stimulation is important not only for the growth of attachment in its own right, but also for the subsequent development of exploratory behavior and instrumental skills. This coincides exactly with Erikson's claim that the development of trust is required for the subsequent development of autonomy (1950). Celia Stendler (1953) pointed out that trust is accompanied by the development of a new motive, dependence, which can be used effectively to encourage the child to develop skill, competence, and a certain amount of independence. The child is dependent on the mother because she has been dependable; he now wishes to please her and remain in her favor. The mother can thus reward (through approval) certain acts. For example, if the child exhibits growing independence through competence or skill, the mother can show her approval by cherishing behavior, reinforcing the development of competence.

As early as 1917, as an alternative to Freud's libido model, Adler postulated the striving motive as the dominant motive in life. Recently, psychologists have reexamined the human need to master unknown aspects of the environment and have found that it is just as important a motive for survival as the need for contact. These researchers emphasize that activities can be rewarding even in the absence of such primary physiological needs as that for sustenence. In his discussion of competence as a motive, Robert White (1959, 1963b) describes the joy that infants display when engaged in new activities. White sees this as a manifestation of a mastery need, out of which competence grows. According to White, the growth of competence proceeds along with exploration, manipulation, and play. Through these activities, the organism begins to have an effect upon the environment; thus, both White (1963) and J. McV. Hunt (1966) speak of an *effectance motive*.

Hunt (1963, 1966) reviews a number of studies which verify that young animals will play, manipulate, explore, and seek new sources of perceptual input without any additional incentive. Harlow's (1950) and Butler and Harlow's (1957) observations of well fed and well watered monkeys revealed amazingly that these primates worked for up to 10 hours disassembling a six-unit puzzle and still showed "enthusiasm for their work" at the end of that time. It would seem that the case for the existence of a mastery need, which is later socialized into a competence or effectance motive, is a strong one.

Differentiation of the competence motive. We have stated earlier that exploration, manipulation, and play are activities important to the development of competence. These activities themselves become differentiated as the person develops, provided there is appropriate practice and training. Examples of exploration can be found in all investigative activity—including the behavior of the experimental scientist and the inventor. Play activity in the child and adult includes sports, games, and creative arts. All skilled acts—crafts that range from domestic to industrial and professional—are examples of the differentiation of manipulative behavior.

One well-documented differentiation of the competence motive is the need for achievement (n-Ach), which will be discussed at length in Chapter 9. A person who demonstrates a strong need for achievement fulfills his motive through achieving. Not all people are achievers. Some find their competence in obtaining status or material goods, in Machiavellianism (having power over others), or in successfully rebelling against the expectations of parents and other authorities.

Appropriate socialization of the competence motive includes the development of that attribute which Erikson called industry. Although the tendency toward activity, coping, and mastery is apparently inherent, the way the competence motive is formulated differs widely from person to person, depending on social training. One way to encourage the development of competence is to *attribute* it to the person. Miller and his co-workers (1972) tried to teach fifth graders to clean up after themselves. An attribution group were told once a day for eight days that they were neat and tidy people (neatness was attributed to them). A persuasion group received lectures on the virtue of neatness. The former group showed much more cleaning up than the latter after two weeks.

Inappropriate socialization in the competence motive through discouragement of the child's natural tendency to activity—either by overindulgence, overanxiety, excessive domination, or rejection—leads to failure to develop skilled behavior. Extremely high standards of achievement, or excessive demands, also discourage the child. Lack of opportunity—as in various minority group settings—also prevents the development of skills and industry. The search for competence in discouraged or unskilled people takes other forms. Their being able to bully or exploit others is sometimes a misguided way of seeking competence. Delinquency and criminal behavior may also fall in this categoy. Such behaviors may reflect attempts of the disaffected person to live up to his own standards of achievement.

Opportunistic and Non-Opportunistic Species

The work of ethologists places this mastery behavior into a broader context. They distinguish between opportunistic and non-opportunistic species. A non-opportunistic species, for example, bees, is high specialized and has almost no capacity for adaptation to changing environmental circumstances. Opportunistic species, on the other hand, are specialists in nonspecialization; they are flexible and show amazing adaptability to environmental change. Morris (1964) noted that opportunistic species display a restless curiosity and a love for the novel and that their nervous systems abhor inactivity. By exploring and sampling they develop ways of adjusting to environments. Primates, especially humans, are the most opportunistic of animals. "Exploration and play are crucial parts of the flexible primate capacity to adapt to and utilize a variety of environmental opportunities" (Breger, 1974, p. 55).

As we ascend the phylogenetic ladder and instinctive patterns become less rigid, curiosity and play increase. Through these exploratory activities the uncommitted cortex (Hebb, 1949) becomes committed and differentiated, expanding cognitive categories and skills. It has clearly been shown by a number of researchers, especially Hebb and his followers, that innate tendencies to mastery require appropriate stimulation for fruition. For example, animals who are raised in a rich, free environment are superior in intellectual performance to animals raised in restricted environments (Forgus & Melamed, 1976). Based on his research with infants and young children, White (1975) has come to the provocative conclusion that cognitive complexity, which forecasts future intelligence, is attained by 3 years of age. This thesis is consistent with Hebb's theory that early experience is overwhelmingly more important than later experience in determining intellectual ability. New cognitions are built upon old ones; the larger the early foundation, the larger the resulting edifice.

The Need for Sensory Variation and the Cognitive Motive

Hunt (1971) has argued that the competence motive depends not only on motor aspects of behavior such as exploration and play, but also on an inherent need for variation in sensory input.

Life is an adaptive process and adaptation requires *information*. The organism can only acquire information when there is a change or variation in incoming stimuli. Thus, researchers have shown that the need for sensory variation is a need like contact and protection. Our concept of death centers around the idea that we will no longer be able to see, hear, experience, or know what is going on. Conceptually, a cessation of information equals death. All living organisms are information receivers and processors. While we agree with Hunt that the competence motive involves the inte-

Figure 5-7   Play is an important medium for developing competence.
Source: Courtesy Marian Bernstein.

gration of sensorimotor activity, the need for information seems also to be
the foundation of another motive—the desire for knowledge—which we
call the *cognitive* motive.

Ever since the classical work of the Gestalt psychologists in the first
quarter of the twentieth century, we have known that there must be sensory variation or heterogeneity in stimulus information in order for the perceptual field to be articulated. In fact, reduced sensory variation leads to
serious malfunction in the perceptual system. A number of research findings integrated by Hebb (1960) points to the inescapable conclusion that
varied sensory stimulation is necessary for the growth of the nervous system, brain function, and effective perception. This research covers a broad
area, including the study of sensory deprivation, the effect of varied early
experience, and curiosity and novelty-discrepancy studies.

Sensory deprivation and sensory variation.   Sensory deprivation occurs
when external sensory stimulation is reduced from heterogeneity to homogeneity. A dramatic set of observations was first reported by Heron (1961),
who asked volunteers to spend time in a small room where sensory varia-

tion was reduced. The reduced environment is shown in Figure 5-8. Not only was the room small, but visual homogeneity was produced by having the room essentially devoid of furniture and enclosed by translucent material which allowed only diffuse light to enter. Auditory homogeneity was produced by making the chamber soundproof and introducing a steady, low-intensity white noise. Kinesthetic and proprioceptive homogeneity was maintained by having the subject lie in bed, most of the time, with his limbs encased in cardboard cylinders. Food and other biological necessities were passed through small partitions when required. The general effect was sensory monotony.

Although subjects were paid $20 a night for participating in the

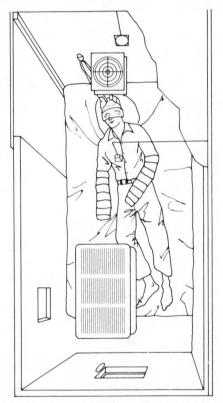

Figure 5-8   Schematic drawing of an experimental cubicle for research in sensory deprivation. The ceiling has been removed and the subject is viewed from above. Source: Solomon et al. *Sensory deprivation.* Cambridge: Harvard University Press, 1961. Copyright © 1961 by the President and Fellows of Harvard College. (Adapted from Heron, 1961.)

study, most subjects wanted to stop after a day or two because of the apparently unbearable emotional and cognitive effects. Most of them reported severe perceptual disturbance, including hallucinatory-like phenomena. The perceptual disturbance included not only a distortion in sensory perception, but also an interference in higher cognitive functioning. Subjects even made an inordinate number of errors in simple arithmetic problems!

It was the reduction in stimuli, not their complete absence, which produced the undesirable perceptual effects, for if the subject was placed in a completely dark room, these effects did not appear (Zubek & MacNeill, 1967). Only under these conditions of a low, monotonous homogeneity of stimulation were the electroencephalograms (brain waves) of subjects abnormal, showing that the electrical activity of the brain was altered (Zubek, 1969).

A certain minimal level of sensory variation is necessary for adequate perceptual functioning. Hebb (1960, 1968) concluded that optimal arousal of the cortex is necessary for both adequate brain functioning and perceptual learning. Thus, sensory variation is necessary for the socialization of the perceptual system.

So far we have reported the results of observational studies which seem to point to sensory variation as a primitive physiological need. Neuropsychological theories also emphasize the necessity and importance of sensory variation for adequate brain function. Sokolov (1960) and Miller, Galanter, and Pribram (1960) have shown that sensory variation results in an alteration of the patterning of brain cortex cell assemblies and thus a change in their functional performance. This is possible because at birth the cortex of higher animals is quite plastic.

The plasticity of cortical coding can be seen from other research. Hubel and Wiesel (1963) obtained the following data. Two kittens were raised from birth under different conditions. The experimental kitten had one eye sutured closed while the other kitten had both eyes sutured. When they were tested, the non-experienced eye of the first kitten exhibited less transfer learning than either eye of the second kitten. It is as if differential experiences in the two eyes are worse than no visual experience for the growth of innate perceptual coding abilities. Moreover, Hirsch and Spinelli (1970) raised cats with hoods over their eyes which occluded certain directional stimuli. The first group's hood let in only horizontal light while the second group was exposed solely to vertical rays. Later testing showed that the receptive cortical fields of the first group would only code horizontal lines, while those of the second group would only code vertical lines.

This work was made possible by the single-cell recording technique developed by Hubel and Wiesel (1959). By implanting micro-electrodes in single cells of the cerebral cortex, they demonstrated that sensory cells are highly selective in their receptivity or coding. Some cells of the visual cortex respond only to movement, others only to a boundary. Still others respond only to a specific color or a specific direction (vertical, horizontal, or diagonal).

Hubel and Wiesel's work is the most direct evidence of built-in perceptual programs. What Hirsch and Spinelli have shown is that these built-in programs can indeed be modified by sensory variation.

Effects of varied early experience on cognition.   Research has shown that different socialization experiences produce a wide variation in the formulation of the cognitive motive. A number of studies verify that animals reared in a rich sensory environment display superior perceptual discrimination and intelligence.

Most of these studies had their origin in the McGill psychology department, under the influence of D. O. Hebb. In one study, Forgus (1954) raised three groups of rats, genetically controlled by litter splitting, under three different conditions. The control groups were raised in a black box with no other objects in the box. Light was admitted only from above. The second group, the perceptual group, were raised in a glass cage through which they could view a variety of objects and movements. The third group, the perceptual-motor group, lived among the objects themselves and could traverse them and play with them. The perceptual and perceptual-motor groups were equally skilled when tested on perceptual-discrimination (differentiating between a circle and square) and perceptual-generalization tasks (recognizing a form even when it was rotated through space). They were both vastly superior to the control group. Moreover, on a task of problem-solving ability in a complicated multiple-unit maze, the two groups were no different from each other and superior to the control group. Hebb (1949) had earlier observed that rich environmental stimulation is an important antecedent of superior intellectual or cognitive function.

Curiosity and novelty discrepancy.   As a result of their studies of curiosity and exploratory behavior, Berlyne (1960) and Jones (1966) have postulated that a need for information exists. Berlyne defines this need as a motivational state which predisposes one to engage in activity that leads to the acquisition of information. Jones and his collaborators (1961) demonstrated that the tendency to seek information increases after the subject has been deprived of information. Volunteers were subjected to conditions of sensory deprivation for varying periods and then exposed to a number of different patterns of colored lights which they could elicit by pressing different buttons. The results showed that there was a correlation between duration of deprivation and visual pattern preference. The longer the deprivation, the more preference was shown for complex, random, unpredictable patterns of lights over simple, predictable, and redundant patterns. However, Jones (1964) also found that under conditions of non-deprivation, subjects preferred patterns of lights from which they could predict a sequence of patterns rather than either random complexity or simple alternation of patterns.

This preference for relative complexity begins in the neonate. Independently (1961a & b), and then with a group of co-workers (1975), Fantz found that when given a choice, infants will attend to the more complex of two visual stimuli. Preferential attention was measured by the length of time the infant would spend looking at one design or another. However, by the age of 2 months, infants clearly show a preference for the human face. Perhaps there is a relationship between the studies of Fantz and those of Jones. The neonate may be like one of Jones' subjects who is deprived—he exists in a state of lack of information. Thus, his preference is for random complexity. After sufficient acquisition of information (as a result of perceptual learning), stable mental schemata are established, which now direct the future search for information. At 2 months, the infant recognizes and prefers the human face. Still later, he prefers the mother's face to other human faces. By the time we are adults, all of us have various aesthetic preferences, which are perhaps differentiations of these original preferences.

If a preference for the familiar develops, what effect does this have on the further search for new information and the growth of knowledge? Empirical studies suggest that the answer lies in the human's tendency to notice and seek (preferential attention) patterns which are slightly discrepant from the familiar. An attempt to explain this tendency has been made by the *discrepancy hypothesis,* which states that attention will be attracted by patterns which are *slightly* discrepant rather than extremely discrepant or by patterns identical to the original (Weatherford & Cohen, 1973; Milewski & Siqueland, 1975; Kagan, 1971). Hebb (1955) provided a neuropsychological parallel for this hypothesis when he contended that the organization of the central nervous system directs the search for stimuli which are "new, but not so new."

There is also a relationship between the search for information and the trait of creativity. When given a choice between simple and complex tasks, people who score higher on tests of creativity will choose the latter. Less creative people choose more routine tasks and satiate more rapidly on routine tasks than creative people do on complex tasks (Levin & Brody, 1966). Creative people have more appetite for novel information. In creative people, the cognitive motive is so organized that it directs pursuit of a wider range of new forms and new patterns of information and knowledge.

The differentiation of the cognitive motive.   We have already discussed one differentiation of the cognitive motive—namely, the increased novelty-seeking behavior of the creative person. The ways in which aesthetic preferences differ among individuals is another example. Aesthetic preference itself depends to some degree upon the level of information (knowledge) the person already has about the field. People well versed in music prefer more varied and complicated music and become quickly satiated with redundant patterns.

The seeking of novelty is a relative matter. Some people prefer certainty to uncertainty. Novel information can be threatening if it does not easily fit into a person's preconceived notions. Other people can tolerate uncertainty and indeed may prefer it. Three different ways of seeking and organizing information can be posited on the basis of analytical and integrative thinking. One individual analyzes by reducing everything to details; at the other extreme is the person who ignores details and focuses on global wholes—the total picture. Somewhere in between is the person who analyzes into sufficient detail but can also integrate across these differentiations into a total picture, a process Lewin described in some detail (Chapter 4).

In the next chapter we will discuss various cognitive styles that have been described in the psychological literature. Each of these styles is an example of how the cognitive motive becomes differentiated. One such example is the *open/closed mind* styles of Rokeach (1960). The open-minded person is generally receptive to new information and is usually trying to find new or additional meanings from the information that is not yet comprehended (what he does not yet understand). The closed-minded person ignores or distorts what he doesn't understand so that new information is avoided or falsified into old stereotypes.

Why Only Four Systems?

Research on the psychobiology of adaptive behavior in mammals indicates that the newborn begins life with a minimum set of instinct-like need systems whose satisfaction is necessary for survival. All human needs seem to fit into these four systems—contact stimulation, protection from danger and excessive stress, manipulation and mastery, and sensory variation. Nature itself has provided a structure to organize these need systems, but it is experience which modifies them into motive systems.

The attachment and security motives grow out of socialization experiences associated with bodily survival needs. The competence motive grows out of the socialization of the need to master. The cognitive motive grows out of the need for sensory variation.

The fact that we limit the motive systems to four is not only a logical extension of the need systems, it is also a parsimonious way of systematizing the full range of human motivation. Murray's classification of needs contains about 33 categories (see Chapter 3). Other theorists from the classical instinct theorists to Cattell have provided classifications of needs in varying numbers. It is our contention that all of the other motives or "needs" can be sorted into one of our four systems. The rest of this book tries to support this view. Table 5-1 is an attempt to sort a representative sample of Murray's needs from the list in Box 3-2 into one of our four motive categories.

Table 5-1   The Basic Motives

Murray's Needs as Defined in Box 3-2	Attachment		Security	Competence	Cognition
abasement	X				
achievement				X	
affiliation	X				
aggression	X	or	X		
counteraction				X	
defendance			X		
deference	X				
dominance	X				
exhibition	X				
harmavoidance			X		
infavoidance				X	
nurturance	X				
order					X
play				X	
rejection	X				
sentience					X
sex	X				
succorance	X				
understanding					X

In later chapters we will discuss how some of these "needs" become symbols of more than one motive at different developmental phases. For example, the intent of aggression behaviors differ. Sometimes aggression can be used in service of the security motive, as well as being a maladaptive deviation of the attachment motive.

In the next chapter we will discuss how these motives are hierarchically organized into personality structure.

6

how the perceptual system organizes personality structure

OVERVIEW

The postulates we proposed in Chapter 1 describe personality as a unique organization which determines its own selection of responses. The perceptual system is at the heart of the structural organization of personality. This system organizes the four motives into a hierarchy. The hierarchies themselves are unique to each individual. The perceived "self" is the phenomenological concomitant of this uniqueness.

Cognitive style is another way of conceptualizing the hierarchical organization of personality. Cognitive style is a perceptual pattern which includes instructions about an individual's self-concept, world view, typical instrumental responses, and ideals. Six different cognitive styles are described in this chapter.

Motivated behavior has an emotional component. Since motives are processed through the perceptual system, it follows that emotions must also be directed by the perceptual system. Thus, this chapter ends with a cognitive-perceptual explanation of emotions.

As the last chapter emphasized, the viability of the biological organism depends upon continuous adaptation to the environment. And in order to function adaptively, the organism must seek and find appropriate information. We have called the process by which this information is extracted and processed *perception.* Baldwin (1969) has pointed out that in principle it is possible to construct laws of perception which relate the stimulus directly to the response without any mediation by a perceptual structure.

In lower organisms, for example, we can discuss a variety of adaptive processes without resorting to the concept of structure. Thus, the root of a plant grows toward water. The presence of water inhibits the formation of a growth auxin (hormone) in that side of the root closest to the water, so that the distant side grows faster and the tip of the root turns toward the water. This mechanism is called a *tropism.* The fledgling herring gull pecks at food by a simple reflex system. The face of the parent gull, a red figure against a yellow background, stimulates a *reflex* pecking response in the fledgling (Tinbergen & Perdeck, 1950). Similar fixed, innate releasing mechanisms have been reported by ethologists for a wide range of animal behavior patterns including aggression and mating (Lorenz, 1958; Eibl-Eibesfeldt, 1970).

Reflex and tropism require no developed programs. In addition, the sexual behavior of lower animals seems to be entirely controlled by hormonal factors. However, in human beings central mediating processes become more important than hormones (as, for example, in homosexuality), and developed programs are necessary for responses to occur. The cerebral cortex has become so dominant in the organization and direction of behavior that all human motives seem to be directed by conceptual thought (Hebb, 1955). Despite some reservations, Baldwin comes to a similar conclusion:

> In the case of mature human behavior, however, since it must be adapted to a wide variety of rapidly changing circumstances, a general cognitive mechanism which represents the distal objects of the environment in a reasonably accurate form would obviously be of great functional value. Similarly, some kind of guided behavior involving a cognitive feedback mechanism is of clear functional value (1969, p. 331).

He elaborates: "The advantage of a cognitive theory lies in the fact that the postulation of a general cognitive mechanism simplifies the explanation of the relationship between the external stimulus and the behavior of the organism" (p. 331).

Baldwin's statement implies that the inclusion of a cognitive mechanism in a theory of human behavior facilitates understanding and predicting such behavior. Our theory of personality advances such a cognitive mechanism, which we call the *perceptual system.*

Thus the domain of personality structure consists of the four motive systems integrated by the perceptual system. We define *motive* as a functional relationship between the person and incentives in his environment, instructions for which are written in the person's perceptual structure. This concept requires a definition of some other terms related to human motivation. In Chapter 5 we discussed how a motive grows out of a need. *Needs* are biological forerunners of motives. *Incentives* are objects in the environment which have the power to influence the direction of behavior. Incentives may be positive or negative for each of the four motives. Lewin and Murray called these incentives valences and values, respectively. These incentives may also be called *goals.* Lewin and Murray both referred to goal-directed movement as vectors.

As the human being develops, the perceptual system gives him instructions about each of the motive systems. As the perceptual system itself becomes more differentiated, these instructions become more specific. We have already seen how the attachment motive becomes differentiated into a number of subsets such as succorance, nurturance, deference, affiliation, and abasement. (These terms are taken from Murray's list of needs. See Table 5-1.) In *succorance,* the child seeks information about whether or not he will obtain what he wants from the parent or other adult. In *nurturance* one person seeks information about how to care for another person. In *deference* the person seeks information about how to establish a subordinate relationship with a superior. In *affiliation,* one seeks information about mutual friendly relationships. In *abasement,* one seeks information about how to abase oneself.

The security motive becomes differentiated into subsets such as defendance, harmavoidance, and aggression. In *defendance,* information is sought about how to protect oneself; in *harmavoidance,* about how to escape from or avoid danger; and in *aggression,* about how to attack in order to destroy a danger. Security can also be represented by financial stability and other safeguards for survival.

The competence motive becomes differentiated into such subsets as achievement, infavoidance (avoiding loss of status), and counteraction. In *achievement,* information is sought about how to compete with one's own standard of excellence; in *infavoidance,* about how to avoid humiliation and subjugation; in *counteraction,* about how to compensate for failure.

The cognitive motive becomes differentiated into understanding, order, sentience, and creativity. In *understanding,* one seeks information about the nature of phenomena; in *order,* about how to classify phenomena; in *sentience,* we seek information that can provide varied and enhanced sensory experience, and in *creativity* we seek novel information.

These four motives and their differentiations are the domain of personality structure—that is, they constitute the structural foundation of motivated behavior. How these motives become organized into a unique, integrated, hierarchical, adaptive whole will depend on the perceptual system.

Perception Organizes Motives

Perception processes the information which permits goal-directed behavior. How is the perceptual system capable of extracting all this necessary and useful information? First, the individual is born with certain sensory capacities which enable him to extract certain primitive, global messages from stimuli which impinge on the senses. For example, the child does not have to learn to see light, hear sound, feel a prick, or feel hunger. However, a child does have to learn to recognize his mother's face, discriminate between musical tunes, or identify a particular word.

Built-in programs code primitive and gross aspects of stimulus categories. With experience and learning, these become changed into modified programs, which allow for a greater range of perceptual information and for more differentiated, more accurate judgment.

This conceptualization of perception as a developing process from built-in to modified programs fits in with Garner's statement that "to perceive is to know" (1966). Perception is more than just information extraction, it is the foundation of all knowledge or cognition. Figure 6-1 diagrams the relationship between perception and other cognitive functions such as learning and thinking.

Figure 6-1 suggests that perception directs our entire search for knowledge. It is remarkable that this view of perception as fundamental to the attainment of knowledge was expressed by Aristotle over 2400 years ago, as the following quotation indicates:

> All men by nature desire to know. An indication of this is the delight we take in our senses; for even apart from their usefulness they are loved for themselves. . . . The reason is that most of all the senses make us know and bring to light many differences between things . . . By nature animals are born with the faculty of sensation and from sensation memory is produced. . . . Now from memory, experience is produced; . . . art (and science) arises when from many notions gained by experience, one universal judgment about a class of objects is produced. . . ." (Metaphysics, Book 1).

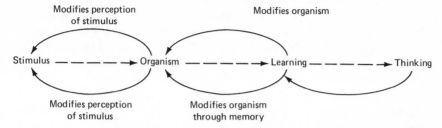

Figure 6-1   The Relationship of Learning and Thinking in the Complex Process of Perception. Stimuli possess potential information which is extracted by the organism as learning. This learning is stored as memory and modifies the organism so that later perception of the same stimuli will be different. The process of thinking (resulting from previous learning) also modifies the organism because new learning occurs; thus the perception of stimuli is modified. Source: After Forgus and Melamed, 1976, p. 4.

Figure 6-1 also implies that perception is a superset of cognition, with learning, memory, and thinking as subsets. Since perception is also the mediator of the basic motives, we can extend the definition of perception to say that perception is the superset of personality organization, with the motive systems as subsets.

Perception subsumes the motive systems.   Until Kelly (1955) postulated his personal construct theory, it was generally accepted that needs organize the direction of perceptions. Kelly theorized that the personal construct system guides how events are anticipated and that anticipation channels action (see Chapter 4). The goal of action is to fulfill the philosophy contained in the personal construct system. Thus, each individual behaves according to his own system of construing. Kelly's theory thus holds that perception organizes needs—and indeed all behavior.

Mancuso (1976), a follower of Kelly, has made Kelly's theory more scientifically viable by relating it to current work in information processing. Data from this field indicate that what we see in the external world is more influenced by preexisting internal schemata (Neisser, 1967) than by the "actual" objects we observe. One example of such work is the theorizing and research of Erdelyi (Erdelyi, 1974; Erdelyi & Appelbaum, 1973) discussed in Chapter 1. In one experiment Jewish students showed an emotion-tinged response to neutral pictures containing either a Star of David or a swastika. The presence of either of these stimuli (by comparison with a picture of a window which was used as a control) resulted in a lower rate of processing (the subjects recognized fewer pictures containing the stimuli when they were asked to tell how many such pictures they had seen). Erdelyi interpreted these findings to mean that the presence of emotionally charged symbols engaged *chronic sets* (what Neisser has called preexisting internal schemata). These sets directed subjects' attention to the meanings associated with the swastika and Star of David, and thus diverted their attention from the neutral pictures.

Why do we not say, however, that the subjects were defending themselves from threatening emotional meanings, as a need → perception theory would postulate? If that were true, we might expect a lower recognition rate for pictures containing the swastika and perhaps a higher than average recognition rate for those containing the Star of David. Yet there was actually no difference in recognition rate between the two.

Erdelyi's work dealt with how perception directs the engagement of emotions. Perception also directs the engagement of motives. Each person formulates his motives differently because different construct systems lead to different anticipations. Some people seek attachment through taking care of others, some through being taken care of, and still others through a combination of the two. Security can be sought through withdrawal or through attacking the danger. Experimental evidence of this differentiation comes from the work of Lazarus, Ericksen, and Fonda (1951). These researchers showed that when people are presented with emotionally threatening words by means of a tachistoscope, some subjects show a lower recognition threshold for these words than for neutral words, while others show a higher recognition threshold.

Competence is also formulated in different symbols. Some seek competence through achievement, while others seek it through successful affiliation. In one study, Matina Horner (1972) found that female students were less interested in achievement than were male students. (This study will be discussed in greater detail in Chapter 10.) Horner's findings have been criticized, however, because she failed to define competence in the same terms for both groups; for the female subjects, competence was not achievement, but successful affiliation with a male. A female would therefore suspect that too much striving for achievement, in the usual male sense, could compromise her success (competence) as a female.

In the area of the cognitive motive, some people search for novelty, while others search for order. For the former, the goal is some degree of change; for the latter, redundancy and routine have high goal value.

Ekman's model of a perceptual program. It is one thing to postulate that schemata and chronic sets exist, it is another to conceptualize their specifics. One such attempt is the Facial Affect Program (FAP). Ekman presented subjects with a set of facial photographs and asked them to identify the emotion displayed in the photograph. Most subjects—even those from different cultures—identified the emotions with a high degree of accuracy. Ekman suggests that this universality of ability to recognize emotions exists because of a Facial Affect Program—that is, an internal mechanism for coding emotions into a pattern of facial expression. Figure 6-2 presents a diagram which shows the steps involved in the programming of perceptual information extracted from facial expressions of emotions. Ekman's (1972) model depicts the interplay between inherent and learned determiners of perceptual programming. Seeing a happy face not only triggers a visual mechanism but also an internal coding mechanism (facial affect program) which sends down a "patterned set of neural impulses to facial muscles . . . triggering a set of muscular movements" (Ekman, 1972, p. 216). One recognizes the other's happiness not only through the spatial organization of the other's face but also through empathic kinesthetic sensation generated by the facial affect program.

Personality Structure Has a Hierarchical Organization

We have just formulated a hypothesis that perception directs the seeking for information which engages the motives. It also organizes the motives into a hierarchy. The basic motives are not necessarily equally developed in all persons. The extent of the development and differentiation of a motive depends on the instructions for engaging the motive contained in the differentiation of the perceptual system. One person's perceptual system may instruct him to value competence more than attachment, so that competence will be at the apex of his hierarchy. Figure 6-3 is an attempt to diagram different motive hierarchies by placing the dominant motive at the apex of a triangle.

An hierarchical system, by its very nature, must have a direction of movement, a preselected ordering of goals. The cognitive theorists de-

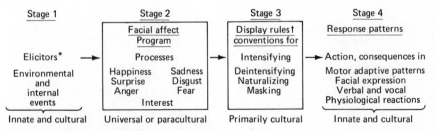

*Elicitors are information in Facial Expressions
†Display rules are cultural rules which direct how emotions are displayed

Figure 6-2   Model describing stages in facial expression of emotions. Source: Reprinted from Forgus and Melamed, 1976; modified from Ekman, 1972, p. 213.

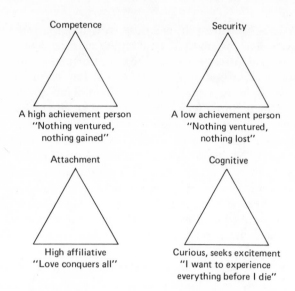

Competence

A high achievement person
"Nothing ventured,
nothing gained"

Security

A low achievement person
"Nothing ventured,
nothing lost"

Attachment

High affiliative
"Love conquers all"

Cognitive

Curious, seeks excitement
"I want to experience
everything before I die"

Figure 6-3　　Varieties of Motive Hierarchies. The reader is challenged to consider the various motive hierarchies in relation to various cognitive styles. People with security as the dominant goal may prefer not to accept this challenge.

scribed in Chapter 4 all offer a central concept to explain this ordering direction of movement. For Goldstein, Lewin, and Angyal, this ordering is in the direction of increased differentiation of the life space; for Kelly it is continuing refinement of the personal construct system; for the existentialists the goal of adaptive behavior is continuous extension and amplification of meanings. For Adler, the target of movement is a dominant goal, subjective and idiosyncratic, that directs personality from the apex of the goal

An infant is raised in an indulgent environment. The parents express their affection by giving him attention, material objects, and approval. His perceptual system associates indulgent treatment with attachment, security, and competence. That is, he *perceives* attachment as provided through what his parents give him; likewise security depends on continuous "getting," and competence means only being able to insure that he continues to "get." "Getting" becomes his dominant goal. Once this perceptual set has been incorporated into memory, all subsequent information is only useful to the extent that it informs about "getting" or "not getting."

A younger sibling is born. The parents now pay equal attention to the newborn. The elder experiences this as a deprivation. He is "not getting." He responds by misbehaving, manipulating the parents into giving him more attention. If he manages once again to "get," this dominant goal will continue to direct his behavior.

hierarchy. All subordinate goals lead to this final goal of the guiding self-ideal.

How are goals mediated? Through the perceptual system, information is organized and direction is given to the other motive systems, in accordance with a guiding self-ideal. Thus, *selective processing* of information allows each person to formulate a hierarchy of values with a dominant final goal at its peak.

All behaviors, no matter how outrageous they may seem to external observers, are organized by the perceptual hierarchical structure with the final goal as its aim (see Figure 6-4). Note that the dominant goal which is filtered through the perceptual system leads not only to action, but also to an affective component in motivated behavior.

There are varieties of dominant goals. The differentiations of the attachment motive, for example, can give rise to several possible dominant goals—to please others, to be taken care of, to be admired, or to be closely affiliated with someone. In each case, the dominant goal becomes the principal director of all goal behavior associated with the attachment motive, and the attachment motive itself will be the most prominent and the most easily engaged of the four motives. A dominant goal may be a differentiation of any of the four basic motives (as achievement is a differentiation of the competence motive); it may also integrate two or more motives, as

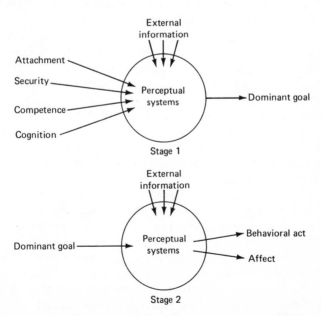

Figure 6-4   How the perceptual system hierarchically organizes personality functioning in motivated behavior.

when a male pursues achievement in order to be more attractive to females (combined competence and attachment motive).

Do we need a construct of "self"?   In discussing the hierarchical organization of personality, we have used constructs such as dominant goal and guiding self-ideal. For many theorists the integrator of personality is the self. Thus, Sullivan speaks of a self-system, Rogers of a self-concept, and Jung labels the self as the final integration of personality structure. Levy (1970) reflects that most perceptual-cognitive theorists have an explicit or implicit postulate of a self construct, but do not specify how this self can be measured. For this reason, it has so far remained a useful but intuitive construct only. The difficulty in measuring such a subjective integrator of personality could be overcome if we found a way of formulating the integrator construct to permit one to subject it to scientific analysis.

In this chapter, we have taken constructs such as dominant goal or guiding self-ideal—also subjective and intuitive concepts—and have tried to translate them into the perceptual-structural components of motives. When perceptual structure is described in the language of information processing, it becomes measurable. One such example of measuring the information in cognitive structure is the study of Forgus and DeWolfe (1969) described in Chapter 1. In that experiment, the researchers used the information obtained from the contents of hallucinations as a measure of cognitive structure which could reliably predict future behavior.

Since we have also described motives in terms of perceptual structure, it should be possible to measure motives by measuring the information in them. A motive has been defined as a relationship between a person and an incentive. The information in the motive, therefore, contains instructions about the nature of this relationship, for instance, what security means, where it can be found, and how to attain it. An example of how the information in motives can be measured is seen in the way McClelland (1971) uses TAT stories to measure the information in the need for achievement (a differentiation of the competence motive). McClelland's work is discussed in greater detail in Chapter 9.

In our theory, motives are hierarchically organized. The most dominant motive has the most differentiated perceptual structure; less differentiated motives are progressively less dominant. The uniqueness of an individual personality is to be found in its peculiar hierarchical organization of motives, with its own unique perceptual organization which directs its dominant goal. This is an operational definition of a unique personality. We can retain the word *self* to mean the subjective, phenomenological concomitant of this uniqueness. In Chapter 8, we will examine the self as an organizer of development.

COGNITIVE STYLES

Cognitive style theory is another way of talking about the hierarchical organization of personality. Such an approach to personality tries to explain both structure and dynamics. A cognitive style is a perceptual organization which includes instructions about an individual's self concept, world view, typical instrumental responses, and ideals. It determines his mode and accuracy of perception, his style of thinking, his goal-directed behavior, his personal belief and myth system, and the focus of his attention. It organizes his emotional life—what arouses emotions, the kinds of feelings he is likely to have, their intensity, and how he copes with emotion.

The following kinds of cognitive styles, all derived from research on perception, have been described.

1. Sharpeners and Levelers

Wulf (1922) reported that the memory for perceived figures undergoes modifications depending on subjects' tendencies either to minimize the differences between figural elements or to accentuate them. He called the former *levelers* and the latter, *sharpeners*. Hebb and Foord (1945) demonstrated empirically that these modifications result from active memory selection and elaboration, not from a passive change in the memory trace. Subsequent studies have related these perceptual tendencies to personality. Holzman and Gardner (1960) reported that sharpeners are cognitively more differentiated. Since they can cope with a wider breadth of stimulus categories and are therefore more adaptive, they are not only cognitively more articulate, but also seek excitement (a differentiation of the cognitive motive) rather than security in the pursuit of their goals. Levelers, who have a narrow range of categories, prefer the familiar, are more conforming and therefore are dominated by considerations of security. Sharpeners are more open to new experience, expend more effort in the pursuit of their goals, and react with more emotional intensity.

While sharpeners probably experience more pleasure, they are also more likely to expose themselves to insecurity, anxiety, and personal danger. Levelers, while "living the safe life," have a smaller repertoire of responses to stress (a less differentiated perceptual structure in that area) and are more vulnerable to the uncertainties of life.

2. Narrow and Extensive Scanners

In their study of attention, Gardner and Long (1962a, b) reported a difference in the scan patterns (how the eyes move back and forth) of individuals attending to a stimulus. Some individuals are wide or *extensive scan-*

ners, while others are *narrow scanners.* Measuring scanning by photographing eye movements or through the subject's ability to resist the habituating effect of repeated perceptual experience, they found that extensive scanners have more frequent shifts in eye fixations, scan more of the field, and are more resistant to stimulus adaptation. Furthermore, they are more accurate in their estimation of perceptual dimensions.

Extensive scanners are also more accurate in the discrimination of other information, such as understanding the behavior of others. They are also less impulsive and are capable of more enduring motivational effort. Since extensive scanners process information more accurately, they cope more effectively with anxiety.

3. Psychological Differentiation

Witkin and his colleagues (1962) described a third cognitive style, *psychological differentiation.* They reported that subjects differed with respect to their reliance on visual and bodily cues in the judgment of the vertical dimension. While visual cues were generally dominant, some subjects also used bodily cues as well. These more differentiated subjects were referred to as *field-independent,* the others as *field-dependent.* Other researchers have indicated that this freedom from a restricted perceptual set or modality is part of a larger class of organization, namely, the articulation or differentiation of the field (Glick, 1968). In general, the less restricted an individual is, the more articulate and differentiated will his perceptual discrimination be. Thus, set-independent individuals are more accurate and adaptive in their perceptions. Since their perceptual structures are more articulated and differentiated, they tend to be more analytical and to have a wider frame of reference. Witkin (1976) has found a number of developmental and personality correlates of this style (see Chapters 7, 8, and 10).

4. Tolerance/Intolerance for Ambiguity (Open versus Closed Mind)

The holocaust in Nazi Germany prompted psychologists to try to understand the aggressors. One early study (Adorno, Frenkel-Brunswick, Levinson & Sanford, 1950) attempted to explain Nazi authoritarianism in psychoanalytic terms—that authoritarian persons are anal characters. Subsequent work has uncovered variables which can be classed as cognitive styles. Rokeach (1960), for instance, used scales to measure attitudes and beliefs. On the basis of repeated and cross-validated findings, he concluded that people differ in being *open-minded* or *closed-minded.* The closed-minded person can be recognized by his dogmatism and authoritarianism. In some respects, Rokeach points out, all of us are dogmatic, because our search for congruence leads us to make judgments in the context of our personal belief systems. Dogmatism is not an either/or property: Tolerance and intolerance exist on a continuous scale which can be measured. Also, we are more tolerant of some things than of others; thus, a person of fundamentalist religious beliefs is more tolerant of a backsliding believer than of an atheist.

Belief systems serve a coping function. The person who is afraid to be alone and worries about the future seeks the certainty of authoritarianism. Without explicit leadership and rules (in the face of ambiguity), the authoritarian or dogmatic person is unhappy. On the other hand, the open-minded person becomes unhappy with doctrinaire or ideological imperatives. Thus, *perceptual differentiation determines affect.* Rokeach and Kliejunas (1972) point out that situational factors interact with cognitive style to determine the dynamics of behavior.

5. Cognitive Consistency

Cognitive consistency has its roots in the cognitive balance theory of Heider (1958). When there is congruence between expectancy and outcome, a state of *cognitive balance* exists. Heider described a number of balance/imbalance situations in which the subject's expectancy of another's behavior—based on the subject's estimate of the person—is either confirmed or denied. If I like a person, I expect him to act according to my value system. If he does, cognitive balance results. The same occurs if someone I dislike acts contrary to my value system. Rosenberg and Abelson (1960) point out that cognitive balance includes an affective component, and whether this is positive or negative depends on whether or not the person is seen as facilitating one's own goal attainment.

Festinger (1957) described another agent of cognitive dissonance. When a person finds himself behaving in a way contrary to his beliefs about himself, cognitive dissonance exists. This discrepant state motivates behavior to remove the dissonance. In trying to make this theory more explicit, Aronson (1972) has added refinements: (1) dissonance can only occur if the discrepancy exists in an area to which the person has made a commitment (the person has decided to make this an important issue for himself), and (2) other things being equal, the dissonance is resolved in the direction of maintaining self-esteem. People differ in where and when they perceive dissonance. This individual variation allows Festinger to consider cognitive consistency a cognitive style variable.

6. Locus of Control

Rotter (1966, 1975) has devised an internal-external (I/E) scale which measures the extent to which an individual attributes causes (*locus of control*) of the results of his own behavior to internal or external sources. Internally oriented people show more freedom of movement. Since freedom of movement depends on the breadth of categories in the person's expectancy repertoire, it qualifies as a cognitive style construct. As described by Phares (1976), for example, internally oriented (high I) people are more responsible and achievement oriented.

If a student fails an examination, he tends to blame himself if he is a high internal and to blame external agents or bad luck if he is a high external. Externals are more subject to anxiety and depression (Naditch, Gargon, & Michael, 1975) while internals are more likely to use denial (Lefcourt, Hogg, & Sordoni, 1975; Phares, 1976). In general, which style is more appropriate depends upon the goal to which the behavior is directed (Rotter, 1975). Prociuk and Lussier (1975) report that this cognitive style has generated more research than any other (277 studies in the 1973–74 period alone).

In order to formulate a more complete description of a cognitive style, the following aspects should be included: (1) Every cognitive style must have a set of percepts (key cognitive categories); (2) these percepts should direct goal-seeking behavior, arouse affect, and provide a set of habitual processes (that is, instrumental acts and perceptual selectivity). In Chapter 11 we will describe ways of measuring cognitive style in this more complete way.

COGNITIVE INFORMATION IN EMOTIONAL AROUSAL

In our discussions of motives and cognitive styles we repeatedly made reference to the affective components of personality structure and implied that emotions are directed by perceptual structures. Others have also advanced cognitive theories of emotion and provided some empirical evidence for this view. Schachter (1964) presented a two-factor theory of emotion which states that emotional expression is a joint function of cognitive definition and physiological arousal. Schachter and Singer (1962) found that individuals given adrenalin (physiological arousal) and placed in a humor-provoking situation (cognitive context) are more likely to express euphoric behavior. Similarly, subjects given adrenalin and put in an anger-provoking situation are more likely to display anger than controls given a placebo.

In an intriguing application of the two-factor theory, Schachter and Latané (1964) performed the following experiments: On the basis of psychiatric and psychological evaluation, they divided prison inmates into *criminally sociopathic* (antisocial personalities) and *non-sociopathic* groups. Individuals in both groups were then given a task of learning a mental maze. Without knowing it, all subjects were randomly shocked on certain "wrong" choices. The researchers were interested in finding out whether the subjects would learn to avoid the shocked choices on subsequent trials. They found that typical avoidance learning occurred for the non-socio-pathic group of criminals, but not for the sociopathic group. In agreement with common opinion, sociopaths do not learn from experience. In spite of punishment, they repeat their mistakes.

The experiment was now repeated with another group of sociopaths and non-sociopaths, but this time each subject was given adrenalin. The result was a drastic reversal of the previous findings. The sociopathic crimi-nals exhibited a steep reduction in errors. By contrast, the non-sociopathic inmates showed disruption of effective avoidance-learning behavior (see Figure 6-5). If we want the sociopath to learn from experience, we must first arouse his emotions. Physical punishment does not arouse the emotion of the sociopath. However, Schmauk (1970) finds that sociopaths can be aroused if the punishment is loss of money rather than electric shock. This suggests an entirely new approach to rehabilitation of criminals, since ap-parently only some kinds of punishment are effective.

Valins (1972) believes that one can reduce Schachter's two-factor the-

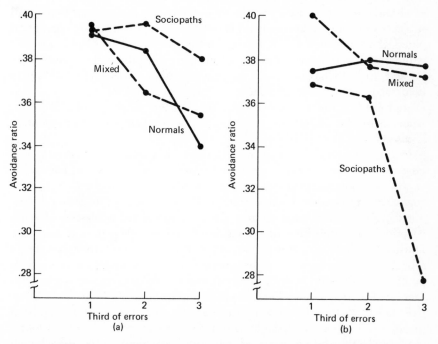

Figure 6-5(a)   Avoidance ratio under placebo by thirds of errors.

(b)   Avoidance ratio under adrenalin by thirds of errors. Source: S. Schachter and B. Latané, 1964, p. 248.

ory to a one-factor theory—with cognition being the basic determinant. In one important study, male subjects were shown photographs of females while they wore earphones which were allegedly monitoring their own heart rates. This, of course, was not true, since the experimenters arbitrarily fed in exaggerated "heart rates" for some of the photographs and not for others. The subjects were then asked to rate the attractiveness of the photographs. Those photographs monitored with the "exaggerated heart rates" were rated as more attractive than others. Even after the subjects were debriefed about the nature of the experiment, they still rated these photographs as more attractive!

In a more complicated experiment, Valins and Ray (1967) showed that the perception of increased emotional reaction also carries with it significant perceptual information. Subjects were presented with slides of snakes in menacing postures. Again, bogus heart rates were fed into the subjects' ears. However, for one group of subjects (the experimental group) the slide was accompanied by the word "shock" every time the heart rate was increased. For another group (the control) this was not the case. It is as if the subject in the experimental group could say to himself, "I am not afraid of a snake because it was the shock that increased my heart rate." All subjects were then asked to express their feelings about snakes. As anticipated, the experimental subjects stated that they were not afraid of snakes while the controls said they were. Furthermore, these statements were backed up by behavior—the experimental subjects were more willing to hold rattlesnakes than the controls. Thus, perceptual information (attributing increased heart rate to electric shock rather than fear of snakes) appears to be the underlying cause of why and when we feel emotionally aroused.

Lazarus (1966) also presents evidence that cognitive intervention can be used to direct or modify emotional states. His notion is that fear, anxiety, or reaction to stress can be reduced by the introduction of effective cognitive intervention. He illustrates this by means of the following experiment. Subjects were exposed to a film which depicted adolescents having deep incisions made into their penises (a ritual in some primitive societies). During the viewing of this movie, subjects were concurrently exposed to a repeated commentary (auditory) which denied that the incisions were painful. This cognitive denial procedure was effective in reducing the autonomic fear reactions to the fear-provoking situation. In order to be effective, however, this denial must precede the film and must be repeated throughout the course of the film. In a similar experiment, Lazarus found that intellectualization was even more effective than denial in reducing anxiety.

A review of these studies which relate cognition to emotion leads to the conclusion that the basic determiner of what we feel is the information that we extract from cues in external stimuli and in our own bodies. That is one way in which perception directs emotion. Earlier in this chapter we mentioned another way, the chronic sets hypothesis of Erdelyi, which states, in essence, that certain internal codes direct us to seek specific emotional meanings in events. Lazarus himself has found individual differences in the response to emotion-arousing information. Some subjects show a heightened response to such information while others show a subdued response. The former are called *sensitizers,* the latter are called *repressors.* As we will discuss in Chapter 9, the sensitizer gives a much more accurate report of what is going on in his own body. Such individuals seem to be more in touch with their feelings, presumably because they have more differentiated perceptual categories for dealing with their emotions.

personality
development I:
conception
to
preadolescence

OVERVIEW

The body constitution provides the underlying foundations of personality. Some constitutional factors are genetic, such as the biochemical individuality of each person. Others have their origin in prenatal experience. The growing fetus is influenced by the mother's experiences: by her emotions and her intake of food and chemicals, and through the transmission of these chemicals and hormones across the placental mesh between mother and fetus. The prenatal environment produces certain predispositions which carry over into postnatal life, affecting postnatal temperament and behavior. These temperamental differences interact with socialization stimulations as the personality of the infant unfolds.

Upon these constitutional foundations, the differentiations of the perceptual system act to become the central organizer of personality development. Through the differentiations of the perceptual structure, the four basic motives unfold into a unique personality hierarchy. The cognitive motive differentiates, through stages similar to those described by Piaget, from ignorance to knowledge. The attachment motive differentiates from early dependency to affiliation. The security motive differentiates from early insecurity to courage, and the competence motive differentiates from potential capacities to actual abilities.

The socialization stimulation begins with the parent-child relationship and the family climate. It proceeds through sibling relationships, peer relationships, the school, and other cultural factors.

This chapter deals with the development of the perceptual structure of personality that we outlined in Chapter 6. Before we begin our discussion proper, however, we should point out that conceptions about human development have changed over the years. Aristotle considered that the sperm contained a fully formed human being of small size which grew to a proper size for birth in the womb (see Figure 7-1). In medieval times, the child was thought of as a miniature adult who was not different in kind from the adult, but would enlarge with time. Since the Enlightenment, the nativistic theorists have conceived of development as not much more than the maturational unfolding of a genetic predisposition. Although changes occur over time, they are predetermined by a genetic clock, not by any environmental influences. Freud's model of instinctual stages is not essentially different from a maturational model. Development consists of the unfolding of sexual instincts and the attempts of the ego and superego to modulate the id impulses. For the supporters of the empiricist position, development consists of the writing of experience on a *tabula rasa,* on which habit patterns develop according to such laws of learning as contiguity and reinforcement. Change is linear and monotonic. Piaget's model, the most influential developmental model since Freud, has some similarities to a maturational model, but concerns itself more with epistemology than any of the others. His theory specifies that cognitive-perceptual changes occur during growth.

PRENATAL FOUNDATIONS

Human development begins with conception as the fertilized egg, called the zygote, begins to grow.

A single-celled zygote contains 46 chromosomes, half from the sperm and half from the egg. These chromosomes are composed of genes (each of which is a coding factor) made up of a specific combination of DNA molecules. This zygote, in 9 months, becomes a newborn infant with billions of cells and a vast array of systems, all produced by the genetic code.

Biochemical Individuality

Individual differences in personality stem partly from the biochemical individuality that is programmed by the genetic code. Williams (1956) introduced the concept *biochemical individuality* to refer to the normal variations that exist in the physiological makeup of individuals. Each individual has a unique biochemical structure. Such uniqueness can be intimated from the large variations in the size of different organs in the newborn.

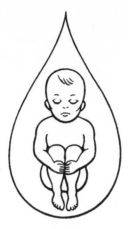

Figure 7-1   Aristotle's Concept of the Homunculus Within the Sperm Cell

These structural variations provide a physical basis for potential individual differences in reactions to stress and emotional stimulation. At birth infants reveal a wide range of emotional states, partially genetic and partially the result of prenatal stimulation. In any case, congenital differences in activity level, irritability, and attention span lead to differential caretaking behavior, which in turn modifies infant behavior (Korner, 1971). Biochemical individuality influences the development of personality.

A longitudinal study spanning the first years of life (Thomas, Chess, Birch, Hertzig, & Korn, 1971; Thomas & Chess, 1977) lends credence to the view that these unique physiological individualities are stable over time. A number of reactive categories (temperamental characteristics) were

---

Box 7-1   Normal Structural Variations in Endocrine Glands in the Newborn

Pituitary: weight varies from 350 to 1,000 mg.
Adrenals: weight varies from 7 to 20 gm. There is further a 10 to 4 variation in thickness of the adrenal cortex.
Thyroid: weight varies from 8 to 50 gm.
Parathyroids: weight varies from 50 to 300 gm. Number of lobes vary from 2 to 12.
Testes: weight varies from 10 to 45 gm.
Ovaries: weight varies from 2 to 10 gm. At birth they contain 30,000 to 400,000 ova!

Source: After Williams, 1956.

consistent from the age of 6 months to 7 years. The categories included: adaptability, regularity of rhythm, approach or avoidance of stimuli, activity level, attention span, intensity of reactions, positive or negative mood, degree of distractibility, and persistence of behavior. These temperamental characteristics readily distinguish between infants at 6 months and continue to distinguish them at 7 years.

Prenatal Development

During prenatal development, a number of principles and factors influence the growth of the embryo and fetus. Allport (1955) summarized two principles of prenatal development: (1) *The principle of "inner secret organization."* This principle states that each region of the fetus is destined to have its own inner function. If a part of the fetus destined to be the eye is surgically transplanted to the back, it will continue to grow into an eye, although nonfunctional. This finding may explain some birth defects. (2) *The principle of timing.* There is a temporal patterning in prenatal development, so that different organs and systems emerge during specific periods. Should any damage—mechanical or chemical—occur to the fetus, the kind of abnormality which may develop will depend not so much on the nature of the traumatic agent but on when the injury occurs. Brain damage is most likely to occur during the first 3 months, while the nervous system is being formed. Correspondingly, circulatory and respiratory weaknesses can occur as late as the seventh month, the time at which these systems are still completing their development.

Prenatal environment. The placental interchange provides contact with the mother's environment, through osmosis across placental membranes. The connection is functional, not anatomical. Ashley Montagu (1950, 1962) has argued that it is through this neurohumoral system, the complex which comprises the integrated nervous and glandular systems, that the mother's reactions may affect the fetus. While some hormones or molecules are too big to pass through the placental mesh, many maternal molecules do gain access (Windle, 1940). Let us now look at some examples of how this *neurohumoral functional connection* operates.

Maternal emotions and fetal activity. Hormones related to the mother's emotional state can pass through the placenta to the baby's bloodstream, affecting his state of activity or arousability. Sontag (1958) found that when mothers undergo severe emotional reactions there is a more than normal increase in the activity of their fetuses. The mothers with the most active autonomic (involuntary nervous) systems also have the most active fetuses. Thus, infants born to mothers who are highly anxious or emotional are probably accustomed to the hyperactivity of their own autonomic nervous systems and this undoubtedly influences postnatal irritability.

Sontag (1941) has also related prenatal maternal emotional upset to feeding problems. In support of this finding, Lakin (1957) found that colic is more likely to occur in babies whose mothers have exhibited strong tension and high anxiety during pregnancy. However, these tense mothers continue to be anxious during feeding of the newborn, confounding Lakin's interpretation.

In Figure 5-3, we presented a conditioning model to explain how the mother becomes a conditioned stimulus for both feeding behavior and emotional behavior. Lakin's finding provides a clinical verification of the hypothesis that negative emotional experiences inhibit the digestive response and influence the onset of colic.

Sontag (1944) also found the infants of upset mothers require more frequent feedings and are hyperactive.

Figure 7-2   Through nurturing the mother fosters succorance and trust, the origin of the attachment motive. Source: Courtesy Marian Bernstein

Nutrition, drugs, and other physical factors.   The health and mental development of the neonate is influenced by the mother's diet during pregnancy (Tompkins, 1948; Kaplan, 1972). Harrell and his co-workers (1955) followed the development of children whose mothers had been either in a diet-enriched or a non-enriched group. At 3 to 4 years, children from diet-enriched mothers showed a significantly higher IQ. Studies on the effects of poor nutrition should not overlook other variables such as poor living conditions, inadequate medical care, lack of cognitive stimulation, and substandard socialization. In addition to the other deficits faced by an individual from a socially deprived background, he also suffers from the direct effect of malnourishment upon his brain.

Montagu (1962) has warned that a number of different chemical agents, among them, nicotine and caffeine, can have harmful effects on the fetus. Addictive drugs such as heroin, methadone, and alcohol pass through the placenta, so that infants born to addicted mothers exhibit withdrawal symptoms (Brazelton, 1970). Helms & Turner (1976) have described a malformation syndrome in the infants of alcoholic mothers—a 20% reduction in body length, malformed facial features, and subnormal intelligence. The effects of some common drugs on the fetus are summarized in Table 7-1.

Some of the other physical factors of prenatal development that have been shown to influence postnatal development include the relationship between the blood types of baby and mother, physical infection in the mother, the age of the mother when the baby is born, severity of labor, and relative prematurity of the infant.

In a well controlled investigation, Koch (1964) studied the mental and emotional state of three groups of 5- to 6-year-old twins who were born at different levels of maturity. Group I weighed under 4½ pounds at birth, and Group II weighed 4½ to 5½ pounds at birth. A third group, full-term controls, were over 5½ pounds at birth. The results indicate that at 5 to 6 years of age the preemies were still smaller in size and tended to have lower IQs. However, those who weighed 4½ to 5½ pounds were more aggressive, intensive, and adult centered. By age 10 the size deficit had been overcome, but the average IQ of the preemies was still lower than that of full-term babies. Somewhere between the ages of 8 and 19, the premature children somehow caught up in their mental development but still evidenced emotional problems. Longitudinal studies such as this one show that human development is grounded in an extended period of socialization, is capable of great plasticity, can lead to a wide variation in final product, has greater freedom of direction, and leaves greater room for error. This extended period of socialization provides room for extensive personality development, itself made possible by the great plasticity at birth of the perceptual structure.

Table 7-1   Effects of Drugs on the Fetus or the Newborn Child

Drug	Effect on the Fetus or Newborn
Narcotics Morphine Heroin Methadone	Depression of fetal respirations. Decreased responsiveness of newborn. Addiction or possible neonatal death.
Barbiturates Phenobarbital Amytal Nembutal	All barbiturates and thiobarbiturates cross the placenta. In usual clinical doses they cause minimal fetal depression. With Nembutal, however, there is decreased responsiveness and poor sucking ability in early neonatal period.
Ethyl alcohol	No neonatal depression. May decrease uterine contractions. Withdrawal symptoms of twitching, hyperirritability, sweating. Fever in babies born to mothers in delirium tremens.
Inhalation anesthetics Ether	Crosses placenta rapidly. Depresses infant by direct narcotic effect. Does not interfere with oxygenation.
Nitrous oxide	No significant depression if concentration of oxygen administered to mother is adequate.
Local anesthetics Procaine (Novocaine)	Cross the placenta readily. Central nervous system may be depressed in infant by direct drug effect or indirectly by causing maternal hypotension if used for regional anesthesia (spinal or epidural anesthesia).
Tranquilizers Chlorpromazine (Thorazine) Meprobamate (Equanil, Miltown) Librium Resperine	 No substantial effects on fetus. Crosses placenta; no effects demonstrated so far. Nasal congestion, excessive mucus lethargy, decreased activity, bradycardia.
Antimicrobial agents Penicillin Ampicillin Streptomycin	 No unfortunate effects. Hearing loss (very rare) in infants whose mothers have been treated for prolonged periods in early pregnancy.
Aureomycin Terramycin	Staining of deciduous teeth. Inconclusive association with congenital cataracts. Potential for bone growth retardation but not proved to occur in utero.
Antithyroid drugs	All antithyroid drugs cross the placenta and can result in fetal goiters and hypothyroidism.

Source: W. A. Bowes et al., The effects of obstetrical medication on fetus and infant, *Monographs of the Society for Research in Child Development*, 1970, 35, No. 4. (Reprinted in Helms & Turner, 1976, p. 48.)

THE ESSENCE OF PERSONALITY DEVELOPMENT
IS THE ARTICULATION OF THE PERCEPTUAL PROGRAM

In reviewing some of the traditional developmental models, Breger (1974) listed the following stages as necessary to a theory of development which does adequate justice to our knowledge of the biology and evolutionary history of the human being. Over time, the organism's biology and psychology develop according to the following specifications:

1. There are *stages* in development such that progression to succeeding stages will be nonoptimal unless previous stages are completed to a specific degree.
2. *Increased differentiation* takes place as the organism develops from a single cell to an interdependent organ system. Presumably analogous differentiation takes place in perceptual structure and the motive systems.
3. *Integration* of the differentiated parts is required in order for effective functioning to take place.
4. Development is *unidirectional;* it is pointed at the final goal. The completion of one stage determines progression to the next. Each stage is the product and creator of experience.
5. There are *critical periods* in development. Certain stimuli and/or experiences must have occurred by a certain age or incomplete development results. For example, infant-mother attachment must be established by eleven months or it will not be established at all. (Levy, 1937).

It is our thesis that there is an ordinal stage hierarchy to development. As we progress from one stage to the next, perceptual structure becomes more differentiated. The articulation of this differentiation includes the establishment of communication channels between the differentiated categories. This permits the system to operate as an integrated unit. The integrated whole develops a definitive structure at some point during its development. The relative articulation of the structure at once establishes constraints as well as freedom of movement for future development. A more articulated structure has a greater potential for growth precisely because both the limits and the freedom of movement are greater.

Perhaps the most important thing which evolves over these developmental stages is that the individual builds a characteristically unique pattern of personality organization. There are a number of variables which can influence formation of this individuality: 1) The individual's inherited biological constitution (e.g., the physical, physiological and biochemical structures); 2) the influence of specific biological conditions which are nongenetic but which result from certain kinds of mechanical or chemical conditions (e.g., pre-natal environment, nutrition during development, and other physiological experiences); 3) maturation, developmental changes predetermined built-in programs; 4) learning experiences; 5) the particular family constellation in the home which includes interaction between the individual and family members; 6) peer and other social relationships; and 7) the institutional practices of the culture.

It is most likely that these seven classes of variables interact in complex ways to determine the total personality system. For example, the physical and intellectual inheritance of the individual can have a decided influence on the attitude which his parents hold toward him and the kind of status he may receive in comparison with his siblings. These biosocial effects in turn influence the kind of activities and skills he pursues.

If a bright child is favored by his parents for his intelligence, then he is more likely to pursue intellectual goals to attain recognition, relegating other activities to secondary importance. By means of the interaction of such variables is laid the foundation of each unique personality.

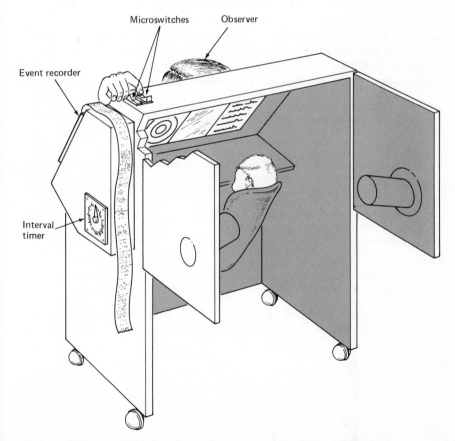

Figure 7-3 Drawing of infant visual-preference apparatus used for paired comparison tests of infants. Source: Forgus and Melamed, 1976, p. 262. Adapted from Fantz, 1961a.

THE PERCEPTUAL (INFORMATION-SEEKING) SYSTEM

The growth of the four motive systems requires that information be extracted from stimuli through perception. A number of changes take place in the perceptual system as the result of maturation and perceptual learning, most notably, acquisition of knowledge, sensorimotor integration, increased specificity of response, and schemata development.

Acquisition of Knowledge

Fantz (1967) has postulated that perceptual development consists of acquisition of knowledge, directed by the attentional selectivity of the organism. In an experiment on form perception (1961), he shows how knowledge is acquired. Infants between the ages of 1 and 15 weeks were tested at weekly intervals in an apparatus which permitted accurate measurement of the infant's preferential attention to one of a pair of stimuli. His apparatus is shown in Figure 7-3. Fantz found, in general, that infants spent more time looking at the more complex of two designs:

1. Infants preferred heterogeneous over homogeneous patterns. While no choice was revealed between a large triangle or a smaller one, or between a circle and a triangle, a checkerboard pattern was preferred over a rectangle of homogeneous color. Moreover there was an age progression toward a preference for more heterogeneity. In comparing a horizontally striped pattern with a bullseye, infants under 2 weeks preferred the former, while older infants shifted until there was a marked preference for the bullseye in the 8-week-old infant.
2. There was a hierarchy of preference for shapes in the 8-week-old infant. The order was human face, printed matter, bullseye, homogeneously colored discs. Pattern, rather than color or brightness, seemed to be the important determiner of preference (see Figure 7-4).
3. Form preference has a functional significance. Infants prefer a human face over a scrambled face, and scrambled features over an oval which is black at the top and reddish at the bottom. The preference for the human face emerges at about 8 weeks of age. Clearly, then, perception exerts a directing influence on the stage differentiation of the attachment system.

More direct evidence for the role of experience comes from Fantz's comparison of dark-reared with normally reared monkeys. The experimen-

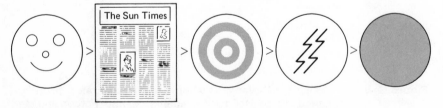

Figure 7-4   Form Preferences in the 8-week-old infant.

172

tal groups were raised in the dark for varying durations from 1 to 11 weeks. Monkeys reared under these conditions for shorter periods of time generally exhibited good spatial orientation after a few hours or days in a normal environment, as well as the usual interest in patterned objects. Those who were left in the dark for longer periods were completely disoriented in space upon their first contact with a normal environment: "They bumped into things, fell off tables, could not locate objects visually—for all practical purposes they were blind" (Fantz, 1961, p. 5).

In addition to their spatial disorientation, those monkeys who had been deprived longest of normal illumination appeared to be more interested in color, brightness, and size rather than pattern—it took them weeks to "learn to see."

The results of this study illustrate the interaction between maturation and learning. Obviously, innate ability cannot be the whole answer, otherwise the dark-reared animals would not be so highly disoriented. Finally, a learning explanation is not sufficient, since those deprived longest took a disproportionately long time to learn to perceive form and space. Evidently there is an interaction between maturation and learning so that the amount and quality of experience interacts with the time at which the experience occurs (critical period) to determine the optimal effectiveness in the growth of form perception.

Bower (1977) points out that the infant already has considerable perceptual ability at birth. This ability is probably dependent on bodily cues such as eye muscle adjustment and movement. Such built-in reactions primarily serve to increase the amount of information the infant can process. Objects become more familiar and the range of cues increases as these built-in programs become modified.

Sensorimotor Integration

Perceptual development produces sensorimotor integration. An ingenious experiment by Held and Hein (1963) illustrates how visuomotor equivalence underlies the growth of sensorimotor integration. In this experiment, one group of kittens was raised in the dark for 10 weeks while the other group was exposed to the patterned interior of the laboratory from 2 weeks of age until training began at approximately 10 weeks. The training for both groups consisted of 3 hours daily exposure in a motion apparatus, in which pairs of kittens were allowed to move through a circular axis as depicted in Figure 7-5. While one member (A) of the pair was allowed to move freely, the passive member (P), connected by a yoke to A, would experience the equivalent sensory, but not the same motor, perceptions. After a number of daily practices, a crucial test of spatial (depth) discrimination was conducted, using the well-known Gibson-Walk "visual cliff" apparatus

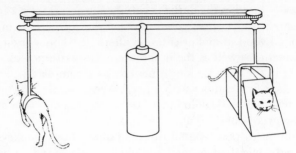

Figure 7-5   Apparatus for equating motion and consequent visual feedback for an active moving (A) and a passively moving (P)
subject. Source: R. Held and A. Hein, 1963, pp. 872-876.
(Reprinted from Forgus, 1975.)

(see Figure 7-6). One hundred percent of the active movement group chose
the appropriate shallow end, the adaptive response, but one-third to one-
half of the passive group chose the deep side, the maladaptive response.
The case for active movement in the development of visuomotor integration is self-evident from these data. A baby learns through active practice
to bring his spoonful of food to his mouth rather than all over his face. Held
and Hein call this practice *visual prehension.*

Increased Specificity of Perceptual Response

Gibson and Gibson (1956) assert that the stimulus contains all the information necessary for perception. Perceptual learning produces increased
specificity; that is, more aspects (features) of the stimulus are perceived.
Using the "visual cliff," Gibson and Walk (1960) have shown that depth
perception starts with a built-in cue which can only operate when either
the object and/or person is moving (motion parallax). With experience,
depth can also be perceived when the field is stationary, on the basis of visual pattern cues. See Figure 7-6(b).

Schemata Development

Kagan (1967, 1970) believes that development leads to the formation
of schemata. In one experiment, he found that 4-month-old infants preferred to look at pictures of human faces which were slightly discrepant
rather than an undistorted human face. McCall and Kagan (1967) interpret these data by using the concept of *schema.* A schema highlights the
most distinctive elements of an event. A person's schema for a particular

Figure 7-6(a)   The visual cliff. Note the baby crawling toward the mother on the shallow side (above) and staying away from the mother on the deep side (see Figure 7-6b on following page).

Figure 7-6(b) Source: After Gibson and Walk, 1960. Reprinted with permission. Copyright 1960, 1961 by Scientific American, Inc. All rights reserved. Photograph courtesy of William Vandivert. (Reprinted from Forgus and Melamed, 1976.)

experience will direct his attention whenever he encounters another such stimulus. The function of schemata in serving the other systems is quite evident. In our example, recognizing the mother's face is important in the formation of attachment.

Developmental Considerations in Cognitive Styles

The studies we have just reviewed were all performed by psychologists who hypothesized that learning has a strong influence on perceptual development. However, the early pioneers of research on perceptual psychology, the Gestalt theorists, held the view that perception was innately organized. Thus, developmental changes would have to be consistent with innate Gestalt principles of organization. An early investigation of this assertion was carried out in Wulf's (1922) study of the memory for perceived forms.

In Wulf's study, subjects were briefly exposed to various visual forms (live figures). After varying intervals of time, one or another of the subjects was asked to draw what he remembered seeing. Wulf reports that the reproduced forms showed increasing change over time. However, Hebb and Foord (1945) replicated the experiments with one modification. *Each* of their subjects was asked to reproduce the figures at a number of time intervals. Their results show that the major change in the reproduced figures occurred after the first reproduction and that there was little change in subsequent reproductions. Thus, there are individual differences in how perceived forms are reproduced. These changes take one of two directions, as illustrated in Figure 7-7. In one case, differences between two parts of the figure were minimized, in the other they were exaggerated. The first perceptual change was called leveling, the second, sharpening.

While Wulf considered these changes examples of spontaneous structural changes in the memory trace, later theorizers (Holzman & Gardner, 1960) saw them as indicative of personality differences, as cognitive style variables. The personality differences between sharpeners and levelers have already been described in Chapter 6. There seems to be no empirical studies on the developmental origin of this cognitive style variable, but in our discussion of the differentiation of the cognitive motive, we have described the search for novelty and the attentional preference for slight discrepancy from the familiar. Furthermore, creative people show more preference for novelty. We can speculate that sharpeners are more creative than levelers, and a number of studies (for example, Hebb, 1949) have shown that an enriched perceptual environment facilitates the growth of creativity. Perhaps sharpeners were developmentally exposed to a richer perceptual en-

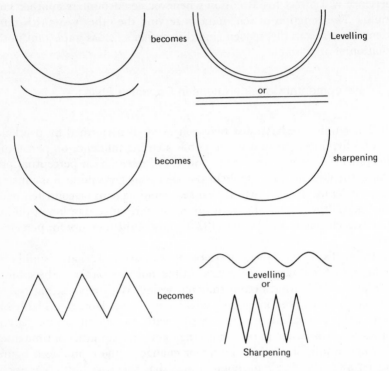

Figure 7-7 Leveling and sharpening changes in the reproduction of perceived forms.

vironment and therefore have more differentiated sets for processing variety or change.

There is some evidence that an enriched perceptual environment may also contribute to the development of extensive scanning. Psychologists generally believe that wealthy children have a more enriched perceptual environment than poor children (Hunt, 1971). Bruner and Goodman (1947) performed a study which compared the ability of children accurately to assess the diameter of a quarter dollar. They found that both wealthy and poor children overestimated the diameter, but poor children overestimated much more. Bruner and Goodman felt that this perceptual exaggeration was the result of a motivational variable—that is, poor children set higher value on a quarter than did wealthy children. However, it is also possible to explain this difference as the result of a perceptual rather than a motivational variable; namely, as a difference in cognitive style. In studies by Gardner and Long (1962a, b), two independent measures of scanning were predictive of the errors children make in estimating the diameter of a circle. Narrow scanners had a greater error of overestimation, just as did the poor children in the Bruner and Goodman study. Therefore, it seems equally plausible to explain the greater error made by the poor children as a consequence of their narrow scanning rather than their greater desire for a quarter.

Another aspect of cognitive style that has been the object of empirical research is the reflectivity/impulsivity dimension. Younger children are more impulsive and less analytical. Growth brings greater reflectivity and more fear of making mistakes (Kagan, 1971). In one study reported by Kagan, American children are developmentally more reflective than their cultural counterparts. Perhaps this finding is related to the fact that American children have higher aspirations for being correct and have more failure anxiety.

Alt (1973), in a study of first- through fifth-grade children, showed that reflectives use more mature problem-solving strategies. Younger reflectives score as well on the 20-question game as older impulsives. However, Adams (1972) found an interaction between age and style variable. While at 6 years, reflectives use more mature strategies than impulsives, at 8 years, this difference no longer exists. At this point the less reflective children have caught up with their more reflective counterparts. In any case, by the time children have become more reflective they have more alternative hypotheses and use more effective strategies (McKinney, 1973).

One possible developmental antecedent of reflectivity can be seen in a study by Campbell (1973). In his study, mothers who show more interest in the learning process are likely to have more reflective children.

A relationship between parental behavior and psychological differentiation has also been reported. In a cross-cultural survey, Witkin (1976) assembled evidence that different methods of child rearing affected this cognitive style. Democratic socialization methods were more likely than autocratic methods to produce field-independent children. Democratic parents permitted their children more freedom of choice and more participation in decision making. Autocratic parents were more likely to command than to instruct.

Field independents also pay more attention to cues coming from the immediate task at hand and are less distracted by cues coming from the outside (Ruble & Nakamura, 1972; Fleck, 1972). Loeb (1975) also related child-rearing practices to locus of control. He noted that sons with external locus of control have parents who are more directive and intruding in the tasks they are performing. Cognitive style develops as cognitive structures become more differentiated with time and experience. More differentiated styles are more effective at environmental tasks.

THE COGNITIVE MOTIVE:
FROM IGNORANCE TO KNOWLEDGE

Stages of Cognitive Development

Developmental theorists have hypothesized that cognition grows with maturation, training, and experience. The growth follows a sequence:

1. There is little if any cognitive organization at birth. Piaget (1952) describes this first stage as the stage of *sensorimotor intelligence.* It is characterized by an absence of inferences and by direct responses to stimuli. Werner (1957) noted a similar quality which he called a *global* response, characterized by its concrete and undifferentiated nature. As we discussed earlier, Kagan (1970) has demonstrated a difference between the impulsive attention to a stimulus at this age and the reflective attention that occurs at later ages. Hebb and his associates have collected an impressive body of evidence to indicate that perceptual learning enables the organism to develop from *sensory domination* to central mediation (Hebb, 1960; Forgus & Melamed, 1976).

2. As development proceeds, processing of information changes. It becomes more differentiated, articulated, and hierarchically integrated (Witkin, 1976). More cognitive categories develop. For Bruner (1964), this differentiation goes through an *iconic phase,* during which the stimulus is represented by an image and hence the organism is less stimulus dominated. More choices become available. For Piaget, representation in this stage is still quite limited. He calls this the *preoperational* stage.

3. When the child has amassed and integrated enough images, a third stage emerges, which Piaget calls the stage of *concrete operations.* As an active manipulator of information, the child now assimilates information into existing schemata. Since new learning is now filtered through existing percepts, the pursuit of knowledge becomes a motive in its own right. However, the child must also accommodate to the environment; that is, modify his own reactions as the conditions and demands of the environment shift. Thus, cognitive growth becomes a balance between *assimilation* and *accommodation.* As this balance is achieved, the focus of attention moves away from centering on self to *decentering*—reorganizing what one encounters into different patterns. Piaget speaks of the objectivity of the external world as being *conserved.* One indication of this is that the child recognizes that even though volume remains the same shape may change. Thus he presumably understands the relationship between form, mass, and other dimensions.

4. Eventually, the child is able to manipulate symbols, a stage Piaget calls *formal operations.* The formal principles of mathematics and syllogistic reasoning are examples of formal operations.

Taken in toto, these four stages indicate that the newborn's global cognitive structure becomes systematically more differentiated with development. Humans have the *capacity* for cognitive growth. Through adequate environmental stimulation and training, which feeds the need for sensory variation, the cognitive motive emerges and cognitive ability grows. In Chapter 5 we reviewed the findings of researchers to the effect that enriched early environment facilitates the differentiation and integration of cognitive ability and that restricted environment does the opposite (for example, Forgus, 1954).

Piaget's model shows us how differentiation proceeds through four cognitive stages as a result of maturation. Bryant (1974), however, has claimed that this development can be slowed down or speeded up as the result of training and appropriate experience.

For Piaget (1964), development takes place in a phylogenetic perspective. Evolution involves the acquisition of a hereditary endowment, providing the individual with physiological and behavioral structures which direct and organize development and learning. Interaction between *genetic endowment* and the *common environment* (shared by the whole species) determines development—which is the emergence of new (cognitive) structures as the organism adapts to the common environment. These new structures are primarily maturational: They provide a knowledge about the environment which all members of the species share, such as the ability to see relationships at the appropriate developmental stage. In possession of these general maturational structures, the individual can now *learn,* as he encounters idiosyncratic aspects of his environment.

For Piaget, learning is *perceptual learning.* In applying Piaget's theory to the nature-nurture controversy, Furth (1974) clarified the relationship between learning and maturation. He concluded that maturational effects determine what kind of learning can take place.

Box 7-2 presents a condensed version of Piaget's stages of cognitive development. His system has attracted both followers and detractors. While there may be inaccuracies in the theory, it is the most comprehensive and systematic theory of cognitive development available.

THE ATTACHMENT MOTIVE: FROM DEPENDENCE TO AFFILIATION

Stages in the Growth of Attachment

Ainsworth (1964), following Bowlby's pioneer work on the growth of mother-infant affection, attempted to establish stages in the development of attachment motive by observing mother-infant interaction at biweekly intervals between the ages of 2 to 15 months. From her observations one can extract the following stages:

1. The first stage, which emerges during the first 8 weeks, consists of *undiscriminating* responsiveness to other people.
2. The second stage, which begins between 8 and 12 weeks, is characterized by *discriminating* responsiveness to the mother, although there is still some responsiveness to others. The social smile, an index of attachment (Gerwitz, 1965; Tautermarova, 1973) emerges. Ainsworth used the baby's crying at the mother's departure as the primary criterion that attachment was present. This stage is firmly established by the time the infant is 6 months old.

Sensorimotor intelligence (0–2 years)	No internal representations until age 2, at which time the child develops sufficient symbolic power to explain discrepancies to himself. Form and pattern schemata become stable and internally represented.
Preoperational stage (2–7 years)	The child uses symbols effectively and improves his ability to form categories, classifications, and concepts. The concept of conservation begins to develop.
Concrete operations (7–12 years)	Understanding of relations emerges. Can break up a Gestalt into its parts and form new Gestalts. The concept of conservation is extended to more categories, for example, the conservation of weight. Ability to abstract relationships and internalize them symbolically.
Formal operations (12 years upward)	Preoccupation with problem solving in a more methodological, deliberate, and systematic way. Increased ability to formulate problems systematically. Logic, mathematics, and deductive reasoning. Creation of higher order operations.

For Piaget, changes in cognitive structure which all children experience as a result of adapting to common environmental obstacles are called *maturation.*

These maturational changes in cognitive structure permit learning to take place. Piaget limits the term *learning* to the effects of the idiosyncratic experiences of each child.

Source: After Piaget (1952, 1964)

3. During the third stage, at about 7 months of age, the child clearly *prefers* his mother and does not respond to other people. This positive attachment is evidenced by a vocalizing and greeting gesture. At this point the infant has developed an attitude of *dependence* toward the mother.
4. The fourth stage, at about 9 months, is characterized by positive attachment to family members, such as siblings and father. Strong preference is evident in the enthusiastic greeting of siblings, versus anxiety in the presence of strangers (*stranger-anxiety*). However, Ainsworth (1973) has subsequently concluded that so-called stranger-anxiety is more a case of reacting to an unfamiliar pattern with excitement. If strangers behave like parents, the infant does not show stranger-anxiety. Moreover strange children do not elicit the anxious response.

Smiling is an early form of communication (Bower, 1977), at first in response to any face, and after 8 weeks, in response to the preferred face of the mother (Fantz, 1961). The critical age period of 7 to 9 months has been verified by the clinical work of Levy (1937). He describes a condition, *affect*

Figure 7-8   Before the end of the first year the child comes to prefer the familiar schemata associated with mother. Source: Courtesy Jim Theologos, Monkmeyer Press

hunger, caused by maternal deprivation. In moderate forms it produces excessive crying, while in extreme forms it produces apathy. If not corrected with adequate mothering between 8 and 11 months, there is permanent and irreversible retardation of the attachment system.

Variables in the Development of Attachment

All the work of Harlow (1971) has pointed to the importance of physical contact in the growth of attachment. Ribble (1943) mentioned the importance of kinesthetic and proprioceptive sensations (rocking the infant) in promoting attachment, as have Korner and Toman (1972) and Pederson and TerVrugt (1973).

Spitz (1946) and Bowlby (1965) have studied the sequential effects of maternal deprivation on infants. In his studies on hospitalized infants, Spitz reported stages similar to those reported by Levy and pointed out that these infants were more susceptible to disease and had a higher mortality rate. Bowlby described a number of effects from varying degrees of separation. Infants who received adequate mothering during infancy but were separated from the mother at age 8 months, because of illness or some other crisis, revealed antisocial behavior which began with attention-getting behavior and progressed, if deprivation continued, to flattened affect. If the deprivation started at 1 to 4 years of age, the children often compensated by stealing and lying. These antisocial tendencies may at times be disguised by a superficial friendliness without real attachment.

There is evidence that other aspects of maternal behavior are related to attachment. Beckwith (1972) found that infants are most socially responsive to mothers who are attentive and respond quickly to the infant's signals, and who allow the infant free expression of impulse and exploratory behavior. Bell and Ainsworth (1972) reported that such maternal behavior leads to a more rapid decline in the frequency and severity of crying during the first year of life. During the first year it seems impossible to spoil the child by giving him attention; on the contrary, abundant mothering at this time prevents bad behavior habits in the child. Mothers who give immediate attention to crying babies produce babies who cry less, contrary to reinforcement theory.

Rheingold (1956) showed that the effects of maternal deprivation can be overcome by intensive mothering. She worked with 16 six-month-old infants living in an institution where they were cared for by many volunteer workers. Half of the children were given special treatment: they were exposed to a substitute mother (Harriet Rheingold herself) for 8 hours a day, 5 days a week, for 8 weeks. During that time she took care of their needs (bathing and diapering) and also provided social stimulation (playing with and smiling at them). The social responsiveness of the treated group increased markedly, not only toward Miss Rheingold, but also toward others. Thus, generalization of the attachment motive occurred. There was no such increase in social responsiveness in the control group during the 8-week period. Harlow (1971) showed that the effects of maternal deprivation can also be remedied by peer contact.

THE SECURITY MOTIVE: FROM FEAR TO COURAGE

Security develops out of the mother's appropriate caretaking and out of the infant's opportunities to master stress successfully, using his own resources.

Maternal Caretaking Variables

Yarrow (1963) studied the effects of three classes of maternal variables. The way these were measured is indicated in Box 7-3. The maternal care variables which show the most consistently high correlation with

Box 7-3.   Maternal Care Variables Catalogued by Yarrow (1963)

A. Variables dealing with *need gratification* and *tension reduction:*
1. *Amount of physical contact,* which was measured in terms of the amount of time during the day and the number of different situations that the child was held by the mother.
2. *Immediacy of response* to the infant's expressed needs, which was a simple measure of how quickly the mother responded to the child's expressed needs with appropriate need-reduction activities.
3. *Degree of soothing,* which was a measure of the extent to which the mother's response to the infant was effective in reducing tension.
4. *Physical involvement,* or closeness, which was a rating of the characteristic way in which the mother held the child—the degree of closeness to the body, and extent to which her manner of holding the child represented an adaptation to the child's characteristics and rhythms.

B. Variables concerned with *stimulation* and *conditions for learning:*
1. *Achievement stimulation,* which was the amount of maternal stimulation that was oriented toward developmental progress; also the extent to which the environment provided the appropriate materials.
2. *Social stimulation,* which was the amount of stimulation oriented toward eliciting social responsiveness, and the amount of time spent in social interaction with the child.
3. *Communications stimulation,* a measure of the extent to which the infant's attempts to express his needs by vocalization or physical activity were encouraged and facilitated by the mother.
4. *Stimulus adaptation,* which was rated in terms of the extent to which materials and experiences given to the infant were adapted to his individual capacities and progress.
5. *Positive-affective expression,* which was an account of the frequency and intensity of expression of positive feelings by the mother, father, and others in the environment.

C. Variables involved with *affectional interchange* (emotional interchange) between mother and infant:
1. *Individualization,* a measure of the extent of maternal awareness of the unique characteristics and sensitivities of the child, as determined by behavior adaptation toward the child's individual characteristics and abilities.
2. *Emotional involvement,* a rating of the extent to which the mother was identified with the child, as expressed through warmth, sensitivity, individualization, and intensity of involvement in the child's future.
3. *Acceptance-rejection,* which was a measure of the extent to which the child's characteristics, abilities, disabilities, and natural background were accepted without question.

many aspects of infant behavior are stimulus adaptation, achievement stimulation, social stimulation, communication, and positive-affective expression, all of which are subclasses of stimulation and conditions for learning. These variables are particularly important in the development of the IQ.

Social initiative (reaching out to people) is determined more by positive-affective expression than by social stimulation per se, exploratory behavior, however, is affected by all of the subcategories in the three major variables. Not only the amount but also the quality of the stimulation given by a caretaker is an important determiner of developmental progress.

We can conclude from Yarrow's study that an infant needs to feel trust and security to be able to explore his environment. All three classes of maternal care variables determine the growth of dependence and trust. He must also be able to cope with stress so that he can handle certain threatening events when he later begins to explore. Yarrow's study shows that need gratification, tension reduction, and affectional interchange facilitate the infant's ability to handle stress.

Infant Stimulation, Resistance to Stress, and Rate of Growth

Yarrow's study does not relate such variables as physical contact and involvement to the infant's ability to cope with stress. A related study that we examined in Chapter 5 found that ability to cope with stress in young rats was closely related to the amount of stimulation, whether handling or shock stimuli, to which the infant rats had been exposed (Levine, 1962). The prolongation of stress response in non-stimulated animals can have severely damaging consequences; stomach ulcers, increased susceptibility to infection, and eventually death due to adrenal exhaustion (Levine, 1962).

There were other findings in Levine's study. Non-stimulated animals have retarded rates of growth because of lower output of somatotropic (growth) hormones. Levine also investigated the question of whether there are critical periods during which infant stimulation is most effective. In one such study, infant rats were handled daily during three different age periods: (a) 2 to 6 days; (b) 6 to 9 days; and (c) 10 to 13 days. Only animals who received handling during the first period showed any evidence that they were capable of appropriate adaptive reactions in the presence of stress. Levine's findings on the importance of infant stimulation have been supported by others (Dennenberg & Karras, 1959; Werboff & Havlena, 1964; Weininger, 1956). The importance of infant stimulation, especially early in life, receives support from work on human infants reported by anthropologists. We already noted Landauer and Whiting's study (1964), which corroborated Levine's findings in a cross-cultural study of 36 societies that stressed infants. Two of the stressing practices were the most reliable: (1) Piercing of nose, lips, or ears; circumcision, inoculation, or scarification; (2) molding (stretching the arms or legs or shaping the head). In societies using these practices the mean heights of adult males was 65.18″ as opposed to 62.9″ for societies which avoided them. The mean difference was statistically significant ($p < .002$).

Anxiety and the Motive Systems

We have examined two ways in which we become secure: through trust in the caretaker and through trust in one's own competence. Anxiety is experienced whenever the previously trusted becomes unreliable. A threat to the attachment motive produces *separation anxiety*. A threat to the cognitive motive, such as a marked discrepancy from the familiar, also produces anxiety, *strangeness-anxiety*. A threat to the competence motive, such as a cue which forecasts a verification of self-doubt, leads to *failure-anxiety*. A threat to the security motive, such as pain, produces *harm-anxiety*. Each motive system influences the others. The attachment motive leads to a desire to please the parent. Parental disapproval may then represent a threat to the child. Thus, behavior growing out of one motive system becomes important in another. The non-confirmation of any motive is a threat which sets into motion appropriate affective responses. The security motive maintains all the motive systems through the mechanism of anxiety, which sets safeguarding behavior into motion. Anxiety is experienced when the direction of the guiding self-ideal is violated (Arnold, 1960). *Courage* is the willingness to risk harm because another motive, more consistent with the guiding self-ideal, takes priority over the security motive.

THE COMPETENCE MOTIVE: FROM INADEQUACY TO COMPETENCE

The development of the competence motive cannot occur without the presence of attachment and security. Dependency (attachment motive) provides the security for exploration of the environment even in the face of distressing experience. That is why mother's kiss has magic healing power.

From Dependence to Independence

Celia Stendler (1953) discusses the progression from dependence to independence. When dependency is established, the child will actively try to please the mother. Stendler points out further that children who have weak dependency motives have inadequate social skills because they have not learned to seek the approval of others. She warns, however, that in cultures which emphasize independence, the need for a stage of dependence is not always recognized. Once dependency is established, the ease with which independence emerges depends on how the parent reacts to the dependency motive. Five misuses of the dependency motive have been noted by Stendler:

Figure 7-9   The security provided by the familiar mother facilitates courageous behavior. Source: Courtesy Marian Bernstein

1. *Impatient parental expectation.* When the child is required to become independent too quickly, adequate dependency and trust do not occur. Individuals so raised later exhibit apparent independence, hiding an underlying fear and resentment of authority. Because they do not trust, they constrict their emotions, are afraid to love or depend on others, fear that they are not loved, and may develop obsessive-compulsive rituals as a "smokescreen" to control the anxiety they feel about being unlovable. Since their attempts to depend were rejected, they develop *counterdependency,* a fear and avoidance of depending on others.
2. *Neglect.* A second negative effect results when the child receives insufficient care as when the mother is inconsistent, emotionally ill, or unprepared for maternal responsibility, or if a new baby comes too early. To compensate for this felt deprivation the child may become *overattached* to any person that offers attention.
3. *Overprotection.* A third undesirable outcome results when the child is kept dependent for too long a period—frequently because the mother is overanxious, overprotective, or oversolicitious. Such a child has insufficient independence training and does not have the opportunity to practice or learn self-reliance. The child therefore exhibits a *lack of confidence.*
4. *Withdrawal of love.* A fourth undesirable effect exists when the mother exploits a strong dependency motive in disciplining or punishing her child (Sears, Maccoby, & Levin, 1957). If a strong dependency motive has been nurtured and

the parent subsequently uses withdrawal of love to discipline the child, the dependency motive is frustrated. This sequence of events leads to distrust and the development of techniques for dominating others by manipulating emotions. Extremes of such patterns are seen in the *hysterical* personality.

5. *Rejection.* Outright dislike of the child, cruel treatment and frustration of the child's attempt to find satisfactory dependence lead to hostility and embitterment. The child may develop an *antisocial* personality; others will be enemies, not objects for attachment.

Dependency can, of course, be used to socialize desirable attributes. Gerwitz and Baer (1958) found that children over the age of 1 year are willing to work harder for social approval when deprived of adult company. In this case, dependency actually helps them become more competent.

Arsenian (1943) has outlined one way to facilitate a smooth transition from dependence to independence. On the first day a child comes to nursery school, it is helpful for the mother to remain in school all day so that the child can quickly adapt to the new environment. If the mother does not stay, it takes longer for the child to overcome separation anxiety and adapt to the school situation. Arsenian also notes that the crucial variable is whether the mother is present on that first day. If so, the child easily develops independence and profits much more from the experience than the child who has not made the transition.

Optimal balance between care and respect. Carol Davis (1966) formulated a child-rearing model based on a longitudinal study of individuals from their early childhood to adulthood (30 months to 25 years). She emphasized the importance of striking a balance between caring for the child's needs and respecting his ability to grow. Observance of this optimal *care/respect balance* produces a reciprocal balance between dependence and self-confidence as indicated in Table 7-2.

Table 7-2 The Relationship Between Reciprocal Trust and Balanced Emancipation
A balance between care and respect effects a balance between reliance (dependence) and self-confidence

Independent Variables	Dependent Variables
The parent CARES for the child →	The child RELIES (depends) on the parent
The parent RESPECTS the child's ability and desire for growth →	The child develops SELF-CONFIDENCE as he emerges

Source: After Davis, 1966.

There are four patterns of imbalance between care and respect, which produce various kinds of maladjustment in the development of independence:

1. *The pampered child.* When the parent has overprotected the child and in so doing discouraged him from relying on his own resources, the child learns to be *overdependent* and distrusts his own abilities. Such an individual can be a model child, compliant with parental wishes, even do well in grade school, only to run into trouble during college when competence, independence, and other demands of adolescence produce more stress.

2. *The rebel.* In this pattern the parent has again cared too much for the child, at the expense of not showing him enough respect. Unlike the previous situation, the child has not "given in" to parental control but has rebelled instead. The counteraction takes the form of a false independence, which actually hides an underlying lack of self-confidence. Since the child fears the negative consequences of dependency, he exhibits an exaggerated concern with "independence," all the while being overly sensitive to the parent's messages.

3. *The neglected child.* In this situation the parent gives too little care and shows a false respect, which probably emanates from the parent's own self-concern. The result is that the child becomes *counterdependent*—that is, he denies the need for parental care. This individual may become too concerned with being self-reliant. Dependence/independence conflicts occur later when the challenge of adolescent-adult intimacy emerges. These individuals seek intimacy with more than one person, often becoming overattached to inappropriate objects.

4. *The overdependent child.* This individual counteracts parental neglect or overambitious demands by becoming *overdependent*, clinging to a dependent way of acting and refusing to become independent.

Play and Experience in the Development of Competence

Hunt (1960) and White (1963) have both pointed out that the competence motive develops out of the child's need to master his environment. An important factor influencing the growth of competence is the amount and kinds of opportunity for exploring and manipulating the environment. Opportunity presents itself first through the quality of the parent-child interaction; second, through the amount of achievement-stimulation in the home (such as the kind of play material); third, the quality of social play; and fourth, the quality of formal education (school). Abundant research shows that early enrichment of the environment leads to superior abilities, as measured by tests of perceptual discrimination and problem-solving ability (Hebb, 1960; Forgus & Melamed, 1976; Fiske & Maddi, 1961). In play, the child exercises his imagination, rehearses various social roles, and practices the art of mastery. Play is not only the exercise of executive abilities, it is also practice in *symbolizing*. Rather than *accommodation* to reality, it *assimilates* reality to the needs of the self (Piaget & Inhelder, 1969). For Piaget, intelligence requires both accommodation and assimilation. Piaget calls this balance between two complementary poles, *equilibration.*

In play, the child assimilates some of the problematic aspects of the real world. Imaginary companions repair loneliness, heroic fantasy feats are an antidote to feelings of weakness, and the distress created by a parent's disapproval is deflected by punishing a doll.

The purpose of education is to create competence, not only in academic achievement, but also in knowledge, values, skills, attitudes, and feelings, all of which facilitate mastery of the process of learning (Grams, 1966). However, the quality of the school may be less important than its social climate. Coleman and his colleagues (1966) studied 600,000 schoolchildren of diverse backgrounds and found that the most important variable in determining test scores of intellect and other skills was the social class composition of the school. Middle-class schools produced more high achievers than lower-class schools. Even poor children who attended middle-class schools become higher achievers. School facilities, class size, teacher skill, and expenditure per pupil make little or no difference. The peer experience and/or teacher expectancies seemed the crucial variables. Coleman's work has been critiqued and extended by Mosteller and Moynihan (1972).

SOCIAL INFLUENCES ON THE MOTIVE SYSTEMS

In addition to the influence of the primary caretaker on the child, there are other important socializing influences. They include family climate, sibling constellation, peer relationships, and as we just mentioned, educational and cultural influences.

Family Climate

The emotional atmosphere in one family may be very different from that in another, even though both may be of the same culture and socioeconomic status. The components of and contributors to this atmosphere include parent-parent interaction (an introduction to the way humans treat one another), parental values (information about what is desirable and undesirable), child-rearing techniques used by the parents (what arouses parents and what they reward and punish), and the parental personalities (affectionate parents, cold and stern parents, or even psychotic parents). Sears, Maccoby, and Levin (1957) presented a classic study on child-rearing practices and their effect on children. They compared middle-class U.S. families to other less puritanical cultures and found that U.S. children were more likely to be constricted and have problems connected with sexual behavior. Inconsistent parental reaction to aggressive behavior is likely to produce an increase in aggressive behavior, and inconsistent nurturance leads to extreme emotional dependence. In an extensive study of the effect of home environment on nursery school children, Baldwin (1949) distinguished between a democratic home atmosphere (permissive, avoided arbitrary decisions, much verbal contact between parent and child) and a controlled home atmosphere (authoritarian restriction of behavior). Children from a democratic environment were more active, competitive, creative, original, aggressive, playful, and nonconforming. Children from authoritarian homes were more quiet, conforming, and nonresistant. Curiosity and originality were restricted.

The effect of fathers has been investigated in several studies. Radin (1973) found that when fathers were restrictive and simultaneously demanded high intellectual achievement from their offspring, the sons actually had lower IQ test scores. Allowing children to expand freely facilitates the growth of competence. McClelland and his associates (1953) found that high-achieving males had warm relationships with their own fathers. On the other hand, deviant behavior in children has been associated with weak fathers who could not discipline (Alkire, 1972). Santrock (1972) found that absence of the father (as a result of divorce or death) impaired cognitive achievement in boys. In the case of divorce, the effect was most marked when the parents separated before the child was 2 years old. The death of the father had its greatest effect when the child was 6 to 9 years old.

Sibling Constellation

Order of birth, number of siblings, age differences between them, gender differences, and sibling interrelationships all affect personality. Schachter (1959) found that first-borns tend to be more dependent, anxious, and tradition-conserving. However, they are less conforming when they face a challenge to their achievement motive (Rhine, 1968).

Of course, all of the variables of the sibling constellation interact. Bigner (1972) found that sex role preference in younger siblings was concordant with the sex of the older sibling. Thus males with older sisters are more likely to exhibit homosexual inclinations, sexual repugnance, and avoidance of sex than males with older brothers (Kahn, Mahrer, & Bornstein, 1972).

Peer Relationships

Peer modeling becomes increasingly important as the child grows older, and peer behaviors that win status are almost certain to be imitated.

In the U.S., boys tend to become more aggressive as they spend more time with peers during middle childhood. Girls—even if they were aggressive to begin with—become less aggressive, in imitation of their peers (Bandura & Walters, 1963). Bronfenbrenner (1970) reviews data which shows that the importance of peers as socializers increases with age and also increases in societies in which parents spend less and less time with their children. Bronfenbrenner expresses alarm at this development; the young become inadequately socialized, failing to learn the traditions and wisdom of the elders, rejecting elders and receiving their values only from peers.

School and Cultural Influences

School is intended by society to be an important socializing institution. How well schools carry out their tasks is open to question (Coleman, 1966; Silberman, 1970). Teachers are meant to be models of adult behavior; textbook and course material also present pre-packaged opinions about various issues. However, schools designed for middle-class children, taught by middle-class teachers, seem to have little relevance to the lives of inner-city minority groups.

Cultural values and institutions help form the child's social world. Indirectly, they influence child-rearing methods, provide values from which one can select, define gender roles, and provide cognitions and precepts that may later become unquestioned beliefs. Bronfenbrenner (1970) has shown some of these differential effects in his comparison of U.S. and Soviet children. Young Americans tend to be more competitive and individualistic but less cooperative than young Russians. This probably reflects the fact that the Soviet Union is still largely a traditional society with authoritarian values.

8

**development
of personality II:
preadolescence
to
old age**

OVERVIEW

As personality development continues, a self emerges. The self is an aspect of perceptual structure which consists of operational instructions for the pursuit of the motives. These operational instructions are codified into a cognitive blueprint (life style). One example of how the self organizes personality can be seen in studies that correlate self-esteem with behavior.

During succeeding developmental stages, the symbols of the motives change. In preadolescence the child pursues competence through industrious activity. He confirms his gender identification as he pursues cognition. He begins to affiliate more with peers, becoming more secure both through his recently acquired skills and his attachments.

The differentiation of motives in adolescence centers around the issue of identity, which influences how the motives are pursued. Peer acceptance and sexuality become differentiations of attachment. In adulthood, the symbols shift to family, career, and community. The relative decline in function that accompanies aging depends on the differentiation that has been achieved; development in the older person is facilitated by the opportunity to continue being active in meaningful pursuits.

Throughout development, the self, which organized the development, remains relatively stable.

From a cognitive standpoint, personality development consists of the increasing differentiation and integration of the perceptual structure. How can this point of view help us to understand development from preadolescence to old age? Since, in our theory, the perceptual structure organizes the basic motives into a hierarchy and determines how the motives are differentiated, one way of following the developmental process as it unfolds is to examine the differing organizations of the motive hierarchy and the differing symbolizations of the motives themselves. Also, at each developmental stage, motives will be represented in a particular way and by specific incentives. Moreover, personality structure is unique and perceptual structure with its motive symbolizations will also differ from person to person.

In addition to increasing differentiation, there is also integration in the direction of a dominant characteristic style for each person. Various theorists have given different labels to this integrative force which acts as an organizing context for understanding all the rest of personality. We have used Adler's terms, *dominant goal, guiding self-ideal,* and *life style,* as names for this integrator. Kelly proposed that development proceeds in the direction of continuous refinement of the personal construct system. All the self theorists postulated that the goal of personality development is the increasing actualization, realization, fulfillment, or authentication of the self. In cognitive terms, the self is *a perceptual mediator which consists of operational instructions* for the pursuit of motive satisfaction.

In tracing the course of development from preadolescence to old age, we will use the construct *self* as the central organizer of both differentiation and integration of the motive systems. We will also examine the differentiation of the motive systems during the major phases of life.

SELF AS AN ORGANIZER OF DEVELOPMENT

As the child grows older, the ways in which motives can be satisfied become more diverse. A number of incentives and goals, some not always compatible, compete for the child's attention, so that he now has to start making choices. These choices are not arbitrary, but progressively reveal the establishment of a plan (which Murray calls the life plan). Without such a plan, incoming information would be chaotic, meaningless, and undirected. This plan is directed by the set of operational instructions which we have called the self. Of all the representations within the perceptual system, the representation of the self is the most important.

Definition and Development of the Self

Horrocks (1976) reviews a number of definitions of self. What they all have in common seems to be contained in the definition of Horrocks and Jackson, which also defines the self from a cognitive standpoint:

> Self is a process by which the organism derives and constructs . . . the organism's interpretation and meaning of itself. . . . [T]he organism is the entity and self is the process that evolves representations of its own entity and related . . . activities. . . . Defining one's self is a continuously evolving product of learning . . . in the form of interacting emotional and cognitive elements. Thus, self is the means by which the organism is aware of and understands itself as a . . . being with a past history and . . . possible future. (1972, p. 95)

Because of the complexity of the human representational system, we can view ourselves as objects and can, therefore, assign a wide range of qualities to ourselves. We can identify, locate, evaluate, interpret, interact with, study, and learn more about ourselves. This objectified self is experienced as having requirements: what we have called the four motives. We want others to like, respect, or recognize us; we want things for ourselves; we want to be safe and to feel capable. As we grow, we continually appraise ourselves and our behavior with respect to these and other wants. In this process we become more or less aware of our real self through various aspects of our being and behavior. These aspects have been described by Allport (1955) and Shulman (1973):

Bodily sense (What is me?). This is the awareness of self as a physical entity with specific boundaries. Allport calls it an "anchor" for self-awareness. One has a body, it can feel pain or pleasure, requires sleep, and so on. One may feel attractive or ugly or even consider his body abnormal and unacceptable. One experiences sexual and other sensations in the body.

Self-identity (What am I?). This is how the person locates himself in his world. One is either child or adult, male or female, black or white, rich or poor, and all the various other ways we have of categorizing ourselves. Self-identity moves through stages. The small child is family dependent for his identity. The young adolescent is peer group dependent. The young adult's identity is more dependent on his intimate relationships, sexual and otherwise. Later identity depends on career, social, and parenting functions.

Box 8-1   Example of a Bodily Sense

Recently, I had as a client an exceedingly attractive young woman. I was struck by the beauty of her face. Her manner of dress and grooming enhanced her whole appearance. I saw nothing unattractive about her. I eventually noticed that she focused attention on her face and away from the lower half of her body. When I came to know her better, I discovered that she considered her body unattractively disproportionate, too large in the thighs and too small in the breasts. Her whole manner of dress and grooming had as its goal to conceal her imagined bodily defects.

Self-image (Who am I?). This is how the person evaluates himself—whether he is a success or failure, competent or incompetent, intelligent or stupid, lovable or unlovable, and so on. The self-image is a judgment the person places on himself, either positive or negative. Developmentally, self-image is a self-fulfilling prophecy, since it leads to behavior which confirms the self-image. The level of self-esteem depends upon the self-image.

Self-interest (What is good for me?). We judge that some things are good for us and some bad. The child feels it is bad to displease the parents. The adolescent feels it is good to conform to the standards of his peer group. One person feels it is good to be educated, another feels it is more important to be popular. Self-interest is not the same as selfishness.

Self-ideal (What do I strive to be?). We strive to be that which is in our self-interest, enhances our self-image, and confirms our self-identity. A discrepancy resulting from low self-image and high self-ideal is experienced as distress, a feeling of inferiority accompanied by unpleasant emotional sensations such as anxiety and guilt. Self-ideal is a relatively permanent aspect of the self, although ways of trying to achieve it may change over time. The self-ideal guides; it functions as the dominant goal of the perceptual system. A person who, at any point in his life span, is more congruent with his ideal, is developmentally more mature for that age.

All these aspects of the self form a *self-concept,* which includes all the views the person holds about himself, whether or not he is consciously aware of them. In addition, each facet of the self contains information and instructions which guide behavior.

Behavioral Correlates and Antecedents of Self-Esteem

Self-esteem, namely, the way in which the person appraises himself, is one aspect of self-image. And, as we have just seen, self-image is itself a differentiation of the self-concept.

Box 8-2   Some Behavioral Correlates of High Self-Esteem

The person with high self-esteem
    shows confidence in his own perception and judgment
    expresses opinions more openly, even when they may be unpopular
    is more assertive and more vigorous in assertion
    is more often a participant than an observer in group discussions
    forms friendships more easily and approaches others more readily
    examines external issues more accurately and processes information
        from external world more readily
    has more free cognitive channels for information extraction because he
        is less preoccupied with himself
Source: Modified after Coopersmith (1967).

The behavioral correlates of self-esteem shown in Box 8-2 are derived from experimental developmental studies by Coopersmith (1967). They all are elaborations of the motive systems. Many of them evolve from the attachment motive, but all of the motive systems are represented, most notably the cognitive motive. There is a clear difference between high and low self-esteem persons. The person with high self-esteem expects success, asserts himself more, and is more actively involved. The opposite happens in low-esteem.

The level of perceptual skill influences self-esteem. The person with low self-esteem is not idly indulging himself in a totally unwarranted self-opinion; his perceptual skills are actually less than adequate. Thus, low self-esteem is associated with decreased ability to recognize when someone is being friendly (Jacobs et al., 1971). These inadequate perceptions also give rise to inadequate social relationships (U'ren, 1971; Coombs, 1969). In one area, high and low self-esteem people are alike: They both want a greater amount of approval from others. On the other hand, the person in the middle of the self-esteem scale is not so strongly concerned with approval (Kimble & Helmreich, 1972).

Antecedents of self-esteem. Coopersmith (1967) reported that development of self-esteem depends upon certain parental variables. When parents themselves have high self-esteem; are emotionally stable, self-reliant, and resilient; are less coercive; provide consistent encouragement and support; establish a reasonable balance between care and autonomy, and evidence a compatible relationship, they are sound models for the development of high self-esteem in their offspring.

Coopersmith also found that high self-esteem in preadolescent boys is associated with attitudes of positive acceptance by their mothers, who nevertheless are also able to be firm when necessary. If these children are punished, the father is the usual agent, and such punishment is likely to be seen by the child as justified.

In his work with both boys and girls, Sears (1970) generally supports the conclusions of Coopersmith. Parental warmth is an especially important source of high self-esteem. Dominating fathers adversely affect the self-esteem of their sons but not of their daughters.

Life Style and the Motive Systems

Each individual develops not only a set of internal representations about himself, but also a schema for perceiving and functioning in the external world. A person's view of the world, and of its operational requirements, together with self-concept, determine his life style. According to

Adler, this perceptual blueprint is a program unique to each individual. Centered on the guiding self-ideal, it contains the perceptual programs that direct the four motives.

As a result of longitudinal studies over the life span of her subjects, Bronson (1966, 1972) concluded that each person is characterized by a life style consisting of characteristic attitudes, abilities, and traits. The central orientations of any life style seem to develop early as a result of the interaction of interpersonal experience, physiological events, and perhaps the unfolding of genetic endowment. Using tests and interviews, as part of the Berkeley Growth Study, she was able to measure a variety of behavioral digressions, for example, cautious/adventurous, grasping/generous, fearful/unafraid. Certain of these scales clustered together, so that Bronson was left with three main clusters. The first cluster was *withdrawal/expressiveness,* a measure of openness to experience and expression. The second, *reactivity/placidity,* concerned itself with the intensity of emotional reaction to environmental information. Both of these behavioral styles were relatively stable over time (from childhood through adolescence into young adulthood). A third cluster, *passivity/dominance,* while loaded with more dimensions, seemed more subject to situational variables.

Gecas (1971) related self-perception to interaction with significant others; through interpersonal contact, the life style becomes consolidated. Self-concept remains more stable if confirmed through interaction with others. A stable self-concept also confers an increased sense of security, leading to a resistance to change in self-perception.

The perceptual program (life style) for each motive system does not change. What does change, over time, is *how the motives are symbolized.* For example, the way an individual responds to a threat to security in specific situations, either by fleeing or by fighting, tends to remain consistent. What we flee from or fight against (symbols of threat), and what we flee to (symbols of security) change with development.

The symbols of attachment change with development. The first attachment is to the mother. Later, the "security blanket" becomes a transitional object. Eventually, the symbol of attachment may be an ideal, a cause that is loved as much as the original attachment object.

Bronson found two main lines of movement toward the competence motive—withdrawal/expressiveness. The withdrawer avoids areas in which he is unsure of himself; the expressive person, on the other hand, will be challenged by difficulty. Competence symbols change over time. The small boy measures his competence according to athletic skills, the adolescent girl according to the standards of her peer group, the young adult by success in a career or personal living.

Differentiation of the Motives

Between the ages of 6 and 12, noticeable changes take place in differentiation, integration, and symbolic representation of the motive systems. Preadolescents are industrious and actively seek to master their world (competence motive). Interestingly enough, although they play in groups, preadolescents do not yet develop strong interest in each other as persons; it is the activity itself which is the focus of interest and which sustains the

Figure 8-1   The preadolescent is a very busy child. Source: Courtesy Marian Bernstein

relationship. Self-classification takes place, abetted by group membership (boys play with boys and girls with girls). Exploratory movements are common, especially as boys try to become brave; girls' efforts in this direction are thwarted to some degree by socialization to seek security through attachment to a protector. Thus aggression is socialized more positively in boys and dependency in girls.

As the child grows larger and stronger he acquires more motor skills. Athletic skills increase. At age 6, only 35 percent can successfully tie the bowknot used in the Stanford-Binet test; at age 9, this becomes 94 percent (Strang, 1959). The ability to exchange ideas with others improves (Alvy, 1968); also an increasing ability to understand relations leads the preadolescent to have a more naturalistic and less magical view of the world. He shows increased ability for abstract thought (symbolization). Word games become fascinating and words themselves become tools for manipulating others.

Reasoning improves. Elkind (1971) found consistent growth in concept development, especially in concepts of classification and relationships. Form and spatial concepts improve (Smith & Smith, 1966; Blake, Wright, & Waechter, 1970). Number concept grows (Cohen, 1972). The growth of all these skills involves differentiation of the competence and cognitive motives. The growing child is learning how to *do;* industry is his major task (Erikson, 1950).

In the middle years of childhood, the child's strong attachment to the mother begins to wane. Hollander (1964) points out that the peer group becomes a supplementary agent of socialization to the family.

Gender role demands encourage different socialization of security-related behavior. Horrocks reasons that preadolescents are learning how to cope with and master others in social situations, by the "law of the jungle" (1976, p. 49). How this coping behavior is expressed shows marked sex differences. Seymour Feshbach (1970) found that boys are more physically aggressive, while girls are aggressive in nonphysical ways. Independently (1969), and in collaboration with her husband (1973), Norma Feshbach concluded that girls use rejection and unfriendliness as expressions of aggression. However, Maccoby and Jacklin (1974) find that boys are more aggressive than girls verbally as well as physically.

Self-Classification and the Process of Identification

As the child approaches puberty, he classifies himself according to his similarities to and differences from others. These may include awareness of race, religion, and socioeconomic class in cultures where these are important. He learns to think of himself as academically skilled or unskilled, strong or weak, pretty or ugly, red-haired or black-haired. All self-classification consists of information about the self. All identifications consist of learning instructions about what one is and what one is supposed to do. Perhaps the most important typing of all is that of gender—male or female.

Gender Identification

All cultures have prescribed roles for males and females. Role specifications are sometimes very rigid and may be very different for each sex. Margaret Mead (1949) found three different types of cultures in her anthropological studies. In one type, male-female roles were similar to ours—that is, males tended to be dominant; in the second type, females were dominant; and in the third type (which was rarer) the sexes had equal status.

Biological studies have linked gender behavior to physiological factors, such as hormones (Maccoby & Jacklin, 1974). The relationship between hormones and sexual behavior is a complicated one. Injection of testosterone in humans increases aggressive behavior in both sexes. However, injection of progestin leads to passivity in the male but increases aggression in the female (Ford & Beach, 1951). Girls born to mothers who received testosterone during pregnancy show less doll play and more aggressive behavior during middle childhood. However, biological males with the external appearance of females (false hermaphrodites) who were raised as females maintained a female identity all through life (Money & Ehrhardt, 1972).

The images of masculinity and femininity differ from subculture to subculture and from age group to age group. Forbes (1966) found clearly delineated masculine and feminine roles in Chicano families. The feminine role required submissive behavior; while the male role took two forms: for the married man, dominance over wife and children and for the single male, evidence of being a successful lover (machismo). In a longitudinal study of such gender role prescriptions, Mussen (1962) found the following: Adolescent males with traditional masculine interests (toughness, disinterest in arts, and so on) showed self-confidence and feelings of adequacy and leadership. At age 30, these same males retained their interests but were lacking in self-confidence, feelings of adequacy and leadership. Indeed, they were no longer of the same high status. Big muscles are important at age 14 but lose their importance by age 30! Some cultures believe that it is unmanly for a boy to express emotions (except anger) freely. In others, men are emotionally expressive without experiencing any loss of masculinity. Any exaggerated or rigid definition of gender-prescribed social behavior seems to be misguided.

Learning and cognition in gender behavior. Gender identification begins at an early age through observational learning and reinforcement of culturally desired behavior by socializing agents. The school-age child clearly understands the concepts male and female and their associated meanings (Hartap & Zook, 1960; Kagan, Hosken & Watson, 1961). Certain behaviors are prescribed for females, while others are prescribed for males. In a cross-cultural survey, Sears, Maccoby, and Levin (1957) document that boys are given more freedom to express aggression, whereas girls are encouraged to express propriety, dependency, and submission. "Prosocial" aggression (preaching moralistic admonition) is acceptable for girls but considered "sissy" for boys.

Barry, Child, and Bacon (1959) found a broad congruence between cultures in socialization pressures for gender behavior with respect to the differentiation of motives. Specifically, nurturance and obedience (differentiations of the attachment motive) are highly loaded for girls, while achievement and self-reliance (differentiations of the competence motive) are highly loaded for boys.

Kohlberg (1966), consistent with his Piagetian view, postulates that the growing child's cognitive structure allows him to enhance certain common features that distinguish one object class from another—in other words, to abstract. For Kohlberg, this process of abstraction determines how children arrive at their own gender identities. In a cognitive context, sextyping, like any other form of typing, simplifies the world and permits more efficient information management. Economy of management is gained at the price of decreased discrimination and inaccuracy. Simplification may become oversimplification; that is, typing may become stereotyping.

Effects of gender identification. Essentially, gender identification consists of acquiring information about how to behave as a male or a female and giving oneself instructions for which role to play. Once gender identity has been established, appropriate practice ensues and sex differences appear. Keough (1965) found a wide range of differences in motor ability. Sex-linked behavior practice is reinforced by the sharp separation between the sexes, their tendency to maintain distance in public, and their open display of contempt for each other (Cohen, 1972).

Changing stereotypes and sex-role bias. In spite of the fact that male/female stereotyping is changing, the traditional attitudes of the past linger on. In one study, Deaux and Emswiller (1974) found that successful performance by a woman of a masculine interest task was attributed to luck, whereas the same performance by a man was attributed to skill. On a feminine task, there was no difference of interpretation.

Like all stereotyping, locking men and women into specific categories or roles has interfered with the socialization of both. A new standard of sex-role behavior may be established around the concept of *androgyny*, a form of behavior relatively free of sex-role stereotype. The androgynous person is more field-independent in sexually stereotyped issues. Maccoby (1966) found that boys and girls who are strongly sex typed (show few of the traits and interests of the opposite sex) have an overall lower intelligence, lower spatial ability, and lower creativity. Bem (1976) studied correlates of androgynous behavior in both men and women. Androgynous persons respond more effectively to more situations than either stereotyped males or females.

Theories of Sex Typing

There are three major approaches to sex-typing behavior: psychoanalytic theory, self-classification (a cognitive approach), and observational learning studies.

Psychoanalytic theory. For Freud, typical sexual behavior grows out of certain developmental events. The little boy discovers that he has a penis, which is a source of great pleasure. He experiences erotic desires for his mother and sees his father as a rival for mother's affection. This triangle constitutes the Oedipal situation, which the child can resolve in one of three ways: (a) repressing the desire for mother out of fear that father will harm him (castration anxiety); (b) denying his desire for mother and shifting his desire to father (the homosexual solution); (c) identifying with the aggressive aspects of father and becoming an aggressive male. Masculine behavior is thus determined by the way the Oedipal situation is resolved. The little girl discovers that she has no penis and wants one. She turns to father in the hope that he will provide one for her. Thus, she tries to please her father and be seductive with him. Since the penis is a thrusting and penetrating organ, it is natural for the male to behave aggressively. The vagina is a receiving organ, so it is natural for the female to be passive-receptive to the male. The male and female social roles thus grow out of the anatomy of each sex.

Self-Classification. Social expectations exert a strong influence on behavior development. The custom of dressing boy infants in blue and girls in pink is only the beginning of a long chain of differing expectations that boys and girls will meet in their development. Parents also define the child to himself, both in words ("You are a boy and boys don't cry") and in interaction with the child (a father will teach his son to play baseball, but is more likely to show off his daughter on a Sunday afternoon walk). These expectations and definitions influence the formation of the child's self-concept. The child learns to classify herself according to sex (Kohlberg, 1966), and then seeks to learn the appropriate role behaviors. Sexual identity is thus largely a matter of self-classification influenced by social definition, social expectations (role demands), social reinforcement, and the imitation of suitable models.

Self-classification is a cognitive operation and will depend upon the child's cognitive categories and style. Undoubtedly, biology, learning, and cognitive variables all influence sex typing. However, cognitive factors seem to have the last word. Homosexual preferences and transsexual surgery are evidence that anatomy is not an absolute ruler.

Observational learning. The small child of either sex imitates the behaviors of the adults around him. Identification thus occurs through *modeling.* In addition, certain behaviors are reinforced by the parents. Masculine behavior in boys wins approval, while feminine behavior arouses disapproval. Later, observational learning occurs with peers of the same sex. Both boys and girls model themselves after admired peers.

Identification and Observational Learning

The foremost exponent of observational learning is Bandura, whose work merits our further inspection because of its vast influence on contemporary psychology.

Academic psychology remained occupied with reinforcement theory until Bandura was able to show that much behavior in the growing child is the result of imitation or observational learning (Bandura, 1969a). He uses the term *observational learning* to explain behavior produced by exposure to models. Synonyms for observational learning are imitation, identification, and modeling. Bandura (1971a) identifies the following sub-processes in observational learning: Attention, retention, reproduction, and motivation. This formulation integrates traditional learning with cognitive considerations. Attention and retention are processes for information extraction and storage. Reproduction, the actual act of imitation, combines information retrieval and usage by recruiting the motor apparatus of the organism.

By including motivation as a sub-process, Bandura distinguishes between knowledge and performance. We don't always act on the basis of what we know and we don't always know the basis on which we act. Whether a person uses what he has learned depends also on the goals he has formulated for himself.

Variables Which Influence Observational Learning. Variables which influence observational learning include the relative nurturance of the model's behavior, the power or influence of the model, similarity between model and observer, reinforcement of imitative behavior, the availability of appropriate models, and the self-esteem and competence of the observer. Bandura and Huston (1961) found that models who display nurturing behavior are more likely to be imitated. Imitation is also more likely when the model has a position of power (exerts control over the child) (Bandura, Ross, & Ross, 1963; Hetherington, 1965; Hetherington & Frankie, 1967): In a study by Mischel and Grusec (1966) children imitated the behavior of a new teacher who was liberal with rewards.

Models of the same sex will have more influence than models of the opposite sex. However, children will imitate the parent or teacher of either sex who seems to be dominant. In addition, we would expect that a model who resembles what the child aspires to be would be more imitated (Mussen, Conger, & Kagan, 1974). Wiggins and his colleagues (1976) point out that people who have low self-esteem, who are incompetent at a particular task, and who are anxious and uncertain, all tend to observe others closely and imitate their actions. There are, no doubt, other variables, not yet identified, which influence modeling.

What Is Imitated?   The development of language in children is an excellent example of observational learning. Children learn the proper use of language from models even without reinforcement (Bandura & Harris, 1966). The fact that observational learning does not require reinforcement has been shown in experiments by Bandura and Walters (1963). Children watched a film in which the model's behavior was rewarded, punished, or had no consequences. In a subsequent free play session, the children imitated the rewarded model the most and the punished model the least. However, upon request, the children were well able to imitate the punished model. Bandura and Walters conclude that learning occurs through observation, even when there is no reinforcement. Reinforcement affects which behaviors are performed, but does not affect ability to learn. What is observed can be learned.

It is obvious that observation contributes to the learning of sex roles and other appropriate social roles. In addition, the evidence suggests that roles which carry power and prestige are often imitated. Styles of interpersonal relationship are learned through observation and modeling. Competence behavior (that which works) is imitated. In addition, ideals are imitated. Keniston (1971) has shown that the so-called radical students tend to come from homes in which the parents hold liberal ideals. Fictitious models in television, motion pictures, or literature can also give rise to observational learning.

A Cognitive Perspective on Observational Learning.   Since the early work of Bandura and Walters (1963), observational learning has been the subject of voluminous research because it offered a viable alternative to the inadequacies of reinforcement theory and psychoanalysis. Reinforcement theory's emphasis on reward seemed to ignore common sense knowledge and cultural wisdom, which tell us that children learn more from watching their parents than from what their parents tell them. Kohlberg (1969) points out that imitation should be viewed in the context of the total adaptive behavior for which cognitive structures exist. In their search for information, these structures provide an intrinsic motivation for imitation. Unlike Freud, who believed that the child imitates because he depends on the parent, Kohlberg believes that the child depends on the parent because he needs a model to imitate.

This linking of imitation and cognition has been subscribed to by Bandura himself (1965, 1976), who hypothesized that reinforcement provides an informational cue which increases imitation because it informs the subject of the consequences of behaving similarly to a model. Liebert and Fernandez (1970) produced experimental verification of this hypothesis. Furthermore, like Kohlberg, Bandura believes that imitation occurs in the first place because innate cognitive structures so predispose the child. Thelen and his co-workers (1972) have shown more specifically that vicarious reward associated with spontaneous imitation of a model only increases spontaneous imitation in subjects who are given an expectancy to perform. Not only does cognition influence imitation, but also the subject can choose to imitate or not. In this context, Stendler's discussion of the link between dependency and competence (see Chapter 5) has a cognitive perspective. The child will choose to please the parent only if it is perceived by the child as consistent with his own goals.

The term *identification* has been used in various, sometimes confusing, ways. Given the cognitive context we have just used, it would probably be better to speak of self-identification—that process by which a person recognizes who and what he is and what he wants to become. Observation influences what is learned; reinforcement, what is acted out; social roles, what one is; but the internal perceptual program identifies who one is and how we perceive ourselves.

ADOLESCENCE

Differentiation of the Motives

As the child enters the period of adolescence, motives become organized around the dominant goal so that certain autonomous differentiations of the motives emerge. These autonomous differentiations of the four motives remain consistent with the life plan formulated in the dominant goal but assume new *symbolizations* (perceptual signs of how the motives are differentiating). Thus the adolescent reveals new ways of seeking satisfaction,

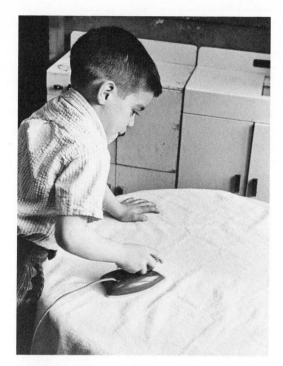

Figure 8-2   Imitation is one way of learning. Source: Courtesy Marian Bernstein

experiencing frustration, and being threatened. Examples of motives which become autonomous and important in adolescence include *status, peer affiliation, emancipation, heterosexuality,* and the search for a meaningful *identity* to provide a sense of direction to one's behavior. These autonomous motives remain interrelated. Horney believes that the search for status is a substitute for the desire for love (attachment motive). For Dreikurs (1971), status is conferred in the normal course of events through social belongingness, while competitive striving for status is a mistaken way of trying to belong (attachment motive). Some evidence for these points of view is offered by Eibl-Eibesfeldt's studies on baboons (1971). In baboons, dominance adheres to that adult who is friendly and able to win the sympathies of others.

The Self as an Organizer of Adolescent Motive Differentiation

Several studies have provided evidence that adolescence is a time when personality becomes increasingly differentiated and hierarchically organized. Gecas (1971) and Levine (1958) studied the evolving self-concept in the adolescent and found that it develops through interaction with the environment in a sequential series of levels of self-perception. All the changes seem to be in the direction of confirming what the adolescent already believes about himself. Degenhardt (1971) and Mullener and Laird (1971) found continuous modification and differentiation of the self-image from age 10 to college. However, such growth is uneven and differs from individual to individual, but always moves in the direction of differentiation, hierarchical integration, and greater flexibility and abstraction of thought (Leskow & Smock, 1970). Horrocks (1976) believes this development is in the service of the main business of adolescence—to build and confirm a stable concept of self. Box 8-3 contains a summary description of the main adolescent tasks.

The adolescent's sense of identity depends on how the motives of adolescence are being satisfied. Jones (1965) found that adolescents who reach physical maturity early (especially boys) have a higher self-image (as part of their sense of identity) and are more at ease with peers. Faust (1975) showed that girls (ages 11 to 14) who matured earlier had more prestige among their peers. Conversely, the late maturer must find other ways to obtain recognition. One instance is the less developed adolescent who attracts attention by becoming the classroom clown.

Box 8-3	Differentiation of Motives during Adolescence
Emancipation	The development of autonomy to the point where one becomes free of the constraints and control of guiding adults. It is a state of independence and of increased self-determination and self-responsibility. *Adolescent rebellion is sometimes directed by the emancipation motive.*
Peer Acceptance	Personal acceptance rather than shared activity. To feel liked and valued for oneself facilitates the formation of identity. Clique formation in high school is an example of a social institution for peer acceptance. It is *a stage in experiential movement toward intimacy and heterosexuality.*
Sexuality	Being acceptable to and successful with members of the opposite sex. It includes erotic and romantic experiences. *It is preparation for long-term love commitments.*
Ideals and Morality	The search for a philosophy of life. It provides a set of rules for behaving in the world, standards to pursue, priorities to order time and activity, criteria by which conflict may be resolved, and directions for action. It is the beginning of the *search for meaning.*
Identity	For Erikson (1968), identity is concerned with who and what one is and negotiating the meaning of one's life. *Identity depends on how the other tasks are met.*

During adolescence, the agency of socialization shifts from the parents to the peer group (Farnsworth, 1967). Gold and Douvan (1969) report that adolescents pick friends who are similar to themselves. In all the studies we have cited so far, the adolescent's preoccupation with security and attachment is a recurring theme. However, cultural and subcultural factors also influence how these motives are differentiated. Maccoby and Modiane (1966), for example, found that the peer group is less important in Mexico than in the United States, so that the competence and attachment motives unfold somewhat differently in these two cultures. Child-rearing styles also influence adolescent behavior in terms of how much control, affection, and interpersonal involvement the young person evidences (Carlson, 1963; Douvan & Adelson, 1966). Mussen and his associates (1963) showed that parental affection was important for the development of security, confidence, and optimal social relationships. Small families tend to produce more independent children (Lefrancois, 1976). Too much or too little parental affection and control lead to adjustment difficulties with peers.

Coleman (1961) and McDill and Coleman (1965) discussed the effect of family and peer experiences on the relative ease of *emancipation.* In general, high school seniors who are confident about their futures (for example, expect to succeed in college) are independent, responsible, and prefer intimate relationships in small groups. The home background is one in which the parents are themselves successful and have a good relationship. Overall, the most effective parental style seems to be an optimum amount of affection, guidance, and respect for the child's skills in a democratic atmosphere.

Sexuality

Sexual behavior in adolescence differs from culture to culture. Margaret Mead (1949) has compared the vast differences in adolescent behavior that exist between the Samoan of the South Pacific and the white American. In the United States, the public acceptability of certain kinds of adolescent sexual behavior has also changed (Kaats & Davis, 1970). Since 1960, there has been an increase in reported premarital sexual intercourse for women. No matter what the cultural customs, heterosexual activity of some type, more or less sanctioned by the culture, is a challenge facing every adolescent as biological promptings and gender role demand.

The heterosexual exploratory behavior of adolescence will lead to the intimacy and caring of adulthood. Adolescents have to learn the skills of heterosexuality well enough to establish affiliation with the opposite sex. One important social institution for establishing such relationships is courting, a vehicle for bringing together the two sexes according to an established code of conduct. Skill in courting depends in part upon how well one learns the code of conduct. Courting experiences prepare the way for later relationships between couples.

Although the adolescent is physically capable of becoming a parent, he is seldom psychologically ready for the responsibilities of parenthood and marriage. In cultures where adolescents marry young, they usually live with older adults who provide a supportive social network. In the United States, teen-age marriages end in divorce three to four times more often than adult marriages (Landers & Landers, 1963). Since in 1977, one out of every two marriages ended in divorce, the outlook for teen-age marriages is poor indeed.

Like all motives, sex and love have their learned symbols. While the elaboration of symbols depends in part on cognitive maturation, it is also heavily influenced by cultural experience. Some cultures have institutions in which adolescents are more adequately trained in the skills necessary for effective heterosexual adaptation. In Kenya, young Masai males and females, following biological puberty, live in heterosexual camps where they learn not only the competencies associated with each adult sex role, but also practice lovemaking and the ingredients of a successful male-female relationship. By the time they marry, they have relatively realistic expectations and adequate perceptual constructs for successful marriage.

Although we live in a society that prizes competence, stresses education for living, and preaches "practice makes perfect," this ideal has not extended to sex. In this area, the adolescent is still left to learn by himself, often furtively, and from his peers who may know less than he. Even adolescents do not know what is being done by their peers. Collins (1974) reports a discrepancy between what adolescents think their peers are doing and their actual behavior. Adolescents consistently overestimated the frequency of heterosexual intercourse among their peers. Girls believed that 66 percent of their peers were engaging in intercourse; the actual figure was 28 percent. For boys, the corresponding figures are 91 and 45 percent. One wonders how often the teen-age girl engages in intercourse because she feels it is the thing to do rather than something she wants to do. Cobliner (1974) found that many adolescent girls became involved in sex simply out of a wish to be accepted or to feel like the "others."

This last study again points to the importance of perception as the determiner of our world view and consequently our behavior. Perceptual expectancy transcends reality. Actually, the heterosexual motive involves all the basic motive systems. It is a form of attachment, provides a feeling of security, and is also used as a measure of competence. Perhaps, above all, the experience itself is that aspect of sexuality we seek the most (cognitive motive).

Cognitive Development and the Symbols of Morality

The perceptual symbols for the sexual motive provide instructions not only for what to do in sexual behavior, but also for what not to do. Some of the instructions fall within the realm of morality. In Box 8-3, we defined the concern with morality and ideals as a search for a philosophy of life, with a set of rules for behaving in the world that would create a positive meaning for life. According to Piaget, moral conscience develops apace with the corresponding stages of cognitive maturation.

Applying Piaget's theory to the basic developmental transformations in cognitive structure, Kohlberg (1969) emphasized that transformations move in the direction of balance (*reciprocity*) between the action of the organism and the environment upon each other. Furthermore, cognitive and affective developments parallel each other.

Kohlberg studied the principle of reciprocity in the development of moral conscience. According to Piaget, moral conscience can only develop when the child understands reversible operations. This understanding rests upon the previous understanding of conservation, which emerges at about 9 years of age (see Chapter 7). By empirical study, Kohlberg tried to demonstrate that the development of moral conscience paralleled the stages of cognitive development. One could not act morally until one had attained a certain logical understanding. Box 8-4 shows the cognitive stages in the development of morality.

Further research demonstrated that the level of moral development depends not only on cognitive ability (Kohlberg & Turiel, 1971; Turiel, 1974) but also on the opportunity to develop reciprocal role-taking skills (Selman, 1971). Adolescents do not reach the top level of Kohlberg's moral

Box 8-4	Relationship Between Cognitive Stage and Moral Understanding*
Conservation:	The child is able to understand that changing the shape, location, or relationship of an object does not change its mass or weight.
Reversibility:	The child understands that if A = B, then B = A.
Reciprocity:	The child understands that what applies to one person can also apply to another. He can recognize that others may have desires similar to his own.
Moral Conscience:	The child understands that the reason for moral behavior is to avoid hurting others.

* Each stage depends upon the attainment of the previous stage.

development scale (Turiel, 1974). This may be related to the fact that not all adolescents have mastered the stage of formal operations.

Turiel (1974) showed that moral conscience continues to develop through adolescence and that the developmental transformations proceed through *disequilibration*—that is, when previous explanations fail to satisfy, the individual must reconsider the situation and arrive at a new explanation. The six stages in the development of moral conscience, related as they are to the maturational sequence, have been systematized by Kohlberg (1976) and are presented in Table 8-1.

Identity, the Self, and Cognitive Style

As the perceptual system develops, it becomes differentiated and less assimilated by the field (Forgus & Melamed, 1976). Adolescents, of course, must also learn to differentiate themselves from the social field, a task that is facilitated by perceptual differentiation. Field independence increases through adolescence, depending partially on the type of socialization experiences available to the subject (Witkin, Goodenough, & Karp, 1967; Witkin, 1976). As formal operations are established, adolescents become more introspective and analytical (Mussen, Conger, & Kagan, 1974); in learning

Table 8-1   Developmental Stages in the Differentiation of Morality According to Kohlberg

Level and Stage	Cognitive Differentiation of the Morality Motive
Level I: Preconventional (concrete opinions)	(Purpose of moral action)
Stage 1. Punishment and obedience orientation	To avoid punishment
Stage 2. Instrumental and individualistic orientation	To win reward or benefit
Level II: Conventional (low level of formal operations)	
Stage 3. Pleasing others orientation	To win approval and avoid disapproval
Stage 4. Law and order orientation	To avoid being considered dishonorable
Level III: Post-conventional, (autonomous or principled level)	
Stage 5. Social contract orientation	To maintain the respect of peers and the community
Stage 6. Universal ethical principle orientation	To avoid violating one's own principles

Source: After Kohlberg (1969, 1976).

to use intellectualization as a coping device, they are often preoccupied with their own thoughts (Blos, 1970; Conger, 1973). While trying to emancipate themselves from parental restrictions, they often fall prey to the tyranny of peer conformity. They may not know how to be comfortable with their own emotions, realistic about their own ideas, or patient with themselves. Nevertheless, optimal development leads to self-identity: confirmation of self-chosen goals, refinement of style, and self-definition (Sealey & Cattell, 1966).

ADULTHOOD

The adult is more settled than the adolescent, more reflective and less impulsive. Because time goes by faster, adults are likely to find it easier to make long-range plans and design projects that will require a number of years to reach fruition. They can consciously direct energies in more persistent ways. If adolescents are more concerned with finding out who they are, psychologically mature adults, having attained a much clearer concept of their own identity, are able to see further into the future and no longer require immediate rewards. The idealistic excesses of adolescence also become tempered by realistic considerations. The person who has matured into psychological adulthood has a more integrated personality: The value and moral systems are usually more in harmony with the motive systems and with behavior.

Differentiation of Motives in Adulthood

In the usual course of events, the young adult acquires a mate, a dwelling place, a family, some material possessions, and a field of endeavor. These are all responsibilities, some of them perhaps to be maintained for the rest of one's life. The greater commitment demanded by one's mate and progeny and the home itself soon supplant in importance all the previous loved ones and close companions. This remarkable change in priorities is a biological adaptation that as a facilitator of species survival is observable in many animal species. The power of love between the sexes is so great that a new bond is formed which loosens old bonds. Both the individual and the species are served.

Love and the Family

Sexual love in couples serves two functions: the preservation of the species and the continued bonding of the couple. In the adult, erotic love becomes important for establishing attachment and maintaining it. Eibl-Eibesfeldt (1971) points out that the practice of maintaining a bond

Box 8-5 Differentiation of Motives in Adulthood

Love: Attachment to a particular person with shared intimacy, sexual activity, and long-term commitment. *Mutual devotion and cherishing is required.*

Marriage and family: A commitment to be responsible for the welfare of others who will constitute a small and important group of people to be cherished. The task includes building and protecting a nest. As in other mammals, parents are never so brave and ferocious as when protecting a nest. Of all human love, *parental love comes the closest to being unconditional,* approaching the love which St. Paul attributed to Jesus.

Career: A commitment to a field of endeavor, whether in pursuit of a gainful occupation or making a home. Talents and interests are expressed in a career, leading to personal satisfaction. Such activity both affords the independence necessary to be a nurturant rather than a succorant and allows the person to make a useful contribution to society. *Through a career, the person satisfies self, family, and society.*

Community: Whereas the adolescent examined society at large, the adult examines the community in which he lives. Adults show more respect for the community and the property of others than teenagers. They will not engage in vandalism because they have developed a *sense of belonging to the community.*

through sex is a peculiarly human characteristic. Other pair-bonding animals do not engage in sexual intercourse except when the female is in heat. The human female is receptive to intercourse at any phase of the estrous cycle, and her sexual appetites are more influenced by psychology than physiology. Appetite in both sexes continues long past the age of fertility. Human beings are by nature more active sexually than other animals (Morris, 1967), partly because the long period of human dependency requires that the female parent have a way of keeping the male parent bonded to her during the time their offspring are maturing. In humans, erotic love not only serves this function but continues to provide a bond for the couple long after the children are reared.

Most of us have had the experience of falling in and out of love. Romance feeds on excitement and novelty rather than on sameness. There must be other incentives as well as erotic love to keep a couple together. The desire to protect and raise children seems to be one of the most important incentives. Erikson (1968) uses the term *generativity* to cover this de-

While our society is monogamous, over 50 percent of the societies studied by ethnologists are polygamous. Apparently, erotic bonding sometimes fades or shifts from one person to another. Bonding may take place with more than one person. According to Eibl-Eibesfeldt (1971), this may be one reason for the high divorce rate in Western society. Insights from anthropology and ethnology may help us better cope with troublesome issues of divorce and marriages in conflict.

velopmental differentiation of attachment. The infant and young child exert a strong attractive influence on both parents and this appeal is hard to resist. The act of cherishing is a pleasant one for parents. The appeal of infantile features has been used by makers of dolls and stuffed animals to make them more attractive (see Figure 8-3).

In addition to the family bond, other factors keep male and female together. Husbands and wives continue to protect and nurture each other. Familiarity and continued close contact produce attachment, security, and comfortable role competence. We prefer that which we know and do well, provided we are successful in the relationship.

The symbols of attractiveness change with changes in social climate and in personal cognitive development. A woman will be attracted by a man's kindness as well as his dominance. A man will be attracted by a woman's yielding as well as her nurturance. A young man will perhaps value a submissive female while an older man may prefer a more spirited one. Current movements toward equality of the sexes may produce great changes in the symbols of attractiveness. As society evolves and social institutions and practices are able to provide increased satisfaction of the basic motives, increased democratization and equality between sexes can permit better solutions to the problems that occur in marital and family life (Dreikurs, 1971).

Successful families. Psychologists such as White (1975) have pointed out that successful parents tend to have successful children, suggesting that some family styles are more conducive to success than others. One empirical study of young college men revealed some of these successful family styles (Heath, 1965). Important antecedent variables of success in young adults include a successful father, harmonious relations between the parents (including satisfactory sexual adjustment between them), and cooperation and mutual respect among the siblings. Successful young adults are autonomous, realistic, have a constructive fantasy life, cope well with anxiety, and prefer small-group intimacy to large-group anonymity. In general, they show broad cognitive schemata. Lewis and his co-workers (1976) stud-

Figure 8-3 The "infant schema": the attributes of a small child (big head in relation to body, high prominent forehead, chubby cheeks, short rounded limbs, small mouth for sucking, etc.) are often greatly exaggerated in the dolls produced by the toy industry, which increases the protectiveness-releasing effect of these "cute" little objects. In commercial art the childish attributes of women are frequently exaggerated as well as the sexual attributes. Source: I. Eibl-Eibesfeldt, (London: Methuen, 1971), p. 21.

ied characteristics of families in which family members functioned well both in their own lives and in their interrelationships (healthy families). Such families evidence affiliative attitudes about human encounter, respect for the views of others, high levels of initiative and problem-solving competency, nonauthoritarian exercise of parental power, shared leadership by parents, closeness, and a strong affectional bond between the parents.

Vocation

Most adults must also engage in career endeavors, and these activities not only help the individual fulfill his motive systems but also contribute to the welfare of the community.

Effects of gender identification on vocation. Some effects of gender identification and sexual stereotyping have been discussed earlier in this chapter. Sex is an important influence in the choice of a vocation. Mead (1949) has pointed out that every known society has divided labor according to whether it is more appropriate for a male or a female—however, not necessarily on the basis of any biological rationale. In some societies women are considered too weak to do heavy work; in others, women carry heavy burdens "because their heads are stronger than men's." Thus the division of labor depends to a great extent upon the particular mores of the culture (Mead, 1949, pp. 7–8). Another factor is whether the culture is pastoral, nomadic, or industrial. In less industrialized societies, the father often need not leave the home in order to work and the son is able, at an early age, to appreciate masculine productivity. By the same token, in cottage industry societies, the mother can be a model not only of a domestic housekeeper, but also of an employed wage earner. Sexual characteristics become stereotyped (Broverman, Vogel, Broverman, Clarkson, & Rosencrantz, 1972).

In our society, women are seen as less competent, independent, objective, and logical than men. The other half of this self-fulfilling prophecy is that men are stereotyped as less sensitive, warm, and emotionally expressive. The traditional prejudice of contemporary society is clearly revealed by the fact that such "male" traits are considered more desirable than "female" traits. Sexual stereotypes continue to exert a major influence on vocational choice.

No matter what division of labor society may wish to assign, some factors have remained relatively constant. In most cultures, women are the caretakers of children and men assume the tasks of providing protection. Aside from any limitations that might attach to this arrangement, there seems to be no necessary relationship between sex and vocation.

One effect of sterotyping in our society is the belief that women are more affiliative than achievement oriented. From her study of the achievement motive in women, Hoffman (1972) concluded that "females have higher affiliative needs . . . and achievement behavior (in females) is motivated by a desire to please." Bardwick (1971) hypothesized that achievement and affiliation are independent motives in men but combined in women, who strive for affiliative achievement and success in interpersonal relationships, especially as mother and wife. Horner (1972) hypothesized that women have a "fear of success," perhaps the result of conflict between competitive strivings and sex-role training to please and affiliate. Most of these research findings are controversial, however, because they have been predicated on procedures dominated by the male outlook. For example, in attempting to arouse achievement fantasies, McClelland uses only pictures of males succeeding at various tasks. There are no pictures of females achieving, and thus the achievement motive in women has never really been tested. Research and cultural bias reflect a lack of clear conception of female vocation except in submissive roles. Tresemer (1973) criticized Horner's methods and conclusions, claiming that she never validated the existence of a "fear of success" motive and that her results can be explained in other ways, for example, that successful affiliation is a symbol of achievement for women.

Other factors that operate in the choice of a vocation are described by Kimmel (1974). They include background factors such as social class, ethnic group, intelligence, and race; role models' personal experience and psychological motives that result therefrom; personal interests and preferences and personality factors.

Some Developmental Considerations of Adult Motive Differentiation

Kuhlen (1968) found that several factors were involved in the unfolding of motives and incentives, among them:

1. *Changes in arousal cues, environmental stimuli, and expectations.* Adults are exposed to stimuli and expectations essentially different from those faced by the adolescent. The adult life situation includes many new categories of experience such as having a home and family of one's own. Different life situations require different arousal cues and foster different expectations.

2. *Satisfaction of motives.* Desire for emancipation and heterosexual activity have usually been established by this time, and the sense of personal identity is solidifying. Thus, the basis upon which one begins to solve problems is quite different from that in adolescence.

3. *Age-related frustration of motives.* As the adult approaches the middle years, some of his aspirations change. Neugarten (1968) found that people who were risk takers at age 40 become accommodators at age 50. Kuhlen points out that women over age 30 see themselves as having less chance for marriage than they did earlier, and men over age 40 see less chance for career success if they

are not already well on their way. Such frustration normally leads to a lowering of aspirations.

4. *Social expectations and realities.* As people grow older, they are faced with a large variety of new realities. Illness, death of an aged parent, job promotion, career changes, and all the other exigencies of life constantly make demands on the adult. As one grows older, role changes occur and even stable roles face minor shifts in role demands and role expectations.

Changes in motives and incentives lead to corresponding changes in personality. As expectancies change, the direction of behavior changes. One such change occurs in the symbolization of motives. The symbols of the attachment motive in adulthood center around the family and the home, which now replace the peer culture. Caretaker roles become reversed. Instead of being parented, the adult will himself become a caretaker.

Vocation and material goods, especially money, become symbols of security. The competence motive is served not only by success in one's activities, but also by material and economic possessions. The new cognitive schemata result in learning more ways to pursue one's self-ideal and improved methods of extracting desired information from stimuli. Diversification of the cognitive motive permits the adult to know much better what will suit him and what he wants.

The Stability and Differentiation of the Self

"The self becomes institutionalized with the passage of time. Not only do certain personality processes become stabilized and provide continuity, but the individual builds around him a network of social relationships which he comes to depend on for emotional support and responsiveness and which maintain him in many subtle ways" (Neugarten, 1964, p. 198).

Several studies have supported the hypothesis that personality remains stable. Woodruff and Birren (1972) examined self descriptions of

---

Box 8-6   Developmental Changes in the Symbols of Competence

Comparison of the self with others is a common way the human evaluates his own *competence*. The symbols of competence change with age. In preadolescent boys, it may be athletic ability. In adolescence, intellectual success in the classroom and successfully "making out" with the opposite sex become common competence symbols. In adulthood, success in vocation and family adjustment replace previous symbols in priority. A specific example of how comparison with others affects aspiration is seen in the "keeping up with the Joneses" motive, in which material display itself becomes a symbol of status and competence.

subjects and found that there was little change in a group who were first tested at a mean age of 19½ and retested 25 years laer. A study by Peck and Berkowitz (1964) found that personality pattern is established well before middle life and continues even through old age. Mischel (1969) concludes from a survey that the stable traits are those that involve cognitive processes—the self-concept, world image, and cognitive style.

While the basic personality remains stable, development does seem to continue. Heath (1965) examines this continuing development from the biological, phylogenetic, and psychological points of view. Biologically, development is continuous throughout life. Phylogenetically, the human lacks well differentiated adaptive instincts so that development must proceed through increasing conscious awareness of experience mediated by increasing differentiation of symbols. Psychological development is in the direction of increased differentiation and greater autonomy from external stimuli. Information from the external environment has less and less ability to affect the personal constructs. According to Heath, a major way of controlling the influence of external information is to focus attention on only certain aspects of stimuli. Carried to the extreme, this may be responsible for the decreased flexibility older persons sometimes exhibit.

From his studies on maturity in young adults, Heath (1965) found certain invariant trends during development. These were increases in stability of organization, integration of new information with the self-organization, allocentricity (responding to the external situation rather than to private needs), and symbolic representations of experience and autonomy (adherence to self-created values). Heath's invariant trends are all cognitive processes.

Apparently, the guiding self-ideal of the personality remains essentially the same throughout development, although its symbolic representations may change.

The self in middle age.   An overview of Butler's (1975) discussion of those features that are salient to middle age is presented in Table 8-2. In each case an issue or developmental challenge is resolved in a positive or negative way, resulting in effective functioning or its distortion. Butler believes that physiological staging is most useful in childhood; while in middle age the situation becomes so complex that there is no clear link between physiology and mental development. New values appear in middle age: character, tenderness, being, wisdom, craftsmanship, and culture. Butler concludes that in middle age, social roles become more rigid (a cultural phenomenon). Identity becomes enforced by society and this identity may become a burden to the person. "Perhaps," he says, "a continuing life-long mild identity crisis may be a . . . valid sign of mental health" (1975).

Table 8-2   Features Salient to Middle Life

Issues	Positive Pole	Negative Pole
Prime of life	Responsible use of power, productivity	Competitiveness
Stock taking	Openness to change, organization of commitments	Closure, fatalism
Fidelity	Commitment to self, others, career, and society; maturity	Hypocrisy: Self-deception
Illness, death	Naturalness regarding body, time	Frantic efforts to be youthful
Credulity	Realistic convictions	Fanatic or overly cynical
Communication complexity	Toward brevity of statement, continuity of dialog	Repetitiveness, closed-mindedness

Source: After Butler (1975).

OLD AGE

Lacking the power and organization to fight back, the elderly have traditionally accepted negative stereotypes imputed to them by our culture. Whereas other societies may make use of the older person's wisdom, grant him a position of status, or provide him with social roles that are useful and dignified, the American culture has sometimes literally discarded the aged person. As humans live longer and illnesses that would kill quickly are replaced by slow killers, a large part of the aged population suffers from chronic illness. The study of personality development must, therefore, distinguish between development that continues in the healthy older person and development that is arrested by illness and approaching death.

In his discussion of the various theories of aging extant in the literature, Bischof (1976) divides them into three types: *biological, psychological,* and *social.* The biological theories are exemplified by the *somatic mutation* theory of Curtis (1966). He hypothesizes that mutations—irreversible changes in body cells—occur ever more frequently with age, so that senescence results when there is a sufficiently large number of inefficient, mutated cells. Bakerman (1969) has pointed out that through disease or wear and tear, the effective number of nonreplaceable cells in the muscle and nervous system is gradually depleted.

Psychological theories include those of Erikson, Jung, and Maslow. For both Jung and Maslow, the process of self-actualization continues as long as the human being is able to think. Buhler (1972) sees aging as a significant part of the developmental life cycle, characterizing the years over 65 as a time when the main issue is concern with the degree of personal fulfillment. Social theories have studied the relationship between aging and culture. Cowgill and Holmes (1972) ask if any valid conclusions about aging can really come from a study carried out within a single culture. In their study of aging in a modern industrial society they found that: (1) one is considered old at an earlier age in nonindustrial societies; (2) longevity and the percentage of elderly persons in the population increase in industrial societies; and (3) the status of the aged is lower and their active participation decreases in modern society.

The Preservation and Decline of Personality Function in Old Age

Cummings and Henry (1961) formulated the notion that the aged person disengages; that is, he begins to withdraw from the external world, expends less energy in activities, and decreases the intensity of his emotional attachments. Maddox (1970) feels, however, that disengagement is not justified as a single explanation of adaptation to aging. His empirical studies suggest, as do those of Cowgill and Holmes, that disengagement is a by-product of industrialized urban society, where the aged person has, perhaps unwillingly, surrendered his roles and attachments. In certain situations (for example, retirement communities) the disengagement concept has been found valid (Kalish, 1972; Poorkaj, 1972; and Scoggins, 1971). Havighurst (1973) and Botwinick (1973) see disengagement as related to personality type. Passive dependency, illness, disability, the absence of close personal attachments and of significant and satisfying roles—all are positively correlated with disengagement.

Many studies (Gutmann, 1964; Rosen & Neugarten, 1964) report that in our culture as well as others there is in old age a movement away from activity and engagement to passivity, self-centeredness, and disengagement. More detailed analysis indicates that there are many causes for this phenomenon and that it is not biologically inevitable. Thus, Neugarten and Miller (1964), in a replication of Rosen and Neugarten's study, found that increased withdrawal (interiority) is related to social conditions.

Physical health is another variable. In a 10-year longitudinal study using the Wechsler Adult Intelligence Scale, Eisdorfer and Wilkie (1974) found complex interactions between physical health, intelligence, and survival. Beginning with people aged 60 to 79, they found that those who were initially brighter survived longer. Moreover, the non-survivors were also in poorer health at the beginning. The causal relation of intelligence to health is not known for certain, but it is equally likely that people who have a stronger desire to live take better care of themselves. In this regard, Hebb (1949) had already noted that brighter people remain active and intelligent into a much older age before they show any decline.

Stability and Integration
of the Self in Old Age

Changes in personality are related to sociocultural conditions, physical health, and also to underlying personality organization. Neugarten (1968) described a change from an active to a passive mode of dealing with the environment. However, Bischof (1976) suggests that such modes are related to preexisting personality, since passive-dependent people disengage earlier.

Whether or not the self-concept changes is related to the individual's level of aspiration, past success or failure, and the social situation (Back & Morris, 1974). Thomae (1973) followed 150 males for a period of 8 years and found that, although major changes occurred in their lives, his subjects tended to work themselves through the same themes over and over again at different periods. Thomae concluded that this was evidence for Adler's life style theory. It is the same personality that meets the physical and social changes brought about by aging, so that these new situations evoke essentially predictable behavior patterns.

Although the self-concept is influenced by aging (self-esteem rises or falls), the self-designed criteria for rising or falling self-esteem have been established much earlier in life. As always, it is the guiding self-ideal that provides the criteria by which one measures one's worth. However, the symbols of the self-ideal shift with aging. Buhler (1968) regards this as a shift in perspective, so that early goals for achievement and activity shift to goals of stability and retirement from continued ambitious striving. This is congruent with Erikson's statement that self-acceptance is a condition for ego-integrity, the task of the last stage of life.

The young adult is *centrifugal*. He propels himself out into the external world. In the middle years, he has a place. He has developed the competence to fit relatively smoothly into his world. The aged adult is *centripetal*. External issues may decline in importance while internal issues (meaning, integrity) become more important (Kimmel, 1974). The adult first achieves, then integrates, then reflects for meanings.

Differentiation of the Motives in Old Age

The attachment motive in the older person is affected both by the change in social situation and the person's emphasis on interiority. Interest in sexual activity may be less frequent and less intense, but is still present.

Declining physical powers are often a threat to the security and competence systems. Increased interiority and attention to spiritual issues become not only new incentives for the cognitive motive, but also give new symbols of security. If these new symbols do not evolve, the sense of being alone and helpless is a reason for anxiety.

Attachments may fade, security may be more tenuous, and competence decline, but the perceptual system continues to function in order to process information and serve the other motives. However, as the senses decline in acuity, attention is more focused and much information is ignored. Brain cells begin to deteriorate and the organism becomes less efficient at processing information. New perceptual symbols are required, a development that is one of the major requirements for adequate functioning in the aged.

Carl Jung pointed out that in most primitive societies the old are the source of wisdom and the guardians of the mysteries and the laws. In our society we have no clear sense of meaning and purpose in old age—thus we attempt, sometimes frantically, to cling to youth. Our culture disregards the competence and attachment motives of the aged and creates a crisis in the security system as well. The resulting loss of external information from the depletion of the motive systems requires the perceptual system to compensate for this loss. This compensation takes place through increased construction of internal information, such as autistic thinking, preoccupation with fantasy, paranoid ideation, and excessive introspection.

The Attainment of Self-Actualization: Approaching the Guiding Self-Ideal

Box 8-7 contains some differentiations of the motives in old age, culminating in self-actualization. Whether or not self-actualization occurs depends on whether or not one's life has a positive meaning.

A major contribution of the existential theorists has been the concept that the absence of positive meaning leads to existential anxiety, which has at its root ontological anxiety—the fear of non-being. The self-actualized life, however, has achieved and created so many meanings that death alone cannot destroy them all. It is the unfulfilled life that is the tragedy, not the death of the self-actualized person who has been child and adult, nurturant and succorant, a parent, friend, lover, teacher, and who even after death remains a model for others—one who dies full of years.

Maslow (1970) studied the lives of people, both living and historical who, in his judgment, were self-actualized. His subjects included Lincoln, Jefferson, Einstein, Eleanor Roosevelt, William James, Albert Schweitzer, Spinoza, and others. Data were collected from historical material, personal documents, and eyewitness reports. Maslow catalogues the following traits as characteristic of self-actualized people: (1) more efficient perception of

Box 8-7 Differentiation of Motives in Old Age

Acceptance of life as lived:	Being able to arrive at a feeling of completion. The feeling of having done one's share and having made a contribution to the whole. *Making peace with oneself.*
Acceptance of death:	To the person who feels complete, death loses its sting (Erikson). The mission has been accomplished and *it is time to pass on.*
Transfer of power and dominion:	One task of aging is to pass the torch to the next generation. This requires giving up one's own preeminence and letting someone younger take the spotlight and the power. It is less a loss than a successful *transfer of leadership to one's successors.*
Transcendance:	Having successfully completed the course, the symbols of the motive systems can develop further. *New meanings* can be elaborated. Issues beyond material human existence come into focus. These new symbols permit a feeling of continuity with the cosmos even after death, a kind of *psychological immortality.*
Self-actualization:	*The completion of life in the direction of the guiding self-ideal. All of life has been a movement toward this moment. A feeling that one's destiny is complete.*

reality; (2) acceptance of self, others, and nature; (3) spontaneity and ingenuousness; (4) problem and task-centeredness; (5) a balance between involvement and detachment; (6) an ability to be autonomous from culture; (7) continued freshness of appreciation; (8) a capacity and desire for peak experiences; (9) a capacity for deep interpersonal relations; (10) a democratic character structure; (11) an ability to discriminate between means and end; (12) an authentic sense of human values; (13) a philosophic sense of humor; (14) creative thinking; and (15) a strong sense of belonging to the human species, comparable to Adler's *Gemeinschaftsgefühl.*

9 | psychodynamics I: goal behavior

OVERVIEW

When motives are aroused by environmental incentives, the dynamics of goal behavior are set into motion. Environmental incentives may be external (in the situation) or internal (such as fantasy).

Response choice is influenced both by what the situation provides and by what the person brings to the situation. Concern over the relative influence of these factors has given rise to the person X situation controversy. Some people are highly consistent across situations. Such internally consistent behavior may be adaptive or maladaptive, depending on the specific behavior involved. Even inconsistency can be a consistent personality variable, and flexibility is a personality disposition that admits of wide variations in behavior across situations, depending upon the individual's perception of what is appropriate.

Tendencies to act are generated when motives are aroused. We have used the achievement model of McClelland and Atkinson as a paradigm to explain movement (action tendencies) in the areas of attachment, competence, and security. Work on intrinsic motivation has shed new light on the cognitive motive. Cognitive style also affects the direction of movement.

Emotions are involved in motivated behavior by virtue of two processes: (1) All emotions contain cognitive information. The meanings extracted from this information influence the arousal, experience, and expression of the emotion. (2) Emotions themselves motivate; they are incentives to action. A number of emotional differentiations and their possible goals are presented. Two of them, frustration and anxiety, are interpreted from a cognitive point of view.

In the last three chapters we discussed the structure of personality and how that structure develops. Personality structure always implies a readiness to behave in a certain way. That readiness is actualized when the personality structure is aroused by environmental stimuli; that is, when the unique motive hierarchy is aroused by appropriate incentives. Thus, the dynamics of behavior are predicated upon the relationship between the personality and environmental stimuli, giving rise to specific response choices. The environmental stimuli contain information. Which information the person will extract from a given stimulus depends in part on the structure of the personality, but it depends also on the information available in the situation.

THE PERSON AND THE SITUATION

Some people respond to environmental stimulation in highly consistent ways. Others reveal great specificity, varying their responses from situation to situation. We may say that the former have easily predictable personalities, no matter what the situation. The latter show more *discriminativeness.* In order to predict their behavior we need to know more about the situation to which they are responding. The existence of cognitive style would seem to point toward behavior consistency, as would a unique motive hierarchy. Another factor that has been suggested is self-concept, which also seems to be a fairly good indicator of how one will be perceived by others. Block (1975), for example, reports that there is a significant correlation between how a person rates himself and how others will rate him. Moreover, these ratings are stable over time.

However, a number of studies have also shown that certain kinds of behavior do not seem to be consistent but vary from situation to situation—that is, tend to be situation specific. In a classic study by Hartshorne and May (1928),—which probably launched the debate over consistency and specificity—school-age children's moral behavior was tested in a variety of situations. The research design of this experimental study is outlined in Box 9-1.

Our experimental critique in Box 9-1 notwithstanding, Hartshorne and May (1928) concluded that moral behavior is relatively specific and does not generalize across situations; that is, they questioned the existence of consistent moral traits in personality. Moral behavior across situations is not unrelated but not completely consistent either. These results are limited not only because of the uncontrolled variable, but also because we cannot generalize about moral (in)consistencies from young children to cognitively sophisticated adults.

One may ask why children are consistent in the classroom and less consistent outside the classroom. It is probable that they were showing compliance behavior in the classroom because of accustomed obedience to teachers as we reasoned in Box 9-1. Were these children actually showing discriminativeness from situation to situation or had they not yet developed the sense of moral judgment that Kohlberg (1969, 1976) describes? It could be they had not yet developed the cognitive sophistication to generalize a common moral principle from situation to situation.

The question of specificity has also been studied in the way motives and attitudes are expressed. Noting that global definitions of sex-typed behavior produce methodological difficulties, Sears, Rau and Alpert (1965) measured some specific behaviors that are presumed to result from sex identification. On the assumption that males are more aggressive and females more dependent, preschool males and females were rated on five kinds of dependent behavior (Sears, 1963). The ratings were:

1. Constructive attention (seeking praise)
2. Seeking contact such as touching and holding
3. Being near, such as following someone
4. Seeking reassurance
5. Disruptive attention-seeking, such as aggression.

The children's behavior was observed in a number of free play sessions and was independently rated with high inter-rater reliability. However, the children who scored high on one measure did not necessarily score high on the others. In fact, intercorrelations between the five measures reached significance in only one of 20 intercorrelations, leading the authors to conclude that the concept of dependency as a unitary personality trait is not valid.

Inspection of the five kinds of "dependency" measures may reveal why these measures are not meaningfully related. There is actually no reason to believe, for example, that the child who seeks praise in constructive ways will show aggression in the same situation; it would not be his style. Similarly, the child who follows and seeks reassurance in this situation is perhaps more insecure and less likely to behave constructively. An earlier study by Beller (1955) had shown that global ratings of dependency in preschool children by their teachers were consistent over a group of sub-measures of dependency. Mischel (1968), however, ascribes these findings to rater bias rather than actual consistency within the child. In fact, he attacks the concept of consistency in personality traits. Yet it is quite possible that global ratings of children by teachers who know them reveal a more accurate knowledge of the child, assimilating and integrating the sub-measures into an identifiable Gestalt.

Some of the People Some of the Time

Some people will be consistent in some situations some of the time, depending on the kinds of behavioral measures taken. A brilliant analysis by Bem and Allen (1974) throws light on one reason why this occurs. They point out first of all that what may be considered important personality dimensions by the researchers may not be considered important by the subjects. Cross-situational consistency will be found only if (1) the subjects agree with the researcher's *a priori* claim that the sampled behavior and situations belong in a common equivalence class, and (2) the individuals agree among themselves on how to scale these behaviors and situations. In their study, subjects were divided into two groups on the basis of their replies to the question of whether they were friendly and conscientious or not. These self-ratings were tested for cross-situational generality by comparing them with reports from subjects' parents, peers, and two independent observers' ratings. The results, shown in Table 9-1, reveal unmistakable con-

Table 9-1 The Search for Cross-Situational Consistencies in Behavior

Each cell shows two values (High / Low).

	Self-report	Mother's report	Father's report	Peer's report	Group discussion	Spontaneous friendliness	All variables
1. Self-Report							
2. Mother's Report	.61 / .52						
3. Father's Report	.48 / .24	.75 / .28					
4. Peer's Report	.62 / .56	.71 / .40	.50 / .34				
5. Group Discussion	.52 / .59	.34 / .41	.50 / .13	.45 / .39			
6. Spontaneous Friendliness	.61 / -.06	.46 / -.18	.69 / -.20	.39 / .09	.73 / .30		
Mean correlations	.57 / .39	.59 / .30	.60 / .16	.54 / .37	.52 / .37	.59 / .01	.57 / .27

Source: D. J. Bem and A. Allen, 1974, p. 514.

sistency. Subjects who saw themselves as consistent were also rated by others as consistent. To support his claim further, Bem (1974) reported that androgynous individuals of both sexes vary their behavior cross-situationally so that they are able to "do well" at all masculine and feminine tasks. Sex-role-typed individuals, on the other hand, do well in situations congruent with their sex-role expectations. Personal consistency, across situations, is largely defined by the person according to his own perceptions.

Snyder and Monson (1975) present other data indicating the importance of the subject's perception. They found that variation in attentiveness to situational guides leads to differences in behavioral expression. Subjects measured for some personality dimensions, including self-monitoring, were asked to join a discussion group. *Self-monitoring* is a trait characterized by the tendency to examine the consequences of one's behavior and then to modify it appropriately. It was found that low self-monitoring subjects were unaffected by discussion context. In another study, raters judged the subjects' generosity, honesty, and hostility in nine relevant situations. High self-monitoring subjects were more influenced by the situation and altered their behavior accordingly. That is, high self-monitoring subjects will be generous, honest, or hostile in a given situation depending on their perception of the appropriateness of such behavior in that situation. Paradoxically, situational variability is caused by self-monitoring, a personality trait. Thus, discriminativeness, which leads to variation from situation to situation, is itself a consistent personality trait.

Personality consistency is *not* the same as behavior consistency. The person who is consistently discriminative will behave differently in different situations. On the other hand, a person who is consistently nondiscriminative will behave the same in different situations.

Interaction between Person and Situation

We have just seen that some people are consistent some of the time depending on their self-perception and discriminativeness. The interaction between person and situation has been examined further. Based on a review of 11 studies and some thoughtful methodological analysis, Bowers (1973) concludes that personality and situation interaction taken together account for more of the variance than either variable alone. He argues that situations are more specific than is commonly recognized—that is, situations are as much a function of the person as the person's behavior is a function of the situation. Bowers points out that we attribute cause to the person—or to the situation—depending on our own cognitive structure. For example, professional mental health workers overassimilate patients' behavior into their conceptual schemes. They often ascribe illness to hospitalized pseudo-patients (Adinolfi, 1971), whereas genuine psychiatric patients are often quite capable of recognizing normal behavior in these pseudo-patients. Thus, cognitive structure determines how a person will view a situation and how he will react. In other words, the situation is a function of the observer in that his cognitive schemes filter and organize the environment. One such scheme is low versus high self-monitoring.

Sarason and his co-workers (1975) point out that when we examine the person versus situation studies carefully, we still have not found out much about why people behave the way they do. Looking at the person-situation relationship tells us more than looking at either person or situation alone, but it does not tell us enough. After an analysis of several studies such as Bowers', they concluded that both person and situation variables account for only a small percentage of behavior. Evidently, we need to find other ways of conceptualizing the person-situation relationship.

Figure 9-1 presents a summary diagram of some of the complex inter-

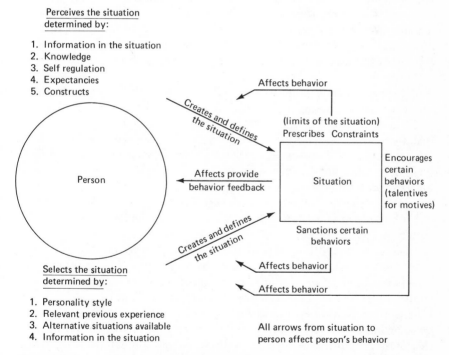

Figure 9-1 The complex interaction between person and environment. The situation provides incentives to behavior or inhibits behavior. Thus the situation is perceived as having positive and/or negative press. The person, in turn, creates and defines the situation through selective perception and attention. The interaction is bi-interactional with constant feedback.

actions between the person and the situation which require conceptual analysis in the future. This interaction is continuous, involving constant interchange between person and situation.

A Cognitive Style Formulation of the Person-Situation Relationship

Saying that personality is consistent does not mean that people do not discriminate from one situation to another. In fact the consistency of cognitive style explains *how* people discriminate from situation to situation. For example, Srull and Karabenick (1975) noted a significant personality-situation interaction in a *locus of control* study. College students divided into high internals and high externals were given opportunities to cheat (that is, falsely report successes) on certain tasks. In one condition, performance was attributed to chance, while in another it was attributed to skill. *The internally controlled subjects cheated more in the skill condition while the externally controlled cheated more in the luck condition.* This is a clear example of the power of a personality variable. The behavior of the subjects depended on their perception of the situation as it interacted with personality style.

How particular people perceive particular environments.   Other studies have revealed that environmental factors do not work automatically, but depend on their perceived effects. Thus, Worchel and Teddlie (1976) studied the effects of three variables independently: felt environmental crowding, varied density, and interaction distance. The first variable was manipulated by varying the number of people per unit space; the second, by varying how close one person was to another—that is, the extent to which personal space was violated. Also, in each condition, the walls of the room either had pictures or were bare. Worchel and Teddlie found that short interaction distance produced a greater feeling of crowding but that this effect was reduced by the presence of distracting pictures on the wall.

A corroborating study is reported by Sundstrom (1975). Subjects interacted in large or small rooms in groups of six: three subjects and three confederates. The confederates intruded by leaning forward, touching subjects, and attempting eye contact 80 percent of the time; they also blocked goals by inattention and interruption while subjects talked; or they did neither of these. Subjects reported discomfort and crowding in the small room. Intrusion led to initial discomfort that decreased with time, and to lower levels of facial regard. Goal blocking also produced lower levels of facial regard, gesturing, and positive head nodding. In this case, however, self-reported irritation increased with time. Contrary to predictions, stress responses to intrusion and goal blocking were not intensified by high room density. Rather, adaptation seemed to involve lower levels of affiliative behavior—an adaptive response, indeed! Thus, work by investigators such as Moos (1973), who stress that environmental conditions and settings (Barker, 1968) affect our behavioral responses to aggression (Galle, Gove, & McPherson, 1972), need to be interpreted in the context of how particular individuals respond to or feel about particular environmental conditions.

Consistency-Specificity as an Individual Difference Variable

Campus (1974) has reasoned that some of the low correlations between behavior across different situations result, in part, from some individuals being highly consistent, while others are not consistent at all. To evaluate this hypothesis she tested a large number of college students on two measures of motives (needs). Subjects were asked to check which adjectives from Murray's list of TAT needs applied to them. They were also asked to give a self-description inventory of their needs. These two measures of personality consistency were correlated.

Three interesting results were obtained: (1) There were low correlations between needs expressed in the two measures. (2) However, a complicated statistical analysis indicated that the low correlations resulted from the fact that some individuals were not consistent at all while others were highly consistent. For the consistent individual, the degree to which responses were determined by personality variables was 70 percent, while it was only 2 percent for the inconsistent individuals. Such extreme inconsistency could, in fact, be considered a personality trait. (3) Consistent personalities shared certain properties while inconsistent personalities shared others. For some people, consistency is highly correlated with a desire to master the environment; for others with conformity and submissiveness. However, consistency is negatively related to overt hostility and hostility turned inward. Furthermore, consistency has a positive correlation with extroversion but a negative one with anxiety.

THE ORGANIZATION OF MOTIVATED BEHAVIOR

The last section pinpointed the pervasiveness of individual differences in goal formulation and pursuit. Which goal is pursued depends on the relationship between consistent motives (defined in Chapter 6) and situational conditions. Our theory of the dynamics of goal pursuit emphasizes the following principles, all consistent with the postulates presented in Chapter 1:

1. Goals are the end points of behavioral movement and are selected by the unique motive hierarchy in interaction with environmental incentives.
2. Motives are hierarchically organized, with the guiding self-ideal at the apex of the hierarchy.

3. Motives interact with each other so that the pursuit of one motive may be affected by other motive systems. For example, the pursuit of competence or attachment may be inhibited by the simultaneous arousal of insecurity.
4. The satisfaction of motives in goal behavior is always directed by the perceptual system.
5. Goal behavior is hierarchically determined. When the motives are engaged, the dominant goal takes precedence over other goals.
6. A goal permits a great variety of situational fluctuation. For example, if the goal is to achieve, then behavior may change from situation to situation depending on what has to be achieved. On the other hand, if the goal is to be evasive, then inconsistent behavior from situation to situation is a direct expression of movement to the goal.

These six principles of organization of motivated behavior inform us that specific behaviors must be interpreted according to which motives in the hierarchy are being served by that behavior. Thus, people have different ways of seeking attachment, security, competence, and cognition. Furthermore, behavior that apparently serves one motive may actually serve another. Thus, sexual activity may often symbolize competence rather than attachment; and, conversely, competence may be sought because it is seen as a requirement for attaining attachment (as in the child who strives for good grades in order to win mother's love). Indeed, the symbols for the four motives are elaborate, as can be seen in Box 9-2.

A reversal can also occur in a motive hierarchy. As the person moves toward the dominant goal, motives interact and compete for saliency. If the dominant goal is to obtain love and the perceived way is through power and status, concerns with competence may take precedence over concerns with love. Similarly, if security is found in interpersonal distance, the pursuit of attachment will be impaired, leading to loneliness and/or bizarre sexual practices. For some people, status concerns even take precedence over survival (for example, hara-kiri as a way of preserving status).

The Achievement Motivation Paradigm

We have just said that different motives have different saliencies for different people. It would be useful to measure the relative saliency of motives, since it would help us to understand and predict what information the person will be inclined to extract from a situation and thus the direction of his behavior. Our outflow theory of perception postulates that relative saliency will depend on the kind of information the perceptual system seeks out. An excellent way to identify the dominant sets in the perceptual system is through the examination of a person's fantasies. In fact, David McClelland asserts that the formalized scoring of fantasy expressions (as in the TAT) provides a more sensitive measure of the person's unique motivation priorities than other indices such as self-report or rater's clinical judgments (McClelland, 1971). In his classical work on measuring the achievement motive, McClelland illustrates this point.

Murray defined the need to achieve as the striving to overcome ob-

Box 9-2 Some Symbols of Motive Differentiation as Incentives

Attachment	Security	Competence	Cognition
Achievement (female)	Achievement	Achievement	
Power (dominance)	Power (dominance)	Power (dominance)	
	Self-esteem	Self-esteem	Self-esteem
Status	Status	Status	
Affiliation	Affiliation	Affiliation (female)	
Approval	Approval	Approval	Approval
Conformity	Conformity	Conformity	Conformity
		Uniqueness	
	Knowledge	Knowledge	Knowledge
	Perfection	Perfection	
Getting	Getting	Getting	
Nurturing	Nurturing	Nurturing	
			Curiosity
			Excitement
		Independence	
Superiority	Superiority	Superiority	
Femininity (masculine)		Masculinity (feminine)	
	Certainty		Certainty
	Control	Control	Control
	Order		Order
Popularity	Popularity	Popularity	
Sex	Sex	Sex	Sentience
Possessions	Possessions	Possessions	
			Novelty
			Consistency
			Closure

Note: This box contains a list of constructs that some psychologists (for example, Murray) have used to catalog human motives. One motive symbol can serve more than one motive system. Indeed, any symbol can probably serve for any motive under the relevant conditions of socialization.

stacles, to exercise power, to strive to do something difficult as well and as quickly as possible. McClelland followed Murray but modified the definition of need to achieve (n-Ach) as involving "success in competition with some standard of excellence" (McClelland, Atkinson, Clark, & Lowell, 1953).

In investigating the achievement motive, McClelland was concerned primarily with the person as an entrepreneur. The standard of excellence against which the person competes is his own rather than any external criterion. The person is not so much concerned with being better than someone else as he is with attaining his own standards.

In measuring the achievement motive, McClelland selects five TAT cards and puts the subject in a situation designed to arouse the achievement motive. For example, the subject is told that he has failed to achieve a desired level of success on some test performance. He is then given the usual instructions for taking the TAT test and asked to write stories for each of the five cards.

The stories are then scored for achievement themes by a method that McClelland devised. After studying a number of people in this way, McClelland could classify subjects on a scale from low n-Ach to high n-Ach. Persons high in n-Ach demonstrated the personality characteristics depicted in Box 9-3.

The individual depicted in Box 9-3 radiates an aura of competence and self-confidence that is revealed through his expectancy of success. In fact, Atkinson (1957), a student of McClelland, who further developed the model, believes that the person high in achievement motive has an *expectancy of success* whereas the low achievement person has a *fear of failure*. These two variables of achievement dynamics are expressed in the following equation.

$$T_A = (M_s \times P_s \times I_s) - (M_{AF} \times P_F \times I_F)$$

where

T_A = is the tendency to approach the achievement task
M_s = motivation to achieve success
M_{AF} = motivation to avoid failure
P_s = probability of success
P_f = probability of failure
I_s = incentive value of succeeding at the task
I_f = incentive value of failing at the task

Note that $P_s + P_f = 1$. The probability is given by the difficulty of the task, the incentive by its challenge, and M_s is measured by the TAT.

The basic paradigm of the achievement motivation theory is that the individual's hope of success is stronger than his fear of failure. This proposition specifies that, in high n-Ach individuals, the motive to be competent is generally stronger than the motive to be secure.

One may raise the question as to whether a fantasy motivation score by one person may mean the same thing as for another person or group.

Box 9-3 Characteristics of Persons High in N-Ach

1. Exercise some control over the means of prediction and produce more than they consume
2. Set moderately difficult goals
3. Maximize likelihood of achievement satisfaction
4. Want concrete feedback on how well they are doing
5. Like assuming personal responsibility for problems
6. Show high initiative and exploratory behavior
7. Continually research the environment
8. Regard growth and expansion as the most direct signs of success
9. Continually strive to improve

Source: After McClelland and Winter, 1969, p. v.

This ultimately raises the question of the validity of measuring saliency through the scoring of fantasy. With respect to the achievement motive, McClelland reports that "in general, studies have confirmed the fact that everywhere men, women, Japanese, Germans, Americans who have high n achievement scores, behave in much the same way" (McClelland, 1971, p. 13).

Atkinson and Cartwright (1964) and Weiner (1970, 1972) have pointed out that the formula for T_A is limited in that it assumes a static personality. As such, it does not allow for carryover from preceding motivational activities. Whether a person has been satiated by previous goal behavior, whether he has succeeded or failed should affect succeeding motivational tendencies. Thus, some correctional factor should be added to the formula to account for carryover. These researchers predict that, in cases where M_s is greater than M_{AF}, failure of goal attainment will result in higher T_A on successive goal attempts. Unfortunately, this prediction does not always hold up empirically, since success in goal activity frequently results in higher subsequent motivational tendencies until, presumably, satiation has been reached. Thus, while the theory of Atkinson and McClelland has generated much research and has been supported by data from many studies (see Atkinson & Feather, 1966), the theoretical foundations are still being refined.

We have theorized earlier that each person has a unique hierarchy of motives with a dominant goal at the apex. For the achievement-oriented person, the competence motive is at the apex, whereas for the fear of failure person, the security motive is at the apex. Other motives can also have priority. Thus, for another individual the attachment motive, in one way or another, may be at the apex. For some people the dominant goal is to please, for others it is to serve, while for still others, it is to be taken care of—all variations of the attachment motive.

All goal behavior is thus hierarchically organized depending on the unique organization of the motive hierarchy. In Chapter 6 we presented diagrams of four different hierarchies, with each of the four motive systems at the apex (see Figure 6-3). The key determiner of the hierarchy of motives for each person is the articulation or differentiation of the perceptual system. That motive which is directed or organized by the most differentiated perceptual structure will give rise to the most dominant goal when motives are set into dynamic action.

Social and Cultural Factors
in Achievement and Other Motives

Horner (1968) conducted an illuminating study which dramatized the extent to which the achievement motive organization and perceptual structure of males and females differ. In her study, female subjects from a large midwestern university wrote stories to the cue, "After first-term finals, Anne finds herself at the top of her Med school class." The stories were scored using the usual TAT criteria. Particular attention was paid to "fear of success" themes, in which the central character suffered social rejection, wondered about normality or sexuality, denied or misrepresented success in various ways, or displayed action that was bizarre or inappropriate. Horner's results showed that 65 percent of the female subjects wrote "fear of success" stories as opposed to only 10 percent of the male subjects. This difference between females and males in "fear of success" has been verified in other studies (among others, Horner, 1972; Feather & Raphelson, 1974).

In a follow-up study, Feather and Simon (1975) obtained data which suggests that the "failure"-related variable has wider implications. Female subjects read stories of males and females failing in qualifying examinations in three professions—medicine, teaching, and nursing. Following this, they were asked to do three things: (1) give a personality description of the characters in the stories; (2) rate the importance of different causes of the failure; and (3) rate the likelihood that various outcomes would follow the failure. Some of the significant results were as follows:

1. A male was seen as less powerful, more obedient, and more feminine if he succeeded or failed at nursing rather than at teaching or medicine.
2. Either sex was seen as more powerful *and* less feminine if he/she succeeded than if he/she failed.
3. Males were evaluated more positively and seen as more powerful and polite if they succeeded.
4. Females, conversely, were evaluated more positively and seen as more powerful and polite, if they failed.
5. Subjects tended to see ability as more determining in male success, luck as more determining in female success, and ability as more determining than failure.

Recall that *all these subjects who saw the female as less favorable than the male were female.* Some of the objections to Horner's findings have already been discussed in Chapter 8. In Chapter 10 we will discuss still other interpretations of Horner's findings.

Application of the Achievement Model to Other Motives

McClelland's use of the TAT can be applied to the other motives. In the original achievement motive model of McClelland-Atkinson, data were collected on subjects who had been informed of previous failure on a task. The experimenters did this because they believed such a situation would arouse the achievement motive if it indeed existed in the subject. In similar ways, this paradigm can be applied to the other motives, as Atkinson and his associates (1954) have done with affiliation (an expression of the attachment motive) and Veroff (1957) and Winter (1971) with power.

Affiliation and fear. Atkinson and his associates (1954) measured affiliation by analyzing TAT stories written by students either in the classroom or in a fraternity. (The latter situation was expected to be more arousing of the motive to affiliate.) Themes written by the fraternity group revealed more concern with attaining friendly relationships and fear of rejection and isolation. Furthermore, unstable and withdrawn individuals in both groups were more likely to reveal a negative fear of rejection rather than the positive desire for friendly relationships—a dimension similar to that found in the achievement motive. Thus, the achievement paradigm can be applied to the competence, security, and attachment motives. In all three cases the person either anticipates *success* or *failure,* depending on whether he has the necessary perceptual categories to pursue success.

Power and dominance. Veroff (1957) adapted the TAT to measure a power motive. The power motive is defined as the desire to influence others and to be in command of a situation. Pictures aimed at arousing such feelings were administered to candidates during a student government election at a college (a situation expected to arouse the power motive). Subjects were also rated independently for "dominance" characteristics by their professors. It was found that those students who scored higher in power motives on the TAT stories also received higher ratings from the professors. People high in the power motive expect to attain positions of control, while those low in this motive expect to be powerless or have no influence and are motivated to avoid the power contest.

Maslow (1968) has argued that people who have a feeling of adequacy about self may be powerful and have leadership capacity, yet maintain a democratic and cooperative rather than a controlling leadership style. Those who have feelings of insecurity about self-worth, love, and recognition are more likely to act in authoritarian ways when they are in a position of power. Perhaps we should make a distinction between internal personal feelings of power and external controlling behavior (an attempt to exert power over others), which implies a compensation for a feeling of inadequacy. In this regard, Sorrentino (1973) has shown that individuals high in the achievement motive (those who compete against their own standard of excellence) display leadership potential. Presumably such persons have an internal sense of personal power.

How the same stimulus can arouse different motives is shown in Table 9-2, which depicts in detail the scoring for achievement, affiliation, and power of stories told to a single stimulus (a picture of a man at a drawing board).

Achievement, affiliation, power, fear of failure, fear of success are all differentiations of attachment, competence and security. To date, no similar ways of measuring the cognitive motive have been devised. However, intrinsic motivation, which was discussed in Chapter 5, can be understood as evidence that a cognitive motive exists.

The Dynamics of the Cognitive Motive: Intrinsic Motivation

In Chapter 5 we introduced the concept of *intrinsic motivation*. Intrinsic motivation is affected by the cognitive motive. Some psychologists have claimed that exploration, stimulus seeking, and related activities are intrinsically rewarding. Harlow (1953) theorizes that such information-seeking behavior is based on innate programs which are evoked by varying environmental stimuli such as novelty, puzzles, and new surroundings. In Chapter 5 we linked such tendencies to the need to master the environment. In a similar manner, Glickman and Schiff (1967) have documented that species, including humans, who must search out food and are not threatened by predators reveal more curiosity than species who obtain food easily and are threatened by predators. Thus, a link is established between adaptive behavior and learning to master the environment. R. White (1959) has seen this need to have effect on the environment as an important determiner of human motivation.

A. Jones independently (1964, 1966) and with his co-workers (1961) has reported experimental data which verify that persons are motivated to *search for information*. When deprived of looking at a varied environment for a period of time, and then given an opportunity to choose what kinds of displays one prefers, the deprived person is more likely to choose more complex rather than less complex displays. Brody (1971) has suggested that this tendency to choose more complex information stimulation is related to the individual's creativity. The degree of creativity is a predictor of information search. More creative individuals will tend to choose more complex stimulation. Implicit in the work of Brody is the notion of cognitive complexity. The more constructs (categories) an individual has, the more cognitively complex that person is. Cognitively more complex people have a low tolerance for boredom and a high threshold for information load

Schroeder (1970) has shown that the desire for cognitive complexity is determined both by personality disposition and the particular environment (as has Berlyne, 1963, 1965). Harvey, Hunt, and Schroder (1963) point out that it is important to realize that the optimal level of information

Table 9-2 Typical Stories Written When Achievement, Affiliation, and Power Motives Have Been Aroused to a Picture of a Man at a Drawing Board.

Achievement Arousal	Affiliation Arousal	Power Arousal
George is an engineer who wants to win a competition in which the man with (need, + 1) (achievement imagery: standard of excellence, + 1) will be awarded the contract to build a bridge. He is taking a moment to think the most practicable drawing how happy he will be if he wins. He has been (goal anticipation, + 1) baffled by how to make such a long span strong, but remembers (block, world, + 1) to specify a new steel alloy of great strength, submits his (instrumental act, + 1) entry, but does not win and (goal state, negative, + 1) is very unhappy.	George is an engineer who is working late. He is (affiliation imagery, + 1) worried that his wife will be annoyed with him for neglecting her. She has been objecting that (block, world, + 1) he cares more about his work than his wife and family. He seems unable to satisfy (block, personal, + 1) both his boss and his wife, (need, + 1) but he loves her very much, and (instrumental act, + 1) will do his best to finish up fast and get home to her.	This is Georgiadis, a (prestige of actor, + 1) famous architect, who (need, + 1) wants to win a competition which will establish who is (power imagery, + 1) the best architect in the world. His chief rival, Bulakovsky, (block, world, + 1) has stolen his best ideas, and he is dreadfully afraid of the (goal anticipation, negative, + 1) disgrace of losing. But he comes up with (instrumental act, + 1) a great new idea, which absolutely (powerful effect, + 1) bowls the judges over, and wins!
Thema + 1, Total n Achievement score = +7	Thema + 1, Total n Affiliation score = +6	Total n Power score = +7

Source: From David C. McClelland, *Assessing Human Motivation*, Morristown, N.J.: General Learning Press, 1971.

processing is not always the most complex level, and will depend on the task criterion. For example, if we have to find something relatively simple, a highly complicated set of hypotheses leads us to overlook the rather simple solution. In general, however, we would expect that the cognitively more complex (more creative) individual is likely to be more competent and more likely to believe that he can influence the environment effectively.

Lepper and Greene (1975) and Calder and Staw (1975) have experimentally investigated the dynamic aspects of intrinsic motivation. Greene and Lepper (1974) have shown that intrinsic motivation decreases when extrinsic rewards such as money are offered. However, Kruglanski and his associates (1975) and Reese and Sushinsky (1976) found that intrinsic motivation may increase if the extrinsic reward is seen as an inherent part of the task.

Calder and Staw (1975) presented subjects with two tasks, picture puzzles and block puzzles. They were either given a reward or no reward for doing each of these tasks. As can be seen from Figure 9-2, there was an interaction between task and external reward. Subjects stated that enjoyment was higher with the picture puzzle (intrinsic motivation) *without* reward. Self-perception is also influenced by many tasks. When a task is challenging we perceive ourselves as intrinsically interested; if not, we need outside incentives. Deci and his colleagues (1975) hypothesize further that extrinsic rewards can affect intrinsic motivation in two ways: (1) when they produce a change in perceived locus of causality, and (2) when they affect one's feelings of competence and self-determination. There need not be a conflict between intrinsic and extrinsic motivation. One can enjoy a task and also enjoy being paid for it. However, if our chief incentive is money, intrinsic rewards may be neglected and vice versa.

Amabile and her associates (1976) have shown that the enjoyment of an intrinsically interesting task can also be modified by other contingencies. Subjects were given intrinsically interesting puzzles under two conditions of time limits and two conditions of unlimited time. In the time-limit condition, half the subjects were given an explicit time limit while for the other half, the time limit was implied. In the unlimited-time condition, subjects were told either to work at their own pace or to work as quickly as possible. Subjects in all four groups finished within the allotted time; however, subjects in the two deadline conditions enjoyed the game less. Intrinsically motivated activities are more satisfying if they are not constrained by time.

Notz (1975) and Calder and Staw (1975) admonish that there are complex interactions between intrinsic and extrinsic motivation, and a variety of other contingencies such as the expectancies and perceptual perspective of the person. In short, the relationship between intrinsic

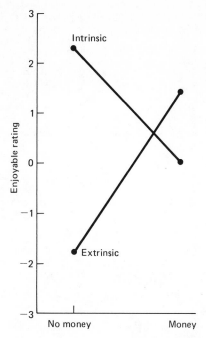

Figure 9-2   Mean ratings of task satisfaction and the interaction between intrinsic and extrinsic motivation. Extrinsic motivation increases with external reward, while intrinsic motivation suffers as a result of conflict between the two types of reward. Source: After Calder and Staw, 1975, p. 602, Figure 1.

motivation and reward in determining such outcomes as satisfaction and performance is not linear, as Figure 9-2 indicates. If the relation were linear, both extrinsic and intrinsic lines would have the same slope.

Cognitive Style and Goal-Directed Behavior

Psychodynamics, in our formulation, is the particular person's style of interaction with the environment, as determined by the motive hierarchy, itself organized by the perceptual system. Cognitive style is one aspect of the perceptual system. Table 9-3 summarizes some important aspects of the psychodynamics of cognitive style. Style interacts with stimulus information in the arousal of goal behavior. Recent data verify some of the relationships predicted in Table 9-3.

In Chapter 6 we mentioned the work of Holzman and Gardner (1960) on sharpeners and levelers. Since sharpeners are cognitively more differentiated, they will seek more novel situations; on the other hand, levelers will

Table 9-3 Dynamics Which We Would Expect to Be Found Associated with Various Cognitive Styles

Style	Stimuli Sought	Stimuli Avoided	Satiated By
Sharpeners	Intense and novel stimuli	Sameness	Routine tasks
Levelers	Low intensity and familiarity	Intensity and novelty	Change and variety
Scanning			
Extensive scanners	Information	Fixation	Homogeneity
Narrow scanners	Limited information	Variation	Heterogeneity
Psychological Differentiation			
Field independence	Freedom from environmental constraint	Constraint	Constraint
Field dependence	Freedom from self-determination	Internal cues	Freedom
Locus of control			
Internal	Self-determination	Environmental control	Forced choice situations
External	Environmental control	Self-determination	Unstructured situations
Tolerance for ambiguity			
High	Freedom from structure	Certainty	Redundancy
Low	Certainty	Ambiguity	Entropy (uncertainty)
Cognitive Consistency	Information congruent with expectancy	Dissonant information which causes incongruence	(not applicable)

seek to avoid new information. Thus, cognitive style directs which stimuli will be selected as well as which response will be chosen.

A similar statement can be made about the extensive and narrow scanning paradigm of Gardner and Long (1962a, b) in Chapter 6 and the construct of *psychological differentiation* (field independence and dependence) of Witkin (1976), as indicated in Table 9-3.

In locus of control studies, Liem (1975) examined how performance and satisfaction were affected by the variables of structure and choice. In an introductory college psychology class, one group of students was permitted to choose the type of recitation section they preferred while another group was assigned by chance. The format of the recitation was either structured or unstructured. The subjects who controlled their choice did better on the examination and expressed more satisfaction. As Table 9-3 predicts, each student will choose more or less structure, depending on his locus of control, and will be more satisfied with his choice. Additional work has shown that perceived control is in turn affected by some other variables. Harvey and Harris (1975) found that perceived control is greater when the subject chooses between positive options than when he chooses between negative options, and also when the difference between the attractiveness of the options is smaller. Finally, Wortman (1975) discovered that when subjects knew beforehand (expectancy) what they hoped to obtain, they perceived themselves as having more control over the outcome.

Locus of control and the arousal power of stimuli. Personality variables influence the arousal capacities of stimuli. Schachter (1975) studied the ways in which obese persons differ from normal and underweight persons in their response to various stimuli including food cues. Obese persons pay more attention to external food cues than do non-obese, but only when the external cues are prominent. When distracted by another task, the obese do not differ from the non-obese in response to food and/or water cues.

Palatability (good taste) is a cue that elicits more response from obese persons (Nisbett, 1972). When given good- and bad-tasting ice cream and cake to try, obese subjects ate much more of the good-tasting food than the bad. Underweight subjects ate approximately equal quantities of the good-tasting and the bad-tasting samples.

Cognitive Consistency Motivates Behavior: A Special Case of the Cognitive Motive

As stated in Chapter 6, Aronson's (1972) interpretation of cognitive consistency led us to classify it as a cognitive style variable. Specifically, he said that the direction of cognitive balance and the resolution of dissonance depends on the nature of the person's self-esteem. Cognitive consistency is that state in which the person's expectancies and outcomes are congruent with each other. The theory of cognitive dissonance is based upon the hypothesis that incongruent cognitions are an aversive stimulus which motivates behavior designed to reduce the congruence (Festinger, 1957). (See Box 9-4.)

Brock and Balloun (1967) had two groups of subjects, smokers and nonsmokers, listen to messages, some of which implied that smoking causes cancer and others which claimed otherwise. The messages were obscured by static, which could be eliminated if the subject pressed a button. Smokers more frequently removed static from the "smoking does not cause cancer" messages, while nonsmokers more frequently removed static from the "smoking causes cancer" messages. According to this study, people are more willing to hear belief-consistent messages than belief-discrepant messages. The study by Brock and Balloun is evidence for the selective inattention hypothesis, according to which a person can tune out a message by inattention—or refuse to tune it in by permitting it to remain unclear. However, whether or not people will tune out threatening information is itself a personality variable. People are either sensitizers or repressers of emotionally loaded information. We will discuss the dynamics of these two different personality styles later in this chapter.

While people tend to construe information so that it is consistent with their cherished beliefs (Kelly, 1955), other researchers have pointed to the

---

Box 9-4   Cognitive Dissonance

You know that elephants cannot fly. If you see an elephant flying by, that observation will be incongruent with the belief that elephants do not fly. The following options (and perhaps others) are open to you:

"I was wrong. Elephants do fly!"

"Elephants don't fly. It must have been a balloon."

"It's a trick. Someone's tricking me!"

"I am hallucinating."

"It couldn't have been an elephant. Must have been a small Zeppelin."

"We are being invaded by creatures from outer space."

"I must have seen it wrong. It couldn't have happened."

"Someone slipped LSD in my coffee."

"The Russians have developed a new weapon!"

The corrective behavior consists of an attempt to reconcile observation and belief so that, as far as possible, cherished beliefs remain intact. *The more cherished the belief, the more necessary to protect it.* A belief is cherished when it satisfies or supports a motive. When a belief would threaten one's feeling of security or competence, one's attachment, or one's whole way of viewing the world, that belief is strenuously protected.

complex relationship that exists between consistency strivings and new information. In effect, receiving a belief-discrepant message and then refuting it results in confirmation of the belief. If an individual can be induced to behave in a way which is later shown to him to be inconsistent with his self-concept or his principles, the individual may either justify his behavior or change his beliefs (Brehm & Cohen, 1962). An individual's beliefs and attitudes can also be manipulated by persuading him to role-play discrepant beliefs and attitudes.

These different findings are not surprising. A perceptual system that is so rigid that it will never entertain a discrepant belief would be a poor mechanism for survival. In order to carry out its judging functions properly, the perceptual system must be ready to evaluate incoming evidence with a certain degree of intelligence. What then are the reasons for the finding that perceptual selectivity and response behavior are indeed often motivated by a striving for cognitive consistency? In our theory, it is because *cognitive dissonance can be a threat to the cognitive motive.* The creation of order out of chaos is a process that facilitates adaptive behavior (see Chapter 6). If belief-discrepant information threatens that order, it actually threatens all the motive systems because it calls into question all organized goal-directed behavior. Therefore, the protection of the individual's orderly way of viewing the world and one's place in it, with the consequent self-selected definition of the guiding self-ideal and the chosen methods for pursuing it, becomes in itself a cognitive motive. A perceptual system which remains constant is much more of an adaptive tool than one which is ever changing; yet rigidity is also maladaptive. A certain amount of flexibility is necessary.

In addition to the desire to maintain internal perceptual order, there is another reason for cognitive consistency strivings, *convenience.* It is simply more convenient to confirm one's expectancies because it requires less effort than changing one's mind. This is especially true when belief-discrepant information is not judged significant enough to constitute a major threat or is not clear enough to permit certainty.

First Instance of Cognitive Consistency Striving—Convenience

You are awakened from a sound sleep by a noise that seems to come from downstairs. You consider investigating but you are very sleepy and don't want to get out of bed. You tell yourself it was probably an outside noise and there is no point in getting out of bed. You return to sleep.

On the other hand, the invalidation of certain beliefs may be experienced as threatening:

Cognitive consistency strivings are thus in the service of the cognitive motive, of convenience, and of preservation of all other cherished motives. However, cognitive dissonance will motivate effectively only when the dissonance is a significant threat to motives or self-interest.

EMOTIONS IN MOTIVATED BEHAVIOR

All motivated behavior has an affective component. Therefore, from our point of view we would expect perception to be an important director of emotions. This view is supported by a cognitive theory of emotion, which has been developed by some of the theorists we will shortly discuss.

The Cognitive Component in Emotions

In everyday life we are accustomed to think that arousal by certain stimuli "causes" emotions which in turn result in a behavioral response. A danger makes us afraid and we run away; the loss of a loved one makes us sad and we mourn; a success makes us happy and we rejoice. The cognitive theorists, however, point out that, in the adult, it is not the actual situation but the information we extract from it that is crucial in determining choice of response. In a situation of danger, we may be blind to the threat; conversely, we may see danger where none exists.

On the other hand, the perception of danger does not automatically lead to fear; sometimes it exhilarates us. The emotion felt in response to a stimulus is obviously a function of expectancy, as McClelland and his associates have shown in their studies of the achievement motive. Emotions, then, are strongly influenced by cognitive factors (Valins, 1972; Lazarus & Averill, 1972). It is, for example, the perception of threat that arouses. Moreover, the perceptual system also influences the *choice of behavioral response* to the perceived stimulus. Coping behavior is chosen behavior. Koriat and his collaborators (1972) exposed subjects to films of accidents which portrayed injury and death to human beings. Half the subjects were instructed to detach themselves emotionally from the viewed film and the other half were instructed to involve themselves. The researchers found that the subjects could indeed regulate their own emotions, as measured by their reported emotional state and by changes in heart rate. The most frequent coping device used for detachment was reminding oneself that the film was a dramatized event and not a reality; another common device was attending to the technical aspects of the production. The most frequently used involvement device was for the subject to imagine that the accidents were happening to him. Subjects were also able to change from involvement to detachment or vice versa in response to instructions. Lazarus (1975) concludes that emotions are self-regulated.

An early theory that considered emotions subsumed under cognitive control was that of Alfred Adler. Adler's theory of emotions has been systematized by Dreikurs:

> We may easily discover the purpose of emotions when we try to visualize a person who has no emotions. . . . He would not be able to take a definite stand, because complete objectivity is not conducive to forceful action . . . we need emotions. They provide the fuel . . . for our actions. . . . We blame emotions for our actions, while actually these emotions are only the servants of our real intentions. . . . We feel driven by them, while we actually create them. . . . A person who loses his temper is under the impression that he cannot control it. . . . However, there is sufficient evidence that a person in rage can suddenly calm down when somebody enters to whom he doesn't want to display his temper (1967, pp. 207–209).

In brief, perception determines the direction of coping behavior and the emotion is self-created to give it impetus. We create the emotion appropriate to what we want to do (see Figure 9-3).

Lazarus: Cognitive intervention to regulate arousal and expression of fear. The determinants of threat appraisal, the way they relate to coping, the way coping feeds back to and modifies threat appraisal and leads to change in emotional response, all lie in the *situation,* the *person,* and the *nature of the coping process employed* (Lazarus, Averill & Opton, 1974). Lazarus (1968) has also demonstrated experimentally that cognitive intervention can be used to regulate fear. In one experiment which we also discussed in Chapter 6, films of a circumcision ritual on adolescent boys were shown to subjects. Heart rate and galvanic skin response (GSR) were used as measures of fear arousal. To one group, only the silent movie was shown. In another group, the film was accompanied by a commentary which continually minimized the amount of pain experienced by the adolescents. In the third group, the subjects were exposed to a similar minimizing commentary before viewing the film. All subjects were then asked to report whether or not circumcision seemed to be a painful procedure. The second and third groups both denied that circumcision was painful, the second group most vehemently.

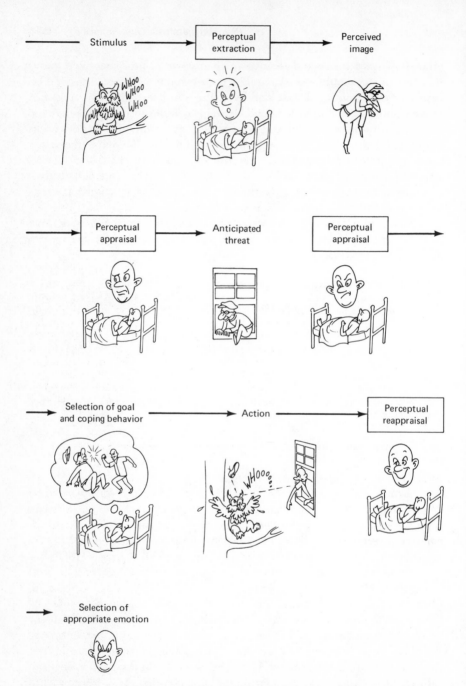

Figure 9-3 A diagram of the stimulus-response chain according to Adler. In each case, the person's imagination arouses an emotion consistent with anticipated and sought-after response. As information changes, continuous-reevaluation occurs.

The results of the experiment suggest that *denial* (a form of cognitive intervention in which verbal information is used to suppress a particular emotion) can be used to lower verbally expressed fear. As pointed out in Chapter 6 and verified in a recognition threshold experiment by Lazarus, Eriksen, and Fonda (1951), some individuals suppress while others enhance emotional information. Could similar personality differences exist in the arousal (GSR) and expression (verbal report) of emotions?

Personality correlates of emotional expression. A reanalysis of six sets of experimental data by Lazarus and his associates (Weinstein, Averill, Opton, & Lazarus, 1968) reveals that external expressions of emotion are not necessarily congruent with internal physiological arousal, but depend on the personality style of the person. Some people are high-denial subjects or "repressors" while others are low-denial subjects or "sensitizers." Repressors will deny fear verbally but simultaneously reveal higher physiological arousal (by direct measures). Conversely, sensitizers will admit fear verbally but reveal a lower degree of physiological arousal.

Buck (1976) discusses and analyzes similar relationships between skin conductance (physiological arousal) and facial expressiveness (external expression) of emotions. He uses the terms *internalizers* (in place of deniers) and *externalizers* (in place of sensitizers). Internalizers have high skin conductance but low facial expressiveness of emotions, while externalizers have low skin conductance but high facial expressiveness.

Thus, there seems to be a personality disposition which differentiates emotional arousal and expression (see Box 9-5).

Box 9-5   Personality Correlates of Emotional Expression

Repressors		Sensitizers
Internalizers		Externalizers
Deny fear verbally	Expression of Emotion	Admit fear verbally
Do not show fear in facial expression		Show fear in facial expression
Higher physiological arousal		Lower physiological arousal

The data of Lazarus and his associates, and of Buck, essentially show that different personalities display a different emotional style as a result of selective attention to information. Sensitizers are verbally coding their emotional arousal more accurately than repressers. Nevertheless, physiological measures show that the repressors are aroused. We do not know if the repressors are lying or are themselves unaware of their own physiological activity; or perhaps they note their sensations, but do not identify them as emotions. This may be considered a cognitive explanation of "unconscious" or "defensive" behavior.

Sources: Lazarus, 1968; Weinstein et al., 1968; Buck, 1976

There are other variables that influence the degree of emotional arousal. These include the person's state of health and general alertness, whether or not he is already aroused by some other stimulus, whether he is satiated with stimuli or relatively deprived, the person's cognitive complexity, and the symbolic value assigned to the stimulus. Let us now consider the relationship between arousal and a number of these variables.

Cognition and arousal. Schachter and Singer (1962) demonstrated that physiological arousal will lead to the expression of a particular emotion based on certain cognitive factors. They injected subjects with epinephrine to produce physiological arousal and exposed them to either an angry confederate or an euphoric one. The physiologically aroused subjects showed either anger or euphoria, depending on the model presented by the confederate. A control group who received a saline injection (which does not produce arousal) was less likely to imitate the emotions of the model. In addition, some of the experimental subjects were informed about the sensations associated with epinephrine injection and this group displayed less arousal. Schachter and Singer conclude that an aroused person will label his emotional state according to whatever perceptual cues are available. As the studies of Valins and Lazarus have shown, perceptual cues may come from physiological sensations as well as from situational information. In this way we can use cognition to explain physiological arousal, extraction of situational information, and personality differences in a one-factor theory.

Berlyne (1966) has also found the arousal is influenced by the kinds of information present in stimuli; namely, whether stimuli are new and unexpected or repetitious and familiar. Novel stimuli produce a higher degree of arousal. Maddi and his associates (1965) point out that our need for variety expresses itself in three ways: (1) the desire for environmental change; (2) exploring more fully the current environment; and (3) use of the imagination to create variety. Using the TAT as an instrument, Maddi found that people differ in the ways they express their need for variety. Some people depend more on external stimuli; others generate their own variety. Style of seeking variety influences the way arousal is created. This style is probably related to Witkin's psychological differentiation; that is, people who produce their own information are more field-independent precisely because they are more psychologically differentiated.

Satiation. Level of arousal is influenced by prior activity. People tend to choose activities dissimilar to their most recent ones (Lewin, 1951). Given a choice, a person will avoid an activity with which he has become satiated in favor of a task which is more immediately novel. Tasks similar to satiated tasks are also avoided (cosatiation). Lewin also found, however, that once a task was started, there was a tendency to complete it. Lewin considered this an example of the tendency to closure and related it to the Gestalt *Law of Prägnanz,* which demands removal of the tension created by an incomplete task. Completion of a task changes its valence from positive to negative.

Stang (1975) studied the effects of continued exposure of a person to a stimulus. His study showed that on first exposure to a symbol that had no valence (an unfamiliar foreign word) the subject's affect level (interest) was low. Repeated exposure led to an increase in interest (affect level). Continued exposure eventually led to satiation and decrease in interest.

Cognitive style and emotional arousal. Cognitive style also influences arousal and performance. It organizes incoming information, arousal style, and response style. Levelers assimilate and dampen down stimulus reception. Sharpeners intellectualize, differentiate more informational categories, and accentuate arousal stimuli (Gardner, Holzman, Klein, Linton, & Spence, 1959).

Kagan, Moss, and Sigel (1963) confirmed the common sense notion that impulsive persons are more easily aroused than reflective individuals, who mobilize their attention and energy more systematically. Impulsive arousal is not always adaptive. Sharpeners are apparently spontaneous but not necessarily impulsive. Witkin and his associates (1962) demonstrated that field-independent people are less aroused by environmental fluctuation because they have more internal frames of reference. We would expect that this would also be true of people with internal locus of control. Box 9-6 explains one instance of clinical behavior in terms of cognitive style.

The Motivational Properties of Emotion

We have just discussed the relation between emotion and cognition. In so doing we took the position that emotions are aroused by information. The information can come from an external stimulus or from a physiologi-

---

Box 9-6   A Clinical Example of a Leveling Cognitive Style

A 32-year-old man receiving psychotherapy for the treatment of a depressive neurosis often began to yawn during the therapy hour. The therapist noted that during these times the patient stopped paying attention to what the therapist was saying. The yawning occurred only when the therapist spoke, never the patient. When the therapist had pointed this out several times, the patient began to observe this phenomenon himself. The yawning and dispersal of attention occurred whenever the therapist was pointing something out that would be emotionally upsetting to the patient or would require him to reevaluate his behavior. The depression itself was a response to a life situation in his job and marriage that would have required a reappraisal of his whole work and marital behavior. His cognitive style was that of a consistent *leveler* who, in one way or another, dampened down information which aroused.

cal stimulus (internal information). Thus, a cognitive theory would predict that emotional arousal, since it contains information for the person experiencing it, would itself instigate actions. In this section we will discuss some of these motivational properties of emotional arousal.

Yerkes-Dodson law. Yerkes and Dodson (1908) found that level of performance is related to degree of arousal. When emotional arousal is absent or low, a subject is poorly motivated to perform. As arousal rises, motivation and, consequently, performance improves. When arousal is too high, however, emotional intensity interferes with effective performance. The relationship between arousal and performance is curvilinear (inverted U). Ducharme (1962) found support for the curvilinear relationship between performance and arousal. Too strong arousal is experienced as unpleasant (Melzack, 1967). Performance is optimal at moderate arousal; Hebb (1955) used this evidence to point out that the seeking of arousal may also be a motivator if the original level is too low.

Differentiation of Emotions
and Their Motivational Properties

The infant's emotions are global; his affect is either positive or negative, signaling either a state of well-being or a state of distress. As the person grows, that polarity becomes differentiated into a variety of affective states,

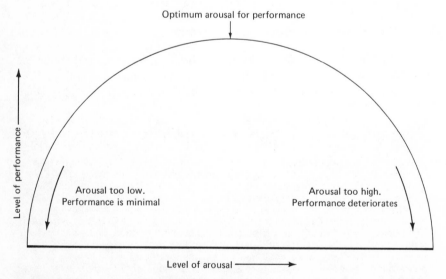

Figure 9-4   The Yerkes-Dodson law.

positive or negative, integrative or segregative, conjunctive or disjunctive. Generally, positive emotions will give rise to approach behavior and negative ones to avoidance behavior. Each emotional state contains specific information for the person experiencing it, about whether the current situation is good or bad, desirable or undesirable. Such information helps in the selection of a direction of movement. In the remainder of this chapter and in part of the next, we will discuss a variety of these emotional differentiations and their motivational or goal properties.

Frustration. Frustration occurs when goal-directed behavior meets a barrier. Mischel defines frustration as a violation of expectancy (1976, p. 373). It is most bitter, he adds, when a person "has built up high hopes and then is prevented from realizing them." That frustration leads to emotional arousal has been shown by several investigators. This arousal is often expressed through an intensification of effort to reach the goal (Amsel & Roussel, 1952; Holton, 1961) or in persistence of effort (Mandler, 1964). Other consequences of frustration include aggression (Barker, Dembo, & Lewin, 1941; Mallick & McCandless, 1966); withdrawal of interest (Barker, Dembo, & Lewin, 1941; Festinger, 1957); and alliance with another sufferer against the frustration (Wright, 1943). The consequences of frustration vary from person to person and situation to situation (see Table 9-4).

Along with frustration, there are other behavioral consequences of failure to attain goals: displacement, substitution, and rationalization. In displacement, the direction of movement is changed to attain the goal—for example, shifting anger from one person to an innocent bystander. In substitution, the goal-object is changed: If Mary turns you down, call up Susie. In rationalization, one convinces oneself that the goal was not desirable after all: "Those grapes are sour anyhow."

Anxiety. Anxiety has been found to motivate behavior in several ways. It often interferes with performance, especially when the stimulus challenge is itself an anxiety-arousing cue (Sarason, 1961). As may be expected, anxiety leads to avoidance behavior. The child who has burned his finger on the hot stove learns to avoid the stove. Fearful avoidance behaviors—either of the original stimulus or of similar stimuli—can be very per-

Table 9-4   Consequences of Frustration

Intensification of effort	"Try harder"
Persistence	"If at first you don't succeed, try, try, again"
Aggression	"If it doesn't work, kick it"
Withdrawal of interest	"I'm bored—let's go get a beer"
Alliance against the frustrator	"Let's go on strike"

sistent (Seligman, 1975). When the subject is unable to avoid the frightening situation, he may just give in and passively submit to the situation. Seligman calls this *learned helplessness.* However, other subjects will fight rather than submit. How one reacts to anxiety depends on person-situation interaction.

Anxiety produces physiological arousal, but there are individual variations which are possibly related to biological constitution. Some individuals demonstrate signs of sympathetic dominance (adrenergic) and others of parasympathetic dominance (cholinergic). The majority show a balance between the two systems (Wenger & Cullen, 1972).

How an individual responds to anxiety is also influenced by personality. Endler and Hunt (1969) administered a self-report anxiety inventory to groups of subjects and analyzed the results. They found that the occurrence of anxiety depends upon the interaction of the stimulus and the typical response style of the person. People respond differently to anxiety-provoking stimuli. What makes one person anxious may have no effect on another; and if both of us are frightened, we each still respond in our characteristic ways.

Defense against anxiety.   Psychoanalytic theory assigns an important role to the various defense mechanisms against anxiety (see Box 2-3 and Table 9-5). However, the concept of defense is not well supported by empirical evidence (Tudor & Holmes, 1973; Holmes, 1974). What Freud called defense mechanisms can be just as well explained in terms of selective perception. Table 9-5 translates Freud's defense mechanisms into cognitive language.

Erdelyi (1974) has incorporated a cognitive explanation of so-called defensive behavior into a more general theory of selective attention. He explains how selective attention, directed by "chronic sets," can account for the motivational and emotional aspects of perception (see Chapter 1).

Anxiety usually leads to some sort of adaptive behavior, but this behavior varies widely as all the above-mentioned studies have shown. Mischel (1976) reviews several studies and points out that cognitive *suppression* of anxiety occurs if adaptation seems impossible, but *vigilance* remains if adaptation seems possible. It is more likely that cognitive suppression is itself a form of adaptation. Several studies referred to in Chapter 6 and earlier in this chapter support the notion that either vigilance or suppression can occur. Eriksen (1951a) found that psychiatric patients who exhibited a high degree of disturbance and avoidance in association to words signifying aggression, homosexuality, and dependence also had higher recognition thresholds for pictures corresponding to these categories. Lazarus, Eriksen, and Fonda (1951) found that subjects who are able freely to interpret sexual aggressive content in the TAT show heightened sensitivity to auditory stimuli that are both hostile and sexual. Whether one suppresses or is vigilant is also a personality characteristic and is not entirely dependent on what is situationally available, as Mischel suggests.

The effect of uncertainty on anxiety. Anxiety is an arousing, vigilance-creating emotion. Therefore, it is most required when the need for vigilance is greatest. It is thus not surprising to find that anxiety is higher when an unpleasant consequence is expected but its time of occurrence and severity are not known. This conclusion is supported by the work of Elliott (1966), who found that subjects are more anxious while awaiting an unpleasant event when they don't know what to expect. In the same vein, Mischel and Grusec (1967) found that, in the face of an unpleasant outcome, subjects prefer to get it over with rather than delay it. These studies were perhaps limited, because obviously there are some unpleasant outcomes we do not care to hurry. We all know that we will someday die, but most of us do not care to hasten the day. The desire to hasten an unpleasant outcome is probably related to our judgment of whether or not we will be better off as a

Table 9-5 Freud's Defense Mechanisms Translated into Cognitive Language

Denial: Seeing but refusing to acknowledge Projection: Attributing one's own feelings to an external agent Displacement: Purposeful unconscious shifting Rationalization: Justification of unacceptable attitudes or behavior	All varieties of *denial.* One perceives what one wishes, confirms one's own expectancies, attributes cause for one's own benefit, and protects cognitive consistency. The perceptual mechanism is selective attention.
Isolation: feeling split off from thought Reaction-formation: An unacceptable impulse is expressed in antithetical ways Regression: Return to a level of functioning used at a previous stage of development	All varieties of *withdrawal.* The challenge stimulus is processed in such a way that the challenge ceases to exist.
Suppression: Conscious decision to avoid attending to a stimulus Repression: Expelling the awareness of the stimulus from consciousness Doing and undoing: Performing forbidden act in symbolic form and then retracting it Dissociation: Drastic modification of consciousness to avoid distress Sublimation: Gratifying an impulse by giving it a socially acceptable aim Intellectualization: Thinking about a feeling instead of experiencing it	All varieties of *controlling.* By selective perception, one can arrange to confuse oneself so that the right hand doesn't know what the left hand is doing. In this way, control is maintained, cognitive dissonance is decreased, and personal constructs are kept valid.

Table 9-6   The Range of Human Emotions and Possible Goal Behaviors

EMOTION			POSSIBLE GOAL
Mild arousal	Moderate arousal	High arousal	
Joy → Elation →	Exaltation →	Ecstasy	Approach behavior
Disappointment → Sadness →	Depression →	Grief	Succorance behavior
Worry → Apprehension →	Anxiety →	Panic	Avoidance behavior
Annoyance → Resentment →	Anger →	Rage	Attack behavior
Squeamishness → Disgust →	Loathing →	Revulsion	Distancing behavior
Envy → Desire			Acquisitive behavior
Liking → Desire →	Lust		Approach behavior
Curiosity → Wonder →	Awe		Explanation-seeking behavior
Doubt → Perplexity →	Confusion →	Bewilderment	Information-seeking behavior and caution
* Alertness → Restlessness →	Irritation → Frustration →	Agitation	Action-oriented behavior
† Boredom ← Dulling →	Apathy		Perceptual excluding behavior

* With increase in arousal, the level of tension rises; with high arousal, agitation occurs.
† Note that the level of arousal here is in the opposite direction.

result. At any rate, certainty can be expected to reduce anxiety (since certainty serves the cognitive motive), provided there is no continuing threat to other motives.

Emotions in the Service of Goals

In this chapter we have discussed only frustration and anxiety as examples of emotional states which motivate behavior. In Chapter 10 we will discuss other emotional differentiations, both segregative and integrative. In everyday life it is easy to think of some emotional experiences as goal-directed. We recognize that anger induces us to attack; fear, to remove ourselves from danger; lust, to approach the desired object; disgust, to eject an unpleasant stimulus; envy, to covet; greed, to possess; love, to cherish the beloved; boredom, to seek stimulation; and so on through the long list of passions that humans experience. We have shown that emotions in the adult are largely under cognitive control and we should expect that these same emotions will serve possible goal behaviors (see Table 9-6).

10

psychodynamics II:
the nature
of
interpersonal
behavior

OVERVIEW

We continue our discussion of psychodynamics by examining various differentiations of the attachment motive in interpersonal behavior, including dependency, affiliation, and aggression and their emotional components. Each of these differentiations represents a distinct way of pursuing attachment. Dependency usually implies a vertical relationship—between a superior and an inferior. Affiliation is usually more horizontal, but dependent relationships can also occur in affiliation. Friendship, love, and sexuality are varieties of affiliation. Aggression is a more complicated form of behavior which includes affiliative and oppositional behavior. It has some relationship to the competence motive and interacts with sexuality in a variety of ways.

Motives can come into conflict, as when two incentives are active at the same time. In a cognitive theory of conflict, perception plays the key role. The information extracted by the perceptual system from the situation is processed to give instructions which lead to incompatible movements.

All interpersonal goal behavior depends on communication. Personality style itself is a form of communication. Each style contains an implicit message which affects the nature of communication and the consequent interpersonal interaction. Messages are carried in verbal as well as nonverbal signals, such as posture, gesture, and facial expression.

There is a reciprocity between communicator and receiver in effective communication and in effective interpersonal relationships.

Interpersonal relationships are an important aspect of life. Much of our goal behavior involves others. In this chapter we will discuss various interpersonal goal behaviors—for example, *dependency, aggression,* and *affiliation*—and their associated emotional components, mainly as differentiations of the attachment motive. Where relevant, we will note how other motives are involved in the interpersonal movements.

DEPENDENCY

Dependent behaviors occur when an individual seeks a supporting social context for his own adaptive responses. The establishment of attachment, as discussed in Chapters 5 and 7, requires a relationship in which the infant can depend on a reliable parenting figure. This same reliability provides the infant with the security to begin exploring his environment. Thus, dependency is also instrumental to the development of competence and cognition (Stendler, 1953; Ross, 1966).

Descriptions of dependent behavior include the following: an increase in deference to others, request for help and reassurance, sensitivity to approval and disapproval, social conformity and suggestibility, and a decrease in autonomy (Murray, 1938; Edwards, 1959; Bernardin & Jessor, 1957; Lang & Laszovik, 1962; Gisvold, 1958; Kagan & Mussen, 1956).

Wiggins and his associates (1971) suggest that dependent behavior may become a central trait of a certain personality type, but all of us may show dependency when the context is appropriate.

Thus, Bandura and Walters (1963) point out that dependency is not based on a common set of motives but may be a useful instrumental response in a specific situation. Furthermore, all of the described dependent behaviors may be socially appropriate at times. To illustrate, the Japanese may show much more deference in their formal behavior but are not necessarily more dependent. Also, sensitivity to approval and disapproval may be appropriate if one's job depends upon the employer's good will.

Variables That Influence Dependency

Anxiety increases dependent behavior. Schachter (1959) divided subjects who were awaiting an electric shock experiment into two groups. One group was presented with information that the shock would be of minimal intensity. The second group was exposed to fear-producing stimuli, such as complicated machinery, heart examinations, and pictures of people who were supposedly experiencing electric shocks. When given a choice of waiting for the shock alone or with others, the latter group was more likely to choose to wait with others.

In a continuation of this experiment, Zimbardo and Formica (1963) found that the high-anxiety subjects chose to wait with others who were also awaiting the shocks—rather than with subjects who had already completed the experiment. Apparently, other things being equal, it is more comforting to be in the company of people who are anticipating the same threat.

Birth Order and Dependency.   Schachter also found that within both of his subject groups firstborns were more likely to choose to wait in the company of others than later borns. Hilton (1967) examined the behavior of 4-year-olds in a setting in which they could interact with their mothers. He found that firstborn and only children were more dependent in their behavior than later born children. Hilton also found, however, that the mothers of first and only children reinforced these dependent behaviors more than the other mothers. The study suggests that the important variable is not birth order, but parental reinforcement.

Gender and dependency.   A number of studies (Maccoby & Jacklin, 1974) found some evidence that dependent behavior was shown more often by females than by males, but Kagan and Moss (1962) point out that this seems the result of cultural expectations for females. As some of the studies on affiliation later in this chapter will show, dependent behavior is reinforced much more in girls than in boys.

Relationship between dependency and modeling.   A study by Bandura and Walters (1963), which rated both parents and their sons on dependency traits, found that parents who were high on dependent traits tended to have sons who were also dependent; the correlation between parents and sons was also high for independence. Apparently the observational learning which takes place in the home may be further influenced by dependency feelings themselves, since people who are more dependent are more likely to imitate others. Ross (1966) confirmed this in a study in which she tried to teach children in a nursery school to play post office. Children previously rated as dependent were much more imitative in their behavior than independent children. Thus, the dependent children imitated many of Ross' incidental behaviors, such as putting a pencil behind her ear, doodling on a pad while pretending to speak on the telephone, and so on. It seems that dependency can be learned by imitation and in turn increases imitation.

Dependency and cognitive style.   An example of the relationship between dependency and cognitive style is shown in some of Witkin's studies on field dependency. Witkin (1962) found that individuals who showed high field-dependence on the rod-frame test also showed other behaviors usually characterized as dependent, such as deferring more to authority and seeking contact with others more often. Wiggins and his collaborators (1971) have offered this correlation as evidence that personality consistency exists and that it cuts across perceptual, emotional, intellectual, motivational, and interpersonal modes of operation. The dependent person is also perceptually dependent upon the field (as upon the position of the frame in the rod-frame test). The ability to differentiate an object from its field is correlated with a more independent perceptual style—more analytic, greater tolerance for ambiguity, more willingness to take risks, and greater creativity (Renner, 1970).

As the research indicates, females and anxious people (of any sex) are more dependent. In some of his studies, Witkin also found that females and anxious people are more field-dependent. Thus, dependency studies and cognitive style studies corroborate each other. It is not surprising that anxious people are more field-dependent, since anxiety narrows perceptual attention (attention is rigidly focused on the threat). Some people are more anxious than others but anyone can become anxious in a threatening situation. Anxiety which triggers field-dependent behavior can come either from the person or the situation.

In our society females are not only reinforced to be more dependent but also to be more conforming—that is, to take the cues for their behavior from the environment rather than from themselves. This also increases field-dependency.

All of the correlates of dependency as a personality disposition may be elaborations of a field-dependent cognitive style.

AFFILIATION

Dependent relationships usually imply a vertical relationship between persons: One is the nurturant and the other is the succorant. Affiliation in general implies a more horizontal relationship, as in friendship. Humans live in groups—families or other kinships; they identify themselves with a society, race, or religion. While intragroup relations are often competitive, group systems have an affiliative component which is experienced by the individual as a sense of belonging together. People seem to join groups because they *want* to be associated with others. The attachment motive, whatever its symbols, remains strong throughout one's life.

In this section we will examine three kinds of affiliative behavior: friendship, love and marriage, and sexual behavior.

Friendship

We do not choose our parents and siblings but we remain more or less attached to them. However, we do choose our friends. Some of the factors that determine choice of friends, supported by research in both primates and humans, are *similarity, peership, reciprocity,* and *complementarity.* Rhesus monkeys choose as playmates those monkeys who have had similar life experiences. Thus, monkeys raised in isolation chose other isolate-reared monkeys while peer-raised monkeys chose other peer-raised individuals as playmates (Pratt & Sackett, 1967). According to Byrne (1961), similar tendencies exist among humans. We are more attracted to people whose attitudes are similar to our own. Similarity of interests and background is a common factor in choice of friends. Strangers working in pairs are most attracted to each other when both are successful in performing a task and when the performances are relatively equal to each other (Senn, 1971). Thus, peership is a factor in attractiveness.

We tend to like others if we see them as having good opinions about us (Aronson & Lindner, 1965). Moreover, liking and disliking are both reciprocated (Lowe & Goldstein, 1970). When others like us, we like them; when others dislike us, we dislike them.

Although the studies cited indicate that similarity is a strong determinant of friendship, most of us also know of friendships between people who are dissimilar or complementary—between an aged person and a young one—or between people whose mutual roles bring them into contact, for example, teacher and pupil or doctor and patient.

Harlow and Harlow (1962) point out that monkey mothers teach their babies social skills which are important for later social relationships. Thus, monkeys raised with terrycloth mothers only, later become autistic and engage in self-destructive behaviors such as biting themselves. On the other hand, if these monkeys are exposed to peers from the first six months of life onward, social and sexual adjustment is slowed, but becomes apparently normal by the time they are adults. It is obvious that peer relationships are important in personality development. As we have discussed in Chapter 8, the ability to make friends is an important motive differentiation in preadolescence and adolescence and influences later sexual relationships.

Love and Marriage

The choice of a heterosexual partner has more complex determinants than does the choice of friends. This is not surprising since mate selection involves not only sexual factors but is also more often in the nature of a permanent decision. The loss of a mate of many years is often the most stressful loss of all.

Some determinants of mate selection.   Murstein (1970) found evidence that men and women with similar qualities will select each other as mates. If a man is not particularly handsome, he will not expect to attract a beautiful woman and will therefore look elsewhere. Kerckhoff and Davis (1962) reported that complementarity is an important factor in mate selection. We look for our mate to have strength where we are weak and to be less strong in those areas where we pride ourselves on strength. A woman who wants to be protected will seek a man who enjoys protecting; a man who feels socially ill at ease will choose a wife who is outgoing and friendly; a low status person may prefer a high status person.

The data indicate that *similarity, complementarity,* and *reciprocity* facilitate mutual attraction. In addition to serving the purposes of love per se, other motives are also served when people seek each other out. The person who wants to be protected finds security in a protector; the socially retiring person solves the problem of social competence by marrying a socially outgoing person.

Rubin (1970) described three components of heterosexual love: affiliative and dependent needs, a predisposition to help, and an exclusive absorption in the partner. However, the first two factors are important in all kinds of love, not only romantic. Dreikurs (1946) proposed that love at first sight is a phenomenon that occurs when one person recognizes in the other a strong symbol of what will help to fulfill one's own guiding self-ideal. The actual psychological reasons for falling in love may not be healthy, nor may we choose mates for healthy reasons. Psychological maturity and cooperation are the minimal requirements for a successful marriage.

Heterosexual love, as distinguished from sexual attraction, requires the development of intimacy. As time passes, physical attractiveness becomes less important while such factors as empathy and mutual interdependency become more important. When these factors are absent, intimacy can become burdensome and a marriage can become unpleasant and unsatisfying.

Sexual Behavior

Sexual behavior is the most intimate form of behavior in which humans engage. Masters and Johnson (1975) point out that in sex partners communicate attitudes, feelings, and goals to each other by their sexual interaction. The biblical use of the term "to know" someone as a euphemism for sexual intercourse is perhaps an accurate description of sexual relationships. Shulman (1973) discussed a number of possible functions of sex, dividing them into prosocial and antisocial functions (see Table 10-1) which he called uses and abuses of sex.

Perusal of Table 10-1 will show that the uses of sex all have the characteristic of facilitating bonding and of permitting friendly relationships. Under these circumstances, sex always seems to be an enjoyable experience. On the other hand, the abuses of sex do not promote bonding, may not lead to enjoyable experience, are self-centered rather than other-centered, and are generally antisocial behaviors. Sexual behavior can thus violate affiliative tendencies or can be a distorted form of affiliation.

Biological factors in sexual behavior.   While females among the lower animals are sexually receptive only during the appropriate phase of the estrus cycle, the human female's ability to be sexually aroused is relatively free of hormonal control. There is some evidence that hormones can produce sexual arousal (Grossman, 1967; Masters & Johnson, 1970), but the studies cited earlier in Chapter 8 suggest that hormones provide only an initial impetus which is modified by social experience to the point that psychosocial factors become more important than physiological factors (Wiggins et al., 1971). Only in certain cases of illness, as in some diseases of the pituitary gland, is there a noticeable loss of sexual interest for physiological reasons.

Social factors in sexual behavior.   Some societies we would consider more primitive allow children to observe sexual behavior between the parents

Table 10-1   Uses and Abuses of Sex

Uses (Prosocial)	*Abuses* (Antisocial)
Reproduction: procreation of children	Mischief: rebellion and willfulness
Pleasure: sensual pleasure	Distance: to avoid intimacy as in sexual exhibitionism
Belonging: bonding and self-esteem	Domination: to assert dominance over another
Sharing experience: bonding	Suffering: as in arranging to be taken advantage of or victimized (a confirmation of one's expectancies)
Consolation: helpfulness to one who is troubled	Demonstration of success: to achieve
Cherishing: loving and gift giving	Demonstration of failure: also a confirmation of one's expectancies
Exercise: physical activity	
Relaxation: to relieve stress	Vanity: to promote self-esteem in the absence of mutuality
Distraction: to relieve preoccupations	Revenge: to get even with someone
Stimulation: for invigoration	Proof of abnormality: also a confirmation of one's expectancies

(for example, the Cantalese in Guatemala). Ford and Beach (1951) have described a number of such societies. In our own society, there is no such clear modeling of sexual intercourse, but there is considerable modeling of how males and females relate to each other in situations of sexual attraction, especially in literature, in films, and on television. There is no doubt that modeling and parental reinforcement affect later sexual behavior, but the primary model and reinforcer in our society is usually the peer group.

Our own cultural standards are in transition. Over a period of four generations our society has moved from mid-Victorian prudery to what seems to us like an astonishing openness about sexual behavior. This change in sexual mores seems to be part of a larger movement involving a change in the social status of women and other previously disadvantaged groups.

Cognitive factors in sexual behavior. There is evidence that perception may be the single most important factor in sexual arousal. Physiological signs of sexual arousal include the usual signs of emotional arousal, such as increased pulse rate, blood pressure, and muscle tension. Some other measures which seem reliably to measure sexual arousal include increased blood flow and pressure in the genitalia themselves. Heiman (1974) used this information to try to discover how aware her subjects were of their own sexual arousal. Having prepared her male and female subjects to be monitored for blood volume and pressure in the penis or vagina, she then had them listen to tapes that described erotic scenes. Among subjects who showed physiological signs of arousal were many who reported no awareness of being sexually aroused. There were more women than men in this non-aware group. Heiman suggests that awareness of sexual arousal requires learning.

Physiological cues actually contain information. The studies on sensitizers and repressors discussed in Chapter 9 show that repressers pay less attention to physiological cues. Perhaps in our society women are trained to pay less attention to physiological cues which suggest sexual arousal.

Emotional Components of Affiliation

In Chapter 9 we reasoned that since emotions contain information that instructs us how to behave, they motivate behavior. This holds true for both integrative (conjunctive) as well as segregative (disjunctive) motions. Anxiety and frustration, discussed in Chapter 9, are segregative emotions. So far in Chapter 10, we have discussed differentiations of the attachment motive which have integrative emotional components. Thus, the motives of dependency, friendship, love, and sexuality lead not only to approach movement but are also accompanied by conjunctive emotions which reinforce the approach movement.

The last differentiation of the attachment motive we will discuss is aggression, a motive which usually gives rise to distancing behavior with its disjunctive emotional component.

AGGRESSION

Aggression is an important but confusing subject. In its worst forms it refers to violent behavior perpetrated by one human being against others. At the other pole, it is considered a desirable quality in competitive situations, a trait that is associated with masculinity, a sign of strength and competence. As in the case of dependency, whether aggression is adaptive or not depends on the person-situation interaction, as can be deduced from Table 10-2.

Variables Influencing Aggression; Biological Roots of Aggression

Aggressive behavior is a fact of existence among many animals. Many ethnologists, among them Lorenz (1966), believe that aggression is instinctive and serves survival purposes: It is important in *sexual selection* (the stronger male wins the most desirable female); it serves the *security* motive by protecting the young; it *procures food, establishes territory,* and *maintains a social order.* Moyer (1971) described eight kinds of aggression human beings commonly display (see Table 10-2).

While Tiger (1969), an anthropologist, argues that male groups aggress instinctively (just as men and women have sexual relations, groups of males aggress against the environment), other authors disagree, finding no compelling evidence that aggression is an instinct (Ziegler, 1964; Scott, 1966; Berkowitz, 1969; Kauffmann, 1970; Montagu, 1976).

There is evidence that *selective breeding* can produce more aggressive animals (Denenberg & Zarrow, 1970), but it is uncertain to what degree this finding will apply to humans. Aggressive behavior seems partly related to hormones. Studies of girls exposed *in utero* to androgens showed that they were distinctly tomboyish (Hamburg, 1971). One cannot yet predict how these girls will behave in adult life. Yalom and his associates (1973) examined the opposite situation: boys who had been exposed to estrogen and progesterone *in utero.* At age 6, there was no important difference between these boys and others, but at age 16 they were less assertive, less prone to anger, engaged in fewer fights, and were less adventurous.

Social modifiers of aggression. The above studies suggest that to a certain extent aggression may be an inborn response. However, psychological

Table 10-2   Categories of Aggressive Behavior*

Predatory	Seeking for prey. Essentially food-seeking behavior.
Fear-induced	Defensive behavior against perceived threat.
Irritable	Aggressive behavior that can appear when a person is frustrated, angry, tired, or harassed.
Territorial	The selection and defense of home territory against trespassers. This kind of aggressive behavior is more common under conditions of excessive crowding.
Maternal	The defense of the young.
Sex-related	This type of aggression occurs both against rivals and against a prospective mate. It may be a part of the courting behavior of some animals and may be necessary to bring about sexual conjugation.
Intermale	Aggression which results in the male dominance hierarchy. In baboons, intermale aggression is most prevalent during the periods when the dominance hierarchy is unsettled. In humans, it occurs most often among younger males.
Instrumental	Aggression which is a learned response to specific situations.

* Moyer's categories may very well not include all forms of aggressive behavior found in humans. Interfemale aggression may be just as common as that among males but would probably be expressed in bickering, criticism, rejection, and exclusion rather than in physical attack. Moyer's last category, instrumental aggression, covers a wide range of aggressive behaviors. It is possible that all aggressive behaviors are learned, or at least partly learned, rather than purely instinctive.
Source: After Moyer, 1971.

studies are much more likely to suggest that it is a learned response. Whatever inborn tendencies are present, it is generally acknowledged that whether or not aggression is actually expressed is much more determined by socialization experience rather than by any inborn mechanism. After all, even the kitten learns to hunt for mice by observing its mother.

In a set of dramatic studies, Kuo (1967) was able to bring the young of different and antagonistic species together: Kittens and puppies, puppies and birds, predatory birds and smaller birds. In the "natural" state, the adults of these species would attack each other or, in the case of predatory birds, kill and eat the smaller ones. When they were raised together, however, they became friendly, even "affectionate."

Denenberg, Paschke, and Zarrow (1968) have shown that the same can occur with mice and rats, natural enemies in the wild. In their study, individual rats were housed with mice from the time of weaning until they were 57 days old, then separated from them. When the rats were 90 days old they were placed with a single mouse for 24 hours. None of these rats killed a mouse, while 45 percent of control rats killed mice. Denenberg and Zarrow (1970) conclude that presumably inborn tendencies can be strikingly modified by socialization.

Anger and aggression. Although there is no direct correlation between anger and aggression, several studies have pointed to a number of relationships. Feshbach and his co-workers (1967) found that if one is angry, it is satisfying to behave aggressively. However, Hokinson, Burgess, and Cohen (1963) are of the opinion that mere expression of aggressive behavior does not drain off anger unless specific satisfaction is obtained. Their experiment showed that the subject's anger did not cease through aggressive behavior unless the aggression was directed at the cause of the anger.

However, anger does not always lead to aggression. Thibaut and Riecken (1955) found that people will aggress more readily against a low status person than against one of high status. Such behavior is reminiscent of pecking orders found among domestic chickens and several other birds. In the pecking order, the high status chicken will peck at a lower status bird, who will in turn peck at one of still lower status. It is, of course, possible that fear will inhibit aggression toward a high status person. Zimbardo (1969) found that fear of retaliation also inhibits anger.

The expression of anger seems to facilitate aggressive behavior, a fact pointed out by Charles Darwin in the nineteenth century. This statement of Darwin's is supported by a study performed by Goldstein and his associates (1975). They found that subjects who thought they were giving electric shocks as part of an experiment increased the intensity of the shocks they gave as they continued to give them. These subjects had not been frustrated or angered before they gave the shocks. The researchers concluded that the continued expression of aggressive behavior led to a phenomenon called *disinhibition:* In other words, continued aggressive behavior loosens the usual inhibitory controls over such behavior.

This study throws into question the popular view held by some scholars that the expression of aggression reduces aggressive tendencies because of its supposed cathartic value. In fact, Staub (1976) has pointed out that training people to be empathic, prosocial, and compassionate is a much more effective way to reduce aggressive tendencies.

There is other evidence that anger and aggression can facilitate each other. Hartmann (1969) studied adolescent delinquents. One group was first provoked to anger, then, along with a control group, viewed films, some containing aggressive scenes, others not. Hartmann found that the angry group showed more aggressive behavior than the controls, and also that the aggression film produced more anger than the nonaggression film. Thus, anger and aggression can facilitate each other.

Viewing aggression can sensitize the viewer. Subjects who viewed aggressive television shows had a tendency to see aggression around them more often than those who did not view aggression shows. Furthermore, they tended to favor the use of aggression as a solution to problems (Greenberg & Gordon, 1972).

Modeling and aggression. As Bandura's studies have shown, any kind of behavior can be learned through imitation. Bandura, Ross, and Ross (1963) showed that nursery school children can learn and will imitate aggressive behaviors by watching adults model these behaviors. Four groups of children were used in this study. The first group saw an adult display violent behavior toward a large inflated rubber Bobo doll; the second group saw a film of the same behavior; the third, a TV cartoon which modeled this behavior, and the fourth served as a control. All groups of children were then frustrated by being allowed to play with some interesting toys for a short while and then having the toys taken away by the experimenter. Each child was taken to another room where there were other toys and a Bobo doll. Then the child's behavior was observed for 20 minutes through a one-way mirror.

The children exposed to the aggressive model all reproduced more aggressive behavior than the control group, but this effect was less in the cartoon group than in the live and film groups. Two other findings appeared: Boys showed more aggressive behavior than girls, and each sex tended more to imitate the same sex model.

Similar results were found in a study by Hanratty and his co-workers (1969), in which children insulted and hit a person dressed as a clown after they had watched similar behavior on a film. It may be argued that the children knew they were not really hurting the Bobo doll or the man dressed as a clown and that they would not behave so if they thought they were doing harm. However, the previously mentioned experiment by Goldstein and his associates seems to indicate that disinhibition of aggression can occur even if subjects believe they are hurting others.

Sexual factors in aggression. Laboratory studies usually find that boys are more often physically aggressive than girls (Moore & Updergraff, 1964; Bandura, Ross, & Ross, 1963). Buss (1963) tested college students for these traits by instructing subjects to give simulated electric shocks to other students. He found that males administered shocks more often than females and shocked other males more often than they did females.

In Table 10-2, one of Moyer's categories of aggressive behavior was called *sex-related.* Two instances of this type of aggression occur when prospective rivals for a mate aggress against each other, or when the sexually aroused male supposedly aggresses against the female. In fact, studies of the relationship between sexuality and aggressive behavior have produced contradictory findings. Barclay (1969) provoked a group of college students to anger and found an increase in the urinary excretion of acid phosphatase (a supposed sign of sexual arousal). On the other hand, Clark and Sensibar (1955) showed slides of nude females to male students and then counted the number of aggressive fantasies in the TAT subsequently given to the students. They found that aroused subjects were *less* likely to compose aggressive stories.

We are all aware that sexual arousal may lead to aggressive behavior.

A small boy who is attracted to a small girl may be as likely to throw a snowball at her as he is to offer to carry her books. Apparently, different people react in different ways. Some people find aggression sexually arousing, others respond with aggressive behavior to sexual arousal. The determining factors seem to have some relationship to how the sexual roles are perceived, how socialization has proceeded, and to the level of arousal itself.

> Society sanctions the display of violent, aggressive behavior in its films, television, and sports contests (boxing, bull fighting, stories in which the hero commits mayhem among the villains, who have already displayed their own violence). The display of overt sexual behavior, on the other hand, is only reluctantly sanctioned. Except for romantic scenes (kissing, hugging), overt erotic behavior is considered pornographic and inappropriate, especially for the young. What would happen if the situation were reversed?

Cognitive Labeling and Aggression

Konečni (1975) found evidence that anger is mediated through cognitive labeling. If a person is first made angry and can also identify or label his emotional experience as anger, then any stimulus which produces arousal—for example, loud tones—will aggravate the angry feelings. Geen and O'Neal (1969) report corroborating data. In situations where a tendency to aggressive behavior already exists, exposure to white noise increases the aggressive responses. In addition to this evidence, we already saw in Chapters 5 and 9 that labeling any emotion will affect how it is expressed in goal-directed behavior (Schachter, 1964).

Cognitive labeling is a perceptual process. Arousal of anger in a particular situation may or may not occur depending upon the selective perception of the individual. To a great extent, whether or not a person expresses aggression will depend upon his self-perception, his perception of the situation, and his perception of what instrumental response is required by the situation.

As in the expression of dependent behavior, aggressive behavior is sometimes a major personality trait, part of a larger personality style.

Humanistic and Non-Humanistic Behavior

It seems necessary to distinguish aggression which promotes survival, such as defense of the young, from aggression which gratuitously injures others and serves no purpose other than personal vanity or a desire for status. The former has a biological rationale, the latter seems to be an aberration. Perhaps the best understanding of this hostile, antisocial behavior can be found in the concepts of George Kelly (1955). Kelly distinguished between aggression and humanistic choice as problem-solving methods. For Kelly, aggression occurs when the individual is threatened and attempts to validate a personal construct that has already been invalidated—for example, punishing others when they don't behave the way we expect them to. Humanistic choice is a nonaggressive way to resolve problems. If one's personal constructs are threatened, it is possible to improve or modify them so that they can once again be confirmed by the events in the field (see Box 10-1). Aberrant aggression is not necessary to survival. Furthermore, humans can be socialized so that aggression between them is minimal. Peaceful behavior *can* be learned.

MOTIVATIONAL CONFLICT

A general definition of conflict has been offered by DiCaprio:

> A conflict exists when two or more incompatible motives, intentions or goals are active at the same time. The specific nature of conflict involves the inability to satisfy opposing needs or to secure competing alternatives. (1974, p. 275)

This incompatibility has been viewed in different ways by different investigators. Thus, Freud's theory postulates a conflict between different parts of the personality structure. It is a theory of *intrapsychic* conflict, between the libidinal and aggressive strivings of the id, the reality demands of the ego, and the moral demands of the superego.

Neal Miller (1944), a reinforcement theorist, described three kinds of conflict, postulating that they resulted from incompatible drives. An indi-

---

Box 10-1   Humanistic Choice Rather than Aggression

You have just come home for the weekend, and you are hardly in the house before your mother starts scolding you for not coming home earlier so you could help her make dinner. She now wants you to set the table, but you would prefer resting a bit before you eat. You feel like telling your mother to keep her dinner, repacking your bag, and taking the late bus back to school.

Instead you ask yourself what is irritating your mother, since her behavior is obviously unreasonable. You go to the kitchen and say, "Mom, you only talk that way when you're very upset by something and you're usually glad to see me when I get home. What's going on?"

You have refused to respond to aggression with aggression. As a result, your mother's anger is defused. She admits she has been irritable all day because of the weather, the mess the neighbor's dog made on the lawn, and because the washing machine didn't work.

vidual either approaches or avoids a cue. Thus, three kinds of conflicts ensue, as depicted in Box 10-2 and Figure 10-1. It is the third conflict which has the most significance for the student of personality. The first conflict is easily resolved. In the second conflict, the individual avoids both unless an external agent compels him to remain in the situation. However, approach-avoidance conflicts are the most difficult to resolve (see Chapter 2). They are characterized by doubt, uncertainty, vacillation, ambivalence, back-and-forth movement, fear, and tension, none of which is conducive to successfully adaptive behavior. Miller's theory, like Freud's, is based upon the hypothesis that incompatible drives exist.

Rogers (1951) has conceptualized conflict as existing between values rather than drives. A person can, according to Rogers, deny his real feelings and try to assume a contradictory attitude contrary to his feelings because he thinks it is better. These conscious but ungenuine values then come into

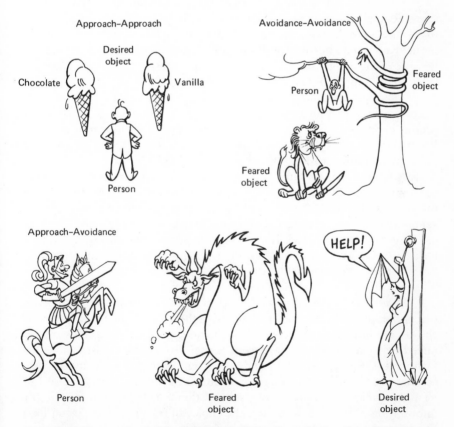

Figure 10-1   A graphic illustration of the three types of conflict according to N. Miller (1944)

conflict with unconscious and genuine feelings. Such a person, says Rogers, will feel tense and out of sorts. Horney (1951) postulated a similar tension between the real self and the ideal self (see Chapter 3).

Conflict and the Basic Motives

We view conflict essentially as a confrontation of incompatible goal movements directed by different motives. It is quite possible for a conflict to exist between the basic motives. For example, a lover may want to rescue his beloved from a burning building (attachment motive) but may hesitate because of the danger (security motive). This situation is, of course, comparable to an approach-avoidance conflict.

The cognitive motive may also conflict with the security motive: curiosity and the search for novelty may tempt us into dangerous situations. A similar conflict may occur between the competence and security motives. We may want to perform a skill task (such as walking along a tightrope) but may hesitate because of the danger of falling.

Another type of related conflict is that between two opposing instrumental methods of trying to pursue a motive. For example, the competence motive may be symbolized in two opposing ways—either successfully to complete a task or never to fail at a task. When faced with a task, the successful completion of which is in doubt, the person may choose to attempt it or choose to avoid it altogether, depending on which symbol of competence is more operative at the time.

A cognitive perspective of conflict. Just as in our definition of motive, perception plays the key role in a cognitive theory of conflict. Motivational choices are directed by perceptual instructions. When the stimulus creates mixed expectancies in the perceiver, a cognitive conflict exists. Since attachment, security, cognition, and competence are organized by the perceptual process, all conflicts can be examined from a perceptual point of view. A conflict can occur because some action is called for but insufficient information is available to permit the choice of response. The person feels he must take some action, but simply doesn't know what. In such cases a person may mark time, putting off the decision until more data are available. If he is forced to make a decision, the person will, as much as possible, maintain his line of movement toward his dominant goal. The more ambiguous the situation, the more determining the internal bias of the person becomes. This vacillating behavior is not so much conflict as it is a decision *not* to respond until the situation becomes less ambiguous. *Ambivalence* (mixed feelings) and its attendant indecision may actually be a way of trying to maintain the status quo until better information is available to permit response selection. One can decide not to decide. One example of such a conflict was given in Chapter 4 when we discussed Adler's theory of psychodynamics (the young woman who is trying to choose between two men).

COMMUNICATION

Interpersonal goal behavior depends on communication, an exchange of information between persons. What is involved in the communication process? One variable is the source of information; whether it arises from the person, the external environment, and/or the relationship between them. A person's style of communicating is another variable. The interaction between communicating styles of two people is still another variable (communicator and receiver characteristics). These variables can be used as *indices of communication,* both verbal and nonverbal.

Measuring the Indices of Communication

As indicated, the principal factors which contribute to an exchange of information in interpersonal communication are the characteristic styles of the persons involved, the reciprocal effects of communicator and receiver on each other, and the structural characteristics of communication.

Characteristic personality style and communication. In Chapters 6 and 9, we used the work of R. S. Lazarus and his associates (Lazarus, 1966; Lazarus and his associates, 1968) to discuss how people differ in the ways they pay attention to information they receive and express (sensitizers and repressors). All of us receive information from internal cognitive and physiological structures as well as from the external environment. And we communicate via internal (physiological) bodily reactions, external bodily expression (facial expression and body language), and verbal statements. Sensitizers pay careful attention to all these sources of information and show consistency between all three measures. For example, if they are confronted with anxiety-provoking information, they reveal, in all three parameters (physiological measures, expressive posture, and verbal statements) that the information was received, processed, and expressed. Repressors tend to censor certain kinds of information, especially that which is emotionally arousing. Although they may verbally deny any fear, yet direct measures will reveal high physiological arousal.

   Some personality styles and implicit communication.   According to the cognitive theory formulated in Chapter 6, each person demonstrates a characteristic personality style which is determined by the organization of his motivational hierarchy. Box 10-3 lists some of the styles that can be identified from clinical and phenomenological observation. The label applied to

---

Box 10-3   Some Common Personality Styles and the Implied Communication in Their Behavior*

The Style	*The Message* (demand characteristic)
The star (supercompetent)	"I'm the best, please applaud."
The aginner	"Right or wrong, I know you're wrong."
The victim	"Things never go right for me."
The getter	"What have you got for me?"
The giver	"Hold still while I force-feed you."
The driver	"Watch my smoke."
The proud one	"I won't stoop to your level."
The lion	"I am the king of the jungle."
The mouse	"Don't frighten me."
The martyr	"Look how I sacrifice for you!"
The critic	"You'll never make it."
The unlovable one	"I'm not lovable."
The undeserving one	"I don't deserve it."
The person who wants to be above reproach	"Don't ever disapprove of me."
The busy beaver	"If I don't do it, it won't get done."
The baby	"I expect you to take care of me."
The prince (princess)	"I'm special."
The good person	"Be pleased by me."
The computer	"These are the facts."
The complainer	"Nobody know the trouble I've seen."
The tower of strength	"If I let up, everybody will fall apart.
The hermit	"I don't need people."
The excitement-seeker	"Whoopee!"

* Each personality style is an example of how perception organizes behavior around a dominant goal. The message transmitted by the behavior, or the interpersonal demand implicit in the behavior, is the communicative aspect of the personality style.

each style is a shorthand term for the way in which the behavioral characteristics are organized in that style.

Behavioral characteristics are themselves conveyors of information that communicate an implicit message to the observer. Box 10-3 also shows the implicit message of each labeled personality style.

Reciprocal effects of communicator and receiver. A number of factors between communicator and receiver (interpersonal) and within each (intrapersonal) affect the accuracy and nature of communication. George Miller has tried to formulate and analyze these factors.

Figure 10-2 shows, in a simplified schema, a heuristic model derived from the technical theory of information and communication suggested by Miller (1953). In this Figure, C sends a message to R. Of course, R sends a message of his own which, in turn, is received by C. T is the transmitted information C and R share in common. The greater the overlap between C and R, the greater the amount of transmitted information, T. *Equivocation* is information the sender has but does not transmit to the receiver, for example, a half-truth or biased message. *Noise* is information added by the receiver, such as inappropriate sets or biased and incorrect interpretation. We can measure the accuracy and quantity of transmitted information by the formula:

$$\text{Transmission} = \text{Total Information} - (\text{Equivocation} + \text{Noise})$$

Structural patterns of verbal communication: Amount and interaction. As we have all observed, social conversation usually consists of an unequal amount of giving and receiving. In studying eight different college student groups, Stephen and Mishler (1952) uncovered a reciprocal pattern between talking and listening. Most of the talking and active listening was done by only two people in each group, who accounted for 40 percent of the total verbal communication taking place. Talkative people are also talked to (hence their active listening), while quiet people are ignored, regardless of what may be going on within them.

Bales (1970) found further that the most talkative people are most likely to become leaders, but that they will not necessarily be the most liked. In an experimental design that held other interpersonal variables constant, Stang (1973) had subjects listen to and rate tapes where the communicator spoke 50, 33, or 17 percent of the time. While the ratings of leadership were linearly related to the amount spoken, the raters liked the middle group the most.

Furthermore, talking and listening tendencies appear to be relatively consistent personality dispositions. David (1972) found that any effect of reinforcing quiet people for talking in one group did not transfer to another interpersonal situation. Whether people talk and engage with one another,

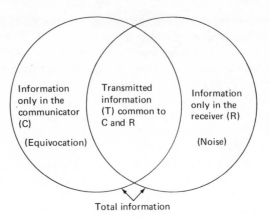

Total information

Figure 10-2 Schematic representation of the accuracy of information transmitted as a function of the communicator's ability and willingness to send complete information and the receiver's ability to decode it. Total information available (both circles) includes equivocation and noise. Source: Modified and simplified from Miller (1953).

including their reaction to situational specifics, is itself a consistent personality disposition.

Patterns of interaction have also been studied in verbal communication. Using the Interaction Process Analysis (IPA) system of Bales (1950), in which raters code verbal interaction patterns in 12 categories, Bales (1958) found marked yet complementary differences between the personality traits of the two most talkative people. While one was friendly, warm, and emotionally supportive (tending to maintain smooth interpersonal flow and movement), the other was a task-oriented confronter, giving information and expressing opinions and suggestions.

Crawford (1974) and Crawford and Haaland (1972) researched the components of one of the more important categories of the IPA, namely, the category "seeks information." An analysis of their results indicates that individuals are most likely to seek information when the structure of verbal interaction has the following components: (1) cooperative group atmosphere; (2) member uncertainty about the correct decision; (3) importance of the decision for which the information is sought; (4) having been rewarded for correct decisions; (5) correctness of previous information given.

Shannon and Guerney (1973) also found *reciprocity* (mutuality) between the kind of stimulus information sought by a communicator and the response given by the responder. These reciprocal patterns seemed in the service of personality tendencies. Thus, statements which express cooperativeness and interdependency are answered by responses expressing advice and leadership. Statements expressing competition and self-assertiveness are replied to with responses expressing argument and self-enhancement.

Cognitive style, trait variables, and reciprocal effects between communicator and receiver are all important in the general process of communication. Similar variables also operate in nonverbal communication.

Nonverbal Communication

While we will limit our discussion of nonverbal communication to facial expressions and a few other aspects of body language, Weiner and his associates (1972) give a general review of the structural components of nonverbal behavior in the flow and maintenance of interpersonal communication. Duncan (1969) has classified these components into three classes of variables: (1) *Kinesics,* the study of expressive body and facial movements, which owes much of its current impetus to the trail-blazing research of Birdwhistell (1970); (2) *proxemics,* the study of the personal and social use of space, summarized and analyzed by Sommer (1969); and (3) *paralanguage,* the study of the nonverbal aspects of speech communication. We will briefly describe some work in kinesics, especially facial expressions, and in proxemics.

Facial expression in communication. Eibl-Eibesfeldt (1971) considers much facial expression innate in humans. He points out that blind and blind/deaf children show normal emotional facial expression. Facial expression is important in communication. Eibl-Eibesfeldt found cross-cultural consistency in greeting expressions (raised eyebrows) as shown in Figure 10-3, in hand gestures, and in other body movements. Eibl-Eibesfeldt's hypotheses are supported by the work on the role of bodily gestures and facial expressions in the pioneering studies on chimpanzees in the natural environment by Jane Goodall (1965, 1968).

The question of innate and learned aspects of facial expressions and their recognition has been dealt with comprehensively by Tomkins (1962, 1963). He hypothesized that there are innate neural programs that link evoking stimuli to the arousal of eight *primary affects*—anger, disgust, fear, sadness, interest, surprise, happiness, and shame. *Secondary affects* are derived from associations among two or more of these primary affects and may thus involve learning and cultural experience.

Studies, such as that of Ekman and his associates (1970), using photographs, videotape, and motion pictures, have substantiated seven of Tomkins' primary effects (all except shame) across cultures. These researchers presented to American and Japanese subjects movie films of autumn leaves and sinus surgery, the latter intended to induce stress.

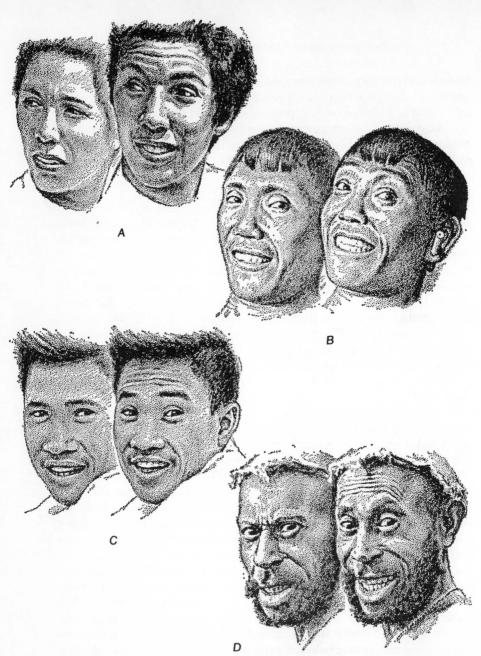

Figure 10-3　　In greeting with the eyes, the eyebrows are jerked upwards for about one-sixth of a second. The series of pictures here is illustrative of the facial expression at the moment of visual contact and on greeting with the eyes. They are drawn from film stills. *A:* Balinese; *B:* Papuan (Woitapmin, photographed by the author); *C:* Frenchwoman (photographed by H. Hass); *D:* Walke Indian (photographed by the author). Source: Eibl-Eibesfeldt, 1971, pp. 14-15.

Unknown to the subjects, their facial expressions were videotaped and subjected to analysis by independent rater coders. The analysis revealed higher scores for anger, disgust, and surprise than for happiness. It is a moot question why stress did not induce fear in these subjects. However, Eibl-Eibesfeldt questions this specific set of categories and the derivation of secondary affects from associations. He points to the need to study spontaneous facial expressions in motion.

Facial expressions communicate many affects and intentions, indeed all the emotions that humans experience. Direct communication can also take place through facial expression (smiling to show pleasure, grimacing to show pain, winking to flirt, and so on).

Gesture. Hayes (1957) studied the communicative aspects of gesture, another aspect of bodily communication. Gesture is probably much less innately programmed than facial expression, but some gestures, such as the raised hand in greeting seem pancultural. Kissing, nose rubbing, touching, patting, and hugging are common gestures in most societies. The threat gesture of shaking the fist, accompanied by a facial scowl, would probably be understood in any society.

Posture. The position of the body in space also communicates information. Katz (1964) conducted a study in which subjects were asked to watch interviewers at work and then rate them according to whether or not they were "understanding." The ratings were done on body posture alone. Katz found that subjects rated interviewers as "understanding" if (1) the head was held in an attentive posture and (2) the body was hunched forward. Spiegel and Machotka (1974) studied the reactions of subjects to various aspects of posture: upright or horizontal posture, arm position, direction of gaze, head position, standing on ground higher or lower than another person, closeness or distance from others, and encounter postures, both group and male-female. Subjects were asked to react to posture in a series of paintings by well-known artists, to diagrams, to mannequins; and themselves to arrange mannequins in their preferred position in various imaginary social contexts. Figure 10-4 shows various arm positions studied by Spiegel and Machotka.

It can be seen that each arm position of Venus evokes a different image. Similar variations in response were found to the other aspects of posture. Table 10-3 shows preferences for and adjectives applied to the various postures in Figure 10-4.

Proxemics: proximity. Hall (1966), a pioneer in proxemics, examined the way humans handle spatial distance between themselves. He divided distance between persons into four categories (see Box 10-4).

Proximity is influenced by culture. Arabs are much more comfortable

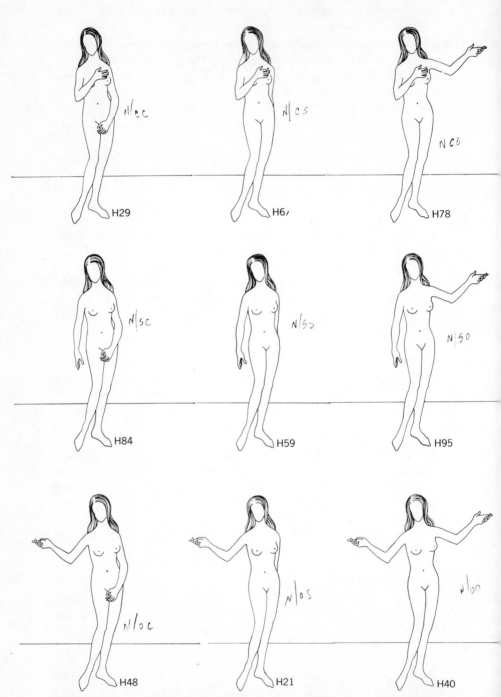

Figure 10-4 The Arms of Venus. Source: Spiegel and Machotka, 1974, p. 198.

Table 10-3   Preferences for and Adjectives Applied to the Various Arm Positions of Venus. The letters N/SS, N/SO, etc. designate the particular postures shown in figure 10-4.

	Most	Second	Second	Most	
Natural	N/SS	N/SO	N/CO	N/OC	Unnatural
Immodest	N/OO	N/SO	N/SC	N/CC	Modest
Receiving	N/OO–N/SS	N/SO	N/OC	N/CC	Rejecting
Self-concerned	N/CC	N/SC	N/OO	N/SO	Other-concerned
Cold	N/CC	N/SC	N/OO	N/SS	Warm
Active	N/OO	N/SO	N/CS	N/CC	Passive
Dramatic	N/OO	N/CO	N/SC	N/SS	Calm
Shy	N/CC	N/SC	N/CO	N/OO	Exhibitionistic
Affected	N/CO	N/OC	N/OS	N/SS	Ingenuous
Unyielding	N/CC	N/OC	N/OO	N/SS	Yielding
Pulled toward	N/SS	N/OS	N/CO	N/CC–N/OC	Pulled away

Source: From Spiegel and Machotka, 1974, p. 194.

at close distance than Westerners. An Arab will show by body posture that he wants to be alone and is less likely to segregate himself in space. The determinants of proxemic behavior are social rules, sensory reception (such as odors), posture, sex identification, voice loudness, the activity pursued, and whether the behavior is sociofugal or sociopetal (away from or toward others).

Mehrabian's Studies

In extensive research on nonverbal communication, Mehrabian (1972) uncovered the following important variables influencing physical patterns of relationships.

Immediacy.   Immediacy cues are concerned with temporal and spatial proximity. In the case of spatial posture and position, immediacy is characterized by more touching, closer position, forward lean, smaller separating distance, and more direct and longer eye contact. Immediacy is also revealed in the implied aspects of verbalization. Thus, the second word of the pair in Box 10-5 reveals more immediacy.

Box 10-4   Hall's Distance Categories

Intimate distance (6 to 18 inches): An uncomfortable distance for most Westerners unless engaged in intimate contact.

Personal distance (1½ to 4 feet): The usual distance we use in working together or talking to each other.

Social distance (4 to 12 feet): A tradesman and customer may use this distance. It is also common in small groups.

Public distance (12 or more feet): A teacher may use this distance in the classroom.

Source: After Hall (1966).

Relaxation.   Certain postures are also characteristic of various internal states. Asymmetrical rather than symmetrical position reveals a more relaxed attitude. Thus asymmetrical arm (or leg) position, sideways lean, openness of arm position, and reclining body position reveal more relaxation than the opposite of these. Using these indices, Mehrabian found we are very relaxed with those we dislike or disrespect, moderately relaxed with those we like or respect, and tense with those who threaten us. In addition, relaxation also reveals status or power. High status or powerful individuals reveal more relaxed postures.

Bodily and facial cues.   Following Ekman and Friesen (1969), Mehrabian studied honesty and deception as revealed by face, arms, and lower extremities. In Mehrabian's experiment, subjects were asked to express their attitudes about abortion. The subjects who expressed the most extreme views were paired and were then instructed to convince their partner about a view *opposite* to their own expressed view—that is, they were required to transmit deceptive information. While this was going on, trained observers were monitoring the bodily expressions of the subjects. When subjects were communicating their true attitudes, the face and arms revealed more information than the lower extremities. However, when deceiving, the legs and feet reveal more information. When we are relaxed, the legs are free. However, when we lie, the legs are kept in a frozen position.

This last finding is not surprising. When we communicate we are more likely to monitor facial expression than the lower part of the body.

A concluding statement on dynamics.   In Chapters 9 and 10 we have organized our discussion of psychodynamics in a way that parallels our discussion of personality structure in Chapter 6. Just as we spoke about differentiation of motives, so we spoke about the differentiation of goal behavior. In discussing how the differentiations of the motives and their associated emotional components motivate behavior, we have focused on the instructions generated by the perceptual system which these motives convey to the person.

Box 10-5   Immediacy (Intimacy) Completion Word

Those (these) people need help.
There (here) is John.
I knew that (this) person.
Those (these) people need help.
They (we) have some problems.
It is your (our) concern.

Source: From Mehrabian, 1972

11

assessment
of
personality

OVERVIEW

In the assessment of personality, it is important to assess both person and situation. In the former case, both overt and covert responses are measured. Different theorists use assessment techniques consistent with their own philosophies. Thus, behavioral assessment is guided by the SORC paradigm, which assesses personality in terms of situation, organism, response and consequences. Behavioral measurements are scored as behavior codes and incorporated into a scoring scale. The behavior codes are made explicit enough so that they have inter-rater reliability.

Cognitive social learning theory is a transition from behavioral assessment methods to methods which pay more attention to measuring internal processes; it combines both objective testing and projective techniques. One of the most frequently used objective tests to measure personality traits is the Minnesota Multiphasic Personality Inventory (MMPI). By contrast, projective techniques try to *infer* underlying personality structure and dynamics from the test material. The TAT is a representative example of a popular projective technique. Personality evaluations derived from a personality inventory such as the MMPI are based on statistical or actuarial norms, whereas the evaluation derived from projective tests depends more on the interpretive skill of the examiner. In the latter case, the examiner's skill and experience will affect the reliability of the test.

Cognitive assessment techniques such as Kelly Rep test give a direct measurement of cognitive constructs, which we consider the core organizers of all behavior. Finally, interview and life history methods give a broad spectrum measure of personality. They give an integrated view of the person in his situation.

The scientific study of any phenomenon usually requires quantitative measurement. In all such measurement, a person has to read or interpret a scale. However, each interpreter has his own personal bias as was pointed out long ago by the founders of experimental psychology. This personal bias influences how a scale is interpreted. In addition, experimenters are subject to experimenter bias—that is, the experimenter has a tendency to interpret results so as to find the outcome he is looking for (Rosenthal, 1966).

An accurate way to predict behavior is to measure both personality and situational variables and the specific nature of their interaction. As explained in Chapter 1, the science of personology must consider idiographic (personality) and nomothetic (situation) variables.

The Importance of Measuring Both Personality and Situation

Using similar logic, Cronbach (1957, 1975) and Bindra and Scheier (1954), have argued convincingly that the most informative psychological research combines the measurement of person variables with traditional experimental methods which measure situational variables. An experiment demonstrating the significance of the interaction between personality and experimental analysis was conducted by Domino (1971). The main features of the research procedure are described in Box 11-1.

Cronbach and Snow (1975) report some generalizations of this interaction. For example, studies have reported many interaction effects between instructor characteristics and student motives for power, afffiliation and achievement. From these studies, Cronbach states that "the constructively motivated student is at his best when an instructor challenges him and then leaves him to pursue his own thoughts and projects. In contrast, the dependent student tends to profit when the instructor lays out the work in detail" (Cronbach, 1975, p. 119).

It should be pointed out further that the treatment X personality de-

---

Box 11-1   The Interaction Between Personality and Teaching Method in Academic Achievement and Satisfaction (after Domino, 1971).

Purpose of Experiment: To study the effect of different teaching methods on different student personalities (a treatment X personality design).

Methodological Design: There were four groups of subjects, each group made up of a particular personality variable exposed to a specific treatment situation. The personality variable was measured by determining whether the person attained achievement through independent effort (Ai) or achievement through conforming to the teacher's demands (Ac). The treatment variable was manipulated by exposing these two personality types to two different classroom situations. In one treatment situation, the teacher stressed and reinforced independent activity on the part of the student. In the other treatment situation, teachers stressed and reinforced conformity to the teacher's wishes (instructor press).

In a study like this, it is important that the teachers applying the treatment have no knowledge of the purpose of the study or of the personalities of the individual students, in order to avoid experimenter bias effects and other confounding conditions which will lead to ambiguous interpretation of results.

Results: Are shown in Table 11-1.

Conclusion: High independent low conforming students (High Ai, low Ac), performed better and expressed more satisfaction when the instructor press encouraged independence, while the High Ac, low Ai students performed better and expressed more satisfaction when the instructor press encouraged conformity. Different personalities respond differently to the specific teaching methods.

Table 11-1 Outcomes of a Psychology Course under Four Combinations of Personality and Treatment

Student pattern	Instruction press	Mean outcome (recorded)*			
		Exam	Course grade	Originality of thought	Student satisfaction
Independent (High Ai, Low Ac)	Independence	98	100	99	100
	Conformity	87	83	100	88
Conforming (Low Ai, High Ac)	Independence	78	66	65	82
	Conformity	100	89	50	94

* The value of 100 was assigned to the average score of the hightest ranking group, and other averages were scaled proportionately. Here, Exam combined a factual multiple-choice test and a quality score for the final essay exam that Domino (1971) reported separately. Likewise, two satisfaction measures have been pooled. (From Domino, 1971, reprinted from Cronbach, 1975, p. 117.)

sign has shown that experimental findings are not necessarily valid across generations, because culturally determined preferences change. For example, Atkinson (1974) points out that the results of Lewin (1944) and his associates on levels of aspiration were valid in Germany and the United States at a time when achievement was probably a dominant motive. This data may be less reproducible today when affiliation may have become relatively more important.

In addition to taking into account the personality X situation interaction and trying to avoid confounding conditions in methodological design, there are other technical concerns in the study and assessment of personality. For example, the measuring scales we use must be reliable and valid. A discussion of these and other technical issues in assessment is best left to text books on the subject of assessment and measurement such as Cronbach (1970), Fiske (1971) and Sundberg (1977).

What Do We Assess When We Assess Personality?
A Cognitive Perspective

Behavior consists of both overt and covert responses—responses that are openly visible and others that are unseen but require that we make inferences. Modern technology has made it possible to use instruments to obtain physiological indices of covert responses. From the work of Lazarus and others summarized in Chapters 9 and 10, we saw that measures of covert and overt behavior may show agreement or disagreement.

Recall that repressers deny an emotion when, in fact, physiological measurements indicate that it is present. Sensitizers, on the other hand, show overt behavior which is consistent with underlying physiological indices. Sensitizers are thus attending to both external and internal sources of information and, according to Lazarus and his associates, are therefore more adaptive.

From our cognitive viewpoint the perceptual system transmits the information about both external and internal behavior; thus the ultimate parameters we want to assess are located in the underlying perceptual and cognitive structure of personality. In order to assess this structure, we must develop methods to measure the person's self-perception, his world view, and the instructions he gives himself about how to behave in the world.

In this chapter we will describe assessment techniques used by different theorists. Thus behavior theorists have developed behavioral assessment techniques which focus primarily on the direct observation of responses made by single subjects.

Social learning theorists such as Bandura and Rotter provide a bridge between traditional behavioral measures and cognitive theory, emphasizing cognitive processes as the foundation of behavioral procedures.

The assessment techniques used by trait theorists are called *objective tests*. Contemporary users of objective tests measure personality by devising tests to measure traits, interests, attitudes, and values.

Projective techniques are used by psychologists whose backgrounds are more clinical. Murray's TAT is an attempt to formulate scales to measure personality from the inferences drawn from fantasy behavior.

The most direct measures of cognitive structure are tests of cognitive style, such as Witkin's psychological differentiation, and measurements of personal constructs as formulated by Kelly.

The final section of this chapter will show how the interview and life history analysis are used to formulate the personality of the individual.

BEHAVIORAL METHODS

Behavioral assessment measures overt behavior directly by observing and measuring responses in natural settings or in the laboratory under controlled conditions. The behavioral assessor asserts that he probably makes the fewest errors since he makes the fewest assumptions. However, he may be more liable to a type two error; that is, his conditions may be so strongly controlled that important underlying determinants of behavior will not be picked up by his tests.

The SORC Paradigm

In addition to emphasizing controlled studies of single subjects, the behavioral assessor is also guided by what is called the *SORC* paradigm—that is, behavior is assessed in terms of situational, organismic, response, and consequence variables. *Situational* variables which elicit differential responses are noted. For example, if a child behaves appropriately in school but not at home, he is responding differentially (discriminating between the cues) to the two situations. Determining what in the home situation instigates the inappropriate behavior becomes part of the assessment. The discrimination may be part of an *organismic* variable, genetically grounded, or may result from past reinforcement contingencies.

The behaviorist distinguishes between two kinds of *responses,* respondents and operants. *Respondents* are emotional and involuntary, while *operants* are voluntary and thus of more interest to the behaviorist. Recent studies have shown that operant techniques can be used to condition even involuntary respondents such as heart rate (Miller, DiCara, Solomon, Weiss, & Dworkiss, 1971). In a behavioral assessment, the frequency, strength, duration, and latency of operants may be measured.

The following specific behavioral assessment techniques are all guided by the SORC paradigm in one way or another. A scoring manual is constructed in each of these techniques which permits the coding of behavioral responses.

Some examples of behavior assessment techniques and their behavior observation codes. Behavioral observation codes have been applied across a wide range of situations. O'Leary and Becker (1967) have trained observers to sit at the back of a classroom and code children's disruptive behavior (noisiness, speaking without raising hands, and pushing). Their scoring manual, revised by O'Leary and O'Leary (1972), has been useful in measuring the effects of token rewards aimed at diminishing disruptive behavior. Lewinsohn and Shaffer (1971), among others, used behavioral observation codes to rate dyadic interaction. The subject's "action" and "reaction" to other family members in the home were recorded by observers and coded using scales on a scoring manual. Indices of action consisted of such categories as criticism, information request, statements of personal problems, and complaint. Reaction indices could be either positive—such as approval, laughter, and interest—or negative—disagreement, criticism, punishment, and ignoring. Inter-scorer reliability for different observers using these codes is quite high (Mariotto & Paul, 1974).

Minimal social behavior scale. The minimal social behavior scale (Farina, Arenbert, & Guskin, 1957) has been applied within a standardized interview situation with hospitalized patients to measure maladjustment and phobias. Observers rate patients on 32 different responses to a simple verbal command, such as, "Drop a pencil on the floor." The response to each item is scored as appropriate or inappropriate. Inter-rater reliability is reported as high.

Behavioral Assessment in a Cognitive Context

Behavior theory has generated much research, and behavior modifiers deserve credit for their empirical studies of assessment procedures. Following the early lead of A. A. Lazarus (1971), who introduced a concern with cognition into the behavioral assessment methods, Mahoney (1974) points to the necessity of a cognitive context for behavior modification. He cites a study by Kaufman, Baron, and Kopp (1966) on how cognitive contingencies affect the outcome of using schedules of reinforcement to alter response patterns.

Five groups of subjects participated in a "concept formation" experiment—that is, they had to discover the unifying concept common to all items in a group. One control group was given minimal instructions (M), and a second was simply told the critical response to make in indicating the concept. Two additional control groups were led to believe (their expectancy) that they would be reinforced at arbitrary intervals (the VI group) or that the reward schedule would depend on how many responses they gave (the VR group). The final group was told that they would be rewarded at a fixed interval of 1 minute (the FI group). In reality, each subject was on this FI schedule. Results are in Figure 11-1.

The cumulative response patterns depended on what the subject thought the consequences of his responses would be rather than what the environmental contingencies actually were. Compare the different patterns of FI and VR. Thus, expectancy, a cognitive factor, becomes a crucial determinant rather than only a reinforcement contingency.

A TRANSITION:
COGNITIVE SOCIAL LEARNING THEORY

The importance of expectancy has been emphasized most strongly by two of the social learning theorists, Bandura and Rotter.

Bandura and Modeling Behavior

As has been already mentioned, Bandura's latest research (1976) has led him to believe that reinforcement represents a subclass of modeling, which in turn is a function present in children because of their cognitive abilities. This view with its experimental support and interpretation is elaborated in Box 11-2.

The study outlined in Box 11-2 indicates that experimental analysis

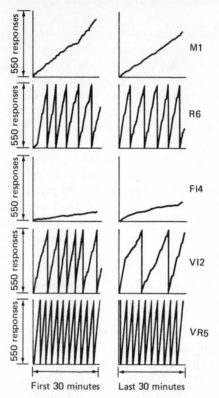

Figure 11-1   Cumulative response records from a representative subject in each of the five experimental conditions. From the top, the conditions illustrated are Minimal instructions (M), Response Instructions (R), Fixed Interval (FI), Variable Interval (VI), and Variable Ratio (VR) Instructions. Digits refer to subject number. The records are taken from the first and last 30 minutes of performance during a three-hour experimental session. Source: Reprinted with permission from Kaufman, Baron, and Kopp, 1966.

and assessment can be useful not only in generating basic data, but also in practical applications to behavior change. Observational learning affects mediating processes so that behavior becomes more adaptive. Thus, it has been shown (Bandura, 1976) that reducing physiological arousal improves performance because it raises expectations of personal efficacy (rather than by eliminating a drive). By such research, Bandura links observational learning with cognition—namely, *one can alter cognitive structure by varying observational learning.*

Assessment in Rotter's Social Learning Theory

Rotter (1966) originally constructed the Internal-External (I-E) control scale to assess whether persons have a predominant tendency to attribute causal events either to their own effort (and responsibility) or to external chance. The test consists of 29 items in which a person must choose between an *a* or *b* response. See Box 11-3.

One response attributes an event to a personal action (internal locus of control), the other to luck or chance (external locus of control). In the example given, the *b* response would be scored as internal (I). Since there are four fillers (items) to guard against habituation, the maximum score for I can be 25, with 14 considered a high score. One can see that the test measures expectancy, so that in effect it yields some evidence of cognitive style.

A number of validation studies using the I-E scale have been conducted, summarized, and evaluated in a review by Phares (1976). For example, Phares (1968) found that when subjects were told that they were in a computer simulation study to match people suited to marry each other, the internals made more use of the information given. Internals are also more sensitive and alert. Ude and Vogler (1969) found that where contingencies of reinforcement were the effective variable, internals utilized that information much earlier than externals.

In addition, internals appear to be confronters in the search for information, even when this information may be uncomfortable. Lefcourt and Wine (1969) required subjects to interview confederates under two conditions: when the interviewee was instructed to have eye contact or when he was instructed to avoid eye contact. It was found that internals looked more often at the persons who were avoiding eye contact. When there are uncertainties in the situation, internals are more likely to pay attention to potentially relevant cues than externals. This perceptiveness of internals was verified in an error scanning task by Wolk and DuCette (1974), who found that internals exhibit more incidental learning than externals.

The above examples are really examples of how internals and externals differ in cognitive style. These reported differences are summarized in Table 11-2

OBJECTIVE TESTS: THE ASSESSMENT OF TRAITS

In contrast to behavioral assessment techniques, which focus on how the person behaves in specific situations, assessors who use objective techniques assume that verbal behavior—in response to written questionnaires, for

Table 11-2   Difference in Cognitive Style of Internal and External Locus of Control

1. Internals are more likely to *seek information.*
2. Internals are more *sensitive* and *alert.*
3. Internals show more *incidental learning.*
4. Internals *pay more attention to relevant cues* when there are uncertainties in the situation.
5. Internals are more responsive to *informational requirements.*
6. Externals are more susceptible to *social influences and social demands.*
7. Internals pursue goals by paying careful attention to demands of the task.
8. Externals pursue goals by relying more on behaviors oriented toward the social agent in the situation.

Source: Adapted from Pines, 1973.

example—is related to *long-term personality characteristics.* By and large it is trait theorists who use these techniques, and their method of analysis is called *psychometric.* The psychometrist believes that verbal responses to written questionnaires can be measured and scored through statistical procedures—thus the approach has also been called *actuarial.* The method for analyzing the meaning of these patterns of scored responses is the correlation method. If a number of items are administered to different criterion groups, one can compute the association between scores on the items among the various criterion groups. If the association is high, one speaks of a high correlation coefficient, or vice versa. Correlation can vary from -1 (perfect inverse association) through 0 (no association) to $+1$ (perfect association). By finding which cluster of items is associated with which criterion groups, we can establish scales for measuring various personality traits. This will become clearer as we describe and briefly examine one of the most popular objective techniques, the MMPI.

The Minnesota Multiphasic Personality Inventory (MMPI)

The MMPI was developed for the differential diagnosis of psychiatric disorders—to assess the type of maladjustment (Hathaway & McKinley, 1940) and its severity or degree (Hathaway, 1965). In standardizing and validating the MMPI, the method of contrasted groups was used. In the original construction 566 items (verbal statements) were administered to normal subjects and psychiatric patients (the contrasted groups), who were asked to mark each statement "true" or "false." From statistical analysis of the answers, clinical scales were established for each distinct patient group, with its own unique characteristics. The standardized scales used in the current version of the MMPI are presented in Table 11-3.

The subject's personality *profile* is identified by the two scale numbers which represent the highest scale scores obtained by the subject. Research on the behavioral and clinical characteristics of these profiles has provided data which permit a description of traits found in each profile. Several profile types are shown in Box 11-4. An atlas containing a number of profiles and behavior descriptions based on actuarial studies has been assembled by Marks, Seeman, and Haller (1974).

The subject's personality *profile* is identified by the two scale numbers which represent the highest scale scores obtained by the subject. Research on the behavioral and clinical characteristics of these profiles has provided data which permit a description of traits found in each profile. Several profile types are shown in Box 11-4. An atlas containing a number of profiles and behavior descriptions based on actuarial studies has been assembled by Marks, Seeman, and Haller (1974).

Box 11-3 is intended only to give a sample of some interpretations.

There are other code types and other systems of classification. A graph depicting the scale score scatter of one subject is shown in Figure 11-2, together with an interpretation of the subject's personality. The same subject will be used for the TAT, interest, and intelligence tests later in this chapter.

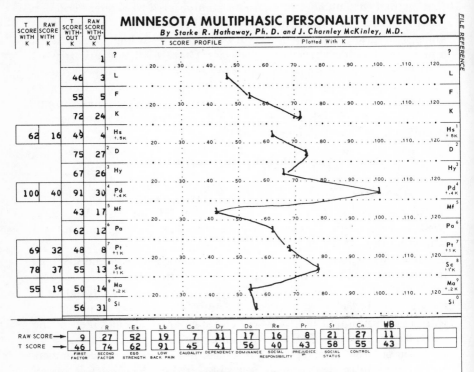

-PATIENT IS AWARE OF AND CONCERNED ABOUT ASOCIAL ATTITUDES AND
EMOTIONAL IMPULSES BUT UNABLE TO CONTROL THEM.
    -TENDS TO MINIMIZE OR SMOOTH OVER FAULTS IN SELF FAMILY AND
CIRCUMSTANCES.
    -PROBABLY SOMEWHAT ECCENTRIC, SECLUSIVE AND WITHDRAWN. MANY
INTERNAL CONFLICTS.
    -MODERATELY DEPRESSED WORRYING AND PESSIMISTIC.
    -SLIGHTLY MORE THAN AVERAGE NUMBER OF PHYSICAL COMPLAINTS. SOME
CONCERN ABOUT BODILY FUNCTIONS AND PHYSICAL HEALTH.
    -SENSITIVE. ALIVE TO OPINIONS OF OTHERS.
    -HAS CAPACITY TO MAINTAIN ADEQUATE SOCIAL RELATIONSHIPS.
    -NORMAL ENERGY AND ACTIVITY LEVEL.
    _NORMAL MALE INTEREST PATTERN FOR WORK, HOBBIES ETC.

MALE AGE 16

Figure 11-2   A graph showing the scale score scatter of an actual subject. The scoring and interpretation are by computer. Source: The Psychological Corporation MMPI Reporting Service.

Table 11-3   Standard MMPI Scales

Scale Name	Abbreviation	Number	Items	Classical Interpretation of Elevated Scores
LIE	L	—	15	Denial of common frailties
FREQUENCY	F	—	64	Invalidity of profile because of expected infrequency
CORRECTION	K	—	30	Defensive, evasive
Hypochondriasis	HS	1	33	Emphasis on somatic complaints
Depression	D	2	60	Unhappy, depressed
Hysteria	Hy	3	60	Hysterical symptomatology
Psychopathic deviancy	Pd	4	50	Lack of social conformity; often in trouble with law
Masculinity-femininity	Mf	5	60	Effeminate (males); masculine orientation (females)
Paranoia	Pa	6	40	Suspicious
Psychasthenia	Pt	7	48	Worried, anxious
Schizophrenia	Sc	8	78	Withdrawn; bizarre mentation
Hypomania	Ma	9	46	Impulsive, expansive
Social introver-sion-Extrover-sion	St	0	70	Introverted, shy

Source: After Gynther and Gynther, 1976, p. 205.

The MMPI has been researched more than any other personality inventory (Dahlstrom & Welsh, 1960; Dahlstrom, Welsh, & Dahlstrom, 1972; Dahlstrom, 1974). Meehl (1954, 1956) believes that inventories like the MMPI are the most reliable ways to assess personality. Although the MMPI manual, using the test-retest method, indicates reliability coefficients from 0.50 to 0.90, split-half methods have achieved reliabilities of only 0.05 to 0.81 (Kleinmuntz, 1969). There is thus some question about the internal consistency of the score scales.

Other personality inventories.   Space precludes a full description of other inventories. The California Psychological Inventory (CPI) initiated by Harrison Gough (1957, 1968) and elaborated empirically by Megargee (1972) is, in a sense, a derivative of the MMPI, having been standardized with similar procedures. Since the scales were based on "folk concepts," it has been shown to have some cross-cultural validity. Gough and Quintard (1974) have shown that their *Socialization Scale* and *Social Maturity Index* reliably distinguish delinquents from nondelinquents in several countries. The Personality Research Form (PRF) by Jackson (1967) is an inventory based on Murray's need system. It has scales for measuring achievement, affiliation, dominance, impulsivity, and order.

Another personality inventory constructed by Cattell (1965) and his

Box 11-4. Profiles or Code Types from MMPI Scales. The Code Type is Identified by Scale Numbers.

Profile—(Code Type	Personality Characteristics	Reference
1-2/2-1	Organically sick; chronic complaints; passive dependent; lack insight; high fatiguability	Halbower, 1955
1-3/3-1	Organically sick; self-centered; passive-aggressive	Halbower, 1955
2-7/7-2	Feeling of inferiority; high motivation for recognition	Halbower, 1955
8-7/7-8	Lack poise and self-confidence; poor defenses; chronic worrying	Halbower, 1955
8-9/9-8	Schizoid; delusional thinking; preoccupied with inner fantasy; over-ideational; regressive dependency	Marks & Seeman, 1963
2-3/3-2	Less conceptually organized; less suspicious; have to be reminded what to do	Lewandowski & Graham, 1972

associates (Cattell, Eber, & Tatsuoka, 1970) is called the 16 PF test. It consists of 16 personality scales such as practical versus imaginative, reserved versus outgoing, suspicious versus trusting. A complete occasional review of such tests can be found in the *Mental Measurement Yearbook* and *Personality Tests and Reviews,* both edited by Buros (see the 1972 reference in the Bibliography).

Interest and value inventories. In addition to assessing traits, one can also measure *values* as Allport, Vernon, and Lindzey (1960) have done. They list six dominant values: aesthetic, economic, political, religious, social, and theoretical. Knowledge of a person's dominant values permits us to predict what vocation would be interesting to him. For example, the highest interest scores of the person, whose MMPI profile is presented in Figure 11-2, are in the areas of law, politics, and business. His highest values are political and economic.

PROJECTIVE TECHNIQUES

Many psychologists have noted that, in contrast both to behavioral assessment, which analyzes behavior as a sample, and to objective (psychometric) methods, which primarily treat data as correlations, "projective techniques emphasize that obtained material is a *sign* of underlying personality structure and dynamics" (Sundberg, 1977, p. 203). The assessor, usually a clinician, makes inferences from these signs. Thus, projective methods are not tests which measure behavior directly but techniques for tapping the projection of covert behavior, from which inferences about personality structure are made. In making inferences, however, the clinician must keep several things in mind—his own perceptual sets, those of the client, how the situation affects the client, and certain contemporary events going on in the client's life.

Projective techniques include: (1) association techniques such as the Rorschach and the Word-Association test, the latter originated by Jung; (2) completion techniques, such as Rotter's Incomplete Sentence Blank (ISB); (3) expressive techniques, such as asking people to draw various figures; these are particularly useful with children or with those whose verbal expression is limited (see Goodenough, 1926; Machover, 1949; and DiLeo, 1973); and (4) construction techniques such as the TAT.

Because they lend themselves more readily to cognitive structure analysis, we will concentrate on the TAT and the ISB.

The Thematic Apperception Test (TAT)

The TAT, a series of pictures of people in various situations, was published by Morgan and Murray in 1935. It is customary to administer eight pictures and ask the subject to write a story about each.

Murray advised that the TAT be scored for both *need* (motive) and *press,* the former referring to an internal goal and the latter to a perceived environmental incentive. Twenty needs and their corresponding social presses can be scored for each story told. Both needs and presses can be scored on a five-point scale of intensity. Although the TAT has no single accepted procedure for scoring and interpretation, elaborate systems do exist for research purposes.

Henry (1947) has added formal and detailed interpretive guidelines. Eron (1950) and Dana (1959) contributed rating scales for evaluating each story. McClelland and his associates (1953) have used the TAT for measuring achievement; Veroff (1957) for measuring power and Atkinson and his co-workers (1954) for measuring affiliation. In a study of TAT validity Eron (1950) administered 20 TAT cards to 150 American male veterans, who produced 3,000 stories. Eron obtained adequate (generally high) inter-rater reliability but could not establish validity, since the fantasy productions do not distinguish between normals and psychiatric patients. In another study of validity, Murstein (1963, 1965) found that fantasied aggression in TAT performance *is* positively related to overt aggression; yet there exist complex interactions with other contingent personality variables (such as guilt and family attitude toward aggression) that complicate the study of the test's validity.

Murstein (1972) has noted that the subject's emotional state will also affect the story told. Thus, hostile college students tell more hostile stories. As with all projective tests, it is important to account for other variables which influence both TAT stories and the tester's interpretations.

From his own experience and a comprehensive review of TAT research, Eron (1977) concluded that the TAT is a useful indicator of general motives, interests, and areas of emotional disturbance, but not a precise assessment technique for measuring specific personality traits of individuals.

It is the view of the present authors that a more molar or organizational approach to the TAT will provide useful information both to the researcher and the clinician. We specifically believe that the cognitive approach to assessment outlined earlier in this chapter can be profitably applied in this direction. Box 11-5 presents a cognitive interpretation of the TAT themes of the 16-year-old adolescent male whose MMPI profile appears in Figure 11-2.

Motive hierarchy, integration, and differentiation in the TAT. Notice that in our cognitive interpretation of the stories in Box 11-5, we have coded the themes or subsets of the basic motive systems. The summary in Box 11-5 shows that security is at the top of this adolescent's motive hierarchy. Attachment (scored as affiliation in the box) is his second most prominent concern. Competence (scored as achievement) is next in line and cognition is the lowest ranking motive. In addition to finding a motive hierarchy from the scored TAT themes, it is also possible to make an estimate of relative differentiation of the motives. In this case, differentiation is low, since the themes mainly revolve around the security motive. Though not well demonstrated in this protocol, it is also possible to estimate from the TAT how integrated the motives are. If the different motives lead to conflicting goal behavior, integration is low. We infer that high motive differentiation and integration represent the most adaptive behavior.

Incomplete Sentence Blank (ISB)

This technique (consisting of 40 completion-type sentences), the most popular example of sentence completion methods, was constructed by Rotter. A manual for scoring responses as *positive, neutral,* and *conflict* was prepared by Rotter and Rafferty (1950). The ISB also lends itself readily to our system for the cognitive analysis of motives. For example, one subject may complete the sentence, "My father ———" with the statement, "still frightens me," while another may complete it with "is very nice." While Rotter would score the first as negative and the second as positive, we would differentiate more finely and score the information in the first case as a negative press with respect to the attachment and/or security motive,

Box 11-5   Representative Cognitive Themes in the TAT Stories of a 16-year-old Male Who "Hated" His Mother and Had a Poor Academic Record

Samples of the stories told in response to the pictures	*Cognitive themes*
1. (Boy with violin). A violin was found by a boy. When he came home he was *wondering* what he was going to do about the lost violin . . . he *returned to the concert hall with the violin*—and the owner *thanked and rewarded him* with $15.	*Self-image:* I am helpful and honest. *Motive:* Affiliation *Press:* Positive. Support from stranger for a good deed.
2. (Farm scene with people) When Beth said she was going . . . to *become a teacher* they *did not pay attention* . . . Beth did, however, *decide to help her mother and father with the farm.*	*Motive:* Achievement. *Press:* Negative. Parents frustrate goals. *Resolution of conflict:* Give into parents' wishes.
3. (Older woman—younger man) Mr. Reynolds was dead. Both Mrs. Reynolds and son knew they would have *to take everything in stride* and *would get over it.*	*Motive:* Security. Concern about losing father. *Resolution:* Resignation and ''bury'' emotions.
4. (Older man—younger man) *Thought* about *what he would look like when he grew old.* Realized that every day you come closer to death whether you *like it or not.*	*Motive:* Security. Concern about aging *Resolution:* Resignation.
5. (Surgery scene) He saw one of the men *holding a knife over his friend.* Took father's gun and said, "Drop the knife or I'll shoot." *They end up in patrol car.*	*World view:* Dangerous. *Motive:* Affiliation. *Ideal self:* To be hero.
6. (Sexual scene) Found his wife *lying naked* in bed . . . had expired. Started to cry . . . then thought he had to call *someone to pick up the corpse.*	*Motive:* Attachment and Security. Concern about losing love. Absence of sex theme. *Resolution:* Burying emotions and being practical.
7. (Abstract picture) Bats and large and small birds surrounded humble house . . . the most common was the wing of the bat. Tom woke up (wondering) if he could have *flown off like a bat.*	*World view:* Big and small organisms competing for space. Outside world is dangerous. *Resolution:* Escape into fantasy.

Brief Summary

   This is a young adolescent male whose achievement motives are frustrated by his parents. His dominant motive is security (fear of death), with affiliation as an instrument for obtaining security. His self-image is of a helpful person caught up in a hostile world; he escapes into fantasy to cope with his own emotions while passively submitting to his presumed fate.

and the second as positive in this subset. In a comprehensive review of 50 validity studies, Goldberg (1965) concludes that sentence completion is probably the most valid of all projective techniques, an opinion which

Murstein (1965) also holds. We agree with their conclusion, because the ISB lends itself so well to scaling and the development of reliable scoring manuals.

COGNITIVE ASSESSMENT TECHNIQUES

Locus of control, ISB, and cognitive methods of scoring the TAT are all ways of assessing personality cognitively. The classical basis for assessing the functional properties of cognitive structure is the concept of differentiation found in the theories of Lewin, Werner, and Piaget, whose work has been described in Chapters 4, 6 and 8. The modern derivative of differentiation, an outgrowth of Kelly's construct theory, is the concept of cognitive complexity—that is, the capacity of the person's cognitive structure to deal with the multidimensionality of events.

Cognitive Complexity

Two different ways of measuring cognitive complexity will be discussed here. Both of them attempt to assess cognitive complexity by measuring the number of dimensions or personal constructs contained in cognitive structure. Crockett (1965) uses a technique in which persons are required to write brief essays about acquaintances who fit certain roles. He measures cognitive complexity by counting the number of different interpersonal adjectives used to describe the acquaintances. Validation studies of Crockett's technique have primarily concentrated on its usefulness in clarifying social perception. Cognitively complex persons are more accurate in processing information about others, in integrating contradictory information about others, and in predicting differences (rather than similarities) between themselves and others.

The above findings suggest that cognitively complex persons are more discriminating in perceptual judgment and should, therefore, be superior in clinical assessment. This implication has been investigated by Bieri, who arrives at a different set of complexity scores (Bieri, 1961; Bieri, Atkins, Briar, Leaman, Miller, & Tripodi, 1966) that do not correlate with scores from Crockett's method (Irwin, Tripodi, & Bieri, 1967).

Bieri's method modifies Kelly's Rep test to provide a measure of the number of functionally different constructs used by a person in construing the behavior of others (rather than his own behavior, as in Kelly's version). A subject is provided with a grid and asked to list a number of acquaintances in the vertical columns. In the horizontal rows, a number of bipolar traits such as adjusted-maladjusted, outgoing-shy are listed. Each of the subject's acquaintances is then rated on these traits, using a six-category rating scale. The similarity of the ratings in each row to every other row is compared—from which a numerical index of cognitive complexity is generated. The less similarity, the more cognitive complexity. Bieri and his associates have conducted empirical studies relating cognitive complexity to clinical judgment, especially when the latter involves reconciling or integrating contradictory information about clients. Bieri's research (1965) provides verified evidence that less complex subjects attempt to form mcre univalent (singular) personality impressions by changing their initial judgments to the most recently presented information. Cognitively more complex subjects, on the other hand, retain both types of (contradictory) information in their personality impression, producing more complicated, if ambivalent, judgments of the other person. In a corroborating study, Tripodi and Bieri (1964) found that cognitively more complex subjects are able to extract more accurate information in clinical inferences than less complex subjects.

How One Scales Subjective Data in Cognitive Assessment

In all of the work reported in this area, subjective data have to be scaled in order to obtain a measure. As Holt (1965) has indicated, the best way to do this is to construct a reliable scoring manual. An actual study by Forgus and DeWolfe (1969) illustrates the stages involved in the construction of scoring manuals for measuring subjective data.

1. *What is the problem?* In Forgus and DeWolfe's study, the problem was to determine whether any reliable information could be obtained from the content of schizophrenic patients' hallucinations.
2. *How to record the subjective experience?* Hallucinating patients were interviewed and the entire interview, including verbatim reports about the hallucinations, was tape recorded.
3. *Creating a scoring manual.* A random sample (10 percent) of the subjective material (hallucinations) was selected as the basis for constructing a scoring manual (see Table 11-4).
4. *Two scorers decide how to use the scoring manual.* Then the scorers rate the rest of the hallucinations independently.
5. *A reliability coefficient between the two scorers is computed.* In this case it was over 0.9. If the reliability is low, the scorers have to iron out their differences. The study cannot continue unless the scoring manual can be used reliably.
6. *The scored subjective experience can then predict unknowns and validity studies can be conducted.* In a preliminary controlled study the Forgus and DeWolfe research found that the themes expressed in hallucinations, as measured by the scoring manual, could also predict relative memory of, or attention to, auditory information which the patients were asked to attend to, retain, and then reproduce verbally. The ability to scale subjective data shows us that this type of data is just as amenable to rigorous scientific analysis as objective data. In fact, such assessment of subjective events goes back to Binet's (1890) first attempt to measure intelligence.

Table 11-4   Samples of Five Scoring Categories for Hallucinatory Themes Used by Forgus and DeWolfe in Their Scoring Manual

---

Conscience disturbance (male 6%, female 67%)

Examples would be voices saying: "you are a tramp," "you have cancer" (implies you are rotten inside), "you are evil," or "repent your sins," etc.

Compensatory grandiosity (male 17%, female 0%)

Ego ideal (grandiose delusions, etc.). Examples: "you are superman, God, etc.," "you are the best person on earth," "you will live forever," "no one can hurt you," or "you will win, no one can stop you," etc.

Level of maturity: Coping with problems (male 56%, female 17%)

Examples for women: patient hears children's voices crying to her for help, or hears children begging her for food, etc.
Examples for men: voices say "stick up for your rights," hears voices say "find a job and get married," etc.

Impulse control problems (male 17%, female 0%)

Examples: voices verbalize to eat, drink, and be merry (or make Harry or Mary). Voices say "go out with no clothes on," "be lascivious," "take a shit," etc.

Impersonal hallucinations (male 6%, female 17%)

Patient does not see the hallucination as related to him. Patient hears "voices of a crowd cheering," "cars being driven noisily," or patient sees "just clouds and spaces," etc.

Note: The percentages shown indicate the proportion of males and females whose hallucinatory themes were in that category. N = 18 males and 12 females.
Source: Forgus and DeWolfe, 1969, pp. 288–292.

A Brief Note on Intelligence Testing

The measurement of intelligence began in 1890 when Alfred Binet was commissioned to devise a way of measuring intellectual ability to be used in making decisions about the education of Paris school children. Even today, IQ test scores have the highest predictive validity for academic performance criteria. The IQ test selected for use in Box 11-6 is the Wechsler Intelligence Scale for Children or *WISC* (Psychological Corporation, 1974), which is the version of the Wechsler Adult Intelligence Scale (*WAIS*) used for individuals under 16 years of age.

The WAIS and WISC consist of two classes of items, each containing five or six sets, which measure verbal ability as learned from educational experience and performance ability—which is assumed to get closer to native ability. Discrepancies between the verbal (VIQ) and performance (PIQ) IQ's have important clinical significance. For example, significantly higher PIQ's are found in students who have more ability than they are using in school. These youngsters are often delinquent and sociopathic and/or underachievers (undermotivated). The young man in Box 11-6 had a significantly higher VIQ than PIQ. He was apparently learning more in school than was reflected in his grades. From this finding, the clinician suspected that anxiety, depression, or other psychological preoccupations might be slowing down his school performance (not his school learning). Box 11-6 shows the steps used by the clinician to track down the personality problems in this case, and his final evaluation.

Role Construct Repertory Test

The Role Construct Repertory Test (called the RCRT or Rep test for short) was developed by George Kelly (1955) and elaborated by others (Bieri, 1961; Bannister & Mair, 1968; Bannister, 1970). The Rep test has

---

Box 11-6   Integrated Personality Evaluation Based on Interview and Various Assessment Instruments

The male client described in this chapter was brought for psychological consultation by his parents because of the following presenting problems: (1) he was doing poorly in school academically; (2) he "hated" his mother and was generally defiant and antisocial in his reactions to both parents.

How the psychologist operated and why he chose the particular assessment techniques:

Following the initial clinical interview to start developing personal rapport and to obtain an overview and perspective on the personality functioning of the young man, the psychologist decided first to administer an intelligence test since the client had a poor academic record. The results of the IQ test indicated clearly that the boy was *not* an underachiever—that is, what he was learning in school was not less than his ability. Rather, he was not showing in his test performance what he was actually learning in school. So it was substandard performance rather than underachievement that was responsible for the poor academic record.

Knowing that underperformance can be caused by a number of factors—psychomotor retardation related to depression, anxiety, or antisocial defiance—the psychologist decided on a battery of tests which could help track down which of these factors were involved.

Analysis of the TAT projective protocol (see Box 11-5) revealed the following salient features: The client perceives himself as a person who wants to be helpful and needs support from adults (his motives) but is continuously frustrated by them (negative press). He expects things to turn out badly, and when they do he passively resigns himself to failure and withdraws into fantasy. The fantasy centers around concerns about his parents which indicate severe insecurity and anxiety. Since he withdraws both from any action aimed at competence and from his parents, he becomes preoccupied with winning favor and approval from affiliation with his friends.

The MMPI psychometric test (see Figure 11-2) threw light on his insecurities, anxiety, and social attitudes, as well as his preoccupation with attachment and withdrawal from competence. It uncovered that he was aware and concerned about his social attitudes and emotional impulses, but felt unable to control them. In addition, he was moderately depressed, worrying, and pessimistic.

been called the most sophisticated example of idiographic measurement (Wiggins, 1973). The test is based on Kelly's personal construct theory, which states that each individual construes the world in a unique fashion (one's personal constructs). A person can be understood to the extent that his system of constructs for ordering and anticipating events can be clarified. The personal constructs organize a person's view of the world, his place in it, and the actions he takes. The Rep test was thus designed to be used as an instrument for eliciting personal constructs.

In the Rep test, the subject selects his own way of evaluating people and relationships rather than using the conceptual system of the assessing psychologist (Sundberg, 1977). The subject is given 20 to 30 role titles such as *your father, your mother, your favorite teacher, a teacher you didn't like, the most successful person you know, a person you pity,* and so on. From these 20 to 30 role titles, three are selected and presented to the subject, who is then asked to describe in what way any two of them are similar and how the third person differs from the other two. This process continues until 15 or more sorts are accumulated. A trained evaluator can determine the subject's construct system from these answers.

The Rep test lends itself well to discovering the unique aspects of a person's way of construing the world. It not only yields idiographic information but permits the measurement of some nomothetic concepts as well. One of these is based on the number of constructs. The larger the number of constructs, the greater a subject's cognitive complexity (Bieri, 1961) and the more differentiated his construct system. A small number of constructs may indicate a lack of versatility in coping with the world.

Another nomothetic issue is the quality of the constructs. Constructs may be permeable (open to the inclusion of new events) or impermeable (relatively closed to new information); tight (closely related to other constructs) or loose; core (the important constructs dealing with identity and self-maintainance) or peripheral. The more important constructs, termed *superordinate,* subsume a number of lesser constructs and are more resistant to change. Box 11-7 shows the modified protocol of a Rep test administered by Kelly (1955).

From the raw protocol it is possible to sort out some of the subject's personal constructs. For example, the subject prefers quiet, easygoing, understanding people and is uncomfortable with people who are critical and ill at ease. Ease of social behavior is thus one dimension along which she views people. Another dimension is how a person seems to feel about herself. People who lack self-confidence are contrasted with those who are confident. Perhaps the subject will show a lack of versatility in her interpersonal relationships. She will probably try to keep her relationships on a friendly, superficial level and avoid more difficult interpersonal tasks.

Box 11-7 Role Construct Repertory Test: Raw Protocol of Mildred Beal (abstracted from her description of figures fitting the role title.)

Sort No.	Similar Figures	Similarity Construct	Dissimilar Figure	Contrasting Construct
1	Boss– Successful person	Are related to me; not at all the same	Sought person	Unrelated
2	Rejecting person– Pitied person	Very unhappy persons	Intelligent person	Contented
3	Father– Liked teacher	Are very quiet and easygoing persons	Pitied person	Nervous, hypertensive
4	Mother– Sister	Look alike; are both hyper-critical of people in general	Boy friend	Friendliness
5	Ex-flame– Pitied person	Feel inferior	Boy friend	Self-confident
6	Brother– Intelligent person	Socially better than adequate	Disliked teacher	Unpleasant
7	Mother– Boss	Hypertensive	Father	Easygoing
8	Sister– Rejecting person	Hypercritical	Brother	Understanding
9	Rejecting person– Ex-flame	Feelings of inferiority	Disliked teacher	Assured of innate worth
10	Liked teacher– Sought person	Pleasing personalities	Successful person	High-powered, nervous
11	Mother– Ex-flame	Socially maladjusted	Boy friend	Easygoing, self-confident
12	Father– Boy friend	Relaxing	Ex-flame	Uncomfortable to be with
13	Disliked teacher– Boss	Emotionally unpredictable	Brother	Even tempera-ment
14	Sister– Rejecting person	Look somewhat alike	Liked teacher	Looks unlike other two
15	Intelligent person– Successful person	Dynamic personalities	Sought person	Weak person-ality

Source: Kelly, 1955, pp. 242–243.

The reliability and validity of the Rep test.   Some studies have found that the Rep test is useful not only in eliciting personal constructs, but also in revealing the structures and internal relationships of the construct system. The studies of Bieri (1965, 1961) on cognitive complexity are one example of this application.

Bonarius (1965) has reviewed research on the Rep test and has concluded that the test is both reliable and valid. He notes that the role figures on the test are actually representative of persons who constitute the subject's social environment, while the constructs are determined by the subject himself.

Landfield (1976) has developed procedures for scoring the differentiation and integration of personal constructs. By measuring the total number of independent personal constructs, one can score the degree of differentiation. The extent of hierarchical integration in the personal constructs is also measurable. In terms of these two indices, the most adaptive personality has moderate differentiation with high integration. By contrast, high differentiation with low integration results in internal confusion and poor interpersonal relationships.

INTERVIEW AND LIFE HISTORY METHODS

The Clinical Interview

The interview is the most important and frequently used assessment tool of the psychiatrist, clinical psychologist, and the other professionals who deal with people's personal problems (MacKinnon & Michels, 1971). It is a face-to-face conversation in which both verbal communication (attitudes, feelings, and other information) and nonverbal messages are exchanged, and which has a consciously selected purpose (Wiens, 1976). Good interviewing is an art the skilled professional has learned by watching his teachers and imitating them, by learning to judge his skills from the responses of his clients, by developing his sensitivity and empathy to others, and by accepting continuing critique from others. Not only what the person says but also what he leaves unsaid, as well as his manner of speaking, posture, and gestures, are data for the interviewer (Sullivan, 1954; Ripley, 1975).

An interview can take many forms, depending upon purpose. A journalist or a personnel counselor may conduct an interview in a different manner from a psychologist who is trying to understand the personality of his client. An interview can be structured or open-ended. The first style is probably more appropriate to the journalist who wants to know where his subject stands on certain issues, or to the employment counselor who needs to know specifics about job skills. The open-ended style is more appropriate to the interviewer who is not trying to fit his subject into any job, but only trying to understand.

Ideally, the behavior of the interviewer will elicit the information sought. Thus, if the client is verbal and actively providing the information, he may simply listen. On the other hand, he may ask questions if he seeks particular answers, or display a sympathetic posture if he wants to encourage. Above all, however, he must be careful not to interfere with the client's free vocalizations or he will inhibit the production of just the information he is trying to elicit (Whitehorn, 1954).

Of course, if certain information is not apparent, the interviewer may actively pursue a topic. For Sullivan (1954), the interviewer is a participant-observer in a dyadic process who constantly does three things: (1) He asks himself what the client's communications could mean; (2) he plans how to phrase what he will say; and (3) he pays attention to the general pattern of interaction between self and client, watching the direction in which the interview is moving.

Different interviewers use different styles, and these vary according to both the interviewer's personality and the client situation. One would not interview a child the same as an adult, or a job applicant as one would a person suffering from depression.

The interviewer who is assessing personality has a definite goal in mind—to understand the personality structure and dynamics of the interviewee, his characteristic ways of thinking, feeling, and acting. To do this he acts like a scientific investigator, sifting clues and looking for new ones until he understands what is happening. Box 11-8, excerpts from an initial interview, demonstrates this process.

The reliability and validity of the interview. Like other assessment instruments, especially projective techniques, the reliability of the interview depends almost entirely on the level of skill of the interviewer. As with all clinical instruments, the correlation between two interviewers will be high if both agree about the information to be elicited during the interview and how to interpret it. The validity of the interview depends on whether the information obtained is, in fact, representative of the client's behavior and personality.

Sundberg (1977) reviewed studies on the reliability and validity of the interview and concluded that psychiatrists using the interview as an assessment tool showed high inter-rater reliability if the assessors were well trained and the diagnostic categories used were broad. Validity studies have shown that screening interviews have been effective in predicting broad categories of maladjustment. Interviews can be structured so that the

Box 11-8   Excerpts From a Sample Initial Interview and Clues Obtained. I = interviewer, C = client.

I. How do you do? My name is————. Won't you come in and sit down?
C. O.K. Where do I sit? (*Note that client asks for instruction, a probable sign that he will engage in cooperative or compliant behavior.*)
I. Any of those chairs you like. (*Will he choose a nearby chair, or one far away? Will he pick a chair in the middle of the room or one in a corner?*)

• • •

I. Has this sort of thing ever happened to you before? (*Is it a repeated pattern of behavior?*)
C. No, I don't like arguments, but this time I lost my temper and said things I was sorry for. (*The client may value harmony in human relationships.*)
I. Don't like to lose your temper? . . . (*an indirect suggestion to the client to elaborate*)
C. Arguments always seem to bring out the worst in people (*a confirmation that the client values harmony*).
I. Tell me more about it.
C. This guy is a stubborn mule. I tried to show him where he was wrong but I should have recognized that he can't stand to be crossed. (*Client expects self to act responsibly.*)

• • •

C. I'll generally go out of my way to please people. I think I'm easy to get along with (*compliance behavior and perhaps a high approval motive*).
I. Did you and he start to have trouble right away?
C. The first day we were paired off as lab partners, he acted like he was taking over. He kept telling me what to do. I didn't care, so I went along. For the first few weeks, he'd accept some of my suggestions about how to run the experiments. I was careful with him because I could see he was touchy and I thought we'd be able to get along (*suggests high compliance behavior with an expectation that the behavior will be appreciated*).
I. Did he seem to like you? (*testing for approval motive*)
C. He doesn't seem to like anybody. That's what gets me (*confirmed*). I did everything I could to keep the work going smoothly (*confirms his own motive to be responsible*). I admit he's a good student and gets high grades. I admire him for that. (*Client tries to be fair in his judgment of others. He is presenting himself as a reasonable, well-intentioned person.*)
    But he's always bitching about something. (*The person who wants to please may experience it as a personal defeat if he doesn't succeed.*)

• • •

C. When he said that, I finally blew up and told him what I thought of him. He yelled back at me and I just walked out of the lab. (*When the high approval motive is not confirmed by response from the lab partner, the latter becomes a threat to the client's motives. The client now engages in aggressive, oppositional behavior himself. He gives up his usual behavior and attacks the disapprover.*)
I. And you feel bad about losing your temper?
C. Yes . . . At home my brother always used to fly off the handle when something bothered him. . . . I never wanted to be like that. . . . It just gets people upset (*a developmental reason for his dislike of open aggression and disharmony*). . . . I sometimes feel angry when I see somebody being mean or taking advantage, but I don't like to fight with people about it.

interviewer is required to rate the client on a number of attributes—for example, hostility, sexuality, dependency, and so on. This procedure increases the validity of the interview for predicting more specific categories
of behavior (Burdock & Hardesty, 1968).

The Life History

According to R. W. White, "The complete description of a person
would amount to nothing less than a full biography" (1972, p. 4). A life
history is such a report that gives special attention to those features that reveal personality. It includes statements about the important events in a
person's life, his reactions to them, his own background, and his
self-description.

Areas covered in the life history.   While different examiners may stress
different aspects of history taking, the following categories appear in all life
histories: autobiographical self-report; description of family interactions;
peer, sexual, and other interpersonal experiences; vocation and schooling;
socioeconomic background; illness or handicaps; and areas of success and
failure.

Life history data consist of a combination of factual material and
subjective perceptions. Even if some details in the history are false, a pattern of personality will still emerge. A full life history may require a number of interviews.

The study of lives.   White (1963, 1975) has been instrumental in promoting the use of this technique for understanding personality. Using life histories as data, he has compared the influence of parental attitudes, family systems, social status, ethnic background, educational experience, and many other factors that affect the total personality.

Studying individuals over the course of years revealed a continuity in personality. Behavior during childhood and adolescence was indicative of how a person would respond to specific situations (for example, stress) later in life. As a prognostic device, then, the life history can be an important tool for educators and others concerned with the socialization and development of the child and adolescent.

White's methods indicate his careful approach to the problem of studying lives and his attempt to reduce interviewer bias. He conducted his studies by first inviting subjects to participate in a personality study, telling them it would take 15 to 20 hours of their time. This gave subjects the opportunity to drop in frequently at the research center where they became friendly with the interviewers. Interviews and tests were conducted by several different workers of both sexes and all ages in order to try to elicit aspects of the self that might be displayed to one interviewer rather than another. The chief investigator conducted several of the interviews and also the subsequent correspondence with the subject.

Each study began with a written autobiography. Several interviews then explored all aspects of the subject's life up to the present. Interviews were recorded so that they could be studied later. In addition to interviews, White rounded out his approach with standardized tests such as the WAIS, TAT, and Rorschach. He also recommended that systematic observation in natural settings, personal writings, and the impressions of other people who know the subject be included in the study of a life.

White admits that the interview has certain defects as a method of assessment. The subject may choose to conceal certain aspects of the self and may defend against revealing some material. However, he believes that his own studies minimize this tendency by using healthy, well-motivated subjects. The second major objection to the interview technique is the interviewer's own bias. White guarded against this by the concurrent use of psychological tests and also by arranging to have the final interpretation be the result of integration by a council of investigators rather than by one person alone.

A final strong point of White's method is that he followed up his initial studies by reexamining subjects at later periods in their lives. It is this longitudinal approach which permits him to discover consistency over time in the themes that concerned his subjects. White's descriptive studies are impressive in tracing the continuity of personality.

Early recollections. Space limitations preclude a consideration of others who have used life history analysis to measure personality. However, one particular aspect of the life history deserves special consideration—early childhood recollections. An analysis of these memories reveals the conclusion the person has drawn about his life—that is, it is an index to his life style.

Early recollections (ERs) are selected by the subject from a vast number of past incidents which he has stored in his memory. They are actually a projection of the client's own perceptions and thus can be used as a projective test to verify material uncovered in the life history (Mosak, 1977).

The following is a set of early memories of an adult male suffering from depression:

ER #1, Age 5	It was a long distance home from school. One day, on the way home I had to move my bowels. I couldn't hold it any longer so I did it in my trousers. I felt ashamed.
ER #2, Age 7	I was left in the car while mother and father went in to visit somebody. I tried to follow them but I didn't know the way. I went back to the car and felt they deserted me and I should hurt myself to make them feel sorry for me.
ER #3, Age 8	I had a fight with a boy and I gave him a bloody nose. Later I was afraid he would get his gang to beat me up.

Interpretation: Life is difficult in all these memories and the patient suffers. Even when he wins (see ER #3), he loses, because now he is even less secure than before. He accuses others of not caring for him properly and demonstrates suffering in order to punish them. He is an angry and frustrated person with little trust either in others or in his own capabilities.

Such a life style shows a high degree of oppositional rather than compliant behavior. The subject was an ambitious, hard-working striver with few friends, none of them close. His heterosexual relationships were rather hostile. He was "out for what he could get" from women, but avoided any real intimacy with them. Driven by loneliness, he sought them out in order to use them. When they began to make demands on him, he protected himself by ending the relationship.

From the earliest childhood recollections it is possible to formulate the subject's self-concept and his world view. He perceives himself as a victim of life and others, while the world itself and the people in it are either hostile or unfair and neglectful. His chosen response style is also revealed in the memories—he fights back. It is possible to describe the subject's life style according to a rubric we have used before: I am _____, Life is _____, Therefore _____. In this case, the blanks can be filled in as follows:

> I am a *suffering victim.*
> Life is *difficult and unfair.*
> Therefore, *I will oppose, punish, and try to protect myself from others.*

This rubric represents a key conclusion the person has reached from his life experiences. Specifically, he believes that people will frustrate his desire for attachment and will victimize him. Thus, the social press is perceived as negative. His method of coping with this state of affairs is to engage in segregative motivational and emotional behavior. Both his intentions and his accompanying emotions are segregative—he keeps himself at a distance from others, distrusts them, and feels justified in being oppositional and vengeful.

Research on Early Recollections

As early as 1912, Adler pointed out that early recollections were an example of retrospective memory selection and that these memories would fit in with and reveal an individual's life style. Liebermann (1957) compared the projective use of early recollections to a test battery composed of three psychological tests and concluded that childhood memories provide essentially similar data about personality and are easier and quicker to obtain. Hedvig (1963) compared early recollections with TAT stories and found that ERs were more stable over time. McCarter and his associates (1961) also found ERs to be a valid method of personality appraisal.

Ferguson (1964) asked assessors who classified themselves as Adlerian, Freudian, or eclectic to match sets of ERs with written descriptions of personality constructed from these same sets. All three types of assessors were able consistently to match the written personality descriptions with the summaries themselves.

The life style formulation, as deduced from the ER, is an attempt to describe some of the core constructs that make up the individual personality: his style of perceiving himself and the world and his style of responding. It is certainly not as complete as a life history nor will it necessarily reveal the same kind of information found in the other methods of personality assessment. However, it is easy to use and seems to give some important information in a short period of time.

12

the maladaptive personality: psychopathology

OVERVIEW

From a cognitive point of view, errors in perception are at the base of maladaptive behavior. Such errors consist of mistaken beliefs, insufficient psychological differentiation, misfocused attitudinal sets, and erroneous instructions about instrumental acts. These perceptual distortions and/or inadequacies lead to dysfunctions in motivated behavior, all of which involve an imbalance in the organization and expression of the basic motives.

Like all goal behavior, maladaptive behavior is a function of person X situation interaction. Impaired brain function is an aspect of the *person* which leads to psychopathology. Other aspects include too little differentiation of the cognitive motive, lack of an integrated motive hierarchy, perceptual dysfunctioning, and so on. What the *situation* contributes can be thought of as stress. One form of stress is whatever is perceived as a threat to a basic motive. Another form of situational stress is any prolonged noxious assault upon the body or person.

The personality disorders are examples of maladaptive behavior in which person factors are significantly more important than situation factors. Such disorders include the paranoid, schizoid, obsessive-compulsive, antisocial, and hysterical personalities. Each of these maladaptive types has a characteristic organization, directed by a set of perceptual instructions about self–world–instrumental acts. In different personality disorders we may expect to find differing cognitive styles and specific kinds of motive imbalance.

Maladaptive deviation is not usually a topic found in a textbook on personality. It is properly a subject for a course in abnormal psychology. However, there are three reasons why we include a discussion of psychopathology in this text. It permits us an opportunity to review the maladaptive personality from three perspectives: (1) The functions of the motive systems in maladaptive deviation; (2) the perceptual instructions in the core rubric—that is, the self–world–action triad, and (3) those personality patterns in which personality factors become far more important than situational factors in psychopathology. Implied in these perspectives is the proposition that certain personality organizations are more adaptive than others.

THE MOTIVE SYSTEMS AND PATHOLOGY

Motives are functional relationships between a person and the incentives in his environment. The nature of these relationships is determined by the person's cognitive structure so that from one stance psychopathology can be viewed as improper functioning of the motive systems. Box 12-1 evaluates some instances of psychopathology in terms of improper motive system functioning. Since in each case malfunctioning can be attributed to mistakes in the reception, processing of, and response to stimuli, psychopathology can result from the faulty processing of information.

A Cognitive Explanation of Maladaptive Behavior

Throughout this book we have tried to show that personality and behavior can be understood and predicted from a cognitive point of view. Kelly (1955) was one of the first to explain maladaptive behavior in this manner. From his personal construct perspective, psychopathology results from mistaken beliefs, insufficient psychological differentiation, misfocused attitudinal sets, or erroneous/deficient instrumental acts.

Box 12-1   Psychopathology Conceived as Improper Motive System Functioning Directed by Inappropriate Perceptual Sets

The inability to form close relationships is a dysfunction in the *attachment* motive.
Avoidance of ordinary life tasks through fear is a dysfunction in the *security* motive.
Inaccurate knowledge about self and world is a dysfunction in the *cognitive* motive.
Ineffective task orientation which leads to personal failure is a dysfunction of the *competence* motive.

In his discussion of schizophrenia, Scher (1957) points out that errors in perception may be at the base of maladaptive behavior. In any perceptual act, the attributes of the item perceived are processed in terms of inner sets. These sets are derived from past experience, involve a set of expectancies which indicate a relationship between events, and are useful for the prediction of probabilities. From these premises, Scher deduces that there are at least four sites where operative error may occur: (1) the perceptual apparatus may be defective, altering the input (as in the effects of some drugs); (2) the wrong information is transmitted (as in selective inattention to undesired information); (3) at higher levels, information may be processed according to inappropriate inner sets (as in paranoid delusions); and (4) an accurate message is directed into mistaken response channels and an ineffective response is chosen.

One way in which cognition and psychopathology are related has been discussed by Beck, a cognitive therapist who reviewed the relationship between cognition, affect, and psychopathology:

> The relationship of cognition to affect in normal subjects is similar to that observed in psychopathological states. Among normals, the sequence perception-cognition-emotion is indicated largely by the demand character of the stimulus situation. In psychopathological conditions, the reaction to the stimulus is determined to a much greater extent by internal processes. The affective response is likely to be excessive or inappropriate because of the idiosyncratic conceptualization of the event. The input from the external situation is molded to conform to the typical schemas activated in these conditions. As a result, interpretations of experience embody arbitrary judgments, overgeneralizations and distortions. Perseverative conceptualizations relevant to danger, loss, unjustified attack and self-enhancement are typical of anxiety neuroses, depression, paranoid states and hypomanic states, respectively (1971, p. 495)

Beck described specific cognitive conditions for the instigation of affects. For example, the arousal of anxiety depends upon the appraisal of a threat to the person's cognitive domain. Anxiety is then enhanced by an appraisal that the person cannot cope with or neutralize the threat, that the threat is immediate, that the exact time of the damage is not completely predictable, and that the result will be noxious. If it is appraised that the damage has already happened, sadness rather than anxiety will result. If both sadness and anxiety are present, then the person feels that damage has already occurred and a continuing threat remains. In each pathological state, a set of cognitive appraisals precedes the pathologic affect.

Beck, Laud, and Bohvert (1974) studied a group of patients suffering from anxiety neurosis to determine the ideational components of the neurosis. In all cases, thoughts about danger were found. In the majority of patients, fantasies with visual images of danger occurred before or during anxiety attacks. These patients were able to work themselves into an anxiety attack with their fantasies. In Chapters 1 and 10, we discussed the experiments of Lazarus and others which showed how cognitive factors influence the arousal and expression of motives. Beck's research extends these findings to show that a significant amount of maladaptive behavior can actually be explained by understanding these operative cognitive factors.

Kelly tried to explain specific kinds of psychopathology according to his personal construct theory. Thus, when the obsessive-compulsive is faced with an unpredictable situation, he "tightens" his personal construct. The schizophrenic, on the other hand, has very "loose" constructs. Note that neither Beck, Scher, nor Kelly deny the existence of other possible factors in maladaptive behavior; they are all trying to show the role that cognition plays in psychopathology. In sum, psychopathology is directed by an incompetent perceptual system, which can result from biological factors, learning factors, or both.

Psychopathology Viewed as Motive Imbalance

Imbalance of motive systems predisposes to pathology. *A motive system may be ineffective to the task.* An inadequate perceptual system will not be able adequately to organize and guide the pursuit of motives. Such examples can be seen in the maladaptive deviation of a person suffering from brain damage or from mental retardation.

The demands of one motive may interfere with the function of another. In the schizoid personality, which we will discuss later, the demands of security lead to a movement away from others. He avoids affiliation in order to be safe.

When one motive is excessively predominant, other motives are neglected. When a person relies on affiliation to serve all his motives, he feels secure only when nurtured and protected by others and develops no sense of self-competence. He often does not rely on himself to extract information, but rather lets his nurturer predigest information for him (he thinks what he is told to think). Such a person is actually incompetent since he does not learn to function independently. When faced with the loss of his protectors and nurturers, he feels lost, abandoned, and unable to care for himself.

The Person in the Situation: Pathology and Stress

In Chapter 9 we saw that goal-directed behavior can be seen as a person-situation interaction. Maladaptive deviation might then be thought of as a subset of this interaction. Sometimes body disease and/or impaired brain function are person variables which lead to dysfunction. Other persons factors which lead to deviation are essentially perceptual—in the words of Kelly (1955), the result of invalid or incomplete personal constructs. What the situation contributes to the person-situation interaction can be thought of as stress. Stress can take two forms: a threat to a consciously perceived motive or enduring stress which remains outside the person's awareness.

An example of the relationship between person and situation stress can be seen in studies of men who suffer from coronary artery disease. Friedman (1969) formulated the hypothesis that a certain behavior pattern (*type A*) distinguishes those prone to coronary attack. This pattern is characterized by extreme competitiveness, drive for success, impatience, restlessness, hyperalertness, and a sense of being pressured by time and commitments. Men with this pattern are also found to have increased cholesterol and increased daytime secretion of noradrenaline. Statistical study shows that type A men are more susceptible to coronary artery disease. Of course, personality factors constitute only one side of the coin—other factors are situational. Lipowski (1975) found that other factors such as job dissatisfaction, status incongruity, and role overload (all situational factors) are equally important, as well as cigarette smoking, overeating, physical inactivity, and a diet high in saturated fats.

Threat to a motive system as situational stress. While the type A person creates stress for himself by the way he approaches the situation, conscious awareness of threat to the motives is another powerful source of stress. Box 12-2 shows examples of situational threat for each of the motive systems.

Box 12-2	Threats to the Motive Systems
Motive	*Threat*
Attachment	Loss of a loved one Rejection by significant others Being alone in a strange place
Security	Life-threatening danger Loss of income and property
Competence	Loss of ability, such as in aging Loss of usual defenses against symbols of threat, as in panic attacks
Cognitive	Loss of stability in the CNS and ANS Novel situations, a new challenge never before experienced Loss of information as in perceptual isolation, blindness, deafness, and so on Invalidation of a personal construct or failure to confirm a motive, especially obstacles in the movement toward the dominant goal (derailment in the pursuit of the guiding self-ideal)

PERSONALITY DISORDERS

It is our conviction that the study of personality disorders is invaluable for understanding the concept of personality itself, for appreciating the consistency of personality, and for showing us how strong personality factors can be in determining behavior, even when such behavior is clearly maladaptive. The personality disorders are not mental illnesses, such as neuroses or psychoses, but extreme personality types. It is the exaggeration of the pattern that designates the maladaptive deviation. Except for the antisocial personality, they do not receive much attention in textbooks of abnormal psychology. For full descriptions of them, one usually has to go to the psychiatric literature. Such descriptions can be found in Brody and Sata (1967), Robins (1967), Winokur and Crowe (1975), and Kleinmuntz (1974). They are life-long behavior patterns much more dependent upon the person than upon the situation. The personality disorders are defined in the *Diagnostic and Statistical Manual of Mental Disorders* (DSM III, in print) as "deeply ingrained maladaptive patterns of behavior that are perceptibly different in quality from psychotic and neurotic symptoms. Generally, these are life-long patterns, often recognizable by the time of adolescence or earlier."

Altogether, ten different personality disorders were listed in DSM II (1968). We will limit our discussion to five of them, which should be sufficient to show how their study is useful for understanding personality: paranoid, schizoid, obsessive-compulsive, antisocial, and hysterical. Taken together, they constitute a representative set of maladaptive deviations which show how motives are engaged to produce movement (goal behavior) which is consequently maladaptive.

Paranoid Personality

Descriptive characteristics. The behavior pattern of the paranoid is characterized by the following traits: suspiciousness, defensiveness, hypersensitivity to slights (real or imagined); a tendency to personalize innocuous events so that the individual feels personally attacked when there is no warrant for such feeling; comparison of self with others with resulting feelings of envy and of being cheated; distrust of those with whom he has close relationships, so that he tries to control their behavior and dominate them through demands and jealous accusations. Forgus and DeWolfe (1969, 1974) found that the themes in the hallucinations and delusions of paranoid patients reveal that they consistently see themselves as liking others and others as disliking them. Other characteristics include a habit of blaming others for whatever goes wrong, inability to tolerate criticism without resentment (Swanson, Bohmert, & Smith, 1970), feelings of inadequacy

compensated for by a habit of searching out the faults of others and belit-
tling them, self-righteousness, and a tendency to distort logic. In short, the
paranoid personality is basically oppositional and insecure. The exaggeration is in the functioning of the attachment and security motives.

It is difficult to find a population of paranoid personalities for research, since they do not consider themselves in need of services and only
come to the attention of the clinician when, under stress, signs of psychosis
appear. Studies of schizophrenia among elderly persons (Kay & Roth,
1961; Herbert & Jacobson, 1967) seem to indicate that at least half of the
patients had premorbid traits that are found in the paranoid personality.

Both Adler (1968) and Sullivan (1956) have described the paranoid
personality as one who suffers from strong feelings of inferiority and who
compensates for these feelings by attributing the cause of any personal failures to inimical external agents. He is at odds with life. Since the world is
hostile, his dominant goal is to preserve himself by defeating his enemies or,
at worst, preserve his pride and go down fighting. He preserves his own
self-esteem by blaming and opposing others.

Interpersonal relationships.   Since this person is generally mistrustful, he
is alert in his relationships for any sign that will confirm his suspicion that
others will abuse him (Brody & Sata, 1967). Being tense in his relationships,
he makes few friends. He guards his privacy and avoids real intimacy. Expecting others to abuse him, he may arrange a series of counterploys (such
as changing the locks on his doors from time to time just in case someone
may have a key). He usually has bad relationships with family members—
parents, siblings, and children. Those who try to be friendly with him are
treated with suspicion and eventually give up their efforts. His interpersonal relationships are thus unhappy, both for himself and others. He is
usually so busy defending himself, he often seems unfeeling and in-
considerate.

Developmental antecedents.   The paranoid has had early training in distrust and defeat (Beck, 1976). Someone, usually a parent, has been unkind
to him and he has felt injured and humiliated by this person. Some studies
of families of paranoid personality have shown that often the opposite sex
parent is domineering and critical while the same sex parent is submissive
and useless to the child as a protector or as a role model (Brody & Sata,
1967). The child grows up angry and hostile. He has not been successful in
pleasing and when he has submitted, he has felt only abused and
dissatisfied.

It is possible to construct a hypothetical core rubric around the self-
perception–world view–instructions for action triad (as developed in Chapter 11) for the paranoid personality:

I am *disliked by others.*

Life is *a competitive struggle against external enemies.*

Therefore, *I will excuse myself from blame and failure by attributing blame to others.*

Schizoid Personality

Descriptive characteristics.   The most characteristic feature of this personality type is the tendency to avoid close or prolonged relationships. The schizoid is seclusive, seems aloof and disinterested. He suffers from strong feelings of personal inferiority (Sullivan, 1956; Adler, 1958; Shulman, 1968; Arieti, 1974). He tends to perceive the world as a puzzling and unsatisfactory place, often hostile. He feels out of place in the world, and functions as a social isolate, as if he were trying to shelter himself from others. Not expecting to find a real place for himself in the social world, he retreats from it to some private corner. He is seldom any trouble to others. He often narrows down the scope of his life so that he goes through the day with as little commotion as possible. Much of his time may be spent in fantasy, which is more pleasant than reality for him. He shows a notable lack of usual ambitions; for example, he may graduate from college and accept a noncompetitive, low level job at which he will remain for many years. In short, the exaggeration in the schizoid lies in the fact that he avoids attachment and is incompetent.

Interpersonal relationships.   These distance-keeping methods are seen in his relation to others. It is unsatisfying to hold a conversation with him. He doesn't talk about himself; he makes little effort to keep the conversation going. He seems to be a "loner," with little desire for companionship. He expects others to misunderstand and reject him, and he doesn't want to take a chance.

Withdrawal from social participation is self-reinforcing. Nonparticipation leads to inadequate development of social skills, so that the schizoid becomes someone who lacks such skills and his social efforts are naive and misfire. He becomes the recluse who lives in a little room by himself and seldom speaks to anyone.

Slater and Roth (1969), in a review of the literature, report that a schizoid personality structure antedates approximately 50 percent of the cases of schizophrenia. Thus, schizoid personality has a relationship to schizophrenia, but many schizoid personalities need never become schizophrenic as Box 12-3 shows.

Developmental antecedents.   The childhood and family relationships of the schizoid personality have been studied more than have those of any other personality disorder. Some investigators believe that this condition involves a biological dysfunction of the central nervous system (Kallman,

1946; Heston, 1970). Others have described certain parent-child relationships that predispose to this personality disorder (Shulman, 1968; Lidz, Fleck, & Cornelison, 1965; Wynne & Singer, 1963; Bateson, Jackson, & Haley, 1956). Whatever the relationship, the schizoid receives early training in complete frustration of his attempts to be a worthwhile autonomous person who is accepted by others. Poorly trained by his parents for socialization or held back by an uneven maturation of his CNS (Churchill, 1971), he finds it difficult to relate well to his peers and is soon rejected by them. He usually finds himself the scapegoat of his peer group and concludes that he will not be able to get along with others. Thus, the withdrawal begins.

Mednick (1970) and Mednick and Schulsinger (1965) studied 207 children of schizophrenic mothers compared with a group of controls. The research was mainly on autonomic responsivity. The 207 children were found to have a more volatile autonomic nervous system than controls, a factor that adversely affects the functioning of the competence system. Schachter and his colleagues (1972, 1975) have also found differences in the nervous systems of such children.

There is some evidence that the schizoid is less resistant to stress and that his withdrawal from stimuli is a protection against stimulus overload. Churchill (1971) has studied schizophrenic children and has found that when such children are working successfully at a task, they show few of the signs that caused them to be classified as psychotic. When they fail at the task, however, remoteness, aloofness, withdrawal, avoidance of eye contact, and other such behaviors appear. Churchill considers that CNS dysfunction may impose a low ceiling on the child's adaptive ability so that he lives in a perpetual "failure" condition, made worse by adult caretakers who do not appreciate the child's limitations. Figure 12-1 shows the increase in avoidance behavior that follows task failure in schizophrenic children.

Some research findings support the view that arousal is disturbed in the schizoid. Situations which represent mild stress arouse the schizophrenic more than the normal (Gruzelier, Lykken, & Venables, 1972). Although the schizoid is not necessarily schizophrenic, he has many personality factors in common with the latter.

Apparently a schizoid personality can be one outcome of an uneven organization of the CNS and ANS. Withdrawal would then be a protective device to avoid stimulus overload and perceptual overinclusion. The failure to withdraw successfully from such stress leads to disturbances of attention, reduced perceptual constancy, and failure of selective perception (McGhie, 1970)—that is, a psychotic state. Fenz and Velner (1970) point out that not all schizophrenics demonstrate such a CNS–ANS imbalance. It seems likely that determining social influences can lead to withdrawal on the part of the child even if his CNS and ANS are perfectly adequate. It is the kind and degree of stress and the possible range of response choices that

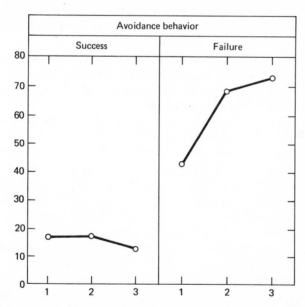

Figure 12-1   Avoidance behavior not only increases markedly in the failure condition but also continues to increase significantly as the failure condition persists. Source: After Churchill (1971).

seem to be the important variables. A child with a defective nervous system will experience more failure. A child with a normal nervous system but with exaggerated levels of aspiration will also experience frequent failure.

A core rubric for the schizoid personality.   As with the paranoid, it is possible to construct a hypothetical core rubric for the schizoid personality which shows his self-perception, perception of the world and the instructions he gives himself about response choices:

> I am *a misfit.*
> Life is a *difficult place and human relationships are troublesome.*
> Therefore, *it is a better for me to keep my distance and maintain a low profile.*

Obsessive-Compulsive Personality (OC)

Descriptive characteristics.   DSM II describes this personality as having an excessive concern with conformity and adherence to standards of concience. The OC personality tends to be fussy and to dislike unclear situations. He likes to organize his life, even to the smallest details. He does not like to take chances, is unhappy with an unpredictable situation, and likes to plan ahead of time rather than leave things to the last minute. He is much more comfortable in unambiguous situations.

The OC personality sees himself as potentially responsible for whatever happens. Therefore, he stands in danger of being blamed for whatever goes wrong. His worth depends upon his ability to avoid being blamed. Competence thus has a high value for the OC.

The most troublesome aspect of the world to the OC personality is its unpredictability. He expects that some day the world will call him to account for all his mistakes and will punish him. He would like to keep everything (the world, other people, his own feelings) under control. If he can control everything, he will be safe. He also tries to avoid blame. Thus, even if he fails to control everything, others will admit that he has at least tried very hard and should not be blamed.

The OC is an arranger and controller. He controls his emotions, which are troublesome because they impel to action. Instead he relies upon thinking. Knowledge becomes a form of power. One can use analysis to understand and what one understands, one can conquer. If one can reduce the techniques for living to recipes, then one can make a cookbook for life and simply follow the instructions. Rituals are appealing to him. He uses them as ways of trying to control the forces of the world.

He tries to be right, because that is also a defense against blame. In any argument he may ask for definitions of terms, or he may object to a word, change the subject, or otherwise overcome any effort to put him in the wrong. One of his chief methods is intellectualization. He will ruminate, analyze, examine, and find flaws in arguments as a way of protecting himself. His ability to use logic makes him a formidable opponent in debate, but when he is about to lose, he twists away on another subject.

Two studies have found a relationship between the OC personality pattern and more serious pathology. Kringlen (1965) studied 91 patients with obsessive-compulsive neuroses. Of these, 72 had a premorbid OC personality. The percentage of OC personality traits among a similar group of controls was much lower. Perris (1966) found that many unipolar depressives (psychotic depressions in which no manic state occurs) showed premorbid OC personality.

Horowitz (1974) studied response to stress in the OC personality. The OC may remain behaviorally calm and emotionless and shift attention in order to control and dampen down emotional arousal. Table 12-1 shows what Horowitz calls *style defects* in the obsessional. The exaggeration of personality in the OC is toward high competence and narrowed cognition.

Interpersonal relations. Brody and Sata (1967) discuss the interpersonal relations of the OC. He may be successful in his work, especially in structured situations where he maintains control. If forced to work under unpredictable conditions, he becomes anxious; thus, if his situation depends on the changing moods of a supervisor, he may respond by becoming stubborn and resentful. If he is a supervisor himself, he may offend those working under him by his pedantic attention to detail and his inability to delegate responsibility. Others may regard him as a rigid, petty, and obstructionist. In general, the OC is a hard worker who usually gets along well with people who consider him trustworthy and respect him for his stability and responsibility. He does not avoid others, can enjoy friends and family, and when he feels secure, he can let himself go and enjoy himself.

Developmental antecedents. The family background has usually included a rigid and domineering parent who expected order and obedience, yet whose demand for order appeared arbitrary to the child. The OC behavior—the stubbornness, opposition, and attention to detail—becomes a way of resisting and defeating the parent. Thus the demand for obedience

Table 12-1   Some Defects of the Obsessional Style in Cognitive Functions

Function	Style as "defect"
Representation	Isolation of ideas from emotions
Translation of images to words	Misses emotional meaning in a rapid transition to partial word meanings
Association	Shifts sets of meanings back and forth
Problem solving	Endless rumination without reaching decisions

Source: After Horowitz (1974).

and respect takes precedence over loving relationships, and the OC child experiences the kind of love that brings demands and restrictions rather than freedom and growth. The child learns to be compliant on the surface while suppressing angry impulses and concealing any overt expression of hostility.

Ehrenwald (1963) studied four generations of one OC family through sustained clinical contact with 13 out of the 14 family members. The family was an upper-middle-class family of business and professional people. In each generation at least two, sometimes more, members showed OC traits. Ehrenwald's clinical study confirmed the exaggerated sense of responsibility, the expectation of obedience to a dominant parent, and the attempt to placate the more powerful person by an outward display of compliance.

Core rubric.   A hypothetical rubric for the OC personality can be constructed as follows:

> I am *liable to be held responsible for what goes wrong.*
> Life is *unpredictable.*
> Therefore, *I have to be on guard against anything that might go wrong.*

Antisocial Personality

Descriptive characteristics.   The antisocial personality functions like an outlaw, in open conflict with his fellow humans. He exploits people ruthlessly and callously, even his "friends." He seems to have no loyalties except to himself and his own glory. He does not regret his own misbehavior—only getting caught at it—and is attracted to criminal behavior, often having repeated brushes with the law. He does not hesitate to lie, deceive, or betray. He is a non-achiever, a troublemaker in school, does poorly on the job (because of a seeming lack of motivation), does not pay bills, and makes a poor spouse. Table 12-2 lists typical behavioral characteristics of the antisocial personality.

The antisocial personality sees himself as a valiant fighter for his own rights. He has a right to make his own laws and oppose those by which others live. He may feel he has been a victim of others and accepts his own malevolence as justified. He feels distressed when he is powerless and constricted and he glories in his ability to overcome restraints. In fact, he is as distrustful of the world as the paranoid or the OC.

He recognizes that people of goodwill exist, but he thinks of them as "suckers" who do not see the world as it really is. He recognizes power, how it works, and the sources from which it emanates. The rules of society are a set of arbitrary restrictions that are unfair and should be opposed. Other people are fair game, because life is a jungle and the laws of the jungle apply.

Table 12-2　　Characteristics and Typical Behavior of the Antisocial Personality

Characteristic	Typical Behavior
Inability to form loyal relationships	Treats persons as if they are objects; may marry but often deserts family
Inability to feel guilt	Feels no pangs of remorse, although he can express sorrow and other emotions
Inability to learn from experience, special attention, or punishment	Commits repeated crimes, and neither punishment nor severe deprivations seem to deter him
Tendency to seek thrills and excitement	Behaves bizarrely and sometimes grotesquely as a rule rather than as an exception
Impulsiveness	Like a child, cannot defer immediate pleasure; cannot tolerate long-term commitments
Aggressiveness	Reacts to frustration with destructive fury
Superficial charm and intelligence	Often qualified for the confidence racket because of winning personality and astuteness
Unreliability and irresponsibility	Unpredictably responsible during some periods but completely irresponsible during others
Pathological lying	Plays many roles—doctor, lawyer, soldier—according to his whims; often confused himself about what he has accomplished or who he really is
Inadequately motivated, antisocial behavior	Impulsively steals and destroys "just for the hell of it"
Egocentricity	Behaves parasitically because of an insatiable need to be believed, served, and supported
Poverty of affect	Incapable of true anger or genuine grief
Lack of insight	Can analyze the motivations underlying the behavior of others—and often does—but has no appreciation of the impact he has on others
Casual but excessive sexual behavior	Has a casual attitude toward sex; and sexual contacts, like most of his behavior, are outlandish and erratic
The need to fail	Has no apparent life plan, except perhaps the need to make a failure of himself

Source: After Kleinmuntz (1974).

Lykken (1957) tested the galvanic skin response (GSR) of prison inmates in anticipation of receiving electroshock. In comparison with other
types, a group that had characteristics of antisocial personality showed
lower levels of GSR response to the conditioned stimulus associated with
the electroshock. These antisocials were less able than others to learn to
avoid the shock. It was as if they could not learn from being punished.
Lykken concluded that the lowered GSR response meant that the antisocial individual had learned to have less autonomic reaction to punishment.
Hare's (1968) research on autonomic responses in antisocials corroborated
the facts that antisocials do not have normal emotional responses, nor do
they benefit from punishment. Chesno and Kilmann (1975) have also verified these findings, as have the experiments of Schachter and Latané (1964)
mentioned in Chapter 6. In another study, however, Schmauk (1970)
showed that antisocials quickly learned how to avoid mistakes when the
punishment was losing money rather than electric shocks. What is punishment for some is not punishment for the antisocial.

Antisocial personality is more often diagnosed in men than in women.
Robins (1967) states the preponderance of males to females approximates a
ratio as high as 10:1.

Interpersonal relations.   The antisocial personality exploits others. His
apparent spontaneity makes him attractive to others and sometimes he can
display loyalty to a friend; more often, however, he feels no real loyalty to
others. He is willing to have a close relationship with a person of the opposite sex, but here he is also disloyal. Since power and impressiveness are
important, he is often a "macho," behaving almost like an adolescent to
show off his masculinity. He is sexually active, sometimes with both sexes.
He may enjoy brawling to show his strength and, in any case, appreciates
his ability to make mischief and to receive the adulation of others. Above
all, he enjoys the excitement of power and of fooling others. Since his relationship to others is predatory, the chief skew in his motive hierarchy is in
the area of the attachment motive.

Developmental Antecedents.   Some twin and adoption studies suggest
that biological relatives of antisocials are more likely to be antisocial
(Schulsinger, 1972; Crowe, 1972; Hutchings & Mednick, 1974). Lee
Robins' (1966) studies indicate that antisocial adults always displayed antisocial traits during childhood. Investigators agree that families which predispose children to antisocial personality structures show a high degree of
antisocial behavior, with broken homes and alcoholism being important
factors (L. Robins, 1966; Oltman & Friedman, 1967). Some investigators
have implicated low socioeconomic status (Dohrenwend & Dohrenwend,

1969), but it must be considered that alcoholism and broken homes are variables that affect low socioeconomic status.

Two psychological factors in childhood seem important. One is the fact that the child has seen antisocial behavior modeled in a parent (Heston, 1970) or older sibling and has seen it rewarded (Bandura, 1969a; Ullman & Krasner, 1969; Yates, 1970). The other is that the child is trained to believe that he is justified in demanding his own way, either because he has been excessively pampered and led to believe he was special, or because having one's own way was a general value for all the people around him.

Buss (1966) identified two types of parental behavior in antisocials. Parents were either cold and distant or were inconsistent and arbitrary in giving affection and punishment, so that there was no relationship between the child's behavior and whether or not he was punished for it. However, the studies on modeling lead us to believe that much antisocial behavior is imitated and it is also quite possible that sometimes such behavior is reinforced by indulgent parents who do not set effective limits to the child's misbehavior. The "black sheep" role is a powerful attention getter in any family.

The role of heredity is still open to question. Crowe (1974) reviewed factors found associated with antisocial personality—early deprivation, parental rejection, a broken family, parental psychopathology, and low socioeconomic status (only the reward of black sheep behavior is omitted from his list)—and concluded that these environmental variables could not adequately account for antisocial behavior. He then initiated a study of a group of children born to female offenders who had been adopted away during infancy. Forty-six such children were compared to an equal number of control adoptees who were exposed to similar developmental conditions. Of the 46 probands (subjects), six were definitely antisocial, while among the controls only one was so diagnosed. The sample is a small one and the difference may not actually be of statistical significance. Further studies are necessary before one can determine what if anything is inherited in the antisocial personality.

Hare (1968) has offered another possible reason for antisocial behavior; namely, that the antisocial person has a low level of emotional arousal, which thus directs him to seek out stimulation. Fenz (1971) examined heart rate response to stress in antisocials and found an "insatiable need for stimulation." Borovec (1970) studied ANS responsivity in the antisocial and also concluded that stimulation seeking is an important motive in sociopathic behavior and that such stimulation seeking is unchecked by a conditioned fear response. The antisocial might, therefore, be called a thrill seeker who has not learned to fear punishment. Studies on ANS sensitivity indicate that the antisocial finds intrinsic motivation in strong stimuli because of a difference in the way his nervous system functions.

Core rubric.   A hypothetical core rubric for antisocial personality can be constructed as follows:

I am *entitled to what I want.*
Life is *a jungle where dog eats dog.*
Therefore, *I will eat before I am eaten and defy their efforts to tame me.*

Hysterical (Histrionic) Personality

Descriptive characteristics.   As if a caricature of a temperamental Hollywood star, the hysteric's behavior is attention seeking and self-dramatizing. Brody and Sata (1967) describe this personality as vain, egocentric, excitable, but with shallow affect. This person often behaves in a sexually provocative way, since sexual display is an effective attention getter. The hysteric responds to small stresses with an exaggerated emotional display which is often intended to influence the behavior of the surrounding people in order to obtain some desired end—to call attention to oneself or to express a desire for service or help from others. Hysterics want conventional things: love, admiration, material wealth, and excitement. They like to make contact with strong, important people upon whom they rely for assistance in obtaining a favored position. They espouse conventional values and know how to behave with propriety. At the same time, they have mastered the techniques of avoiding unpopularity; they avoid taking an unpopular stand, sacrifice principle for expediency, try to please whenever possible, and display open opposition to others only when it is safe. All of these behaviors reveal the hysteric's dependence upon others for approval. He may thus be said to negotiate all of life through the attachment motive.

Descriptions of the hysterical personality have been offered by Alarcon (1973), Verbeek (1973), Chodoff (1974), and Slavney and McHugh (1974). Horowitz (1974) listed examples of how hysterical style affects cognitive functions in hysterical personality (see Table 12-3).

Interpersonal relations.   Interpersonal relations are stormy because of the excessive demands and temperamental displays. As the antisocial per-

Table 12-3   Some "Defects" of the Hysterical Style in Cognitive Functions

Function	Style as "Defect"
Perception	Global or selective inattention
Representation	Impressionistic rather than accurate
Translation of images and enactions to words	Limited
Problem solving	Short circuit to rapid, often erroneous conclusion; avoids topic when emotions are strongly unpleasant

Source: After Horowitz (1974).

sonality is more commonly found in males, so the histrionic personality is most often seen among females, perhaps because of cultural factors. Thus, coquetry, seductiveness, childish ways of speaking, and other contact-seeking behaviors are frequent. Divorce, desertion, and conflict are common in marriages with an hysterical partner. Under stress, psychotic symptoms may appear, associated with elaborate and fantastic wishful thinking; however, anxiety, depression, and other neurotic symptoms are more common. Hysterics may be impulsive, opportunistic, unreliable, and high-pressure in their demands and, when frustrated, can be angry and caustic.

Since they feel no need to be precise or exact, they are late rather than punctual (preferring a dramatic entrance) and approximate rather than accurate in their statements ("Well, that's what I meant even if I didn't say it right and you should have known what I meant"). The value they place on convenience allows them to shade the truth with impunity.

Miller and Magaro (1977) composed a test battery to determine if operational definitions of personality styles would cluster in a predictable way. They found that there was indeed something that could be called a hysterical style. It was characterized by global cognitive and affective processes, high suggestibility, naiveté, and interpersonal dependency.

Because outward social appearance is so important, and because they have a high approval motive and external locus of control (Jones & Shranger, 1968), hysterics tend to imitate the behavior of those they consider proper. They want to be members of the "in-group." They bolster their own security by joining with similar others to exclude those who are different and to look down on them. They cannot afford isolation, so seek friends. They are generally gregarious, social, and talkative, although they can also be shy when the situation demands it. They like excitement and like to be in the center of it as long as there are no unpleasant consequences.

Developmental antecedents. One origin of these personality disorders lies in a family situation in which the young child is discouraged from self-reliance and rewarded with attention and indulgence for those behaviors that later become the characteristics of the adult personality. Parental behavior seems to have been overprotective and overindulgent. The child was valued for his dependent and childlike behavior, not for any constructive attempts to establish himself as a productive and helpful person. There is no doubt that hysterical behavior is also modeled by parents and that cultural factors may reinforce hysterical tendencies in females. There are as yet no significant empirical studies which shed further light on the developmental antecedents of the hysterical personality even though it is one of the more frequent personality disorders.

Core rubric. A hypothetical core rubic for the hysterical personality would read something like:

I am *sensitive.*

Life *makes me nervous.*

Therefore, *I am entitled to special care and consideration.*

COGNITIVE STYLE AND PSYCHOPATHOLOGY

The relationship between specific maladaptive behaviors and their corresponding cognitive styles has been investigated in a number of studies. Silverman (1964) has pointed out that paranoids are *extensive scanners* and *high field articulators.* Witkin's (1968) studies indicate that personalities whose fields are more articulated use specialized defenses, such as isolation and intellectualization, while more global personalities use primitive denial (they refuse to look at the facts). Witkin claims that the *level of differentiation* determines the form of pathology. Field-independents would tend to be obsessive-compulsive, while globals tend to be inadequate and emotionally unstable (more hysterical).

In locus of control studies, Phares (1976) concludes that high internals can tolerate more environmental stimuli without stress. In a study by Staub, Turasky, and Schwartz (1971), high externals tolerated fewer and less intense electric shocks than internals. In another study, Houston (1972) divided subjects into two groups. One group was told there was no way they could avoid electric shock. The second was told they could avoid shock if they made no mistakes. The former group showed anxiety, the latter, a higher level of physiological arousal. Apparently, the nature of the situation influences the locus of control. Hersch and Scheibe (1967) found externals to be more maladjusted. While they rate high on succorance and abasement, they are lower in defensiveness, achievement striving, dominance, endurance, and orderliness. Table 12-4 shows some relationships between cognitive style, maladaptive deviation, and the various personality disorders.

THE MOTIVE SYSTEMS IN THE PERSONALITY DISORDERS

Earlier in the chapter we discussed some of the relationships between the motive systems and psychopathology. We claimed that psychopathology could be seen as an imbalance in the motives or as an improper functioning of the motives. It is also possible to examine some of the specific disturbances of the motive systems we would expect to find in particular personality disorders. In our description of the paranoid, for example, we can see that suspicious and antagonistic human relationships obviously interfere with the attachment motive. Not finding security in attachments, he must

Table 12-4 Some Relationships Between Cognitive Style, Psychopathology, and Personality Disorders

Cognitive Style	Maladaptive Tendency If Style Is Extreme	Personality Disorder in Which Such Extreme Styles Exist
Sharpeners	Excitement seeking	Antisocial, hysterical
Levelers	Excessive order and control	Obsessive-compulsive, schizoid
Extensive scanners	Overcautiousness, doubting, suspicion	Paranoid, obsessive-compulsive, antisocial
Narrow scanners	Withdrawal, impulsivity	Schizoid, hysterical
Field-independent	Isolation, controlling	Paranoid, obsessive-compulsive
Field-dependent	Dependency	Hysterical
Internal locus of control	Self-blame, excessive feeling of responsibility	Obsessive-compulsive
External locus of control	Feelings of helplessness and dependency	Hysterical, paranoid
High tolerance for ambiguity	Lack of order, poor planning	Hysterical, antisocial
Low tolerance for ambiguity	Excessively critical behavior	Obsessive-compulsive, schizoid, paranoid
Reflective	Constricted	Schizoid, obsessive-compulsive
Impulsive	Acting out	Hysterical, antisocial

protect himself against the harm he expects from others. He tends to find his security in avoiding defeat, shame, or embarrassment at the hands of supposedly hostile others. He preserves his own status by projecting blame elsewhere. He functions as if he has a perceptual disability: he sees danger where there is no real danger and he attributes cause to external agents (Witkin, 1968; Phares, 1976). He is too concerned with personal security to worry overly about his competence in any task.

The most obviously affected system in the schizoid is also the attachment system. His contacts are limited, distant, and tenuous. He avoids attachments in order to feel secure. This lack of social participation leads to social incompetence. On the other hand, the competence motive becomes more important than either security or attachment for the obsessive-compulsive. If he is not competent, he expects to be in danger and to be rejected by others.

The antisocial personality also shows impaired attachment, since he views others as competitors rather than helpful allies. His security, therefore, depends upon his ability successfully to resist others, and his competence on his ability to outdo them. To the hysteric, however, attachments are exceedingly important. Successful affiliation provides security and is an indication of competence.

Table 12-5 shows some of the relationships between the personality disorders we have discussed and how the motives function in each. In each

Table 12-5 Some Relationships Between Personality Disorders, Dominant Goal, and Motive

Personality Disorder	Perception of Self and Others	Dominant Goal (Guiding Self-Ideal)	Attachment	Security	Competence
Paranoid	Self: endangered Others: hostile	Protecting self against blame and loss of status	Hostility	Avoiding defeat	Depends on his security
Schizoid	Self: unacceptable Others: rejecting and hurting	Protecting self against damage by others	Distance	In avoidance of people	Absent
Obsessive-Compulsive	Self: responsible for events Others: create confusion	Controlling life	Controlled	Depends on his competence	Through control
Antisocial	Self: one of the predators in the jungle Others: natural prey	Overpowering the rules	Manipulates others	There is none anyway	In defeating the rules
Hysterical	Self: requires cherishing Others: potential audience	Being center of attention	Demands attention	Through being cherished only	In winning attention and love

case, the cognitive motive is described as if it were composed of the three parts of the core rubric; self-perception, perception of others, and the dominant goal that determines response choice. Under each of the other motives is listed the kind of behavior such a personality uses in goal behavior.

Personality Disorders As Maladaptive Personalities

The personality disorders we have reviewed in this chapter are only some of the ways in which maladaptive behavior is expressed. We have singled out these disorders because they seem to represent most clearly that form of psychopathology which stems from personality rather than from situational variables. Personality disorders are maladaptive personalities. It is, therefore, not surprising that in these disordered personalities we can find evidence of maladaptive functioning of the motives and of maladaptive perceptual programs which organize them.

13

changing behavior and personality

OVERVIEW

Different theories conceptualize personality change in different ways. For us, behavior change can be achieved through altering the cognitive components of personality structure and dynamics. Methods suitable to these goals include somatic methods, meditative and hypnotic methods, alteration of belief systems, behavior modification, and psychotherapy. In all of these methods, the central change is a change in the way the person processes information. Some treatment techniques consist of direct cognitive intervention and training in giving oneself more effective instructions.

Among the factors that influence behavior change are the cognitive style of the client, the behavior of the therapist, and the interaction between the two.

Not all change in behavior represents a change in personality; there may also be a change only in behavioral response. Our theory of behavior postulates that all behavior is directed by perceptual structure, which is the core of personality. Thus, change in personality necessarily includes change in perceptual structure, not only change in response. We have seen that the various theories about the genesis of behavior focus on personality as an organizer of behavior to a lesser or greater extent. This relative emphasis or deemphasis on personality as an organizing variable quite naturally carries over to the meaning of change in behavior or personality (see Box 13-1).

While Box 13-1 highlights the central emphasis of major theoretical groups, it is important to keep in mind that each theory has subsidiary or moderator propositions, that theories have changed and to some extent converged, and that each major theoretical orientation has its own philosophy about the basic nature of human behavior. Thus, Burton (1976), in summarizing a symposium on behavior and personality change, concludes that the emphasis on libidinal and unconscious determination, so central in Freudian or other so-called psychodynamic theories, has decreased to peripheral importance in contemporary theorizing. Conversely, Mahoney (1974), Meichenbaum (1973), Krasner (1976), and A. Lazarus (1977) are examples of major theorists in behavior therapy who have broadened their

Box 13-1   Representative Theoretical Conceptions of Behavior Change

Theory	Major structural change postulated when behavior or personality changes
Psychoanalysis (Freudian)	Resolution of intrapsychic conflict between various parts of personality (id, ego, superego) and change in contents of conscious and unconscious, particularly bringing the latter into awareness
Behavior theory	Changes in response to environment as a result of changes in conditioning or reinforcement contingencies
Social learning theorists (Bandura, Rotter)	Changes in response to situations because of a change in expectancies
Trait theorists	Change in primary personality factors or types, or in the pattern of the profile depicting various scale positions for each factor
Cognitive theorists	Change in personal constructs, cognitive differentiation, or cognitive complexity
Existentialism	Change in the person's "being-in-the world"

scope to make cognition of central determining importance. We have already noted how the social learning theory of Bandura and Rotter places direct emphasis on expectancy, a perceptual variable.

The increasing attention to cognitive structure in personality theorizing and research has by no means relegated response and environment to negligible importance. As we saw in our discussion of person–situation interaction in Chapter 9, we need to conceptualize and measure behavior in terms of both the person and the environment. Sundberg (1977) puts it the following way: What kind of person will make what kind of response in what kind of situation? This triple interaction between personality structure, response, and environment is important to keep in mind when trying to effect behavior change. People of different dispositions (for example, different aptitudes) will respond differently to different treatments (aimed at changing behavior). That is the focus of the Aptitude-Treatment Intervention (ATI) studies of Cronbach (1975), a paradigm which has been extended to the therapy-counseling situation by Owens (1968) and to all person-environment interactions by Hunt (1975). In this context, behavior change can be effected by intervening at four levels: the person's physiology, his cognitive structure, the responses he makes, or the social environment.

THE COGNITIVE MODEL OF PERSONALITY CHANGE

The conclusion of our introductory paragraphs suggests that there are a number of levels at which we can try to intervene in order to change behavior—for example, somatic, meditative, belief systems, behavioral responses, and psychotherapy. The key proposition which guides our formulation of behavior change states that all human motives are cognitively directed because they are filtered or mediated through the perceptual system, which directs both the structure and dynamics of personality. In this context, behavior change will be achieved by altering the cognitive components of personality structure and dynamics, as exemplified in Box 13-2.

Personality and the Self Are Resistant to Change

Personality change is difficult to achieve. Even people who come to a therapist for help seem to resist alteration of basic personality. Many of the cognitively oriented theorists—for example, Sullivan, Heider, Kelly, and Festinger as well as Beck (1976)—believe that the underlying cause of this resistance to change is the desire for cognitive consistency, or the striving to avoid cognitive dissonance.

Kelly (1955) stressed that we hold on to our cherished personal constructs even after they have been invalidated. If we do not have a relevant construct, we have to process information in terms of what we do have, even if it is invalid. Sullivan pointed out the coping significance of maintaining the self-system. If a person loses his self-system, he undergoes a deintegration—colloquially, "loses his mind." Thus, the person will choose to distort reality rather than alter any aspects of the self-system. The self-system is the main system for coping with anxiety. Furthermore, change itself produces anxiety.

Adler's life style serves a similar purpose. Adler believed that all information is coded in the context of the life style, the cognitive blueprint. Information is extracted and processed according to the commands of the life style; therefore, new information input tends to confirm the life style rather than contradict it. For all these theorists, the perceptual system organizes personality. Since any perceptual system tends to seek its own confirmation, it is difficult for us to change our points of view; our subjective bias directs how we search for reality.

Techniques for producing change in personality and behavior include the following:

1. *Somatic methods.* Work directly on the body through such agents as drugs, hormones, or electroconvulsive shock.
2. *Meditative and hypnotic methods.* Use normal physiological processes to produce change in physiological activity through such procedures as relaxation training, meditation, suggestion, and hypnosis.
3. *Altering belief systems.* Uses certain educational techniques for altering people's beliefs (religious conversion, mass media, and propaganda).
4. *Behavior modification.* Applies experimentally based principles, including conditioning, reinforcement contingencies, and modeling, to produce changes in behavior. Cognitive intervention techniques are used both in behavior modification and psychotherapy.
5. *Psychotherapy.* Uses dialogue to catalyze personality change.

Somatic Methods

Somatic methods are aimed at changing behavior through direct intervention into the person's physiological system. Masserman (1955) has astutely pointed out that ultimately all physical methods aimed at producing behavior change have their effects mediated through altering perceptual functioning. Drugs, alcohol, and electroconvulsive and insulin shock produce some alteration in the subject's perceptual state. It is in this context that the somatic techniques should be viewed.

One instance of such perceptual mediation can be seen in the studies of Betz and Whitehorn (1956; Whitehorn & Betz 1960). These researchers found that physicians working with schizophrenics were more successful if they were warm, outgoing, and intervening. These physicians had 82 percent success whether they used somatic adjuncts or not. Less warm physicians had only 34 percent success without somatic adjuncts, but 82 percent if they used insulin treatment as well.

Fisher and his associates (1962) compared the effect of a placebo and meprobamate, a tranquilizer, on dropout rate (dropping out of therapy) among patients. With placebos, the dropout rate was 32 percent. When the meprobamate was given by physicians who were instructed to have an experimental attitude, the dropout rate was still 32 percent. However, it was reduced to 16 percent when the physician adopted a therapeutic attitude, again demonstrating the interaction between drugs and therapist attitude. The therapeutic attitude consisted of showing interest and concern.

Masserman concludes, "many drugs employed clinically, as adjuncts to psychiatric therapy, have one psychodynamic action in common, they dull perception, prevent the formation of elaborate associations, and probably disorganize complex behavior patterns . . ." (1955, pp. 459–460). More modern researches, however, have shown that drugs such as amphetamines can also speed up perception (Kaplan, Sadock, & Freedman, 1975). The next section indicates that physiological and perceptual states can be altered without artificial stimuli—that is, by using the natural physiological processes of the body.

Meditative and Hypnotic Techniques

Meditative and hypnotic techniques are ancient tools for producing behavior change. Hypnosis fell into partial disrepute after it was popularized as a parlor or exhibition hall display, and has only recently regained its respectability. Meditative techniques have been an integral part of religious rituals in the Western world as well as in Asia, but were most often practiced in Hindu and Buddhist cultures, where the practice took many forms. Yoga, Zen meditation, and other forms have been studied. The best known in the Western world today is Transcendental Meditation.

Transcendental Meditation (TM). Transcendental meditation is another way of intervening in the physiological process by using psychological techniques—that is, by training the person in mental concentration and attention. During the years since its inauguration into the United States in 1959, over a half million people have begun to practice TM (Bloomfield, 1976). Benson (1975) has pointed out that the religious trappings are not necessary; that the main influence on physiology is the practice of relaxation.

Although the first few years were met by skepticism among professionals, the 1970s brought more favorable reception as a result of empirical research on objective behavior changes following TM. Independently (1970) and in joint studies (1971, 1972), Wallace has reported a number of physiological changes associated with TM. Figure 13-1 compares change in metabolic rate following hypnosis, sleep, and TM.

Other changes in bodily function following TM include a marked decrease in blood lactate levels, an increase in the brain's alpha activity (confirmed by Banquet, 1973), and fewer spontaneous galvanic skin responses (Orme-Johnson, 1973). All of these bodily changes indicate that TM gives rise to greater stability of the autonomic nervous system. The profound state of relaxation is followed by increased alertness and responsiveness to external stimuli, heightened perceptual acuity, and greater efficiency. There is also greater resistance to environmental stress and psychosomatic disease, and an increase in general health that is accompanied by clearer perception and thought (Bloomfield, 1976).

This increase in health includes psychological health. Anxiety, as

Levels of rest

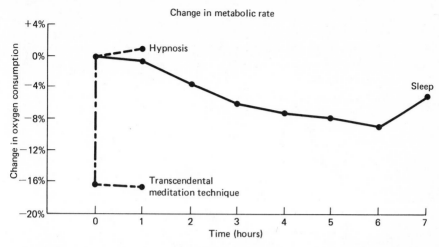

Note: 0% refers to the resting (normal level) of metabolism as measured by oxygen consumption. Once TM has been established there is a 16 percent drop in oxygen consumption — metabolism slows down and relaxation sets in — with no additional change over time. In contrast, there is a more gradual and slower decrease in metabolism during sleep, and a slight increase under hypnosis.

Figure 13-1   Changes in metabolic rate during sleep, hypnosis, and the transcendental meditation technique. Source: "The physiology of Meditation" by Robert Keith Wallace and Herbert Benson. Copyright © 1971 by Scientific American, Inc. All rights reserved.

measured by the Cattell anxiety scale, shows a significant decrease (Ferguson & Gowan, 1976). Meditation also produces greater directedness, spontaneous expression, and acceptance of feeling and capacity for intimate contact (Seeman, Nidich, & Banta, 1972). There are also reduced levels of depression and neuroticism.

Bloomfield (1976) reports on a 23-year-old woman who had been suffering from anxiety attacks since age 17. These attacks were accompanied by the usual exaggerated autonomic signs: panic, tension, and insomnia. Following a year's meditation, these symptoms were drastically reduced. Figure 13-2 shows scores on the MMPI scales prior to and following meditation. Notice particularly the sharp drop in hysteria, depression, and hypochondriasis scores. The previously high scores for depression and hypochondriasis were undoubtedly related to the severe anxiety she experienced.

In summary, after TM: (1) the ANS becomes more stable; (2) basal metabolism decreases; (3) there is a change in brain wave patterns in the electroencephalogram (EEG); (4) anxiety, tension, and depression are re-

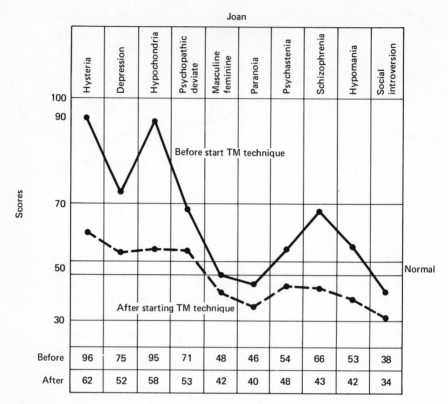

Figure 13-2   One subject's MMPI scores before and after learning TM techniques. Source: Bloomfield, 1976, p. 103.

duced; (5) the person becomes more receptive to information, giving rise to greater creativity and self-determination—that is, develops more internal locus of control.

These lofty claims for TM require additional studies to assess their validity. Yet the implication of Bloomfield's reviews and conclusions is that TM changes physiology and behavior by making ANS functioning more stable, thereby reducing anxiety. "The key to successful therapy lies in creating psychological and physiological conditions that optimize the natural tendency of the nervous system to stabilize itself" (Bloomfield, 1976, p. 194). He cautions that TM should be accompanied by periodic reevaluation in psychotherapy until the intensity of the disturbing thoughts lose their frightening quality. He notes, in contrast, that tranquilizers such as Valium and Librium sedate the patient, make him feel listless and groggy, and may even be addicting. He believes that TM, on the other hand, has a restorative power. The net result is not just a cumulative decline in anxiety but greater stability, adaptability, integration, and growth.

Hypnosis and suggestion. As originally conceived by Charcot and Janet, the predecessors of Freud, the hypnotic state was believed to alter the subject's psychological balance by supposedly reducing voluntary control over behavior. Barber (1971) points out, however, that most research which attributes a variety of psychophysiological effects to hypnosis fails to determine the relative contribution of the following variables.

1. *Suggestions* that certain physiological effects are forthcoming
2. *Instructions* intended to produce positive motivation to respond to suggestions
3. Suggestions of *relaxation*
4. Suggestions that the subject is entering a *deep trance* or a state of hypnosis

The fourth variable, deep trance, is usually considered to be the "cause" of hypnotic phenomena. This conclusion is now under serious criticism, since similar physiological effects have been reported without the so-called trance being present. It has been found that direct or indirect suggestions, given under *either* hypnotic *or* waking conditions, are sufficient to produce certain physiological manifestations. Kliman and Goldberg (1962) recorded visual recognition thresholds under base-line conditions (normal state) and under hypnotic and waking treatment conditions. There was no appreciable difference in threshold for the recognition of tachistoscopically presented words between hypnotic and waking suggestion conditions. However, words which are hard to recognize in the waking condition are easier to recognize in the hypnotic condition whereas words that are easier to recognize under base-line conditions are still more easily recognized when the subject receives a suggestion either in the waking or hypnotic state.

Physiological correlates of the hypnotic state per se. Barber (1971) concludes that whether any physiological changes takes place—and especially the direction of the change—depends on whether the subject carries out the suggestion given, not on the trance state per se. Hypnotic subjects show an elevated level of palmar conductance when they carry out suggestions which involve effort or activity (Barber & Coules, 1959; Davis & Kantor, 1935). If the subject accepts literally the suggestion to relax, there is a fall in palmar conductance; if not, it remains unchanged. Barber (1958) reports that if hypnotized subjects show lethargy, drowsiness, or other signs of trance, these characteristics can be readily removed and the good subject will continue to carry out whatever hypnotic performances are instructed, for example, "Be perfectly awake, come out of 'trance' but continue to obey my commands."

"Appropriately predisposed persons do not need hypnotic-induction procedure and need not appear to be in trance to carry out many, if not all, of the behaviors which have been historically associated with the term hypnosis" (Barber, 1971, p. 242).

Barber (1971) thus concluded that *suggestion* (presumably which can also be self-induced) is the important variable. The emphasis on suggestion gives us a cognitive interpretation of hypnotic effects, just as we found in our discussion of somatic intervention and TM, where we saw the importance of attention to perceptual state and locus of control.

A cognitive conclusion about somatic intervention, meditation, and hypnosis.   The major conclusion arising from the work on all three techniques is that cognitive intervention can be used to regulate natural physiological processes. Biofeedback techniques have produced similar findings, including control of alpha waves in the EEG (Nowlis & Kamiya, 1971).

All these scientific demonstrations have important therapeutic implications. Through cognitive intervention we can train ourselves to diminish physiological conditions which produce noxious psychological states, and to enhance physiological processes which produce increased psychological health.

Altering Belief Systems

Franks (1976) distinguishes between humanistic-scientific and transcendental belief systems. The first kind is dealt with by the science of personology and social psychology (as in the work of Rokeach), while the second occurs in certain religious experiences.

Open and closed minds.   In his study of the contents of human thought, Rokeach (1960) concerned himself with the nature of cognitive structure that underlies belief systems. He postulates that belief systems can theoretically be scaled according to three dimensions. The first is the *belief-disbelief* scale, which gives the individual instructions about what to believe and what not to believe. The second is the *central-peripheral* dimension, which consists of three regions (a conceptualization similar to K. Lewin's personality theory described in Chapter 4). The regions are central, intermediate, and peripheral. The central region contains information about behavior which is closest to the person's self-perception, self-interest, and self-system. This region is the hardest to change, a point noted also by Rogers and Sullivan (see Chapter 3). Regions two and three, of some importance to the social psychologist, contain messages incorporated from cultural authorities and, therefore, reveal the extent to which the person's attitudes conform to the dictates of these authorities. In his book, Rokeach (1960) reviews data which supports the view of clinicians that social attitudes are not as difficult to change as self-invested attitudes. Rokeach's third dimension—*time perspective*—relates to whether the person lives primarily in the past, present, or future. Preoccupation with the first or last is conducive to

nonadaptive, stagnating behavior. The adaptive person, as the existentialist emphasizes, is concerned with present existence but anticipates future
action with considered reflection from past experience.

One way to study the relative rigidity or plasticity of a belief system is
to study a person's openness to experience, the open–closed mind dimension. For this purpose Rokeach constructed his Dogmatism Scale, a questionnaire designed to measure the extent to which a person holds flexible or
dogmatic beliefs about personal and social issues. The advantage of Rokeach's scale is that it presents us with an agenda for researching the contents of cognitive structure and can thus help us understand which kinds of
cognitive organization are more susceptible to adaptive change. In general,
persons who are open to new experiences but can at the same time integrate them into ongoing cognitive organization are more adaptive.

Religious and other forms of conversion. Other than what we said about
transcendental meditation, transcendental belief systems are beyond the
scope of this book. We note in passing, that Benson, Beary, and Carol
(1975) have seen similarities among the effects of meditation, relaxation
and mystical experiences. Some psychiatrists and psychologists have compared psychotherapy and religious conversion, noting that the second experience deals more deeply with the fundamental anxiety concerning death
and being—ontological anxiety (May, 1959).

Caruso (1952), an existentialist psychiatrist, expressed the opinion
that psychotherapy is a preliminary to a religious *metanoia* (conversion);
that a rebirth is the logical end of a psychotherapeutic experience which
leads to a change in values. The various religious traditions have all demanded not only certain types of behavior, but certain types of perceptual
experience from their adherents. Religious rituals have, as one purpose, to
elicit a suitable experiential awareness.

Nicoll (1967), a Christian thinker, states that the human being must
die and be reborn. He must die to his pride and love of status and be reborn
to a new sense of wholeness and goodness. Religious conversion is thus a
basic change in personality. Does personality actually change through genuine religious conversion? William James (1958), one of America's first psychologists, discussed this issue in his classic, *The Varieties of Religious
Experience,* first published in 1902. James described many "cases" of conversion and concluded that personality can indeed change as a result.
The convert's typical ways of behaving change; self-perception and world
view change. The world and the self are experienced in new and different
ways.

There is little significant research on this subject, but subjective reports abound. A conversion experience apparently can be an intense stress
experience which leaves a person permanently changed thereafter.

Behavior Modification

Behavior therapy began as an attempt to base psychological treatment upon sound scientific principles. The major treatment method in use when behavior therapy received its main impetus (in the 1950s and 60s) was psychoanalysis. Some behaviorists felt that psychoanalysis was a dogmatic belief system rather than a science. Behavior therapy drew upon the hypothesis that all behavior, normal and abnormal, was learned, and thus the paradigms of stimulus-response and response-reinforcement became the foundation of early behavior therapy. Most of the procedures of behavior therapy derive from principles of learning. They are used to modify maladaptive behavior and to foster acquisition of more adaptive behavior patterns. These procedures confront maladaptive behavior in the here and now rather than focusing on the patient's past and highlight the impact of the environment on the patient's behavior. Some major proponents are Bandura (1969), Kanfer (1970), Mischel (1976), Lazarus (1973), and Ullman and Krasner (1969).

The Nature of Behavior Therapy
(Behavior Modification)

Each of the behavior therapists emphasizes a different treatment technique. One of the pioneers of behavior modification, Wolpe (1969) limits it to the application of experimentally-established principles of learning for the purpose of changing unadaptive behavior Arnold Lazarus (1971), the originator of "broad spectrum behavior therapy" includes, in addition to the objective techniques, all the usual or traditional psychotherapeutic techniques. The behavior therapists with a social learning orientation, such as Bandura (1969) and Ullman and Krasner (1969), consider the relevant social learning histories of their patients when they plan behavioral treatment strategies.

Recent developments have introduced far-reaching modifications to this stimulus-response and response-reinforcement paradigm—modern behavior therapy has become much more sophisticated. One development has been to incorporate new behavior techniques in addition to those of classical and operant conditioning. Another has been in the direction of broadening the theoretical base of behavior therapy to allow for contributions from related fields such as systems theory, group dynamics, communications theory, and cognitive studies. Foremost among these proponents of new developments are Bandura (1976), A. Lazarus (1977), Meichenbaum (1977), and Mahoney (1974).

356

Techniques of Behavior Modification

Systematic desensitization. Wolpe (1969) introduced *reciprocal inhibition* or *systematic desensitization* as a way of eliminating unwanted neurotic behavior. The technique involves replacing the unwanted behavior with more desirable and incompatible behavior. For example, it is impossible to be both tense and relaxed at the same time (reciprocal inhibition). Through gradual and·systematic relaxation training, Wolpe teaches his clients how to reduce tension and anxiety. Practicing relaxation has enabled many of Wolpe's patients to ameliorate other symptoms, such as sexual dysfunction.

Wolpe (1976) claims that desensitization is nothing but a form of conditioning. However, it is always accompanied by relaxation training, which includes a set of instructions about how to behave. In the desensitization procedure, Wolpe asks the patient to construct a fear hierarchy—a list of situations in which the person experiences fear. The patient assigns a rating of severity to the fears on a scale of 0 to 100. Zero means that the patient does not experience fear, while a rating of 100 indicates the situation the patient finds the most fear provoking. Desensitization usually begins with the least fearful situation and proceeds gradually to the most. Wolpe also uses a form of guided imagery (a cognitive intervention) when he instructs the patient to imagine himself in frightening situations while he is practicing relaxation.

Assertiveness training. This technique has been used as an integral part of systematic desensitization. In this procedure, the patient is taught to act in more self-assertive ways through instructions by the therapist and also by repeated practice of such behavior, first in non-threatening situations and later in the situations feared by the patient. The therapist models the assertive behavior and the patient role-plays it before using it.

Rimm and Masters (1974) claim that assertive behavior appears to inhibit interpersonal anxiety as reliably as does deep muscle relaxation. Percell, Berwick, and Beigel (1974) studied the effect of assertiveness training on self-concept and anxiety. Comparing an assertiveness training group to a more traditional therapy group, they found that after eight sessions the former showed more assertiveness and self-acceptance and less anxiety. Assertive behavior inhibits fear behavior and vice versa. Once one resolves to confront, getting indignant in the process, one no longer feels afraid. The client practices assertive behavior by practicing behavior which is the opposite of his usual behavior.

Implosion therapy. Implosion and flooding have been introduced by Stampfl and Levis (1967, 1968). *Implosion therapy* involves exposing the patient, for prolonged periods of time, to anxiety-provoking scenes (such as by projection of these scenes onto a screen). *Flooding* exposes the patient to the actual anxiety-arousing situation. By experiencing the anxiety-arousing situation without the expected occurrence of disaster, the patient's reactions to the feared situation change. While in systematic desensitization, anxiety was relieved gradually, in implosion and flooding, there is no such gradual approach; the exposure to the stimulus is pervasive and intense.

Operant techniques. The use of *differential reinforcement* (reinforcement practice) has been shown to alter anorexia nervosa (nervous loss of appetite), agoraphobia (fear of open spaces), and other neurotic behavior. The therapist withholds reinforcement until behavior, other than the symptom pattern is expressed (Callahan & Leitenberg, 1970; Leitenberg, Agras, Butz, & Winze, 1971; Leitenberg, 1973). Leitenberg (1972) summarizes the philosophy guiding this technique: "When *expectations* of success are combined with repeated practice in the feared situation together with praise and feedback, all the ingredients for an effective treatment of phobia are present."

Token economy is a special case of reinforcement practice. Ayllon and Azrin (1965) set up a system in a mental hospital in which patients could earn tokens for the display of appropriate and responsible behavior. These earned tokens (secondary reinforcers) could then be used to purchase a variety of reinforcers such as food, privacy, recreation, and sustained scheduled attention from a therapist. Tokens were instrumental in generating high rates of performance on previously rejected jobs. If reinforcement was given regardless of the rate of job performance, however, decrease in job adequacy resulted. Increased quantity of reinforcement produced an increase in rate of adequate performance. This is an application of a well-known principle of reinforcement, namely, that the strength of the response is a function of the quantity of the reward. Atthowe and Krasner (1968) were able to establish an effective token economy system with chronic patients in a VA hospital that sustained itself over a 2-year period.

Changes in behavior produced by operant techniques remain under the regulation of environmental reinforcement contingencies. This has been demonstrated experimentally by using the ABAB design. In this design, A is a control condition and B is an experimental treatment condition.

An ABAB design experiment that involved the self-destructive behavior of a psychotic 9-year-old boy was performed by Tate and Baroff (1966). During the A condition, the boy's destructive behavior was simply ignored for 4 days. During the B condition, the behavior therapists would remove themselves from the boy when he exhibited self-destructive behavior (negative reinforcement). This also lasted for 4 days. Then A and B were repeated. The results are shown in Figure 13-3.

Negative reinforcement drastically reduced the self-destructive be-

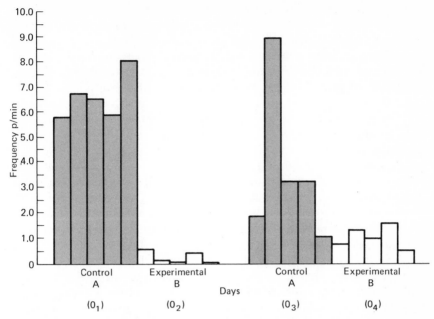

Figure 13-3   Effects of the contingent punishment procedure in Tate and Baroff's study, illustrating experimental effects within a single-subject design. (The individual bars are data for each day of the experiment.) Source: Tate and Baroff, 1966. (Adapted from Neale and Liebert, 1973, p. 153.)

havior. When this reinforcement contingency was removed, the self-destructive behavior returned, but could again be reduced by reintroduction of negative reinforcement treatment.

Behavior Modification Techniques
Developed from Social Learning Theory

Bandura and his students have developed behavior modification techniques based on Bandura's social learning theory. The techniques combine the use of modeling with guided performance and refinement through successful practice, leading eventually to a complete, positive experience (Bandura, 1976). In describing his technique, Bandura points out that the therapist models the desired behavior for the client, guides the client through the performance of the behavior, and provides opportunities for the client to perform the new behavior successfully. Successful performance is also facilitated by providing the client with repeated modeling in graduated sub-tasks of increasing difficulty, arranging protective conditions to allay anxiety (for example, holding the head and tail of the snake securely so the phobic client will be more willing to approach) and by joint performance (doing the task together with the client).

The more such aids the therapist uses, the faster are new behaviors learned, attitudes changed, and anticipatory fears reduced. Bandura, Jefferey, and Wright (1974) compared groups of adult phobics exposed to the same amount of participant modeling treatment and found that progress was more rapid when the therapist used more of these response induction aids. Bandura considers that successful performance is the primary vehicle of change in the participant modeling approach.

As the client improves, response induction aids are phased out until, finally, the client's performance is self-directed. Successful self-directed performance produces more general and durable behavior and attitude change (Bandura, Jefferey, & Gajdos, 1975). Bandura, Blanchard, and Ritter (1969) compared the effectiveness of participant modeling to standard desensitization procedures by studying adults and adolescents with snake phobias. One group was treated with systematic desensitization. A second group repeatedly viewed a film of people interacting with snakes and used self-induced relaxation until they could view the scenes without anxiety. The third group was treated by means of live modeling and guided performance. The therapist himself handled the snakes and gradually led the clients to do so. A fourth group served as untreated controls. An analysis of the results showed that untreated controls remained fearful and avoided approaching snakes. Groups 1 and 2 were both more willing to approach snakes than the untreated group, but group 3 subjects were dramatically more powerful in eliminating phobic behavior.

Behavior Therapy: A Subset of Cognitive Therapy

Although radical behaviorists insist that only environmental contingencies and events can influence behavior—and Wolpe (1976) insists that conditioning is the basis of all behavior change—other behavior therapists do not agree. A. Lazarus (1977) points out that the most current view is that conditioning is cognitively mediated. Lazarus has recommended multimodal or "broad spectrum" behavior therapy (1976) which includes, among other techniques, cognitive intervention. For example, he uses rational images to help a person reduce self-upsetting ideation. "Above all, *stop telling yourself that* because you are a fallible human being this means that you are worthless, useless and a complete failure" (A. Lazarus, 1971, pp. 179–180). This technique is similar to the rational-emotive therapy of A. Ellis (1971). Mahoney (1974) reviews behavior theory and research and concludes that an unmediated stimulus-response theory is conceptually inadequate and other models must be considered. One such model is the cognitive learning model, as used by Bandura (1969), Meichenbaum (1977), and others previously mentioned.

Beck (1976) has explicitly used a cognitive learning approach to behavior change. Although he is a psychotherapist, the techniques he uses strongly resemble behavior therapy techniques. Calling himself a cognitive therapist, he directs his technique to modifying the ideational content involved in the symptom; namely, the irrational inferences and premises. He trains his client to recognize his spontaneous verbal and pictorial cognitions (automatic thoughts). He also uses induced as well as spontaneous images to pinpoint the patient's misconceptions and to reality-test his distorted views of himself and his world (Beck, 1970a, c). Thus change is seen as occurring in the conceptual system of the patient. Brown (1967) had a female patient who felt fear and guilt at the sight of male genitals. He instructed her to visualize a series of scenes of male genitalia from a nude little boy through a nude statue to a nude adult male. These exercises changed her attitude toward male genitalia. Beck believes that systematic desensitization leads to the same gradual change in attitudes. In a similar vein Leitenberg and his associates (1969) point out that instructions in systematic desensitization define, for the patient, what behaviors are of interest, while he receives constant feedback from his own observations. They reason that such self-observed signs (a perceptual act) of improvement account for much of the success of all graduated behavior therapy. *Thus the patient participates as an active thinker.*

Beck (1976) points out that systematic desensitization enables the patient to increase his objectivity, for example, to discriminate between a real danger and a fantasied one. Patients who are questioned at the termination of an individual fantasy generally construe the threatening situation differently and more realistically than before, owing to a modification or shift in their ideational system. Assertiveness training, role playing, and modeling all lead to a change in the patient's self-concept, because, as he prac-

---

Box 13-3   An Example of an Irrational Inference Based on Faulty Generalization

A young man who likes a female classmate discovers that she prefers to sit and talk to another man in the college union building. He concludes that women in general will find him less attractive than other males.

Beck would try to teach the young man that there are other possible reasons for the young woman's behavior and that the behavior of one woman cannot be generalized to all women. These types of ideations, according to Beck, lead to symptoms such as anxiety and depression. Repeated cognitive intervention by the therapist, and teaching the patient to intervene in his own cognitions, corrects the irrational inference and its corresponding pathological emotional states.

tices the desired behavior he gradually changes his view of himself in relation to others.

Consistent with Beck's analysis, Goldfried and his collaborators (1974) point out that in order to be effective, behavior modification must include a cognitive restructuring. Goldfried and Goldfried (1975) review some of the outcome studies (including Meichenbaum, 1972, and Trexler & Karst, 1972) which show that systematic rational restructuring can be effective.

As behavior therapy and theory evolve, various cognitive issues play increasingly important roles. What has not changed, fortunately, is its scientific bases. A. Lazarus (1977) lists these "behavioral principles" as: due regard for scientific objectivity, extreme caution in the face of conjecture and speculation, a rigorous process of deduction from testable theories and a fitting indifference to persuasion and hearsay.

Skinner, the father of operant conditioning, never denied that thought existed, but considered it difficult to study directly through experimental analysis. He did state that changes in response brought about through operant procedures could feed back to alter thought. Modern behavior therapists have demonstrated that experimentally rigorous techniques can be used to intervene in thought directly.

Psychotherapy

The main procedure used in psychotherapy is a dialogue between the therapist and the client. Each of the theoretical schools of psychotherapy offers its own explanation of how psychotherapy helps and what changes occur in the client, but in all schools, the relationship between client and therapist is considered central. The therapist may be active (make interpretations and give instructions) or passive (listen while the client engages in free association). There are numerous techniques of psychotherapy. A common one is *interpretation,* in which the therapist explains the client's behavior, dreams, feelings, or other productions in whatever theoretical language he usually uses. In Chapters 2 through 4 we reviewed the various approaches different psychotherapies take to the issue of behavior change.

Originally, psychotherapy was almost always a dialogue. Recent developments, however, have included group and family therapies and a mixture of dialogue, role playing, and expression of feeling techniques as in the Gestalt therapy techniques of Perls (Polster & Polster, 1973), the transactional analysis of Berne (1966), marriage counseling, and various other group procedures.

Marmor (1976) has tried to describe the operational factors in the many and diverse approaches to psychotherapy. He believes there are eight major factors operative in all the psychotherapeutic approaches. He defines these as: (1) A good patient-therapist relationship in which the patient is motivated for change; (2) release of tension and expectation of help (relief of distressing feelings and increase in morale); (3) cognitive learning; (4) operant conditioning (as through approval-disapproval cues from the therapist); (5) suggestion and persuasion; (6) observational learning from what the therapist models; (7) repeated rehearsal and practice; and (8) emotional support from the therapist.

What changes in psychotherapy? Box 13-4 summarizes the key concepts of several theorists about what changes in therapy and how change is facilitated by the therapist.

All of the above theories in Box 13-4 evidently postulate that psychopathology results from some kind of imbalance—be it oppressive superego, psychic disharmony, inflated self-system, blocked self-realization, incomplete Gestalt, distorted life style, or maladaptive ideation. These exaggerations in structure and dynamics are paralleled by distortions in perception and diffficulty in attaining the goals directed by the basic motives. The strategies and tactics of psychotherapy are aimed at correcting these unhappy outcomes of personality imbalance.

In psychoanalysis it is postulated that a transference neurosis develops when the patient transfers the neurotic conflict to the therapeutic situation. Working through the transference neurosis and resulting resistance eventually leads the patient to accept some and renounce others of his libidinal desires, in this way reducing the conflict. For Jung, successful psychotherapy increases the process of individuation (self-actualization). One-sidedness decreases so that greater intrapsychic harmony is achieved (structure becomes more balanced). Furthermore, the complexes are resolved, giving rise to more balanced perception—that is, the increased processing of more accurate information. For example, a man with a masculinity complex allows his *anima* to surface as a complement to his *animus*. He thus accepts the notion that masculinity can include tender feelings as well as aggressiveness.

As a result of the therapist's interpretation of parataxic distortions and the interpersonal experience with the therapist, Sullivan's patient develops more interpersonal skills—leading to increased security and satisfaction.

For Rogers, the person becomes more fully functioning and the self-concept is enhanced. The Gestalt therapists similarly believe that the person becomes more complete. His perceptions are broader so that he is more capable of dealing with all of reality. The transactional therapists use the giving and withholding of strokes, so that maladaptive scripts and tapes are replaced by more effective ones for processing information during interpersonal transactions. Self-concept changes from "I'm not OK" to "I'm OK,"

Box 13-4   Theoretical Constructs of Therapeutic Change

Theory	What Changes	How It Is Changed
Freud	Unconscious id and superego; forces become more amenable to ego management	Interpretation makes the unconscious conscious, and "working through" permits acceptance of self
Jung	One-sidedness changes toward intrapsychic harmony; complexes are resolved	Analysis of dreams and art work lead to recognition and acceptance of archetypes
Sullivan	Parataxic distortion changes to syntaxic thought; less inflation of self-system.	Revealing and exposing parataxic distortion
Rogers	Self-concept improves, permitting greater self-realization	Unconditional positive regard; reflection of feeling and empathic listening
Gestalt (Perls)	The Gestalt becomes more complete; parts of the personality form a more integrated whole, unmet "needs" are satisfied	Gestalt operates to reorganize the figure/ground relationships; new values become salient
Berne	The script and the tapes change so that more adult ego states emerge	Exposing games and script; giving and withholding strokes
Adler	Life style; dominant goal changes from personal superiority to social interest.	Disclosure of mistaken assumptions and fictitious goals; encouragement
Kelly	Personal constructs become permeable and comprehensive	Present constructs are reviewed and altered and/or new ones are formulated, using the therapist as a validating agent
Beck Mahoney Meichenbaum	Cognitive categories change: automatic ideation changes to awareness of how one can control self and life	Confront, disclose, and analyze irrational beliefs; homework assignments involve sequential analysis of thought and practice in self-initiated cognitive intervention
Rotter	Expectancies, reinforcement values	Verbal reinforcement of desired behaviors, not rewarding maladaptive behaviors, interpretation of inappropriate expectations

and this improvement in self-confidence facilitates the satisfaction of human motives which make life more complete, rewarding, and fulfilling.

In Adler's theory, the life style changes in therapy. Since life style depends upon perceptual categories, the therapist aims at correcting the client's mistaken assumptions. Kelly thought of therapy as a "reconstruing process" in which personal constructs are reveiwed and altered and/or new ones are formulated, until the client has a comprehensive and permeable set of constructs which are capable of processing a wide range of events.

A social learning approach to psychotherapy. We have previously pointed out that both Rotter and Bandura are social learning theorists. However, Bandura fits more properly into a discussion of behavior therapy, while Rotter's methods are primarily psychotherapeutic. For Rotter (1954, 1970), psychotherapy is a learning process and the therapist's function is to increase the client's freedom of movement and reduce the value of detrimental goals. Rotter proposes to accomplish this by changing the client's expectancies and reinforcement values. If the client avoids a situation because of a high expectancy of failure, changing the expectancy may permit the client to approach the situation. If the client persistently gets himself into trouble because he does not see the consequences of his own behavior, helping him to understand the consequences may provide strong negative reinforcement for the previous thoughtless behavior.

In addition to employing many of the traditional psychotherapeutic techniques, including interpretation, Rotter aims to change expectancies through (1) direct reinforcement, usually verbal; (2) placing the client in situations where he can observe different behaviors, as in group therapy; (3) teaching the client alternative behaviors; and (4) trying to increase his expectancies that alternative behaviors will be more effective. The therapeutic relationship itself, as well as interpretation and exploration of past behaviors, is used to help change reinforcement values. Rotter's method is thus a direct application of social learning theory to the process of psychotherapy itself.

Outcome research in psychotherapy: cognitive perspective. The most central controversy among psychologists about psychotherapy has been whether it really improves adaptive behavior and, if it does, how enduring the improvement is. One important reason for the controversy is that some of the claims on behalf of psychotherapy have been based upon subjective reports of improvement by clients themselves. The scientist requires that such subjective reports be independently verified before he can accept their validity. Some recent studies have addressed this question. Mahoney (1974) reviewed research on cognitively oriented therapy. In one example, a review of outcome studies of the rational-emotive therapy of Ellis (1971, 1973a,

1973b), he concluded that while patients have generally reported improvement following psychotherapy, the ability to obtain reliable and valid measures of improvement through direct behavioral measures has remained elusive. There is a discrepancy between self-reports and direct behavioral measures.

.The studies reviewed by Mahoney lacked adequate controls and therefore gave inconclusive results. More recent, better designed studies of outcome use more reliable and more valid methods, as shown in the following representative examples.

Self-instructional training in cognitive intervention. Meichenbaum (1969) originally tried to teach schizophrenics to stop using private words and language that others do not understand (non-consensual communication). Following this work, Meichenbaum and his associates (1973a, b; 1974; 1975) developed a successful method for changing inappropriate behavior through training the patient to intervene verbally in his own words, behavior, and thoughts. In this procedure, when the patient makes a psychotic statement, the therapist first models a more appropriate way of talking (which differs from the patient's "crazy talk and conceptions") and then instructs the patient to imitate, through repeated practice, the more appropriate language and thinking of the therapist. The patient is thus taught to use self-instruction to change his thinking and verbal behavior.

In one research application of this cognitive training strategy, Meichenbaum and Cameron (1973a) obtained impressive results. The performance of five cognitively trained schizophrenics on a variety of direct behavior measures was compared with that of five matched controls (also schizophrenic) who were given equal attention but no training in self-instruction. The behavior of these two groups was assessed by an experimenter who knew nothing about the patients' condition or assignment. The results are depicted in Figure 13-4. The five sets of graphs reveal, and statistical analysis supports, that the cognitively trained subjects improved in all behavioral indices except digit recall in the absence of distraction. The fact that such training in how to intervene in one's own cognitions can improve communication (interview), logical understanding (proverb test), reality perception (inkblot test), and immediate memory under distraction has important implications for the theory and practice of psychotherapy. Most significantly, it suggests that one ought to pay more attention to what the patient can do to help himself.

Using Personal Construct (Rep) scores as a guide to effective psychotherapy. Landfield (1971), in some interesting clinical research, has applied Kelly's personal construct theory and Rep test to assess some of the conditions facilitating successful therapeutic outcome. In Kelly's theory, the

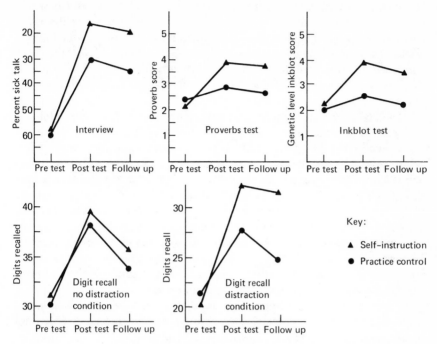

Figure 13-4 Performance measures at pretreatment, post-test, and follow-up stages. Source: Reprinted with permission from Meichenbaum and Cameron, 1973a.

healthy personality is adaptive and well integrated. Adaptivity is measured by the number of distinctly different concepts the person employs, and degree of integration, by their relationships to one another. The person should have a sufficient number of constructs and there should be sufficient integration among them so that his thinking is not scattered. These Functionally Independent Constructs (*FIC*) can be measured. It has been empirically demonstrated by Landfield's data reviews that adaptive persons and therapists have an average FIC score of 14, with significant deviation above that indicating maladaptive personality functioning. Landfield compares a successful therapeutic outcome to an unsuccessful one and relates successful/unsuccessful outcome of psychotherapeutic intervention to changes in the FIC score (1971, pp. 114–130). The successful client, Pam, had an original FIC score of 18. Constructs in her original Rep test revealed that she was "seriously questioning *whether or not she could cope with life*," and had problems in sex identification. After a few weeks of psychotherapy, her FIC score had decreased 8 points. The constructs in her second Rep test revealed that she had gained more confidence in coping with her problems and organizing her life. The unsuccessful client, Doug, had an extremely high original FIC score of 26. His constructs indicated a highly self-reliant, cognitively complex person, who was alienated and lonely. After several weeks of psychotherapy, there was no decrease in the high FIC score. There was instead an increase in the number of constructs that involved moralistic thinking. There is no evidence that psychotherapy helped him.

The behavior of the therapist.   According to Landfield, an important difference that affected the outcomes of the two cases was the way the therapist's own construct system enabled him to respond to the client. It has been theorized that the therapist's experience rather than his theoretical orientation is the crucial variable in therapeutic success (Fiedler, 1950). Rogers (1957) and others (Truax & Mitchell, 1971; Scheid, 1976) have verified empirically that such therapist personality variables as warmth, competence, interpersonal climate, comfort, and client satisfaction are instrumental in a successful outcome (see also Carkhuff & Berenson, 1967; Luborsky & Spence, 1971). The therapist's attitude of understanding and empathic feedback induces an enhanced patient concept of self-worth, which in turn improves confidence and competence.

Active therapist intervention is another significant aspect of effective therapeutic outcome, as originally pointed out by Rogers (1957) and Rogers and Dymond (1956). Research has verified that what the therapist responds to actively tends to be discussed and thought about further by the patient. An analysis of taped interviews showed that active intervention by the therapist correlated with more improvement in the client.

Clarifying cognitive sequences in psychotherapy.   Beck (1976) illustrates his views on cognitive intervention therapy by discussing the treatment of severely depressed patients. One female patient had the typically poor self-image and feelings of being unlovable usually associated with clinical depression. Her current depression began when a male friend called to postpone a date. The therapist directed her to examine her sequence of thoughts. As a result she began to realize that her feelings of rejection were exaggerated distortions resulting from illogical connections. When Beck asked her to keep a journal, she was able to see from her record that the greater percentage of her experience was, in fact, positive. Her memory retrieved primarily the negative incidents because her perceptual sets selectively focused on information which confirmed her expectancy of being unlovable. This method of sequential analysis and cognitive intervention, similar to that of Meichenbaum, plus *reinterpretation* helped abate the depression. In his clinical work, Raimy (1976) has come to a similar conclusion: repeatedly encouraging patients to seriously review and consider their misconceptions, both during and between visits to the therapist, will facilitate effective personality change following psychotherapy.

Expectancy. Research by Frank (1961) and Goldstein (1962a, b) found that patients' expectancies also play an important determining role in psychotherapy. Patients who receive instructions that instills high expectancy of a successful psychotherapeutic outcome are more likely to benefit. Moreover, Heilbrun (1972) and Sloane and his associates (1970) have found that simply preparing the patient with an explanation of how psychotherapy works and what he can expect from the therapist already begins to produce beneficial effects. In a critical review of research on expectancy effects in psychotherapy, Wilkins (1973), supports the conclusion that expectancy is an important determiner of outcome. Expectancy effects, which is a cognitive variable, confirms the well-known psychological phenomenon of "self-fulfilling prophecy."

A comparative study of psychotherapies. Luborsky, Singer, and Luborsky (1975) reviewed the literature on outcome studies of psychotherapy in order to compare as much as possible the different theoretical schools. Included in the review were also outcome studies of behavior therapies. In their preface the authors admit the difficulties of making such a comparison and note that their selection of studies included only those that met reasonable research design criteria. They further refined their review by using studies dealing with only adults, the majority of whom were nonpsychotic and therefore of the type more often treated with psychotherapy. The research literature they reviewed was of impressive quantity (over 100 studies) and ranged from 1936 to the present. They conclude that all forms of psychotherapy and behavior therapy seem to have some beneficial effect—the net effect is a "tie score" between them, probably because they all contain the required operative factors.

COGNITIVE STYLE AND BEHAVIOR CHANGE

If, as we have seen in earlier chapters, cognitive style is related to behavior, both normal and abnormal, then it is reasonable to expect that it also influences what happens when a client seeks a therapist for the purpose of changing his behavior. Cognitive style can be expected to influence how the client will behave in the treatment situation, which treatment techniques will be more effective, and the outcome of his attempt to seek change.

Cognitive Style Studies of Behavior Change

Studies of the effect of cognitive style in therapy have come largely from two areas: psychological differentiation and locus of control. Many of the other cognitive styles we have discussed have not been researched in terms of their relationship to therapy. For example, the work on reflec-

tive/impulsive styles has been carried out largely in the field of development, not in the clinic. Nevertheless, these two groups of studies present
evidence that cognitive style is indeed a factor in therapy.

Psychological differentiation: Field-independent versus field-dependent. Several studies show that the field-dependent client is less likely to benefit from
psychotherapy. In one study on alcoholics, Karp, Kissin, and Hustmyer
(1970) found that field-dependents stay in a therapy program a shorter period of time than field-independents. Kissin, Platz, and Su (1970) concluded that independents do better in psychotherapy, while dependents do
better with pharmacological treatment.

A more direct test of therapeutic outcome was performed by Pardes
and his co-workers (1974). Sixty acute psychotics hospitalized for treatment
were given an overall clinical assessment and a rating of psychological differentiation, based on test data. A significant correlation was obtained:
Undifferentiated patients stayed in the hospital an average of 86 days,
while differentiated patients stayed an average of only 51 days.

What are the possible reasons for these findings? Are undifferentiated
clients simply unsuitable for psychotherapy? Greene (1972) reports that
differentiated patients are more likely to be assigned to insight therapy,
while less differentiated ones are more likely to be assigned to supportive
therapy. Is this an indication of perceptive clinical judgment on the part of
the clinician—or is it rather a sign that the therapist's own expectations
prejudice him against the undifferentiated client?

Witkin, Lewis, and Weil (1968) found that the greatest frequency of
undesirable verbal exchange (interruptions, pauses, number of words used)
occurred in the least differentiated patient-therapist dyad and the lowest
frequency occurred in the most differentiated dyad. With more differentiated patients, verbal flow is smoother and communication more effective.
The therapist who is relatively passive and waits for the client to take the
lead would ordinarily find himself frustrated with a passive client.

A study by Russakoff and his associates (1976) verified the hypothesis
that undifferentiated patients would be less satisfied with therapeutic
structure and would, therefore, respond less well to psychotherapy. Furthermore, in such undifferentiated styles there would be less mutual attraction between therapist and patient. Russakoff used techniques devised
by Witkin to assess the psychological differentiation of non-psychotic patients. Immediately following the first therapeutic interview, the therapists
filled out a 43-item questionnaire concerning each patient's appropriateness for psychotherapy. Less differentiated patients were less satisfied and
were also found less appropriate for psychotherapy. In essence, the less differentiated patient wanted more things from the therapist, and the therapist more frequently reported, "I did not know what to do." The last two

findings are consistent with those of Gates (1971) and Sousa-Poza and Rohrberg (1976), who found that less differentiated patients want the therapist to lead and initiate.

In all these studies it is regrettable that no comparison was made between experienced and less experienced therapists in the treatment of field-dependents. The field-independent client may certainly change more easily with any kind of treatment, but a highly experienced therapist may have good results with field-dependents as well. It is also possible that undifferentiated clients may respond to behavior therapy as well as the differentiated ones and one hopes some empirical studies on this subject will soon be available.

Locus of control: Internal/external.   Lefcourt (1966) recognized that the development of internal locus of control would facilitate adaptive personality change in psychotherapy. Conversely, successful psychotherapy would be accompanied by an increase of internal locus of control, since such persons would be more adaptive and cope better with life. Support for such a deduction comes from the work of Smith (1970), which found that individuals who experienced acute life crises showed a decrease in external locus of control following psychotherapy. This finding did not hold true for people in therapy who did not have immediate life crises.

In another study with patients in psychotherapy, an increase in internal locus of control was found to result from an emphasis on reeducative strategies or changing actions (Dua, 1970). This was particularly true of the action-oriented therapy groups. In a similar kind of research design, Foulds (1971) compared the pre- and post-I-E scores of 30 undergraduate college students who were in four weekly half-hour group therapy sessions for 8 months with a matched control group who were not treated. The experimental group showed a significant increase in internal scores by comparison with the control group. While findings such as those of Dua and Foulds are encouraging, the absence of some kind of activity in the non-treated, control groups makes the reliability of these findings somewhat questionable. Replication with more adequate controls is required.

An interesting study of Helweg (1971) found that students and patients who were more intrinsically controlled and less dogmatic (according to Rokeach) chose therapists (on the basis of viewing films of their interaction) who were more client oriented than directive in their approach. High externals and dogmatics preferred the latter kind of therapist.

As in the studies on psychological differentiation, Dowds and his associates (1977) have shown that locus of control influences the judgments that therapists make about patients. When the patient was a high external, the therapist was more likely to decide that he was unsuitable for therapy. In their study, 39 male patients in a Veterans Administration hospital were

Box 13–5   Intuitive Analysis of Client Behavior and Therapist's Response in Various Cognitive Styles

Cognitive style	Response to Psychotherapy Process	What the therapist can do
Sharpeners	Will look for exciting insights and novelty; Will be bored if novelty is missing	Does not allow discussion to remain on one subject too long; therapist himself becomes an interesting figure to client
Levelers	Avoid emotionally arousing material; do not desire much change	Step-by-step procedure; does not ask client to move fast.
Extensive scanners	Want to understand everything before they move	Explains in detail, links, clarifies, and discloses the client's reluctance to move and excessive demand for information.
Narrow scanners	Limited by the narrowness of their percepts; have trouble understanding psychotherapy; do not see alternatives	Shows client other points of view and alternatives: uses self as a model: answers questions about concepts and methods
Field-independent	Quick learners; use *themselves* as a frame of reference	Help client to consider other points of view
Field-dependent	Want therapist to do all the work	Point out what the client must do; acting as a guide, the therapist assigns tasks which lead to greater self-reliance in the patient
Internal locus of control	Tend to take charge of therapy	Accept client's lead as long as there is therapeutic movement; resume leadership when movement stops.
External locus of control	Expect therapist to make magic	Same as field dependent
High tolerance for ambiguity	Do not work methodically; jump around	Brings client back to subject
Low tolerance for ambiguity	Concrete approach; hard to deal with abstract concepts; do not understand concept of unconscious determinants	Gives specific instructions; keeps situation very clear and the rules precise
Reflective-analytic	Intellectualization without movement or emotional expression—''philosophizers''	Sets limits to ''philosophizing'' and assigns actions tasks; tries to arouse emotions
Impulsive-global	Global emotional arousal— avoid unpleasant information and want immediate satisfaction	While giving emotional support, provides positive feedback for more disciplined behavior.

assigned to six male psychiatric residents and psychology trainees. Each therapist completed a questionnaire after his initial interview with the patient. The patients themselves were tested for a number of factors, including psychological differentiation and locus of control. Those patients found less suitable for therapy after the initial interview were generally field-dependent and externally oriented.

This last study suffers from the same defect mentioned previously. While psychiatric residents and psychology trainees may have some experience as therapists, they can hardly be considered experienced therapists. Until similar studies are performed, using therapists with much more experience, no definite conclusion can be drawn. All we can say at the moment is that the particular therapists used in the studies are more adept at helping the differentiated and internal client than the dependent and external client. It is possible that the therapist's experience may be even a more important variable than the client's cognitive style.

Cognitive Style and the Therapist-Client Dyad

It is tempting to speculate that if we knew enough about the topic, we could assess the prospective client's cognitive style and would know exactly what kind of therapeutic procedure to use with him. Unfortunately, as Luborsky and his co-workers (1975) point out, such information is not yet available. From what we do know and from what we can extrapolate, perhaps we can intuitively describe some of the expected behavior of the client and how the therapist could respond to it. Box 13-5 is an exercise in speculation. We have guessed that certain client behaviors will be found in each cognitive style and we have described maneuvers and strategies that the therapist can use in order to counteract the possible negative effects of these behaviors. Such tactics are hopefully a part of the armamentarium of an experienced therapist.

bibliography

ADAMS, W. V. Strategy differences between reflective and impulsive children. *Child Development*, 1972, *43*, 1076–1080.

ADLER, A. *Understanding human nature.* New York: Greenberg, 1927.

ADLER, A. *What Life Should Mean To You.* New York: Grosset and Dunlap, 1937.

ADLER, A. *Social interest: A challenge to mankind.* New York: Capricorn Books, 1964.

ADLER, A. *The practice and theory of individual psychology.* Totowa, N.J.: Littlefield, Adams, 1968.

ADLER, A. *The science of living.* Garden City, New York: Anchor Books, 1969.

ADLER, K. A. Life style in schizophrenia. *Journal of Individual Psychology*, 1958, *14*, 68–72.

ADINOLFI, A. A. Relevance of person perception research of clinical psychology. *Journal of Consulting and Clinical Psychology*, 1971, *37*, 167–176.

ADORNO, T. W., E. FRENKEL-BRUNSWICK, D. J. LEVINSON, and R. N. SANFORD. *The Authoritarian Personality.* New York: Harper, 1950.

AINSWORTH, M. D. Patterns of attachment behavior shown by the infant in interactions with his mother. *Merrill-Palmer Quarterly*, 1964, *10*, 51–58.

AINSWORTH, M. D. Attachment and dependency: A comparison. In *Attachment and Dependency*, ed. J. L. Gerwitz. Washington D.C.: Winston, 1972, pp. 97–137.

AINSWORTH, M. D. Anxious attachment and defensive reactions in a strange situation and their relationship to behavior at home. Paper presented at the Meeting of the Society for Research in Child Development, Philadelphia, 1973.

ALARCON, R. D. Hysteria and hysterical personality: How come one without the other? *Psychiatric Quarterly*, 1973, *47*, 258–275.

ALKIRE, A. A. Enactment of social power and role behavior in families of disturbed and non-disturbed preadolescents. *Developmental Psychology*, 1972, *7*, 270–276.

ALLPORT, G. W. *Personality: A psychological interpretation.* New York: Holt, Rinehart & Winston, 1937.

ALLPORT, G. W. *Becoming: Basic considerations for a science of personality.* New Haven, Conn: Yale University Press, 1955.

ALLPORT, G. W. *Pattern and growth in personality.* New York: Holt, Rinehart and Winston, 1962. (a)

ALLPORT, G. W. The general and the unique in psychological science. *Journal of Personality*, 1962, *30*(3), 405–422. (b)

ALLPORT, G. W., P. E. VERNON, and G. LINDZEY. *A study of values.* Boston: Houghton Mifflin, 1960.

ALT, R. L. Problem-solving strategies of reflective, impulsive, fast-accurate and slow-inaccurate children. *Child Development*, 1973, *44*, 259–266.

ALVY, K. Relation of age to children's egocentric and cooperative communication. *Journal of Genetic Psychology,* 1968, *112,* 275–286.

AMABILE, T., M. W. DE JONG, and M. R. LEPPEL. Effects of externally imposed deadlines on subsequent intrinsic motivation. *Journal of Personality and Social Psychology,* 1976, *34,* 92–98.

AMSEL, A., and J. S. ROUSSEL. Motivation properties of frustration: I, Effect on a running response of the addition of frustrations to the motivational complex. *Journal of Experimental Psychology,* 1952, *43,* 363–368.

ANGYAL, A. *Neurosis and treatment.* New York: Viking, 1965.

ANSBACHER, H., and R. ANSBACHER *The Individual Psychology of Alfred Adler.* New York: Basic Books, 1956.

ARGYLE, M. *The psychology of interpersonal behavior.* London: Penguin Books, 1967.

ARIETI, S. An overview of schizophrenia from a predominantly psychological approach. *American Journal of Psychiatry,* 1974, *131,* 241–249.

ARNDT, W. B. *Theories of personality.* New York: Macmillan, 1974.

ARNOLD, M. *Emotions and personality.* New York: Columbia University Press, 1960.

ARONFREED, J. *Conduct and conscience: Socialization of internalized control over behavior.* New York: Academic Press, 1968.

ARONSON, E. *The social animal.* San Francisco: W. H. Freeman, 1972.

ARONSON, E., and J. M. CARLSMITH. Performance expectancy as a determinant of actual performance. *Journal of Abnormal and Social Psychology,* 1962, *65,* 178–182.

ARONSON, E., and D. LINDNER. Gain and loss of esteem as a determinant of interpersonal attraction. *Journal of Experimental Social Psychology,* 1965, *1,* 156–171.

ARSENIAN, J. M. Young children in an insecure situation. *Journal of Abnormal Social Psychology,* 1943, *38,* 225–249.

ATKINSON, J. W. Motivational determinants of risk-taking behavior. *Psychological Review,* 1957, *64,* 359–372.

ATKINSON, J. W. Motivational determinants of intellectual performance and cumulative achievement. In *Motivation and Achievement,* ed. J. W. Atkinson and J. O. Raynor. Washington, D.C.: Winston, 1974.

ATKINSON, J. W., and D. CARTWRIGHT. Some neglected variables in contemporary conceptions of decision and performance. *Psychological Reprints,* 1964, *14,* 575–590.

ATKINSON, J. W., and N. T. FEATHER (Eds.). *A theory of achievement motivation.* New York: Wiley, 1966.

ATKINSON, J. W., R. W. HEYNS, and J. VEROFF. The effect of experimental arousal of the affiliation motive on thematic apperception. *Journal of Abnormal and Social Psychology,* 1954, *49,* 405–410.

ATTHOWE, J. M., and L. KRASNER. Preliminary report on the application of contingent reinforcement procedures (token economy) on a "chronic" psychiatric ward. *Journal of Abnormal Psychology,* 1968, *73,* 37–43.

AYLLON, T., and N. H. AZRIN. The measurement and reinforcement of behavior of psychotics. *Journal of Experimental Analysis of Behavior,* 1965, *8,* 357–383.

BACK, K. W., and J. D. MORRIS. Perception of self and the study of whole lives. In *Normal aging, II,* ed. E. Palmore. Durham, N. C.: Duke University, Press, 1974.

BAKERMAN, S. (Ed.). *Aging life processes.* Springfield, Ill.: C C Thomas, 1969.

BALDWIN, A. L. The effect of home environment on nursery school behavior. *Child Development,* 1949, *20,* 49–62.

BALDWIN, A. L. In *Handbook of Socialization Theory and Research,* ed. Goslin, D. A. Chicago: Rand McNally, 1969, p. 331.

BALES, R. F. *Interaction process analysis: A method for the study of small groups.* Reading, Mass.: Addison-Wesley, 1950.

BALES, R. F. Task roles and social roles in problem-solving groups. In *Readings in social psychology,* 3rd ed., ed. E. E. Maccoby, T. M. Newcomb, and E. L. Hartley. New York: Holt, Rinehart and Winston, 1958.

BALES, R. F. *Personality and interpersonal behavior.* New York: Holt, Rinehart and Winston, 1970.

BANDURA, A. Influence of models' reinforcement contingencies on the acquisition of imitative responses. *Journal of Personality and Social Psychology,* 1965, *1,* 585–589. (a)

BANDURA, A. Vicarious processes: A case of no-try learning. In *Advances in experimental social psychology,* ed. L. Berkowitz. New York: Academic Press, 1965, Vol. II, pp. 3–55. (b)

BANDURA, A. A social learning interpretation of psychological dysfunctions. In *Foundations of abnormal psychology,* ed. P. London and D. Rosenhan. New York: Holt, Rinehart & Winston, 1968, pp. 293–344.

BANDURA, A. Social learning theory of identificatory processes. In *Handbook of socialization theory and research,* ed. D. A. Goslin. Chicago: Rand McNally, 1969, pp. 213–262. (a)

BANDURA, A. *Principles of behavior modification.* New York: Holt, Rinehart and Winston, 1969. (b)

BANDURA, A. Analysis of modeling processes. In *Psychological modeling,* ed. A. Bandura. Chicago: Aldine-Atherton, 1971, pp. 1–62. (a)

BANDURA, A. *Social learning theory.* Morristown, N.J.: General Learning Press, 1971. (b)

BANDURA, A. A psychotherapy based upon modeling principles. In *Handbook of psychotherapy and behavior change,* ed. A. E. Bergin and S. Garfield. New York: Wiley, 1971, pp. 653–708. (c)

BANDURA, A. Behavior theory and the models of man. *American Psychologist,* 1974, *29,* 859–869.

BANDURA, A. Social learning perspective on behavior change. In A. Burton (ed), *What makes behavior change possible?* New York: Brunner/Mazel, 1976, pp. 34–57.

BANDURA, A. *Personal Communication* 1976

BANDURA, A., E. G. BLANCHARD, and B. RITTER. Relative efficacy of desensitization and modeling approaches for inducing behavioral, affective, and attitudinal changes. *Journal of Personality and Social Psychology,* 1969, *13,* 173–199.

BANDURA, A., AND N. B. HARRIS. Modification of syntactic style. *Journal of Experimental Child Psychology,* 1966, *4,* 341–352.

BANDURA, A., and A. C. HUSTON. Identification as a process of incidental learning. *Journal of Abnormal and Social Psychology,* 1961, *63,* 311–318.

BANDURA, A., R. W. JEFFERY, and E. GAJDOS. Generalizing change through self-directed performance. *Behavior Research and Therapy,* 1975, *13,* 141–152.

BANDURA, A., R. W. JEFFERY, and C. L. WRIGHT. Efficacy of participant modeling as a function of response induction aids. *Journal of Abnormal Psychology,* 1974, *83,* 56–64.

BANDURA, A., D. ROSS, AND S. A. ROSS. A comparative test of the status, envy, social power, and secondary reinforcement theories of identificatory learning. *Journal of Abnormal and Social Psychology,* 1963, *67,* 601–607.

BANDURA, A., D. ROSS, and S. A. ROSS. Imitation of film-mediated aggression models. *Journal of Abnormal and Social Psychology,* 1969, *66,* 3–11.

BANDURA, A. and R. WALTERS. *Social learning and personality development.* New York: Holt, Rinehart and Winston, 1963.

BANNISTER, D. The nature and measurement of schizophrenic thought disorders. *Journal of Mental Science,* 1962, *108,* 825.

BANNISTER, D. *Perspectives in personal construct theory.* London: Academic Press, 1970.

BANNISTER, D., and J. M. M. MAIR. *The evolution of personal constructs.* New York: Academic Press, 1968.

BANQUET, J. P. Spectral analysis of the EEG in meditation. *Electroencephalography and Clinical Neurophysiology,* 1973, *35,* 143–151.

BARBER, T. X. Hypnosis as perceptual-cognitive restructuring: II, "Post"-hypnotic behavior. *Journal of Clinical and Experimental Hypnosis,* 1958, *6,* 10–20.

BARBER, T. X. Physiological effects of hypnosis and suggestion. In *Biofeedback and Self-Control, 1970,* ed. J. Stoyva, T. Barber, L. Dicara, J. Kamiya, N. Miller, and D. Shapiro. Chicago: Aldine-Atherton, 1971.

BARBER, T. X., and J. COULES. Electrical skin conductance and galvanic skin response during "hypnosis." *Int. J. Clin. Exp. Hypnosis,* 1959, *7,* 79–92.

BARCLAY, A. M. The effect of hostility on physiological and fantasy responses. *Journal of Personality,* 1969, *37,* 651–667.

BARDWICK, J. M. *Psychology of women: A study of biocultural conflicts.* New York: Harper & Row, 1971.

BARKER, B. M., H. R. BARKER, JR., and A. P. WADSWORTH, JR. Factor analysis of the items of the state-trait anxiety inventory. *Journal of Clinical Psychology,* 1977, *33,* 450–455.

BARKER, R. G. *Ecological psychology.* Stanford: Stanford University Press, 1968.

BARKER, R. G., T. DEMBO, and K. LEWIN. Frustration and regression: An experiment with young children. Iowa City: *University of Iowa Studies in Child Welfare,* 1941, *18,* 386.

BARRY, H., I. CHILD, and M. BACON. Relation of child training to subsistence economy. *American Anthropologist,* 1959, *61,* 51–63.

BATESON, G., D. D. JACKSON, and J. HALEY. Toward a theory of schizophrenia. *Behavioral Science,* 1956, *1,* 251–264.

BEACH, F. A. Current concepts of play in animals. *American Naturalist, 1945, 79,* 523–541.

BECK, A. T. Cognitive therapy: Nature and relation to behavior therapy. *Behavior Therapy,* 1970, *1,* 184–200. (a)

BECK, A. T. The core problem in depression: The cognitive triad. In *Depression: Theories and therapies,* ed. J. Masserman. New York: Grune and Stratton, 1970. (b)

BECK, A. T. Role of fantasies in psychotherapy and psychopathology. *Journal of Nervous and Mental Diseases,* 1970, *150,* 3–7. (c)

BECK, A. T. *Cognitive therapy and the emotional disorders.* New York: International Universities Press, 1976.

BECK, A. T. Cognition, affect and psychopathology. *Archives of General Psychiatry,* 1971 *24,* 495–500.

BECK, A. T. Cognitive therapy: Nature and relation to behavior therapy. *Behavior Therapy, 1,* 184–200 1970a.

BECK, A. T. Role of fantasies in psychotherapy and psychopathology. *J. Nerv. Ment. Dis., 150,* 1970c, 3–7.

BECK, A. T., R. LAUDE, and M. BOHNERT. Ideational components of anxiety neurosis. *Archives of General Psychiatry,* 1974, *31,* 319–325.

BECK, S. J. How the Rorschach came to America. *Journal of Personality Assessment,* 1972, *36,* 105–108.

BECKWITH, L. Relationships between infants' social behavior and their mothers' behavior. *Child Development,* 1972, *43,* 397–411.

BELL, S. M., and M. D. AINSWORTH. Infant crying and maternal responsiveness. *Child Development,* 1972, *43,* 1171–1190.

BELLER, E. K. Dependency and independence in young children. *Journal of Genetic Psychology,* 1955, *87,* 25–35.

BEM, D. J. The measurement of psychological androgyny. *Journal of Consulting and Clinical Psychology,* 1974, *42,* 155–162.

BEM, D. J., and A. ALLEN. On predicting some of the people some of the time: The search for cross-situational consistencies in behavior. *Psychological Review,* 1974, *81,* 506–520.

BEM, S. L. Probing the promise of androgyny. In *Readings toward a psychology of androgyny,* ed. A. G. Kaplan and J. P. Bem. Boston: Little, Brown and Co., 1976, pp. 47–62.

BENSON, H. *The relaxation response.* New York: William Morrow and Co., 1975.

BENSON, H., J. F. BEARY, and M. P. CAROL. Meditation and the relaxation response. In *Psychiatry and mysticism,* ed. S. R. Dean. Chicago: Nelson-Hall, 1975.

BERKOWITZ, L. Simple views of aggression: An essay review. *American Scientist,* 1969, *57,* 372–383.

BERLYNE, D. E. *Conflict, Arousal and Curiosity.* New York: McGraw-Hill, 1960.

BERLYNE, D. E. Motivational problems raised by exploratory and epistemic behavior. In *Psychology: A Study of a Science,* Vol. V, ed. S. Koch. New York: McGraw-Hill, 1963.

BERLYNE, D. E. *Structure and direction in thinking.* New York: Wiley, 1965.

BERLYNE, D. E. Conflict and arousal. *Scientific American,* 1966, *215* (2), 82–87.

BERNARDIN, A. C., and R. JESSOR. A construct validation of the EPPS with respect to dependency. *Journal of Counseling Psychology,* 1957, *21,* 63–67.

BERNE, E. *Principles of group treatment.* New York: Grove Press, 1966.

BETZ, B. J., and J. C. WHITEHORN. The relationship of the therapist to the outcome of therapy in schizophrenia. *Journal of Psychiatric Research Reports,* 1956, *5,* 89–105.

BIERI, J. Complexity-simplicity as a personality variable in cognitive and preferential behavior. In *Functions of varied experience,* ed. D. W. Fiske and S. Maddi. Homewood, Ill.: Dorsey Press, 1961.

BIERI, J. Cognitive complexity: Assessment issues in the study of cognitive structure. Paper presented at the meeting of the American Psychological Assoc., Chicago, Sept. 1965.

BIERI, J. Cognitive complexity and personality development. In *Experience, structure and adaptability,* ed. O. J. Harvey. New York: Springer, 1966.

BIERI, J., A. L. ATKINS, S. BRIAR, R. L. LEAMAN, H. MILLER, and T. TRIPODI. *Clinical and social judgment.* New York: Wiley, 1966.

BIGNER, J. J. Sibling influence on sex-role preferences of young children. *Journal of Genetic Psychology,* 1972, *121,* 271–282.

BINDRA, D., and I. H. SCHEIER. The relation between psychometric and experimental research in psychology. *American Psychologist,* 1954, *9,* 69–71.

BINSWANGER, L. *Being in the world, Selected papers of L. Binswanger.* New York: Basic Books, 1963.

BIRDWHISTELL, R. L. *Kinesics and context.* Philadelphia: University of Pennsylvania Press, 1970.

BISCHOF, L. J. *Adult psychology.* New York: Harper & Row, 1976

BLACKBURN, R. Personality in relation to extreme aggression in psychiatric offenders. *British Journal of Psychiatry,* 1968, *114,* 821–828.

BLAKE, F. G., F. H. WRIGHT, and G. H. WAECHTER. *Nursing care of children.* Philadelphia: J. B. Lippincott, 1970.

BLOCK, J. Recognizing the coherence of personality. Paper presented at the International Conference on International Psychology, Saltjönsfrn, Derfrn, 1975.

BLOOMFIELD, H. H. Application of the Transcendental Meditation Program to Psychiatry. In *Modern Therapies,* ed. V. Binder, A. Binder, and B. Rimland. Englewood Cliffs, N.J.: Prentice-Hall, 1976.

BLOS, P. *The young adolescent: Clinical studies.* New York: Free Press, 1970.

BONARIUS, J. C. J. Research in the personal construct theory of George A. Kelly: Role construct repertory test and basic theory. In *Progress in experimental personality research,* ed. B. A. Haner. New York: Academic Press, 1965, pp. 1–46.

BOROVEC, T. D. Autonomic reactivity to sensory stimulation in psychopathic, neurotic and normal juvenile delinquents. *Journal of Consulting and Clinical Psychology,* 1970, *35,* 217–227.

BOSS, M. *Psychoanalysis and daseinsanalysis.* New York: Basic Books, 1963.

BOTWINICK, J. *Aging and behavior: A comprehensive integration of research findings.* New York: Springer, 1973.

BOWER, T. G. R. *A primer of infant development.* San Francisco: W. H. Freeman, 1977.

BOWERS, K. S. Situationism in psychology: An analysis and a critique. *Psychological Review,* 1973, *41,* 287–303.

BOWLBY, J. Separation anxiety. *International Journal of Psychoanalysis,* 1960, *41,* 89–113.

BOWLBY, J. Processes of mourning. *International Journal of Psychoanalysis,* 1961, *42,* 317–334.

BOWLBY, J. *Child care and the growth of love.* London: Penguin, 1965.

BOWLBY, J. *Attachment and loss, Vol. I Attachment.* New York: Basic Books, 1969.

BRAZELTON, T. B. Effects of prenatal drugs on the behavior of the neonate. *American Journal of Psychiatry,* 1970, *126,* 1261–1266.

BREGER, L. *From instinct to identity: The development of personality.* Englewood Cliffs, N.J.: Prentice-Hall, 1974.

BREHM, J. W., and A. R. COHEN. *Explorations in cognitive dissonance.* New York: Wiley, 1962.

BROCK, T. C., and J. L. BALLOUN. Behavioral receptivity to dissonant information. *Journal of Personality and Social Psychology,* 1967, *6,* 413–428.

BRODY, E. G., and S. L. SATA. Personality disorders: Trait and pattern disturbances. In *Comprehensive textbook of psychiatry,* ed. A. M. Freedman and H. I. Kaplan. Baltimore: Williams and Wilkins, 1967.

BRODY, N. Information theory, motivation and personality. In *Personality theory and information processing,* ed. H. M. Schroder and P. Suedfeld. New York: Ronald Press, 1971.

BRONFENBRENNER, U. *Two worlds of childhood—U.S. and U.S.S.R.* New York: Russell Sage Foundation, 1970.

BRONSON, W. C. Central originations: A study of behavior organization from childhood to adolescence. *Child Development,* 1966, *37,* 125–155.

BRONSON, W. C. The role of enduring orientations of the environment in development. *Genetic Personality Monographs,* 1972, *86,* 3–80.

BROVERMAN, I. K., S. R. VOGEL, D. M. BROVERMAN, F. E. CLARKSON, and P. S. ROSENCRANTZ. Sex role stereotypes: A current appraisal. *Journal of Social Issues,* 1972, *28,* 59–78.

BROWN, B. Cognitive aspects of Wolpe's behavior therapy. *American Journal of Psychiatry,* 1967, *124,* 854–859.

BRUNER, J. S. Course of cognitive growth. *American Psychologist,* 1964, *19,* 1–15.

BRUNER, J. S. Personality and perception. In *Perception: An approach to personality,* ed. R. R. Blake and G. V. Ramsay. New York: Ronald Press, 1951.

BRUNER, J. S. You and your constructs. *Contemporary Psychology,* 1956, *1,* 355–356.

BRUNER, J. S., and C. C. GOODMAN. Value and need as organizing factors in perception. *Journal of Abnormal and Social Psychology,* 1947, *42,* 33–44.

BRYAN, J. H., and T. SCHWARTZ. Effects of film material upon children's behavior. *Psychological Bulletin,* 1971, *75,* 50–59.

BRYANT, P. *Perception and understanding in children.* New York: Basic Books, 1974.

BUCK, R. *Human motivation and emotion.* New York: Wiley, 1976.

BUHLER, C. The developmental structure of goal setting in group and individual studies. In *The course of human life,* ed. Charlotte Buhler and F. Massarik. New York: Springer, 1968.

BUHLER, C. The course of human life as a psychological problem. In *Developmental psychology: A book of readings,* ed. W. R. Looft. New York: Holt, Rinehart and Winston, 1972.

BURDOCK, E. I., and A. S. HARDESTY. Psychological Test for Psychopathology. *Journal of Abnormal Psychology*, 1968, *73*, 62–69.

BUROS, O. K. (Ed.) *The seventh measurements yearbook*, Vols. 1 and 2. Highland Park, N.J.: Gryphon Press, 1972.

BURTON, A. (Ed.). *What makes behavior change possible?* New York: Bruner/Mazel, 1976.

BURTON, R. V. Generality of honesty reconsidered. *Psychological Review*, 1963, *70*, 481–499.

BUSS, A. H. Physical aggression in relation to different frustrations. *Journal of Abnormal and Social Psychology*, 1963, *67*, 1–7.

BUSS, A. H. *Psychopathology.* New York: Wiley, 1966.

BUTLER, R. A. and H. F. HARLOW. Discrimination learning and learning sets to visual exploration incentives. *Journal of General Psychology*, 1957, *57*, 257–264.

BUTLER, R. N. Psychiatry and psychology of the middle-aged. In *Comprehensive textbook of psychiatry, II,* ed. A. M. Freedman, H. I. Kaplan, and B. J. Sadock. Baltimore: Williams and Wilkins, 1975, pp. 2390–2404.

BYRNE, D. Interpersonal attraction and attitude similarity. *Journal of Abnormal and Social Psychology*, 1961, *62*, 713–715.

CALDER, B. J., and B. M. STAW. Self-perception of intrinsic and extrinsic motivation. *Journal of Personality and Social Psychology*, 1975, *31*, 599–605.

CALLAHAN, E. J., and H. LEITENBERG. Reinforced practice as a treatment for acrophobia: A controlled outcome study. *Proceedings of the American Psychological Association*, 1970, *5*, 533–534.

CAMPBELL, S. B. Mother-child interaction in reflective, impulsive and hyperactive children. *Developmental Psychology*, 1973, *8*, 341–349.

CAMPOS, J. Heart rate: A sensitive tool for the study of emotional development. In *Developmental psychobiology: The significance of infancy,* ed. L. Lipsitt. Hillsdale, N.J.: Erlbaum, 1975.

CAMPOS, J., R. EMDE, T. GAENSBAUER, and C. HENDERSON. Cardiac and behavioral interrelationships in the reactions of infants to strangers. *Developmental Psychology*, 1976, *11*, 589–601.

CAMPUS, N. Transitional consistency as a dimension of personality. *Journal of Personality and Social Psychology*, 1974, *29*, 593–600.

CARKHUFF, R. R., and B. G. BERENSON. *Beyond counseling and therapy.* New York: Holt, Rinehart and Winston, 1967.

CARLSON, R. Identification and personality structure in preadolescence. *Journal of Abnormal and Social Psychology*, 1963, *67*, 567–573.

CARPENTER, C. R. The Howlers of Barro Colorado Island. In *Primate behavior: Field studies of monkeys and apes,* ed. I. DeVore. New York: Holt, Rinehart and Winston, 1965, pp. 250–291.

CARUSO, I. A. *Psychoanalyse und Synthese zur Existenz,* Wien: Herder Verlag, 1952.

CATTELL, R. B. *The scientific analysis of personality.* Baltimore, Md.: Penguin Books, 1965.

CATTELL, R. B. Personality theory derived from quantitative experiment. In *Comprehensive textbook of psychiatry, II,* ed. A. M. Freedman, H. M. Kaplan, and B. J. Sadock. Baltimore: Williams and Wilkins, 1975. Pp. 669–687.

CATTELL, R. B., H. W. EBER, and M. M. TATSUOKA. *Handbook for the sixteen personality factor questionnaire (16 PF)*. Champaign, Ill.: Institute for Personality and Ability Testing, 1970.

CATTELL, R. B., K. RICKELS, C. WEISE, B. GRAY, and R. YEE. The effects of psychotherapy upon measured anxiety and regression. *American Journal of Psychotherapy*, 1966, *20*, 261–269.

CHESNO, F. A., and P. R. KILMANN. Effects of stimulation on sociopathic avoidance learning. *Journal of Abnormal and Social Psychology*, 1975, *84*, 144–150.

CHODOFF, P. The diagnosis of hysteria: An overview. *American Journal of Psychiatry*, 1974, *131*, 1073–1078.

CHURCHILL, D. W. Effects of success and failure in psychotic children. *Archives of General Psychiatry*, 1971, *25*, 208–214.

CIMINERO, A. R., K. S. CALHOUN, and H. E. ADAMS (Eds.). *Handbook for behavioral assessment*. New York: Wiley, 1976.

CLARK, R. A., and M. R. SENSIBAR. The relationship between symbolic and manifest projections of sexuality with some incidental correlates. *Journal of Abnormal and Social Psychology*, 1955, *50*, 327–334.

CLARKE, A. D. B., and A. M. CLARKE. Cognitive changes in the feebleminded. *British Journal of Psychology*, 1954, *45*, 173–179.

CLARKE, A. D. B., and A. M. CLARKE. Recovery from the effects of deprivation. *Acta Psychologica*, 1959, *16*, 137–144.

CLARKE, A. D. B., and A. M. CLARKE. Some recent advances in the study of early deprivation. *Journal of Child Psychology and Psychiatry*, 1960, *1*, 26–36.

CLARKE, A. D. B., A. M. CLARKE, and S. REIMAN. Cognitive and social changes in the feebleminded: Three further studies. *British Journal of Psychology*, 1958, *49*, 144–157.

COBLINER, W. G. Pregnancy in the simple adolescent girl: The role of cognitive functions. *Journal of Youth and Adolescence*, 1974, *3*, 17–29.

COHEN, D. *The learning child*. New York: Vintage Books, 1972.

COLEMAN, J. S. *The adolescent society*. New York: Free Press, 1961.

COLEMAN, J. S. ed. Equality of educational opportunity. Washington, D.C.: U.S. Government Printing Office, 1966.

COLLINS, J. K. Adolescent dating intimacy: Norms and peer expectations. *Journal of Youth and Adolescence*, 1974, *3*, 317–328.

CONGER, J. S. *Adolescence and youth: Psychological development in a changing world*. New York: Harper & Row, 1973.

COOMBS, R. H. Social participation, self-concept and interpersonal valuation. *Sociometry*, 1969, *32*, 273–286.

COOPERSMITH, S. *Antecedents of self-esteem*. San Francisco: W. H. Freeman, 1967.

COWGILL, D. O., and L. D. HOLMES (Eds.). *Aging and modernization*. New York: Appleton-Century-Crofts, 1972.

CRAWFORD, J. L. Task uncertainty, decision importance and group reinforcement as determinants of communication processes in groups. *Journal of Personality and Social Psychology*, 1974, *29*, 619–627.

CRAWFORD, J. L., and G. A. HAALAND. Pre-decisional information seeking and subsequent conformity in the social influence process. *Journal of Personality and Social Psychology*, 1972, *23*, 112–119.

CROCKETT, W. H. Cognitive complexity and impression formation. In *Progress in experimental personality research,* Vol. II, ed. B. A. Maher. New York: Academic Press, 1965.

CRONBACH, L. J. The two disciplines of scientific psychology. *American Psychologist,* 1957, *12,* 671–684.

CRONBACH, L. J. *Essentials of Psychological Testing,* New York: Harper and Row, 1970.

CRONBACH, L. J. Beyond the two disciplines of scientific psychology. *American Psychologist,* 1975, *30,* 116–127.

CRONBACH, L. J., and R. E. SNOW. Aptitudes and instructional methods. *American Psychologist,* 1975, *30*(2), 116–127.

CROWE, R. R. The adopted offspring of women criminal offenders: A study of their arrest records. *Archives of General Psychiatry,* 1972, *27,* 600.

CROWE, R. R. An adoption study of antisocial personality. *Archives of General Psychiatry,* 1974, *31,* 758–791.

CUMMINGS, G., and W. G. HENRY. *Growing old: The process of disengagement.* New York: Basic Books, 1961.

CURTIS, H. J. A Composite theory of aging. *The Gerontologist,* 1966, *6,* 143–149.

DAHLSTROM, W. G. MMPI handbook, Volume II: A sneak preview. Invited presentation at the Ninth Annual MMPI Symposium, Los Angeles, California, February 1974.

DAHLSTROM, W. G., and G. S. WELSH. *An MMPI handbook: A guide to use in clinical practice and research.* Minneapolis: University of Minnesota Press, 1960.

DAHLSTROM, W. G., G. S. WELSH, and L. E. DAHLSTROM. *An MMPI Handbook, Vol. I: Clinical interpretation,* rev. ed. Minneapolis: University of Minnesota Press, 1972.

DANA, R. H. The perceptual organization: TAT score, number, order and frequency. *Journal of Projective Techniques,* 1959, *23,* 307–310.

DAVID, K. H. Generalization of operant conditioning of verbal output in 3-man discussion groups. *Journal of Social Psychology,* 1972, *87,* 243–249.

DAVIS, C. *Room to grow.* Toronto: University of Toronto Press, 1966.

DAVIS, R. C., and J. R. KANTOR. Skin resistance during hypnotic states. *Journal of General Psychology,* 1935, *13,* 62–81.

DEAUX, K., and T. EMSWILLER. Explanation of successful performance on sex-linked tasks: What is skill for the male is luck for the female. *Journal of Personality and Social Psychology,* 1974, *29,* 80–85.

DECI, E. L., W. F. CASCIO, and J. KRUSELL. Cognitive evaluation theory and some comments on the Calder and Staw critique. *Journal of Personality and Social Psychology,* 1975, *31,* 81–85.

DENENBERG, V. H., and G. G. KARRAS. Effects of differential infantile handling upon weight gain and mortality in the rat and mouse. *Science,* 1959, *130,* 629–630.

DENENBERG, V. H., R. E. PASCHKE, and M. X. ZARROW. Killing of mice by rats prevented by early interaction between the species. *Psychonomic Science,* 1968, *11,* 39.

DENENBERG, V. H., and M. X. ZARROW. Rat pax. *Psychology Today,* 1970, *3,* 45–47; 66–67.

Diagnostic and Statistical Manual of Mental Disorders (DSM-II). Washington, D.C.: American Psychiatric Association, 1968.

Diagnostic and Statistical Manual of Mental Disorders (DSM-III). Washington, D.C.: American Psychiatric Association, in press.

DiCAPRIO, N. S. *Personality theories: Guides to living.* Philadelphia: Saunders, 1974.

DIGENHARDT, A. Zur Veränderung des Selbstbildes von jungen Mädchen beim Eintritt in die Reifezeit. *Zeitschrift für Entwicklungspsychologie und Pädagogische Psychologie,* 1971, *3,* 1–3.

DINKMEYER, D., and G. D. McKAY. *Raising a responsible child: Practical steps to successful family relationships.* New York: Simon & Schuster, 1973.

DOHRENWEND, B. P., and B. S. DOHRENWEND. *Social status and psychological disorder: A causal inquiry.* New York: Wiley, 1969.

DOLLARD, J., L. W. DOOB, N. E. MILLER, O. H. MOWRER, and R. R. SEARS. *Frustration and aggression.* New Haven: Yale University Press, 1939.

DOLLARD, J., and N. E. Miller. *Personality and psychotherapy.* New York: McGraw-Hill, 1950.

DOMINO, G. Differential prediction of academic achievement in conforming and independent settings. *Journal of Educational Psychology,* 1968, *59,* 256–260.

DOMINO, G. Interactive effects of achievement orientation and teaching style on academic achievement. *Journal of Educational Psychology,* 1971, *62,* 427–431.

DOUVAN, E., and J. ADELSON. *The adolescent experience.* New York: Wiley, 1966.

DOWDS, B. N., A. F. FONTANA, M. RUSSAKOFF and M. HARRIS. Cognitive mediators between patients' social class and therapists' evaluations. *Archives of General Psychiatry,* 1977, *34,* 917–920.

DREIKURS, R. *The challenge of marriage.* New York: Hawthorn, 1946.

DREIKURS, R. *Psychodynamics, psychotherapy and counseling.* Chicago: Alfred Adler Institute, 1967.

DREIKURS, R. *Social equality: The challenge of today.* Chicago: Henry Regnery, 1971.

DUA, P. S. Comparison of the effects of behaviorally oriented action and psychotherapy reeducation on introversion-extraversion, emotionality and internal-external control. *Journal of Counseling Psychology,* 1970, *17,* 567–572.

DUCHARME, R. Inaction et Activation: Leur Influence sur l'activité instrumentale. Unpublished Doctoral Dissertation, University of Montreal, 1962.

DUNCAN, O. D. Inheritance of poverty or inheritance of race? In *On understanding poverty,* ed. D. P. Moynihan. New York: Basic Books, 1969.

EDWARDS, A. L. *Edwards Personal Preferences Schedule.* New York: Psychological Corporation, 1959.

EHRENWALD, J. *Neurosis in the family and patterns of psychosocial defense.* New York: Harper & Row, 1963.

EHRHARDT, A. A., K. EVERS, and J. MONEY. Influence of androgen and some aspects of sexually dimorphic behavior in females with a late-treated adrenogenital syndrome. *Johns Hopkins Medical Journal,* 1968, *122,* 115–122.

EIBL-EIBESFELDT, I. *Ethology: The biology of behavior.* New York: Holt, Rinehart and Winston, 1970.

EIBL-EIBESFELDT, I. *Love and hate.* London: Methuen, 1971.

EISDORFER, C., and F. WILKIE. Intellectual changes. In *Normal aging, II,* ed. E. Palmore. Durham, N.C.: Duke University Press, 1974, pp. 95–103.

EKMAN, P. Universals and cultural differences in facial expressions of emotion. In *Nebraska Symposium on Motivation*, ed. J. K. Cole. Lincoln: University of Nebraska Press, 1972.

EKMAN, P., and W. V. FRIESEN. Non-verbal leakage and clues to perception. *Psychiatry*, 1969, *32*, 88–106.

EKMAN, P., W. V. FRIESEN, and E. J. MALMSTROM. Facial behavior and stress in two cultures. Unpublished manuscript. Langley Porter Neuropsychiatric Institute, San Francisco, 1970.

EKMAN, P., W. V. FRIESEN and P. ELLSWORTH. *Emotion in the Human Face*. New York: Pergamon, 1972.

ELKIND, D. Measuring young minds. *Horizon*, 1971, *13*, 35.

ELLIOT, R. Effects of uncertainty about the nature and advent of a noxious stimulus (shock) upon distress. *Journal of Personality and Social Psychology*, 1966, *3*, 353–356.

ELLIS, A. *The essence of rational psychotherapy: A comprehensive approach to treatment.* New York: Institute for Rational Living, 1970.

ELLIS, A. *Growth through reason: Verbatim cases in rational-emotive psychotherapy.* Palo Alto, Calif.: Science and Behavior Books, 1971.

ELLIS, A. Are cognitive behavior therapy and rational therapy synonymous? *Rational Living*, 1973, *8*, 8–11.(a)

ELLIS, A. *Humanistic psychotherapy: The rational-emotive approach.* New York: Julian Press, 1973.(b)

ENDLER, N. S., and J. McV HUNT. Generalizability of contributions from sources of variance in the S-R inventories of anxiousness. *Journal of Personality*, 1969, *37*, 1–24.

ERDELYI, M. H. A new look at the new look: Perceptual defense and vigilance. *Psychological Review*, 1974, *81*(1), 1–25.

ERDELYI, M. H., and A. E. APPELBAUM. Cognitive masking: The disruptive effect of an emotional stimulus upon the perception of continuous neutral items. *Bulletin of the Psychonomic Society*, 1973, *1*(*1-B*), 59–61.

ERICKSEN, C. W. Perceptual defense as a function of unacceptable means. *Journal of Abnormal and Social Psychology*, 1951, *46*, 557–564. (a)

ERIKSEN, C. W. Some implications for TAT interpretation arising from need and perception experiments. *Journal of Personality*, 1951, *19*, 283–288. (b)

ERIKSEN, C. W. Perception and personality. In *Concepts of personality*, ed. J. M. Wepman and R. W. Heine. Chicago: Aldine, 1963, pp. 31–62.

ERIKSON, E. *Childhood and society.* New York: Norton, 1950.

ERIKSON, E. H. *Identity: Youth and crisis.* New York: Norton, 1968.

ERON, L. D. A normative study of the Thematic Apperception Test. *Psychological Monographs*, 1950, *64*(9).

ERON, L. D. Quoted in N. D. Sundberg, *Assessment of persons.* Englewood Cliffs, N.J.: Prentice-Hall, 1977.

EXNER, J. E. *The Rorschach: A comprehensive system.* New York: Wiley, 1974

EYSENCK, H. J. *Dimensions of personality.* London: Routledge & Kegan Paul, 1947.

EYSENCK, H. J. *The scientific study of personality.* London: Routledge & Kegan Paul, 1952.

EYSENCK, H. J. The inheritance of extraversion-introversion. *Acta Psychologica,* 1956, *12,* 429–432.

EYSENCK, H. J. Learning theory and behavior therapy. *Journal of Mental Science,* 1959, *105,* 61–75.

EYSENCK, H. J. The effects of psychotherapy. In *Handbook of abnormal psychology,* ed. H. J. Eysenck. New York: Basic Books, 1961, pp. 697–725. (a)

EYSENCK, H. J. (Ed.). *Handbook of abnormal psychology.* New York: Basic Books, 1961. (b)

EYSENCK, H. J. The measurement of emotion: Psychological parameters and methods. In *Emotions: their paramteres and measurement,* ed. L. Levi. New York: Raven Press, 1975.

FANTZ, R. L. The origin of form perception. *Scientific American,* 1961, *204,* 66–72. (a)

FANTZ, R. L. Pattern vision in newborn infants. *Science,* 1963, *140,* 296–297.

FANTZ, R. L. A method for studying depth perception in infants under 6 months of age. *Psychological Record,* 1961, *2,* 17–32. (b)

FANTZ, R. L. Visual perception and experience in early infancy: A look at the hidden side of behavior development. In *Early behavior: Comparative and development approaches,* ed. H. W. Stevenson et al. New York: Wiley, 1967.

FANTZ, R. L., J. F. FAGIN, and S. B. MIRANDA. Early visual selectivity. In *Infant perception: From sensation to cognition,* ed. L. B. Cohen and P. Salapatek. New York: Academic Press, 1975.

FARINA, A., D. ARENBERT, and S. A. GUSKIN. A scale for measuring minimal social behavior. *Journal of Consulting Psychology,* 1957, *21,* 265–268.

FARNSWORTH, D. L. Are our present adolescents a new breed? *New England Association Review,* 1967, *15,* 4–10.

FAUST, M. S. Developmental maturity as a determinant in prestige of adolescent girls. In *Contemporary issues in adolescent development,* ed. J. J. Conger. New York: Harper & Row, 1975, pp. 17–27.

FEATHER, N. T., and A. C. RAPHELSON. Fear of success in Australian and American student groups: Motive or sex-role stereotype? *Journal of Personality,* 1974, *42,* 190–201.

FEATHER, N. T., and J. G. SIMON. Reactions to male and female success and failure in sex-linked occupations: Impressions of personality, causal attributions and perceived likelihood of different consequences. *Journal of Personality and Social Psychology,* 1975, *31,* 20–31.

FENZ, W. D. Heart rate response to a stressor: A comparison between primary and secondary psychopaths and normal controls. *Journal of Experimental Research in Personality,* 1971, *5,* 7–13.

FENZ, W. D., and J. VELNER. Physiological concomitants of behavior indexes in schizophrenia. *Journal of Abnormal Psychology,* 1970, *76,* 27–35.

FERGUSON, E. D. The use of early recollections for assessing life style and diagnosing psychopathology. *Journal of Protective Techniques and Personality Assessment,* 1964, *28,* 403–412.

FERGUSON, E. D. *Motivation: An experimental approach.* New York: Holt, Rinehart & Winston, 1976.

FERGUSON, P., and C. G. GOWAN. TM: Some preliminary findings. *Journal of Humanistic Psychology,* 1976, *16,* 51–60.

FERSTER, C. B. A functional analysis of depression. *American Psychologist,* 1973, *28,* 857–879.

FESHBACH, N. Sex differences in children's modes of aggressive responses toward outsider. *Merrill Palmer Quarterly,* 1969, *15.*

FESHBACH, S. The stimulating effects of a vicarious aggressive activity. *Journal of Abnormal and Social Psychology,* 1961, *63,* 381–385.

FESHBACH, N. Aggression. In *Carmichael's manual of child psychology,* ed. D. Mussen. New York: John Wiley, 1970. Pp. 159–260.

FESHBACH, S., and N. FESHBACH. The young aggressors. *Psychology Today,* 1973, *6*(11).

FESHBACH, S., W. B. STILES, and E. BITTER. The reinforcing effect of witnessing aggression. *Journal of Experimental Research in Personality,* 1967, *2,* 133–139.

FESTINGER, L. *A theory of cognitive dissonance.* Palo Alto, Calif.: Stanford University Press, 1957.

FIEDLER, F. E. A comparison of therapeutic relationship in psychoanalytic, non-directive and Adlerian therapy. *Journal of Consulting Psychology,* 1950, *14,* 436–445.

FISHER, S. and R. P. GREENBERG. *Scientific credibility of Freud's theory and therapy.* New York: Basic Books, 1977.

FISHER, S., J. O. COLE, K. RICKLES, and E. H. UHLENHUTH. Drug-set interactions: The effect of expectations on drug response in outpatients. Paper used at Colloquium of International Psychopharmacology, Munich, 1962.

FISKE, D., and S. MADDI. *Functions of varied experience.* Homewood, Ill.: Dorsey Press, 1961.

FLANDERS, N. A., B. N. MORRISON, and G. L BRODE. Changes in people's attitudes during the school year. *Journal of Educational Psychology,* 1968, *59,* 334–338.

FLECK, J. R. Cognitive styles in children and performance on Piagetan conservation tasks. *Perceptual Motor Skills,* 1972, *35,* 747–756.

FORD, C. S., and F. A. BEACH. *Patterns of sexual behavior.* New York: Harper & Row, 1951.

FORGUS, R. H. The effect of early perceptual learning on the behavior organization of adult rats. *Journal of Comparative Psychology,* 1954, *47,* 331–336.

FORGUS, R. H. *Perception.* New York: McGraw-Hill, 1966.

FORGUS, R. H. *Perception.* New York: Harper and Row, 1975.

FORGUS, R. H. and A. S. DEWOLFE. Perceptual selectivity in hallucinatory schizophrenics. *Journal of Abnormal Psychology,* 1969, *74,* 288–292.

FORGUS, R. H., and A. S. DEWOLFE. Coding of cognitive input in delusional patients. *Journal of Abnormal Psychology,* 1974, *83*(3), 278–284.

FORGUS, R. H. and L. E. MELAMED. *Perception: A cognitive-state approach,* 2nd ed. New York: McGraw-Hill, 1976.

FOULDS, M. L. Changes in locus of internal-external control: A growth experience. *Comparative Group Studies,* 1971, *2,* 293–300.

FRANK, J. D. *Persuasion and healing.* Baltimore: Johns Hopkins University Press, 1961.

FRANKS, C. M. Foreword. In *Multimodal behavior therapy: Theory and practice,* ed. A. A. Lazarus. New York: Springer, 1976.

FREUD, S. *Standard edition of the complete psychological works of Sigmund Freud*, London: Hogarth Press, 1953–1966.

FRIEDMAN, M. *Pathogenesis of coronary artery disease.* New York: McGraw-Hill, 1969.

FURTH, H. G. Two aspects of experience in ontogeny: Development and learning. *Advances in Child Development and Behavior*, 1974, *9*, 47–67.

GALLE, O. R., W. R. GOVE, and J. M. MCPHERSON. Population density and pathology: What are the relations for man? *Science*, 1972, *176*, 23–30.

GARDNER, R. W., P. S. HOLZMAN, G. S. KLEIN, H. B. LINTON, & D. P. SPENCE. Cognitive control: A study of individual consistencies in cognitive behavior. *Psychological Issues*, 1959, *1*, 4.

GARDNER, R. W., and R. I. LONG. Control defence and centration effect: A study of scanning behavior. *British Journal of Psychology*, 1962, *53*, 129–140. (a)

GARDNER, R. W., and R. I. LONG. Cognitive control of attention and inhibition. *British Journal of Psychology*, 1962, *53*, 381–388. (b)

GARNER, W. To perceive is to know, *American Psychologist*, 1966, *21*, 11–19.

GATES, D. W. Verbal conditioning, transfer and operant level "speech style" as functions of cognitive style. *Dissertation Abstracts International*, 1971, *32B*, 3634.

GECAS, V. Parental behavior and dimensions of adolescent self-evaluation. *Sociometry*, 1971, *34*, 466–482.

GEEN, R. G., and E. C. O'NEAL. Activation of cue elicited aggression by general arousal. *Journal of Personality and Social Psychology*, 1969, *11*, 289–292.

GELB, A., and K. GOLDSTEIN. *Psychologische Analyse hirnpathologischer Fälle.* Leipzig: Barth, 1920.

GERWITZ, J. L. The course of infant smiling in four child-rearing environments. In *Determinants of infant-behavior*, Vol. II, ed. B. M. Foss. London: Methuen, 1965, pp. 205–206.

GERWITZ, J. L., and D. M. BAER. The effect of brief social deprivation on behavior for a social reinforcer. *Journal of Abnormal and Social Psychology*, 1958, *56*, 49–56.

GIBSON, E. J., and R. D. WALK. The "visual cliff." *Scientific American*, 1960, *202*(4), 64–71.

GIBSON, J. J., and E. J. GIBSON. Perceptual learning: Differentiation or enrichment? *Americana*, 1956, *2*, 83–94.

GILL, M. M., and P. S. HOLZMAN (Eds.). *Psychology versus metapsychology: Psychoanalytic essays in memory of George S. Klein.* New York: International Universities Press, 1976.

GISVOLD, D. A validity study of the autonomy and deference subscales of the EPPS. *Journal of Consulting Psychology*, 1958, *22*, 445–447.

GLICK, J. An experimental analysis of subject-object relationships in perception. *Contemporary Research and Theory on Visual Perception*, ed. R. N. Haber. New York: Holt, 1968.

GLICKMAN, S. E., and B. B. SCHIFF. A biological theory of reinforcement. *Psychological Review*, 1967, *74*, 81–109.

GOFFMAN, E. *The presentation of self in everyday life.* Garden City, New York: Doubleday, 1959.

GOLD, M., and E. DOUVAN. *Adolescent development: Readings in research and theory.* Boston: Allyn and Bacon, 1969.

GOLDBERG, P. A review of sentence completion methods in personality assessment. *Journal of Projective Techniques and Personality Assessment,* 1965, *29,* 12–45.

GOLDFARB, W. Infant rearing and problem-solving. *American Journal of Orthopsychiatry,* 1943, *13,* 249–266.

GOLDFRIED, M. R., E. T. DECENTECEO, and L. WEINBERG. Systematic rational restructuring as a self-control technique. *Behavior Therapy,* 1974, *5,* 247–254.

GOLDFRIED, M. R., and A. P. GOLDFRIED. Cognitive change methods. In *Helping people change,* ed. F. H. Kanfer and A. P. Goldstein. New York: Pergamon Press, 1975.

GOLDSTEIN, A. P. Patient expectancies in psychotherapy. *Psychiatry,* 1962, *25,* 72–79. (a)

GOLDSTEIN, A. P. *Therapist-patient expectancies in psychotherapy.* New York: Pergamon Press, 1962. (b)

GOLDSTEIN, J. H., R. W. DAVIS, and D. HERMAN. Escalation of aggression: Experimental studies. *Journal of Personality and Social Psychology,* 1975, *31*(1), 162.

GOLDSTEIN, K. *The organism.* New York: American Book Co., 1939.

GOLDSTEIN, K. *Human nature in the light of psychopathology.* Cambridge, Mass.: Harvard University Press, 1940.

GOODALL, J. New discoveries among Africa's chimpanzees. *National Geographic,* 1965, *128,* 802–831.

GOODALL, J. In *Primates: Studies in adaptation and variability,* ed. P. C. Jay. New York: Holt, Rinehart and Winston, 1968.

GOODENOUGH, F. *The measurement of intelligence by drawings.* Yonkers-on-Hudson, N.Y.: World Book Co., 1926.

GOUGH, H. G. An interpreter's syllabus for the California Psychological Inventory. In *Advances in psychological assessment,* Vol. I, ed. P. McReynolds. Palo Alto, Calif.: Science and Behavior Books, 1968, pp. 55–79.

GOUGH, H. G. *California Psychological Inventory Manual.* Palo Alto, Calif.: Consulting Psychologists Press, 1957.

GOUGH, H. G., and G. A. QUINTARD. A French application of the CPI Social Maturity Index. *Journal of Cross-Cultural Psychology,* 1974, *5,* 247–252.

GOULDNER, A. W. The norm of reciprocity: A preliminary statement. *American Sociological Review,* 1960, *25,* 161–178.

GRAMS, A. *Facilitating learning and individual development.* St. Paul: Minnesota Dept. of Education, 1966.

GREENBERG, B. S., and T. F. GORDON. Children's perceptions of television violence: A replication. In *Television and social behavior,* Vol. V: *Television's effects: Further explorations,* ed. C. A. Cornstock, E. A. Rubinstein, and J. P. Murray. Washington, D.C.: Government Printing Office, 1972.

GREENE, D. M. and M. R. LEPPER. Effect of extrinsic rewards on children's subsequent intrinsic interests. *Child Development,* 1974, *45,* 1141–1145.

GREENE, M. A. Client perception of the relationship as a function of worker-client cognitive styles. *Dissertation Abstracts,* 1972, *33A*(III), 3030–3031.

GROSSMAN, S. P. *A textbook of physiological psychology.* New York: Wiley, 1967.

GRUZELIER, J. H., D. T. LYKKEN, and P. H. VENABLES. Schizophrenia and arousal revisited. *Archives of General Psychiatry,* 1972, *26,* 427–432.

GUTMANN, D. L. An exploration of ego configurations in middle and late life. In *Personality in middle and late life,* ed. Bernice L. Neugarten et al. New York: Atherton Press, 1964.

GYNTHER, M. D., and R. A. GYNTHER. Personality inventions. In *Clinical methods in psychology,* ed. I. B. Wiener. New York: Wiley, 1976, pp. 187–279.

HALBOWER, C. C. A comparison of actuarial versus clinical prediction to classes discriminated by MMPI. Unpublished Ph.D. dissertation, University of Minnesota at Minneapolis, 1955.

HALL, E. T. *The hidden dimension.* Garden City, N.Y.: Doubleday, 1966.

HALL, C. and G. LINDZEY. *Theories of Personality.* New York: Wiley, 1957.

HAMBURG, D. A. Recent research on hormonal factors relevant to human aggressiveness. *International Social Science Journal,* 1971, *23,* 36.

HANRATTY, M. A., R. M. LICKERT, L. W. MORRIS, and L. E. FERNANDEZ. Imitation of film-mediated aggression against live and inanimate victims. *Proceedings of the 77th Annual Convention of the American Psychological Association,* 1969, pp. 76–79.

HARE, R. D. Detection threshold for electric shock in psychopaths. *Journal of Abnormal Psychology,* 1968, *73*(3), part 2, 1–24.

HARLOW, H. F. Learning and satiation of response in intrinsically motivated complex puzzle performance in monkeys. *Journal of Comparative Physiological Psychology,* 1950, *43,* 289–294.

HARLOW, H. F. Mice, monkey, men and motives. *Psychological Review,* 1953, *60,* 23–32.

HARLOW, H. F. *Learning to love.* San Francisco: Albion Press, 1971.

HARLOW, H. F., and M. K. HARLOW. Social deprivation in monkeys. *Scientific American,* 1962, *207,* 137–146.

HARRELL, R. F., E. WOODYARD, and A. I. GATES. *The effect of mother's diet on the intelligence of the offspring.* New York: Teachers College, Columbia University, 1955.

HARRISON, R. Cognitive change and participation in a sensitivity-training laboratory. *Journal of Consulting Psychology,* 1966, *30,* 51–520.

HARTAP, W. W., and E. A. ZOOK. Sex role preferences in three- and four-year-old children. *Journal of Consulting Psychology,* 1960, *24,* 420–426.

HARTMANN, D. Influence of symbolically modeled instrumental aggression and pain cues on aggressive behavior. *Journal of Personality and Social Psychology,* 1969, *11,* 280–288.

HARTMANN, H. *Essays on ego psychology,* New York: International Universities Press, 1964.

HARTSHORNE, H. and M. A. MAY. *Studies in the nature of character.* Vol. 2 *Studies in service and self-control.* New York: Macmillan, 1928.

HARVEY, J. H., and B. HARRIS. Determinants of perceived choice and the relationship between perceived choice and expectancy about feeling of internal control. *Journal of Personality and Social Psychology,* 1975, *31,* 101–104.

HARVEY, O. J., D. E. HUNT, and H. M. SCHRODER. *Conceptual systems and personality organization.* New York: Wiley, 1963.

HATHAWAY, S. R. Personality inventories. In *Handbook of clinical psychology,* ed. B. B. Wolman. New York: McGraw-Hill, 1965, pp. 451–476.

HATHAWAY, S. R., and McKINLEY, J. C. A multiphasic personality schedule (Minnesota); I. Construction of the schedule. *Journal of Psychology*, 1940, *10*, 249–254.

HAVIGHURST, R. J. Social roles, work, leisure, and education. In *The psychology of adult development and aging*, ed. C. Eisdorfer and M. P. Lawton. Washington, D.C.: American Psychological Association, 1973.

HAYES, F. Gestures: A working bibliography. *Southern Folklore Quarterly*, 1957, pp. 218–317.

HEATH, D. H. *Explorations of maturity.* New York: Appleton-Century-Crofts, 1965.

HEBB, D. O. Emotions in man and animals: An analysis of the intuitive processes of recognition. *Psychological Review*, 1946, *53*, 88–106.

HEBB, D. O. *The organization of behavior.* New York: Wiley, 1949.

HEBB, D. O. *Drives and the CNS* (conceptual nervous system). *Psychological Review*, 1955, *62*, 243–254.

HEBB, D. O. The American Revolution. *American Psychologist*, 1960, *15*, 735–745.

HEBB, D. O. Concerning imagery. *Psychological Review*, 1968, *75*, 466–477.

HEBB, D. O., and E. N. FOORD. Errors of visual recognition and the nature of the trace. *Journal of Experimental Psychology*, 1945, *35*, 335–348.

HEDVIG, E. Stability of early recollections and Thematic Apperception stories. *Journal of Individual Psychology*, 1963, *19*, 49–54.

HEDVIG, E. Children's early recollections as a basis for diagnosis. *Journal of Individual Psychology*, 1965, *21*, 187–188.

HEIDEGGER, M. *Existence and being.* Chicago: Henry Regnery, 1949.

HEIDER, F. *The psychology of interpersonal relationships.* New York: Wiley, 1958.

HEILBRUN, A. B. Effects of briefing upon client satisfaction with the initial counseling contact. *Journal of Consulting and Clinical Psychology*, 1972, *38*, 50–56.

HEIMAN, J. Facilitating erotic arousal: Toward sex-positive sex research. Paper presented at meeting of the American Psychological Association, New Orleans, 1974.

HELD, R., and A. HEIN. Movement-produced stimulation in the development of visually guided behavior. *Journal of Comparative Physiological Psychology*, 1963, *56*, 872–876.

HELMS, D. B. and J. S. TURNER. *Exploring Child Behavior.* Philadelphia: W. B. Saunders, 1976.

HELWEG, G. C. The relationship between selected personality characteristics and perceptions of directive and non-directive psychotherapeutic approaches. Doctoral dissertation, University of Michigan, Ann Arbor, Mich.: University Microfilms, 1971, No. 71-26 965.

HENRY, W. E. The Thematic Apperception technique in the study of culture-personality relations. *Genetic Psychology Monographs*, 1947, *35*, 3–135.

HERBERT, M. E., and S. JACOBSON. Late paraphrenia. *British Journal of Psychiatry*, 1967, *113*, 461.

HERON, W. In *Sensory deprivation*, ed. R. L. Soloman et al. Cambridge: Harvard University Press, 1961.

HERSCH, P. D., and K. E. SCHEIBE. Reliability and validity of internal-external control as a personality dimension. *Journal of Consulting Psychology*, 1967, *31*, 609–613.

HESTON, I. The genetics of schizophrenia and schizoid disease. *Science,* 1970, *167,* 249.

HETHERINGTON, E. M. A developmental study of the effects of sex of the dominant parent on sex-role preference, identification, and imitation in children. *Journal of Personality and Social Psychology,* 1965, *2,* 188–194.

HETHERINGTON, E. M. and G. FRANKIE. Effect of parental dominance, warmth and conflict on imitation in children. *Journal of Personality and Social Psychology,* 1967, *6,* 119–125.

HILTON, I. Differences in the behavior of mothers toward first and later born children. *Journal of Personality and Social Psychology,* 1967, *7,* 282–290.

HIRSCH, H. V. B., and D. N. SPINELLI. Visual experience modifies distribution of horizontally and vertically oriented receptive field in cats. *Science,* 1970, *168,* 769–781.

HOFFMAN, L. W. Early childhood experiences and women's achievement motives. *Journal of Social Issues,* 1972, *28,* 129–195.

HOKINSON, J. E., M. BURGESS, and M. F. COHEN. Effect of displaced aggression on systolic blood pressure. *Journal of Abnormal and Social Psychology,* 1963, *67,* 214–218.

HOLLANDER, E. P. Individuality and social identity: Extra-familial agents of social influence on children. Final report to the *National Institute of Child Health and Human Development,* Grant HD00887. Buffalo: Department of Psychology, State University of New York, 1964.

HOLMES, D. S. Investigations of repression: Differential recall of material experimentally or naturally associated with ego threat. *Psychological Bulletin,* 1974, *81,* 632–653.

HOLT, R. R. Experimental methods in clinical research. In *Handbook of clinical psychology,* ed. B. Wolman. New York: McGraw-Hill, 1965.

HOLTON, R. B. Amplitude of an instrumental response following the withholding of reward. *Child Development,* 1961, *32,* 107–116.

HOLZMAN, P. S., and R. W. GARDNER. Leveling and sharpening and memory organization. *Journal of Abnormal and Social Psychology,* 1960, *61,* 176–180.

HORNER, M. S. Sex differences in achievement motivation and performance in competition and non-competitive situation. Unpublished doctoral dissertation, University of Michigan at Ann Arbor, 1968.

HORNER, M. S. Toward an understanding of achievement-related conflicts in women. *Journal of Social Issues,* 1972, *28,* 157–176.

HORNEY, K. *The neurotic personality of our time.* New York: Norton, 1937.

HORNEY, K. *Neurosis and human growth.* London: Routledge and Kegan Paul, 1951.

HOROWITZ, M. Stress response syndromes: Character style and dynamic psychotherapy. *Archives of General Psychiatry,* 1974, *31,* 768–773.

HORROCKS, J. E. *The psychology of adolescence.* Boston: Houghton Mifflin, 1976.

HORROCKS, J. E., and D. W. JACKSON. *Self and role: A theory of self-process and role behavior.* Boston: Houghton Mifflin, 1972.

HOUSTON, B. K. Control over stress, locus of control and response to stress. *Journal of Personality and Social Psychology,* 1972, *21,* 249–255.

HUBEL, D. H., and T. N. WIESEL. Receptive fields of single neurons in the cat's striate cortex. *Journal of Physiology,* 1959, *148,* 574–591.

HUBEL, D. H., and T. N. WIESEL. Shape and arrangement of columns in cat's striate cortex. *Journal of Physiology*, 1963, *165*, 559–568.

HUBEL, D. H., and T. N. WIESEL. Receptive field and functional architecture of monkey striate. *Journal of Physiology*, 1968, *195*, 215–243.

HUESMANN, L. R., L. D. ERON, M. M. LEFKOWITZ, and L. O. WALDER. Television violence and aggression: The causal effect remains. *American Psychologist*, 1973, *28*, 617–620.

HULL, C. L. *Principles of behavior.* New York: Appleton-Century-Crofts, 1943.

HUNT, D. E. Person-environment interaction: A challenge found wanting before it was tried. *Review of Educational Research*, 1975, *45*, 209–230.

HUNT, J. McV. Piaget's observations as a source of hypotheses concerning motivation. *Merrill-Palmer Quarterly*, 1963, *9*, 263–275.

HUNT, J. McV. The epigenesis of intrinsic motivation and early cognitive learning. In *Current research in motivation,* ed. R. W. Haber. New York: Holt, Rinehart and Winston, 1966.

HUNT, J. McV. Intrinsic motivation: Information and circumstances. In *Personality theory and information processing,* ed. H. M. Schroder and P. Suedfell. New York: Ronald Press, 1971, pp. 85–130.

HUTCHINGS, B., and S. A. MEDNICK. Registered criminality in the adoptive and biological parents of registered male adoptees. In *Genetic research in psychiatry,* ed. R. R. Fieve, H. Brill, and D. Rosenthal. New York: University Press, 1974.

IRWIN, M., T. TRIPODI, and J. BIERI. Affective stimulus value and cognitive complexity. *Journal of Personality and Social Psychology*, 1967, *5*, 444–448.

JACKSON, D. N. *Personality research form manual.* Goshen, New York: Research Psychologists Press, 1967.

JACOBS, L., G. BERCHEID, and G. WALSTER. Self-esteem and attraction. *Journal of Personality and Social Psychology.* 1971, *17*, 84–91.

JAMES, W. *The varieties of religious experience.* New York: New American Library, 1958.

JASPERS, K. *General psychopathology.* Manchester, England: Manchester University Press, 1963.

JONES, A. Drive and incentive variables associated with the statistical properties of sequences of stimuli. *Journal of Experimental Psychology*, 1964, *67*, 423–431.

JONES, A. Information deprivation in humans. In *Progress in experimental personality research,* Vol. III, ed. B. A. Maher. New York: Academic Press, 1966.

JONES, A., H. J. WILKINSON, and I. BRADEN. Information deprivation as a motivational variable. *Journal of Experimental Psychology*, 1961, *62*, 126–137.

JONES, M. C. Psychological correlates of somatic development. *Child Development*, 1965, *36*, 899–911.

JONES, S. C., and J. S. SHRANGER. Locus of control and interpersonal evaluations. *Journal of Consulting and Clinical Psychology*, 1968, *32*, 664–668.

JUNG, C. G. *The Practice of Psychotherapy.* London: Routledge and Kegan Paul, 1954.

JUNG, C. G. *Alchemical studies.* London: Routledge and Kegan Paul, 1967.

KAATS, G. R., and K. E. DAVIS. The dynamics of sexual behavior of college students. *Journal of Marriage and the Family*, 1970, *32*, 330–339.

KAGAN, J. The growth of "face" schema: Theoretical significance and methodological issues. In *Exceptional infant*, Vol. I; *The normal infant*, ed. J. Hellmuth. Seattle: Child Publications, 1967.

KAGAN, J. Attention and psychological change in the young child. *Science*, 1970, *170*, 826–832.

KAGAN, J. *Understanding children, behavior, motives and thoughts*. New York: Harcourt Brace Jovanovich, 1971.

KAGAN, J., B. HOSKEN, and S. WATSON. The child's symbolic conceptualization of the parents. *Child Development*, 1961, *32*, 625–636.

KAGAN, J., and H. A. MOSS. *Birth to maturity: A study in psychological development*. New York: Harper & Row, 1962.

KAGAN, J., H. MOSS, and I. SIGEL. Psychological significance of styles of conceptualizations. *Monographs of the Society for Research in Child Development*, 1963, *28*, 73–112.

KAGAN, J., and P. H. MUSSEN. Dependency themes on the TAT and group conformity. *Journal of Consulting Psychology*, 1956, *20*, 29–32.

KAHN, M. H., A. R. MAHRER, and R. BORNSTEIN. Male psychosexual development: Role of sibling sex and ordinal position. *Journal of Genetic Psychology*, 1972, *121*, 187–196.

KALISH, R. A. Of social values and the dying: A defense of disengagement. *Family Coordinator*, 1972, *21*, 81–94.

KALLMAN, F. The genetic theory of schizophrenia. *American Journal of Psychiatry*, 1946, *103*, 309.

KANFER, F. H. Self-monitoring: Methodological limitations and clinical applications. *Journal of Consulting and Clinical Psychology*, 1970, *35*, 148–152.

KAPLAN, B. J. Malnutrition and mental deficiencies. *Psychological Bulletin*, 1972, *78*, 321–334.

KAPLAN, H. I., B. J. SADOCK, and A. M. FREEDMAN. Neurochemistry of behavior: Recent advances. In *Comprehensive textbook of psychiatry, II*, ed. A. M. Freedman, H. I. Kaplan, and B. J. Sadock. Baltimore: Williams and Wilkins, 1975.

KARP, S. A., B. KISSIN, and F. E. HUSTMYER. Field dependence as a predictor of alcoholic therapy dropouts. *Journal of Nervous and Mental Disorders*, 1970, *150*, 77–83.

KATZ, I., and S. COHEN. Some determinants of cross-racial helping behavior. *Journal of Personality and Social Psychology*, 1976, *32*(6), 964–970.

KATZ, R. Body language: A study in unintentional communication. Unpublished doctoral dissertation, Harvard University, 1964.

KAUFFMAN, H. *Aggression and altruism*. New York: Holt, Rinehart and Winston, 1970.

KAUFMAN, A., A. BARON, and R. E. KOPP. Some effects of instructions on human operants. *Psychological Monograph Supplements*, 1966, *1*, 243–250.

KAY, D., and M. ROTH. Environmental and hereditary factors in the schizophrenics of old age ("late paraphrenia") and their bearing on the general problem of causation in schizophrenia. *British Journal of Psychiatry*, 1961, *107*, 649.

KELLY, E. L. Consistency of the adult personality. *American Psychologist*, 1955, *10*, 659–681.

KELLY, G. A. *The psychology of personal constructs,* Vol. I. New York: Norton, 1955.

KENISTON, K. *Youth and dissent: The rise of a new opposition.* New York: Harcourt, Brace, Jovanovich, 1971.

KEOUGH, J. *Motor performance of elementary school children.* Los Angeles: University of California, Dept. of Physical Education Monographs, 1965.

KERCKHOFF, A. C., and K. E. DAVIS. Value consensus and need complementarity in mate selection. *American Sociological Review,* 1962, *27,* 295-303.

KIMBLE, C., and R. HELMREICH. Self-esteem and the need of social approval. *Psychonomic Science,* 1972, *26,* 339-342.

KIMMEL, D. C. *Adulthood and aging: An interdisciplinary developmental view.* New York: Wiley, 1974.

KISSIN, B., A. PLATZ, and W. H. SU. Social and psychological factors in the treatment of chronic alcoholism. *Journal of Psychiatric Research,* 1970, *9,* 13-27.

KLAUS, M., R. JERAULD, N. KREGER, W. MCALPINE, M. STEFFA, and J. KENNEL. Maternal attachment: Importance of the first post-partum days. *New England Journal of Medicine,* 1972, *286,* 460-463.

KLEIN, G. S. Freud's two theories of sexuality. In *Clinical-cognitive psychology,* ed. L. Breger. N.J.: Prentice-Hall, 1969, pp. 136-181.

KLEINMUNTZ, B. *Personality measurement: An introduction.* Homewood, Ill.: Dorsey, 1969.

KLEINMUNTZ, B. *Essentials of abnormal psychology.* New York: Harper & Row, 1974.

KLIMAN, G., and E. L. GOLDBERG. Improved visual recognition during hypnosis. *Archives of General Psychiatry,* 1962, *7,* 155-162.

KLINE, P. *Fact and fantasy in Freudian theory.* London: Methuen, 1972.

KOGAN, N., and M. A. WALLACH. Group risk taking as a function of members' anxiety and defensiveness levels. *Journal of Personality,* 1967, *35,* 50-63.

KOHLBERG, L. A cognitive developmental analysis of children's sex-role concepts and attitudes. In *The development of sex differences,* ed. E. E. Maccoby. Stanford: Stanford University Press, 1966, pp. 82-173.

KOHLBERG, L. The cognitive-developmental approach to socialization. In *Handbook of socialization theory and research,* ed. D. A. Goslin. Chicago: Rand McNally, 1969, pp. 3-24.

KOHLBERG, L., and E. TURIEL. *Research and moral development: A cognitive developmental approach.* New York: Wiley, 1971.

KONEČNI, V. J. The mediation of aggressive behavior: Arousal level versus anger and cognitive labeling. *Journal of Personality and Social Psychology,* 1975, *32*(4), 706.

KORIAT, A., R. MELKMAN, J. R. AVERILL, and R. S. LAZARUS. The self-control of emotional reactions to a stressful film. *Journal of Personality,* 1972, *44,* 601-619.

KORNER, A. F. Individual differences at birth: Implications for early experience and later development. *American Journal of Orthopsychiatry,* 1971, *41*(4), 608-619.

KORNER, A. F., and E. B. TOMAN. The relative efficacy of contact and vestibular proprioception in soothing neonates. *Child Development,* 1972, *43,* 443-453.

KRASNER, L. On the death of behavior modification: Some comments from a mourner. *American Psychologist,* 1976, *31,* 387-388.

KRETSCHMER, E. *Physique and temperament.* London: Routledge and Kegan Paul, 1936.

KRINGLEN, E. Obsessional neurotics. *British Journal of Psychiatry,* 1965, *3,* 709.

KRUGLANSKI, A. W., I. WRITER, D. ARIZI, R. AGASSI, J. MONTEQIO, I. PERI, and M. PERETZ. Effects of task intrinsic rewards upon extrinsic and intrinsic motivation. *Journal of Personality and Social Psychology,* 1975, *31,* 699–705.

KUHLEN, R. G. Developmental changes in motivation during the adult years. In *Relations of development and aging,* ed. J. E. Birren. Springfield, Ill.: Charles C Thomas, 1964.

KUHLEN, R. G. Developmental changes in motivation during the adult years. In *Middle age and aging,* ed. Bernice L. Neugarten. Chicago: University of Chicago Press, 1968, pp. 115–136.

KUO, Z. Genesis of cats' responses to rats. *Journal of Comparative Psychology,* 1931, *11,* 1–35.

KUO, Z. *The dynamics of behavior development.* New York: Random House, 1967.

LAKIN, M. Personality factors in mothers of excessively crying (colicky) infants. *Monographs of the Society for Research in Child Development,* 1957, *22,* No. 1.

LANDAUER, T. K., and W. M. WHITING. Infantile stimulation and adult-stature of human males. *American Anthropologists,* 1964, *66,* 1007–1028.

LANDERS, T. J., and N. G. LANDERS. *Building a successful marriage.* Englewood Cliffs, N.J.: Prentice-Hall, 1963.

LANDFIELD, A. W. *Personal construct systems in psychotherapy.* Chicago: Rand McNally, 1971.

LANDFIELD, A. W. Interpretive man: The enlarged self-image. In *Nebraska Symposium on Motivation,* ed. J. K. Cole and A. W. Landfield. Lincoln, Nebraska: Nebraska University Press, 1976, pp. 127–178.

LANG, P. J., and A. D. LAZOVIK. Personality and hypnotic suggestibility. *Journal of Consulting Psychology,* 1962, *26,* 317–322.

LAWICK-GOODALL, J. VAN. The behavior of free-living chimpanzees in the Gombe Stream Reserve. *Animal Behavior Monographs,* 1968, *1* (3), 165–311.

LAWICK-GOODALL, J. VAN. *In the shadow of man.* Boston: Houghton Mifflin, 1971.

LAZARUS, A. A. *Behavior therapy and beyond.* New York: McGraw-Hill, 1971.

LAZARUS, A. A. Multimodal behavior therapy: Treating the "basic id." *Journal of Nervous and Mental Disease,* 1973, *156,* 404–411.

LAZARUS, A. A. *Multimodal behavior therapy.* New York: Springer, 1976.

LAZARUS, A. A. Has behavior therapy outlived its usefulness? *American Psychologist,* 1977, *32,* 550–554.

LAZARUS, R. S. *Psychological stress and the coping process.* New York: McGraw-Hill, 1966.

LAZARUS, R. S. Emotions and adaptation: Conceptual and empirical relations. In *Nebraska Symposium on Motivation,* ed. J. W. Arnold. Lincoln: University of Nebraska Press, *16,* 1968, 175–270.

LAZARUS, R. S. The self-regulation of emotion. In *Emotions: Their parameters and measurements,* ed. L. Lennart. New York: Raven Press, 1975, pp. 47–68.

LAZARUS, R. S., and J. R. AVERILL. Emotion and cognition: with special reference to anxiety. In *Anxiety: Current trends in theory and research,* Vol. II, ed. C. D. Spielberger. New York: Academic Press, 1972.

LAZARUS, R. S., J. R. AVERILL, and E. M. OPTON, JR. Towards a cognitive theory of emotion. Paper presented at the third International Symposium on Feelings and Emotions. Chicago, October, 1968.

LAZARUS, R. S., J. R. AVERILL, and E. M. OPTON, JR. The psychology of coping: Issues of research and assessment. In *Coping and adaptation*, ed. G. V. Coelho, D. A. Hamburg, and J. E. Adams. New York: Basic Books, 1974.

LAZARUS, R. S., C. ERIKSEN, and C. P. FONDA. Personality dynamics in auditory perceptual recognition. *Journal of Personality*, 1951, *19*, 471–482.

LEFCOURT, H. M. Belief in personal control: Research and implications. *Journal of Individual Psychology*, 1966, *22*, 185–195. (b)

LEFCOURT, H. M., E. HOGG, and C. SORDONI. Locus of control, field-dependence and the conditions arousing objective versus subjective awareness. *Journal of Research in Personality*, 1975, *9*, 21–36.

LEFCOURT, H. M., and J. WINE. Internal versus external control of reinforcement and the deployment of attention in experimental situations. *Canadian Journal of Behavioral Science*, 1969, *1*, 167–181.

LEFRANÇOIS, G. *Adolescence.* Belmont, Calif.: Wadsworth, 1976.

LEITENBERG, H. Positive reinforcement and extinction. In *Behavior modification: Principles and clinical applications*, ed. W. S. Agras. Boston: Little, Brown, and Co., 1972.

LEITENBERG, H. The use of single-case methodology in psychotherapy research. *Journal of Abnormal Psychology*, 1973, *82*, 87–101.

LEITENBERG, H., W. S. AGRAS, D. H. BARLOW, and D. C. OLIVEAU. Contribution of selective positive reinforcement and therapeutic instructions to systematic desensitization therapy. *Journal of Abnormal Psychology*, 1969, *74*, 113–118.

LEITENBERG, H., W. S. AGRAS, R. BUTZ, and J. WINCZE. Relationship between heart rate and behavioral change during the treatment of phobias. *Journal of Abnormal Psychology*, 1971, *78*, 59–68.

LEPPER, M. R., and D. M. GREENE. Turning play into work: Effects of adult surveillance and intrinsic rewards on children's intrinsic motivation. *Journal of Personality and Social Psychology*, 1975, *31*, 479–486.

LESKOW, S., and C. D. SMOCK. Developmental changes in problem solving strategies: Permutation. *Developmental Psychology*, 1970, *2*, 412–422.

LEVIN, J., and N. BRODY. Information deprivation and creativity. Paper presented at the Eastern Psychological Association, New York, April, 1966.

LEVINE, J. Representation des étages du developement et conscience de soi chez l'enfant. *Enfance*, 1958, No. 2, pp. 85–114.

LEVINE, S. Infantile experience and resistance to physiological stress. *Science*, 1957, *126*, 403.

LEVINE, S. Stimulation in infancy. *Scientific American*, May 1960, p. 86.

LEVINE, S. Psychophysiological effects of infant stimulation. In *Roots of behavior*, ed. E. L. Pliss. New York: Hoeber, 1962.

LEVY, D. Primary affect hunger. *American Journal of Psychiatry*, 1937, *94*, 643–652.

LEVY, L. *Conceptions of personality: Theories and research.* New York: Random House, 1970.

LEWANDOWSKI, D., and GRAHAM, J. R. Empirical correlates of frequently occurring two-point MMPI code types: A replicated study. *Journal of Consulting and Clinical Psychology,* 1972, *39,* 466–472.

LEWIN, K. *A dynamic theory of personality,* trans. Donald K. Adams. New York and London: McGraw-Hill, 1935.

LEWIN, K. *Field theory in social science: Selected theoretical papers.* New York: Harper, 1951.

LEWIN, K., T. DEMBO, L. FESTINGER, and P. S. SEARS. Level of aspiration. In *Personality and the behavior disorders,* ed. J. V. McHunt. New York: Ronald Press, 1944, pp. 333–378.

LEWINSOHN, P. M., and M. SHAFFER. Use of home observations as an integral part of the treatment of depression: Preliminary report and case studies. *Journal of Consulting and Clinical Psychology,* 1971, *37,* 87–94.

LEWIS, J. M., W. R. BEAVERS, J. T. GOSSETT, and V. A. PHILLIPS. *No single thread: Psychological health in family systems.* New York: Brunner/Mazel, 1976.

LIDZ, T. S., T. FLECK, and A. R. CORNELISON. *Schizophrenia and the family.* New York: International Universities Press, 1965.

LIEBERMAN, M. A., I. D. YALOM, and M. B. MILES. Encounter: The leader makes a difference. *Psychology Today,* 1973, *6* (10), 69–72, 74, 76.

LIEBERMAN, M. G. Childhood memories as a projective technique. *Journal of Projective Techniques and Personality Assessment,* 1957, *21,* 22–26.

LIEBERT, R. M., and L. E. FERNANDEZ. The effects of vicarious consequences on imitative performance. *Child Development,* 1970, *41,* 847–852.

LIEM, G. R. Performance and satisfaction as affected by normal control over silent decisions. *Journal of Personality and Social Psychology,* 1975, *31,* 232–260.

LIPOWSKI, Z. T. Psychophysiological cardiovascular disorders. In *Comprehensive textbook of psychiatry, II,* ed. A. M. Freedman, H. I. Kaplan, and B. J. Sadock. Baltimore: Williams and Wilkins, 1975, pp. 1660–1667.

LOEB, R. C. Concomitance of boys' locus of control examined in parent-child interactions. *Developmental Psychology,* 1975, *11,* 353–358.

LORENZ, K. The evolution of behavior. *Scientific American,* 1958, *199,* 67–83.

LORENZ, K. *On aggression.* New York: Harcourt, Brace and World, 1966.

LOVAAS, O. I., J. P. BERBERICH, B. F. PERLOFF, and B. SCHAEFFER. Acquisition of imitative speech by schizophrenic children. *Science,* 1966, *151,* 705–707.

LOWE, C. A., and J. W. GOLDSTEIN. Reciprocal liking and attributions of ability: Mediating effects of perceived intent and personal involvement. *Journal of Personality and Social Psychology,* 1970, *16,* 291–297.

LUBORSKY, L., B. SINGER, and L. LUBORSKY. Comparative study of psychotherapies: Is it true that "everyone has won and all must have prizes?" *Archives of General Psychiatry,* 1975, *32,* 995–1008.

LUBORSKY, L., and B. P. SPENCE. Quantitative research on psychoanalytic therapy. In *Handbook of psychotherapy and behavior change,* ed. A. E. Bergin and S. L. Garfield. New York: Wiley, 1971, pp. 408–438.

LYKKEN, D. T. A study of anxiety in the sociopathic personality. *Journal of Abnormal and Social Psychology,* 1957, *55,* 6–10.

MCCALL, R. B., and J. KAGAN. Stimulus schema discrepancy and attention in the infant. *Journal of Experimental Child Psychology,* 1967, *5,* 381–390.

McCarter, R. E., S. S. Tomkins, and H. M. Schiffman. Early recollections as a predictor of the Tomkins-Horn picture arrangement test performance. *Journal of Individual Psychology,* 1961, *17,* 177–180.

McClelland, D. C. *Assessing human motivation.* Morristown, N.J.: General Learning Press, 1971. (a)

McClelland, D. C. *The drinking man.* New York: Free Press, 1971. (b)

McClelland, D. C., J. W. Atkinson, R. A. Clark, and E. L. Lowell. *The achievement motive.* New York: Appleton-Century-Crofts, 1953.

McClelland, D. C., and D. Winter. *Motivating economic achievement.* New York: Free Press, 1969.

McDill, E. L., and J. S. Coleman. Family and peer influence in college plans of high school students. *Journal of the Sociology of Education,* 1965, *38,* 112–116.

McGhie, A. Attention and perception in schizophrenia. In *Progress in experimental personality research,* Vol. 5, ed. B. A. Maher. New York: Academic Press, 1970.

McKinney, J. D. Problem-solving strategies in impulsive and reflective second-graders. *Developmental Psychology,* 1973, *8,* 145.

Maccoby, E. E. Sex differences in intellectual functioning. In *The development of sex differences,* ed. E. E. Maccoby. Stanford: Stanford University Press, 1966, pp. 25–55.

Maccoby, E. E., and C. N. Jacklin. *The psychology of sex differences.* Stanford: Stanford University Press, 1974.

Maccoby, M., and H. Modiane. On culture and equivalence. In *Studies in cognitive growth,* ed. J. S. Bruner. New York: Wiley, 1966.

Machover, K. *Personality projection in the drawing of the human figure.* Springfield, Ill.: Charles C Thomas, 1949.

MacKinnon, R. A., and R. M. Michels. *The psychiatric interview in clinical practice.* Philadelphia: Saunders, 1971.

Maddi, S. R. *Personality theories: a comparative analysis.* Homewood, Ill.: Dorsey Press, 1976.

Maddi, S. R., B. S. Propst, and I. Feldinger. Three expressions of the need for variety. *Journal of Personality,* 1965, *33,* 82–98

Maddox, E. L. Themes and issues in sociological theories of human aging. *Human Development,* 1970, *13,* 17–27.

Mahoney, M. J. *Cognition and behavior modification.* Cambridge, Mass.: Ballinger Publishing Co., 1974.

Mahoney, M. J. Self-reward and self-monitoring techniques for weight control. *Behavior Therapy,* 1974, *5,* 48–57.

Mallick, S. K., and B. R. McCandless. A study of catharsis of aggression. *Journal of Personality and Social Psychology,* 1966, *4,* 594–596.

Mancuso, J. C. Current motivational models in the elaboration of personal construct theory. In *Nebraska Symposium on Motivation,* ed., J. K. Cole (Ed.), Lincoln, Nebraska: University of Nebraska Press, 1976, pp. 43–98.

Mandler, G. The interruptions of behavior. In *Nebraska Symposium on Motivation,* ed. D. Levin. Lincoln, Nebraska: University of Nebraska Press, 1964, pp. 163–219.

MARIOTTO, M. J., and G. L. PAUL. A multimethod validation of the inpatient multidimensional psychiatric scale with chronically institutionalized patients. *Journal of Consulting and Clinical Psychology,* 1974, *42,* 497–508.

MARKS, P. A., and W. SEEMAN. *The actuarial description of personality: An atlas for use with the M.M.P.I.,* Baltimore: Williams and Wilkins, 1963.

MARKS, P. A., W. SEEMAN, and D. L. HALLER. *The actuarial use of the MMPI with adolescents and adults.* Baltimore: Williams and Wilkins, 1974.

MARMOR, J. Common operational factors in diverse approaches to behavior change. In *What makes behavior change possible?* ed. A. Burton. New York: Bruner/Mazel, 1976, pp. 3–12.

MASLING, J., L. RABIE, and S. H. BLONDHEIM. Obesity, level of aspiration, and Rorschach and TAT measures of oral dependence. *Journal of Consulting Psychology,* 1967, *31,* 233–239.

MASLING, J., C. JOHNSON, and C. SATURANSKY. Oral imagery, accuracy of perceiving others and performance in Peace Corps training. *Journal of Personality and Social Psychology,* 1974, *30,* 414–419.

MASLOW, A. H. *Toward a psychology of being.* Princeton, N.J.: Van Nostrand, 1968.

MASLOW, A. H. *Motivation and personality.* New York: Harper & Row, 1970.

MASSERMAN, J. H. *Practice of dynamic psychiatry.* Philadelphia: Saunders, 1955.

MASTERS, W. H., and V. E. JOHNSON. *Human sexual inadequacy.* Boston: Little, Brown, 1970.

MASTERS, W. H., and V. E. JOHNSON. *The pleasure bond.* Boston: Little, Brown and Co., 1975.

MATARAZZO, J. D. *Wechsler's measurement and appraisal of adult intelligence,* 5th ed. Baltimore: Williams and Wilkins, 1972.

MAY, R. Contributions of existential psychotherapists. In *Existence: A new dimension in psychiatry and psychology,* ed. R. May, E. Angel, and H. F. Ellenberger. New York: Basic Books, 1958.

MAY, R. The existential approach. In *American handbook of psychiatry,* Vol. II, ed. S. Arieti. New York: Basic Books, 1959.

MAY, R. *Love and will.* New York: Norton, 1973.

MEAD, M. *Male and female.* New York: William Morrow and Co., 1949.

MEDNICK, S. A. Breakdown in individuals at high risk for schizophrenia: Possible predispositional perinatal factors. *Mental Hygiene,* 1970, *54,* 50–63.

MEDNICK, S. A., and F. SCHULSINGER. A longitudinal study of children with a high risk for schizophrenia: A preliminary report. In *Methods and goals in human behavior genetics,* ed. S. Vandenberg. New York: Academic Press, 1965.

MEEHL, P. E. *Clinical versus statistical prediction: A theoretical analysis and a review of the evidence.* Minneapolis: University of Minnesota Press, 1954.

MEEHL, P. E. Wanted—a good cookbook. *American Psychologist,* 1956, *11,* 263–272.

MEGARGEE, E. I. *The California Psychological Inventory handbook.* San Francisco: Jossey-Bass, 1972.

MEHRABIAN, A. *Nonverbal communication.* Chicago: Aldine-Atherton, 1972.

MEICHENBAUM, D. The effects of instructions and reinforcement on thinking and language behavior of schizophrenics. *Behavior Research and Therapy,* 1969, *7,* 101–114.

MEICHENBAUM, D. H. Cognitive modification of test-anxious college students. *Journal of Consulting and Clinical Psychology*, 1972, *39*, 370–380.

MEICHENBAUM, D. Cognitive factors in behavior modification: Modifying what clients say to themselves. In *Annual review of behavior therapy and practice*, Vol. I, ed. C. M. Franks and G. T. Wilson. New York: Bruner/Mazel, 1973, pp. 416–431.

MEICHENBAUM, D. Self-instructional methods. In *Helping people change*, ed. F. H. Kanfer and A. P. Goldstein. New York: Pergamon Press, 1975.

MEICHENBAUM, D. *Cognitive behavior modification*. New York: Plenum, 1977.

MEICHENBAUM, D., and R. CAMERON. Training schizophrenics to talk to themselves: A means of developing attentional controls. *Behavior Therapy*, 1973, *4*, 515–534. (a)

MEICHENBAUM, D., and R. CAMERON. An examination of cognitive and contingency variables in anxiety relief procedures. Unpublished manuscript, University of Waterloo, Waterloo, Canada, 1973. (b)

MEICHENBAUM, D., and R. CAMERON. The clinical potential of modifying what clients say to themselves. In *Self-control: Power to the person*, ed. M. J. Mahoney and C. E. Thoresen. Monterey: Brooks/Cole, 1974, pp. 263–290.

MELZACK, R. Brain mechanisms and emotion. In *Neurophysiology and emotion*, ed. A. C. Glass. New York: Rockefeller University Press, 1967, pp. 60–69.

MILEWSKI, A., and E. R. SIQUELAND. Discrimination of color and pattern novelty in one-month human infants. *Journal of Experimental and Child Psychology*, 1975, 19, 122–136.

MILLER, G. A. What is information measurement? *American Psychologist*, 1953, *8*, 3–11.

MILLER, G. A., E. GALANTER, and K. PRIBRAM. *Plans and the structure of behavior.* New York: Holt, Rinehart and Winston, 1960.

MILLER, I. W., and P. A. MAGARO. Toward a multivariate theory of personality styles: Measurement and reliability. *Journal of Clinical Psychology*, 1977, *33*, 460–466.

MILLER, N. E. Experimental studies of conflict. In *Personality and the behavior disorders*, Vol. I, ed. J. McV. Hunt. New York: Ronald Press, 1944, pp. 431–465.

MILLER, N. E. Theory and experiment relating psychoanalytic displacement to stimulus-response generalization. *Journal of Abnormal and Social Psychology*, 1948, *43*, 155–178.

MILLER, N. E. Comments on theoretical models: Illustrated by the development of a theory of conflict behavior. *Journal of Personality*, 1951, *20*, 82–100.

MILLER, N. E., L. V. DiCARA, H. SOLOMON, J. M. WEISS, and B. DWORKISS. Learned modification of autonomic functions: A review and some new data. In *Biofeedback and self-control*, Annual Journal, 1970, Chicago: Aldine Atherton, 1971, pp. 351–359.

MILLER, N. E., and J. DOLLARD. *Social learning and imitation.* New Haven, Conn.: Yale University Press, 1941.

MILLER, W. R., and M. E. P. SELIGMAN. Depression and the perception of reinforcement. *Journal of Abnormal Psychology*, 1973, *82*, 62–73.

MISCHEL, W. *Personality assessment.* New York: Wiley, 1968.

MISCHEL, W. Continuity and change in personality. *American Psychologist*, 1969, *24*(11), 1012–1018.

MISCHEL, W. *Introduction to personality.* New York: Holt, Rinehart & Winston, 1976.

MISCHEL, W., and J. GRUSEC. Determinants of the rehearsal and transmission of neutral and aversive behaviors. *Journal of Personality and Social Psychology,* 1966, *3,* 197–205.

MISCHEL, W., and J. GRUSEC. Waiting for rewards and punishments: Effect of time and probability on choice. *Journal of Personality and Social Psychology,* 1967, *5,* 24–31.

MONTAGU, A. Constitutional and prenatal factors in infant and child health. In *Symposium on the healthy personality,* ed. M. J. Senn. New York: Josiah Macy, Jr., Foundation, 1950.

MONTAGU, A. *Prenatal influences.* Springfield, Ill.: Charles C Thomas, 1962.

MONTAGU, A. *The nature of human aggression.* New York: Oxford, 1976.

MOORE, S., and R. UPDERGRAFF. Sociometric status of preschool children related to age, sex, nurturance, giving and dependency. *Child Development,* 1964, *35,* 519–524.

MOOS, R. H. Conceptualizations of human environments. *American Psychologist,* 1973, *28,* 652–665.

MORGAN, C., and H. A. MURRAY. A method for investigating phantasies: The Thematic Apperception Test. *Archives of Neurology and Psychiatry,* 1935, *34,* 289–306.

MORRIS, D. The response of animals to a restricted environment. *Symposium of the Zoological Society of London,* 1964, *13,* 99–118.

MORRIS, D. *The naked ape.* New York: Dell Publishing Co., 1967.

MOSAK, H. H. *On purpose.* Chicago: Alfred Adler Institute, 1977.

MOSAK, H. H., and B. H. SHULMAN. *Introductory individual psychology, a syllabus.* Chicago: Alfred Adler Institute, 1961.

MOSTELLER, F., and D. P. MOYNIHAN (Eds.). *On equality of educational opportunity.* New York: Vintage Books, 1972.

MOYER, K. E. *The physiology of hostility.* Chicago: Markham, 1971.

MULLENER, N., and J. D. LAIRD. Some developmental changes in the organization of self-evaluations. *Developmental Psychology,* 1971, *5,* 233–236.

MURRAY, H. A. *Explorations in personality.* New York: Oxford University Press, 1938.

MURRAY, H. A. The personality and career of Satan. *Journal of Social Issues,* 1962, *28,* 36–54.

MURRAY, H. A., and L. A. KLUCKHOHN. Conception of personality. In *Personality in nature, society and culture,* ed. C. Kluckhohn, H. Murray, and D. M. Schneider. New York: Knopf, 1956, p. 30.

MURSTEIN, B. I. *Theory and research in projective techniques (emphasizing the TAT).* New York: Wiley, 1963.

MURSTEIN, B. I. (Ed.). *Handbook of projective techniques.* New York: Basic Books, 1965.

MURSTEIN, B. I. Stimulus—value role: A theory of marital choice. *Marriage and the Family,* 1970, *32,* 465–481.

MURSTEIN, B. I. Normative written TAT responses for a college sample. *Journal of Personality Assessment,* 1972, *36,* 109–147.

MUSSEN, P. H. Long-term consequents of masculinity of interests in adolescents. *Journal of Consulting Psychology*, 1962, *26*, 435–440.

MUSSEN, P. H., J. J. CONGER, and J. KAGAN. *Child development and personality.* New York: Harper & Row, 1974.

MUSSEN, P. H., H. YOUNG, R. GADDINI, and L. MORANTE. The influence of father-son relationships on adolescent personality and attitudes. *Journal of Child Psychology and Psychiatry*, 1963, *4*, 3–16.

NADITCH, M. P., M. A. GARGON, and L. B. MICHAEL. Denial, anxiety, locus of control and the discrepancy between aspirations and achievements as components of depression. *Journal of Abnormal Psychology*, 1975, *84*, 1–9.

NEISSER, U. *Cognitive Psychology.* New York: Appleton-Century, 1967.

NEALE, J. M., and R. M. LIEBERT. *Science and behavior. An introduction to methods of research.* Englewood Cliffs, N.J.: Prentice-Hall, 1973.

NEUGARTEN, B. L., and ASSOCIATES. Adult personality: Toward a psychology of the life cycle. In *Middle age and aging*, ed. B. L. Neugarten. Chicago: University of Chicago Press, 1968, p. 137.

NEUGARTEN, B. L., and D. L. MILLER. Ego functions in middle and late years: A further exploration. In *Personality in middle and late life: Empirical studies*, ed. B. L. Neugarten et al. New York: Atherton Press, 1964, pp. 105–113.

NICOLL, M. *The new man: An interpretation of some parables and miracles of Christ.* London: Stuart and Watkins, 1967.

NISBETT, R. E. Eating behavior and obesity in men and animals. *Advances in Psychosomatic Medicine*, 1972, *1*, 173–93.

NOTZ, W. W. Work motivation and the negative effects of extrinsic rewards: A review with implications for theory and practice. *American Psychologist*, 1975, *39*, 884–891.

NOWLIS, D. P., and J. KAMIYA. The control of electroencephalographic alpha rhythms through auditory feedback and the associated mental activity. In *Biofeedback and self-control, 1970.* Chicago: Aldine-Atherton, 1971.

NUNNALLY, J. C., and L. C. LEMOND. Exploratory behavior and human development. In *Advances in Child Development*, Vol., III, ed., H. W. Reese. New York: Academic Press, 1973.

O'LEARY, K. D., and W. C. BECKER. Behavior modification of an adjustment class: A token reinforcement program. *Exceptional Children*, 1967, *33*, 637–642.

O'LEARY, K. D., and S. G. O'LEARY (Eds.). *Classroom management.* Elmsford, N.Y.: Pergamon Press, 1972.

OLTMAN, J., and S. FRIEDMAN. Parental deprivation in psychiatric conditions. *Diseases of the Nervous System*, 1967, *28*, 298–303.

ORME-JOHNSON, D. W. Autonomic stability and Transcendental Meditation. *Psychosomatic Medicine*, 1973, *35* (4), 341–349.

OWENS, W. A. Toward one discipline of scientific psychology. *American Psychologist*, 1968, *23*, 782–785.

PARDES, H., D. S. PAPERNICK, and A. WINSTON. Field differentiation in inpatient psychotherapy. *Archives of General Psychiatry*, 1974, *31*, 311–315.

PASSINI, F. T. and W. T. NORMAN. A universal conception of personality structure? *Journal of Personality and Social Psychology*, 1966, *4*, 44–49.

PAVLOV, I. P. *Conditioned reflexes.* London: Oxford University Press, 1927.

PECK, R. F., and H. BERKOWITZ. Personality and adjustment in middle age. In *Personality in middle and later life: Empirical studies,* ed. B. L. Neugarten. New York: Atherton Press, 1964, pp. 15–43.

PEDERSON, D. R., and D. TERVRUGT. The influence of amplitude and frequency of vestibular stimulation on the action of the 2-month-old infant. *Child Development,* 1973, *44,* 112–128.

PERCELL, L. P., P. T. BERWICK, and A. BEIGEL. The effects of assertiveness training on self-concept and anxiety. *Archives of General Psychiatry,* 1974, *31,* 502–504.

PERRIS, C. (Ed.). A study of bipolar (manic-depressive) and unipolar recurrent psychoses. *Acta psychiatrica Scandinavica,* 1966, *42* (supplement 194), 1.

PERVIN, L. A. Rigidity in neurosis and general personality functioning. *Journal of Abnormal and Social Psychology,* 1960, *61,* 389–395.

PHARES, E. J. Differential utilization of information as a function of internal-external control. *Journal of Personality,* 1968, *36,* 649, 662.

PHARES, E. J. A social learning theory approach to psychopathology. In *Applications of a social learning theory of personality,* ed. J. B. Rotter, J. Chance, and E. J. Phares. New York: Holt, Rinehart and Winston, 1972, pp. 436–469.

PHARES, E. J. *Locus of control in personality.* Morristown, N.J.: General Learning Press, 1976.

PIAGET, J. *The origins of intelligence in children.* New York: International Universities Press, 1952.

PIAGET, J. Development and learning. In *Piaget rediscovered,* ed. R. E. Ripple and V. N. Rockcastle. Ithaca: Cornell University Press, 1964, pp. 1–12.

PIAGET, J., and B. INHELDER. *The psychology of the child.* New York: Basic Books, 1969.

PINES, H. A. An attributional analysis of locus of control orientation and source of informational dependence. *Journal of Personality and Social Psychology,* 1973, *26,* pp. 262–272.

POLSTER, E., and M. POLSTER. *Gestalt therapy integrated: Contours of theory and practice.* New York: Bruner/Mazel, 1973.

POORKAJ, H. Social-psychological factors and "successful aging." *Sociology and Social Research,* 1972, *56,* 289–300.

PRATT, C. L., and G. P. SACKETT. Selection of social partners as a function of peer contact. *Science,* 1967, *155,* 1133–1135.

PRIBRAM, K., and M. M. GILL. *Freud's project reassessed. Preface to Contemporary cognitive theory and neuropsychology.* New York: Basic Books, 1976.

PROCIUK, T. J., and R. J. LUSSIER. Internal-external locus of control: An analysis and bibliography of two years of research (1973–1974). *Psychological Reports,* 1975, *37,* 1323–1337.

RADIN, N. Observed paternal behavior as antecedent of intellectual functioning in young boys. *Developmental Psychology,* 1973, *8,* 369–376.

RAFMAN, S. The infant's reaction to imitation of the mother's behavior by the stranger. In *The Infant's Reaction to Strangers,* New York: International Universities Press, 1974, pp. 117–148.

RAIMY, VICTOR. Changing misconceptions as the therapeutic task. In *What Makes Behavior Change Possible,* A. Burton, ed. New York: Brunner/Mazel, 1976.

REESE, S., and L. W. SUSHINSKY. The comparing response hypothesis of decreased play effects: A reply to Lepper and Greene. *Journal of Personality and Social Psychology*, 1976, *33*, 233–244.

RENNER, V. Effects of modification of cognitive-style on creative behavior. *Journal of Personality and Social Psychology*, 1970, *14*, 257–262.

RHEINGOLD, HARRIET L. The modification of social responsiveness in institutional babies. *Monographs of the Society for Research in Child Development*, 1956, *21* (2), Serial No. 63.

RHINE, W. R. Birth order differences in conformity and level of achievement arousal. *Child Development*, 1968, *39*, 987–996.

RIBBLE, M. *The rights of infants.* New York: Columbia University Press, 1943.

RIMM, D. C., and J. C. MASTERS. *Behavior therapy.* New York: Academic Press, 1974.

RIPLEY, H. S. Psychiatric interview. In *Comprehensive textbook of psychiatry*, II, ed. A. M. Freedman, H. I. Kaplan, and B. J. Sadock. Baltimore: Williams and Wilkins, 1975, pp. 715–724.

ROBINS, E. Personality disorders: Sociopathic type. In *Comprehensive textbook of psychiatry*, ed. A. M. Friedman and H. I. Kaplan. Baltimore: Williams and Wilkins, 1967, pp. 951–958.

ROCK, I., and I. KREMENT. A re-examination of Rubin's figural after-effect. *Journal of Experimental Psychology*, 1957, *53*, 20–30.

ROGERS, C. R. Client-centered therapy. Boston: Houghton Mifflin, 1951.

ROGERS, C. R. The necessary and sufficient conditions of therapeutic personality change. *Journal of Consulting Psychology*, 1957, *21*, 95–103.

ROGERS, C. R. *On becoming a person.* Boston: Houghton Mifflin, 1961.

ROGERS, C. R., and R. R. DYMOND (Eds.). Psychotherapy and the placebo effect. *Psychological Bulletin*, 1956, *61*, 65–94.

ROKEACH, M. *The open and closed mind.* New York: Basic Books, 1960.

ROKEACH, M., and P. KLIEJUNAS. Behavior as a function of attitude-toward-object and attitude-toward-situation. *Journal of Personality and Social Psychology*, 1972, *22*, 194–201.

ROSEN, J. L., and B. L. NEUGARTEN. Ego functions in the middle and late years: A Thematic Apperception study. In *Personality in middle and late life*, ed. B. L. Neugarten et al. New York: Atherton Press, 1964, pp. 309–310.

ROSENBERG, M. J., and R. P. ABELSON. An analysis of cognitive balancing. In *Attitude organization and change*, ed. M. J. Rosenberg et al. New Haven, Connecticut: Yale University Press, 1960.

ROSENTHAL, R. *Experimenter Effects on Behavior Research.* New York: Appleton-Century-Crofts, 1966.

ROSENWALD, G. C. Effectiveness of defenses against anal impulse arousal. *Journal of Consulting and Clinical Psychology*, 1972, *39*, 292–298.

ROSS, D. Relationships between dependency and incidental learning in preschool children. *Journal of Personality and Social Psychology*, 1966, *4*, 374–381.

ROTTER, J. B. *Social learning and clinical psychology.* New York: Prentice-Hall, 1954.

ROTTER, J. B. Generalized expectancies for internal versus external control of reinforcement. *Psychological Monographs*, 1966, *80* (1, Whole No. 609), 1–28.

ROTTER, J. B. Some implications of a social learning theory for the practice of psychotherapy. In *Learning approaches to behavior change,* ed. D. J. Levis. Chicago: Aldine, 1970, pp. 200–241.

ROTTER, J. B. Some problems and misconceptions related to the construct of internal versus external control of reinforcement. *Journal of Consulting and Clinical Psychology,* 1975, *43,* 56–57.

ROTTER, J., J. E. CHANCE, and E. J. PHARES (Eds.). *Application of a social learning theory of personality.* New York: Holt, Rinehart and Winston, 1972.

ROTTER, J. B., and J. E. RAFFERTY. *Manual: The Rotter Incomplete Sentences Blank.* New York: Psychological Corporation, 1950.

RUBIN, Z. Measurement of romantic love. *Journal of Personality and Social Psychology,* 1970, *16,* 265–278.

RUBLE, D. N., and C. Y. NAKAMURA. Task orientation versus social orientation in young children and their attention to relevant social cues. *Child Development,* 1972, *43,* 471–480.

RUSSAKOFF, L. M., A. F. FONTANA, B. W. DAWDS, and M. HARRIS. Psychological differentiation and psychotherapy. *Journal of Nervous and Mental Diseases,* 1976, *163,* 329–333.

RYCHLAK, J. *Introduction to personality and psychotherapy: A theory construction approach.* Boston: Houghton Mifflin, 1973.

SACKETT, G. P. Unlearned responses, differential rearing experiences, and the development of social attachments by rhesus monkeys. In *Primate behavior,* Vol. I, *Developments in field and laboratory research,* ed. L. A. Rosenblum. New York: Academic Press, 1970, pp. 111–140.

SALMON, P. A study of the social values and differential conformity on primary schoolboys as a function of maternal attitude. Unpublished Ph.D. thesis, University of London, 1967.

SANFORD, N. Personality: Its place in psychology. In *Psychology: Study of a science,* Vol. V, ed. S. Koch. New York: McGraw-Hill, 1963.

SANTROCK, J. W. Relation of type and onset of father absence to cognitive development. *Child Development,* 1972, *43,* 455–469.

SARASON, I. G. The effects of anxiety and threat on the solution of a difficult task. *Journal of Abnormal and Social Psychology,* 1961, *62,* 165–168.

SARASON, I. G., R. E. SMITH, and E. DIENER. Personality research: Components of variance attributable to the person and the situation. *Journal of Personality and Social Psychology,* 1975, *32,* pp. 199–204.

SARNOFF, I. *Testing Freudian concepts.* New York: Springer, 1971.

SCHACHTER, J., J. KERR, J. M. LACHIN, and M. FAER. Newborn offspring of a schizophrenic parent: Cardiac reactivity to auditory stimuli. *Psychophysiology,* 1975, *12,* 483–492.

SCHACHTER, J., J. KERR, J. LACHIN, Z. KHATOCHOTURIAN, T. WILLIAMS, and M. FAER. Heart rate reactivity of newborn offspring of schizophrenic patients. *Psychophysiology,* 1972, *9,* 273.

SCHACHTER, S. *The psychology of affiliation.* Stanford: Stanford University Press, 1959.

SCHACHTER, S. The interaction of cognitive and physiological determinants of emotional states. In *Advances in experimental psychology,* Vol. I, ed. L. Bekonilly. New York: Academic Press, 1964, pp. 49–80.

SCHACHTER, S. *Emotion, obesity and crime.* New York: Academic Press, 1975.

SCHACHTER, S., and LATANÉ, B. Crime, cognition and the autonomic nervous system. In *Nebraska Symposium on Motivation,* ed. D. Levine. Lincoln: University of Kansas Press, 1964, pp. 221–272.

SCHACHTER, S., and J. E. SINGER. Cognitive, social and physiological determinants of emotional state. *Psychological Review,* 1962, *69,* 221–272.

SCHEID, A. B. Clients' perception of the counselor: The influence of counselor introduction and behavior. *Journal of Counseling Psychology,* 1976, *22* (6), 503–508.

SCHER, J. M. Perception: Equivalence, avoidance and intrusion in schizophrenia. *Archives of Neurology and Psychiatry,* 1957, *77,* 210–217.

SCHMAUK, F. J. Punishment, arousal and avoidance learning. *Journal of Abnormal and Social Psychology,* 1970, *76,* 325–335.

SCHROEDER, S. R. Selective eye movements to simultaneously presented stimuli during discrimination. *Perception and Psychophysics,* 1970, *7,* 121–123.

SCHULSINGER, F. Psychopathy: Heredity and environment. *International Journal of Mental Health,* 1972, *1,* 190.

SCOGGINS, W. F. Growing old: Death by installment plan. *Life-threatening behavior,* 1971, *1,* 143–147.

SCOTT, J. P. Agonistic behavior in mice and rats: A review. *American Zoologist,* 1966, *6,* 683–701.

SEALY, A. P., and R. B. CATTELL. Adolescent personality trends in primary factors measured on the 16 PF and the HSPQ questionnaires through ages 11–23. *British Journal of Social and Clinical Psychology,* 1966, *5,* 172–184.

SEARS, R. R. Survey of objective studies of psychoanalytic concepts. *Social Science Research Council Bulletin,* 1943, No. 51.

SEARS, R. R. Experimental analysis of psychoanalytic phenomena. In *Personality and the behavior disorders,* Vol. I, ed. J. McV. Hunt. New York: Ronald Press, 1944, pp. 326–332.

SEARS, R. R. Dependency motivation. In *Nebraska Symposium on Motivation,* ed. M. R. Jones. Lincoln: University of Nebraska Press, 1963.

SEARS, R. R. Relation of early socialization experiences to self-concepts and gender role in middle childhood. *Child Development,* 1970, *41,* 267–289.

SEARS, R. R., E. E. MACCOBY, and H. LEVIN. *Patterns of child rearing.* New York: Harper & Row, 1957.

SEARS, R. R., L. RAU, and R. ALPERT. *Identification and child rearing.* Stanford: Stanford University Press, 1965.

SECHREST, L. The psychology of personal constructs. In *Concepts of personality,* ed. J. M. Wepman and R. W. Heine. Chicago: Aldine, 1963, pp. 206–233.

SEEMAN, W., S. NIDICH, and T. H. BANTA. Influence of transcendental meditation on a measure of self-actualization. *Journal of Counseling Psychology,* 1972, *19*(3), 184–187.

SEISS, T. F., and D. N. JACKSON. The Personality Research Form and vocational interest research. In *Advances in psychological assessment,* Vol. II, ed. P. McReynolds. Palo Alto, Calif.: Science and Behavior Books, 1971, pp. 109–132.

SELIGMAN, M. E. P. *Helplessness in depression, development and death.* San Francisco: W. H. Freeman, 1975.

SELMAN, R. L. The relation of role taking to the development of moral judgment in children. *Child Development,* 1971, *42,* 79–91.

SENN, D. J. Attraction as a function of similarity-dissimilarity in task performance. *Journal of Personality and Social Psychology,* 1971, *2,* 15–16.

SHANNON, J., and B. GUERNEY, JR. Interpersonal effects of interpersonal behavior. *Journal of Personality and Social Psychology,* 1973, *26,* 142–150.

SHIELDS, J., and C. W. SHERIF. *Social Psychology.* New York: Harper & Row, 1969.

SHIPLEY, T. E., and J. VEROFF. A projective measure of need affiliation. *Journal of Experimental Psychology,* 1952, *43,* 349–356.

SHULMAN, B. H. *Essays in schizophrenia.* Baltimore: Williams and Wilkins, 1968.

SHULMAN, B. H. *Contributions to individual psychology.* Chicago: Alfred Adler Institute, 1973.

SHULMAN, B. H., and H. H. MOSAK. Various purposes of symptoms. *Journal of Individual Psychology,* 1967, *23,* 79–87.

SILBERMAN, C. E. *Crisis in the classroom.* New York: Random House, 1970.

SILVERMAN, J. The problem of attention in the research and theory of schizophrenia. *Psychological Review,* 1964, *71,* 352.

SKINNER, B. F. *The behavior of organisms: An experimental analysis.* New York and London: D. Appleton-Century Company, 1938.

SKINNER, B. F. *Walden Two.* New York: Macmillan, 1948.

SKINNER, B. F. *Science and human behavior.* New York: Macmillan, 1953.

SKINNER, B. F. *Cumulative record.* New York: Appleton-Century-Crofts, 1959.

SKINNER, B. F. Autobiography. In *A history of psychology in autobiography,* eds. E. G. Boring and G. Lindzey. New York: Appleton-Century-Crofts, 1967, pp. 385–414.

SKINNER, B. F. *Beyond freedom and dignity.* New York: Knopf, 1971.

SKINNER, B. F. *About behaviorism.* New York: Knopf, 1974.

SKINNER, B. F. *Particulars of my life.* New York: Knopf, 1976.

SLATER, E. and M. ROTH. *Clinical Psychiatry.* Baltimore: Williams and Wilkins, 1969.

SLATER, P. *Earth walk.* New York: Bantam, 1976.

SLAVNEY, P. R., and P. R. McHUGH. The hysterical personality. *Archives of General Psychiatry,* 1974, *30,* 325–329.

SLOANE, R. B., A. H. CRISTOL, M. C. PEPERNIK, and F. R. STAPLES. Role preparation and expectation of improvement in psychotherapy. *Journal of Nervous and Mental Diseases,* 1970, *150,* 18–26.

SMITH, O., and P. SMITH. Developmental studies of spatial judgments by children and adults. *Perceptual and Motor Skills,* 1966, *22,* 3–73.

SMITH, R. E. Changes in locus of control as a function of life crisis resolution. *Journal of Abnormal Psychology,* 1970, *75,* 329–332.

SNYDER, M., and T. C. MONSON. Persons, situations and the control of social behavior. *Journal of Personality and Social Psychology,* 1975, *32* (4), 637–644.

SOKOLOV, E. W. In *The central nervous system and behavior: Transactions of the third conference,* ed. M. A. B. Brazier. New York: Josiah Macy, Jr., Foundation, 1960.

SOLOMON, R. H., and L. C. WYNNE. Traumatic avoidance learning: The principles of anxiety conservation and partial irreversibility. *Psychological Review,* 1954, *61,* 353–385.

SOMMER, R. *Personal space: The behavioral basis of design.* Englewood Cliffs, N.J.: Prentice-Hall, 1969.

SONTAG, L. W. The significance of fetal environmental differences. *American Journal of Obstetrics and Gynecology,* 1941, *42,* 906–1003.

SONTAG, L. W. War and fetal maternal relationship. *Marriage and Family Living,* 1944, *6,* 1–5.

SONTAG, L. W. Maternal anxiety during pregnancy and fetal behavior. *Physical and Behavioral Growth,* 26th Ross Laboratories Pediatric Research Conference, Columbus, Ohio, 1958, 21–24.

SONTAG, L. W., C. T. BAKER, and V. L. NELSON. Mental growth and personality: A longitudinal study. *Monographs of the Society for Research in Child Development,* 1958, *23* (68), 1–143.

SORRENTINO, R. An extension of the theory of achievement motivation to the study of emergent leadership. *Journal of Personality and Social Psychology,* 1973, *26,* 348–368.

SOUSA-POZA, J. F., and R. ROHRBERG. Communicational and interactional aspects of self-disclosure in psychotherapy: Differences related to cognitive style. *Psychiatry,* 1976, *39,* 81–91.

SPIEGEL, J., and P. MACHOTKA. *Messages of the body.* New York: Free Press, 1974.

SPITZ, R. A. Hospitalization: A follow-up report on investigations described in Vol. I, 1945. In *The psychoanalytic study of the child,* Vol. II, eds. A. Freud et al. New York: International Universities Press, 1946, pp. 113–117.

SPITZ, R. A. and WOLF, K. M. Anaclitic depression: an inquiry into the genesis of psychiatric conditions in early childhood, II. In *The psychoanalytic study of the child,* Vol. II, eds. A. Freud et al. New York: International Universities Press, 1946, 313–342.

SROUFE, L. A., E. WALTERS, and L. MATAS. Contextual determinants of infant affective response. In *The origins of fear,* eds. M. Lewis and L. Rosenblum. New York: Wiley, 1974, pp. 49–72.

SRULL, T. K., and S. A. KARABENICK. Effects of personality: Situation and locus of control congruence. *Journal of Personality and Social Psychology,* 1975, *32*(4), 617–628.

STAMPFL, T. G. Implosive therapy: An emphasis on covert stimulation. In *Learning approaches to therapeutic behavior change,* ed. D. J. Levis. Chicago: Aldine, 1970, pp. 182–304.

STAMPFL, T. G., and D. J. LEVIS. Essentials of implosive therapy: A learning-theory-based psychodynamic behavioral therapy. *Journal of Abnormal Psychology,* 1967, *72,* 496–503.

STAMPFL, T. G., and D. J. LEVIS. Implosive therapy: A behavioral therapy? *Behavior Research and Therapy,* 1968, *6,* 31–36.

STANG, D. J. Effects of interaction rate on ratings of leadership and liking. *Journal of Personality and Social Psychology,* 1973, *27,* 405–408.

STANG, D. J. Effects of "mere exposure" on learning and affect. *Journal of Personality and Social Psychology,* 1975, *31*(1), 7–12.

STAUB, E. Predicting prosocial behavior: How do personality characteristics and situations determine conduct? Paper presented at XXI International Congress of Psychology, Paris, 1976.

STAUB, E., B. TURASKY, and G. E. SCHWARTZ. Self-control and predictability: Their effects on reactions to aversive stimulation. *Journal of Personality and Social Psychology*, 1971, *18, 157–162.*

STAYTON, D., M. D. S. AINSWORTH, and M. MAIN. Development of separation behavior in the first year of life: Protest, following and greeting. *Developmental Psychology*, 1973, *9,* 213–225.

STENDLER, C. *Child development.* New York: Harcourt Brace, 1953.

STEPHAN, F. F., and E. G. MISHLER. The distribution of participation in small groups: An exponential approximation. *American Sociological Review*, 1952, *17,* 203–207.

STRANG, R. *An introduction to child study*, 4th ed. New York: Macmillan, 1959.

STRASSBERG, D. S. Relationships among locus of control, anxiety and valued-goal expectations. *Journal of Consulting and Clinical Psychology*, 1973, *41,* 319.

SULLIVAN, H. S. *An interpersonal theory of psychiatry.* New York: Norton, 1953.

SULLIVAN, H. S. *The psychiatric interview.* New York: Norton, 1954.

SULLIVAN, H. S. *Clinical studies in psychiatry*, ed. H. S. Perry, M. L. Bawel, and M. Gibbon. New York: Norton, 1956.

SUNDBERG, N. D. *Assessment of Persons.* Englewood Cliffs, New Jersey: Prentice-Hall, 1977.

SUNDSTROM, E. An experimental study of crowding: Effects of room size, intrusion and goal blocking on nonverbal behavior, self-disclosure and self-reported stress. *Journal of Personality and Social Psychology*, 1975, *32* (4), 645–654.

SWANSON, B. W., T. J. BOHMERT, and J. A. SMITH. *The paranoid.* Boston: Little, Brown, and Co., 1970.

TATE, B. G., and G. S. BAROFF. Aversive control of self-injurious behavior in a psychotic boy. *Behavior Research and Therapy*, 1966, *4,* 281–287.

TAUTERMAROVA, M. Smiling in infants. *Child Development*, 1973, *44,* 701–704.

THELEN, M. H., D. L. RENNIE, J. L. FRYNEAR, and D. McGUIRE. Expectancy to perform and vicarious reward: The effects on imitation. *Child Development*, 1972, *43,* 699–703.

THIBAUT, J., and H. RIECKEN. Authoritarianism, status and the communication of aggression. *Human Relations*, 1955, *8,* 95–120.

THOMAE, H. Determinants of consistency and change in personality development. *Revista de Psicologia Generale Applicada*, 1973, *28,* 3–16.

THOMAS, A., and S. CHESS. *Temperament and Development.* New York: Bruner/Mazel, 1977.

THOMAS, A., S. CHESS, H. G. BIRCH, M. E. HERTZIG, and S. KORN. *Behavioral Individuality in Early Childhood.* New York: New York University Press, 1971.

THORNDIKE, E. L. *The elements of psychology.* New York: A. G. Seiler, 1905.

TIGER, L. *Men in groups.* New York: Random House, 1969.

TINBERGEN, N., and A. C. PERDECK. On the stimulus situation releasing the begging response in the newly hatched herring-gull chick. *Behavior*, 1950, *3,* 1–38.

TOMKINS, S. *Affect, imagery and consciousness: The positive affects,* Vol. I. New York: Springer, 1962.

TOMKINS, S. *Affect, imagery and consciousness: The negative affects,* Vol. II. New York: Springer, 1963.

TOMPKINS, W. T. The clinical significance of nutritional deficiencies in pregnancy. *Bulletin of the New York Academy of Medicine,* 1948, *24,* 376–388.

TRESEMER, D. Fear of success: Popular but unproven. In *The female experience* (a special publication of *Psychology Today*). Del Mar, Calif.: Communication Research Machines, Inc., 1973, pp. 58–62.

TRIPODI, T., and J. BIERI. Information transmission in clinical judgements as a function of stimulus dimensionality and cognitive complexity. *Journal of Personality,* 1964, *32,* 119–137.

TREXLER, L. D., and T. O. KARST. Rational-emotive therapy: Placebo and no-treatment effects on public-speaking anxiety. *Journal of Abnormal Psychology,* 1972, *79,* 60–67.

TRUAX, C. B., and K. M. MITCHELL. Research on certain therapist interpersonal skills in relation to process and outcome. In *Handbook of psychotherapy and behavior change,* eds. A. E. Bergin and S. L. Garfield. New York: Wiley, 1971, pp. 299–344.

TUDOR, T. G., and C. S. HOLMES. Differential recall of successes and failures: Its relationship to defensiveness, achievement, motivation and anxiety. *Journal of Research in Personality,* 1973, *7,* 208–224.

TURIEL, E. Conflict and transition in adolescent moral development. *Child Development,* 1974, *45,* 14–29.

UDE, L. K., and R. E. VOGLER. Internal versus external control of reinforcement and awareness in a conditioning task. *Journal of Psychology,* 1969, *73,* 63–67.

ULLMAN, L. P., and L. KRASNER. *A psychological approach to abnormal behavior.* Englewood Cliffs, N.J.: Prentice-Hall, 1969.

U'REN, R. C. A perspective on self-esteem. *Comprehensive Psychiatry,* 1971, *12,* 466–472.

VALINS, S. Persistent effects of information about internal reactions: Ineffectiveness of debriefing. In *The cognitive alteration of feeling states,* ed. R. H. London and R. E. Nisbett. Chicago: Aldine, 1972.

VALINS, S., and A. RAY. Effects of cognitive desensitization in avoidance behavior. *Journal of Personality and Social Psychology,* 1967, *7,* 345–350.

VERBEEK, E. Hysteria. *Psychiatrica clinica,* 1973, *6,* 104–120.

VEROFF, J. Development and validation of a projective measure of power validation. *Journal of Abnormal and Social Psychology,* 1957, *54,* 1.

WALLACE, R. K. Physiological effects of transcendental meditation. *Science,* 1970, *167,* 1751–1754.

WALLACE, R. K., H. BENSON, and A. F. WILSON. A wakeful hypometabolic physiologic state. *American Journal of Physiology,* 1971, *221*(3), 795–799.

WALLACE, R. K., and H. BENSON. The physiology of meditation. *Scientific American,* 1972, *226*(2), 94–90.

WALTERS, R. H. Some conditions facilitating the occurrence of imitative behavior. In *Social facilitation and imitative behavior,* eds., E. C. Simmel, R. A. Hoppe, and G. A. Milton. Boston: Allyn and Bacon, 1968, pp. 7–30.

WASHBURN, S. L., and D. A. HAMBURG. Aggressive behavior in old world monkeys and apes. In *Primates: Studies in adaptation and variability,* ed. P. Jan. New York: Holt, Rinehart and Winston, 1966, pp. 458–478.

WEATHERFORD, M. J., and L. B. COHEN. Developmental changes in infant visual preferences for novelty and familiarity. *Child Development,* 1973, *44,* 416–424.

WEINER, B. New conceptions in the study of achievement motivation. In *Progress in experimental personality research,* Vol. V, ed. B. A. Maher. New York: Academic Press, 1970.

WEINER, B. *Theories of motivation.* Chicago: Markham, 1972.

WEINER, B., I. FREIZE, A. KUKLA, L. REED, S. REST, and R. ROSENBAUM. Perceiving the causes of success and failure. In *Attribution: Perceiving the causes of behavior,* eds. E. Jones, D. Kanouse, H. Kelley, R. Nisbett, S. Valins, and B. Weiner. Morristown, N.J.: General Learning Press, 1972.

WEININGER, O. The effects of early experience on behavior and growth characteristics. *Journal of Comparative Physiological Psychology,* 1956, *49,* 1–9.

WEINSTEIN, J., J. R. AVERILL, E. OPTON, JR., and R. S. LAZARUS. Defensive style and discrepancy between self-report and physiological indices of stress. *Journal of the Personality and Social Psychology,* 1968, *10,* 405–413.

WENGER, M. A., and T. O. CULLEN. Studies of autonomic balance in children and adults. In *Handbook of psychophysiology,* eds. N. S. Greenfield and R. A. Sternback. New York: Holt, Rinehart & Winston, 1972, p. 535.

WERBOFF, J., and J. HAVLENA. Febrile convulsions in infant rats and later behavior. *Science,* 1964, *142,* 684–685.

WERNER, H. The conception of development from a comparative and organismic point of view. In *The concept of development,* ed. D. Harris. Minneapolis: University of Minnesota Press, 1957, pp. 125–148.

WHITE, R. W. Motivation reconsidered: The concept of competence. *Psychological Review,* 1959, *66,* 297–333.

WHITE, R. W. Competence and the psychosexual stages of development. In *Nebraska Symposium on Motivation,* ed. M. Jones. Lincoln: University of Nebraska Press, 1960.

WHITE, R. W. (Ed.). *The study of lives: Essays on personality in honor of Henry A. Murray.* New York: Atherton Press, 1963. (a)

WHITE, R. W. Ego and reality in psychoanalytic theory. *Psychological Issues,* 1963, *3*(3), Monograph No. 11. (b)

WHITE, R. W. *The enterprise of living: Growth and organization in personality.* New York: Holt, Rinehart and Winston, 1972.

WHITE, R. W. *Lives in progress: A study of the natural growth of personality,* 3rd ed. New York: Holt, Rinehart and Winston, 1975.

WHITEHORN, J. C. Guide to interviewing and clinical personality study. *Archives of Neurology and Psychiatry,* 1954, *52,* 197–216.

WHITEHORN, J. C., and B. J. BETZ. Further studies of the doctor as a crucial variable in the outcome of treatment with schizophrenic patients. *American Journal of Psychiatry,* 1960, *117,* 215–223.

WIENS, A. N. The assessment interview. In *Clinical methods in psychology,* ed. I. B. Weiner. New York: Wiley, 1976.

WIGGINS, J. S. *Personality and prediction: Principles of personality assessment.* Reading, Mass.: Addison-Wesley, 1973.

WIGGINS, J. S., K. E. RENNER, G. L. CLORE, and R. J. ROSE. *The psychology of personality.* Reading, Mass.: Addison-Wesley, 1971.

WIGGINS, J. S., K. E. RENNER, G. L. CLORE, and R. J. ROSE. *The psychology of personality,* 2nd ed. Reading, Mass.: Addison-Wesley, 1976.

WILKINS, W. Expectancy of therapeutic gain: An empirical and conceptual critique. *Journal of Consulting and Clinical Psychology,* 1973, *40,* 69–77.

WILLIAMS, R. J. *Biochemical individuality.* New York: Wiley, 1956.

WINDLE, W. F. *Physiology of the fetus.* Philadelphia: Saunders, 1940.

WINOKUR, G., and R. R. CROWE. Personality disorders. In *Comprehensive textbook of psychiatry,* II, eds. A. M. Freedman, H. I. Kaplan, and B. J. Sadock. Baltimore: Williams and Wilkins, 1975, pp. 1279–1297.

WINTER, D. G. The need for power in college men. In *Alcohol and human motivation,* eds. D. C. McClelland, W. N. Davis, R. Kalin, and H. E. Wanner. New York: Free Press, 1971.

WITKIN, H. A. Psychological differentiation and forms of pathology. In *Reviews of research in behavior pathology,* ed. D. S. Holmes. New York: Wiley, 1968.

WITKIN, H. A. Socialization and ecology in the development of cross-cultural and sex differences in cognitive style. Prepared for presentation at the 21st International Congress of Psychology, Paris, July 18–25, 1976.

WITKIN, H. A., R. B. DYK, H. F. FATERSON, D. R. GOODENOUGH, and S. KARP. *Psychological differentiation.* New York: Wiley, 1962.

WITKIN, H. A., D. R. GOODENOUGH, and S. A. KARP. Stability of cognitive style from childhood to young adulthood. *Journal of Personality and Social Psychology,* 1967, *7,* 291–300.

WITKIN, H. A., H. B. LEWIS, and E. WEIL. Affective reactions and patient-therapist interactions among more differentiated and less differentiated patients early in therapy. *Journal of Nervous and Mental Diseases,* 1968, *146,* 193–208.

WOLFENSBERGER-HÄSSIG, C. *Verhaltensforschung im Kinderzimmer.* München: Wilhelm Goldmann Verlag, 1974.

WOLK, S., and J. DUCETTE. Intentional performance and incidental learning as a function of personality and task dimensions. *Journal of Personality and Social Psychology,* 1974, *29,* 90–101.

WOLPE, J. The systematic desensitization treatment of neuroses. *Journal of Nervous and Mental Diseases,* 1961, *132,* 189–203.

WOLPE, J. *The practice of behavior therapy.* New York: Pergamon Press, 1969.

WOLPE, J. Conditioning is the basis of all psychotherapeutic change. In *What makes behavior change possible?* ed. A. Burton. New York: Bruner/Mazel, 1976, pp. 58–72.

WOODRUFF, D. S., and J. E. BIRREN. Age changes and cohort differences in personality. *Developmental Psychology,* 1972, *6,* 252–259.

WORCHEL, S., and C. TEDDLIE. The experience of crowding: A two-factor theory. *Journal of Personality and Social Psychology,* 1976, *34 (1),* 30–40.

WORTMAN, C. B. Some determinants of perceived control. *Journal of Personality and Social Psychology,* 1975, *31,* 282–294.

WRIGHT, M. E. The influence of frustrations upon the social relations of young children. *Character and Personality,* 1943, *12,* 111–122.

WULF, F. Über die Veränderung von Vorstellugen (Gedächtnis and Gestalt). *Psychologische Forschung*, 1922, *1*, 333–373.

WYNNE, L. C., and M. T. SINGER. Thought disorder and family relations of schizophrenics, II: A classification of forms of thinking. *Archives of General Psychiatry*, 1963, *9*, 199–206.

YALOM, I. D., R. GREEN, and N. FISK. Prenatal exposure to female hormones: Effective psychosocial development in boys. *Archives of General Psychiatry*, 1973, *28*, 554.

YARROW, L. J. Research in dimensions of early maternal care. *Merrill-Palmer Quarterly*, 1963, *9*, 101–114.

YATES, A. J. *Behavior therapy*. New York: Wiley, 1970.

YERKES, R. M., and J. D. DODSON. The relation of strength of stimulus to rapidity of habit formation. *Journal of Comparative Neurological Psychology*, 1908, *18*, pp. 459–482.

ZIEGLER, H. P. Displacement activity and motivational theory: A case study in the history of ethology. *Psychological Bulletin*, 1964, *61*, 362–376.

ZIMBARDO, P. G. The human choice: Individuation, reason and order versus deindividuation, impulse and chaos. In *Nebraska Symposium on Motivation*, eds. W. J. Arnold and D. Levine. Lincoln: University of Nebraska Press, 1969, pp. 237–307.

ZIMBARDO, P. G., and R. FORMICA. Emotional comparison and self-esteem as determinants of affiliation. *Journal of Personality*, 1963, *31*, 141–162.

ZUBEK, J. P., and M. MACNEILL. Perceptual deprivation phenomena: Role of the recumbent position. *Journal of Abnormal Psychology*, 1967, *72*, 147–150.

ZUBEK, J. P. (Ed.). *Sensory deprivation: Fifteen years of research*. New York: Appleton-Century-Crofts, 1969.

ADDITIONAL REFERENCES

ATTNEAVE, F. Some informational aspects of visual perception. *Psychological Review*, 1954a.

DiLEO, J. H. *Children's drawings as diagnostic aids*. New York: Brunner/Mazel, 1973.

FORBES, J. D. *Mexican-Americans: A handbook for educators*. Berkeley, Calif.: Far West Laboratory for Educational Research & Development, 1966.

HALL, C. and G. LINDZEY. *Theories of personality*, 2nd. ed. New York: Wiley, 1970.

KOCH, H. L. A study of twins born at different levels of maturity. *Child Development*, 1964, *35*, 1265–1282.

KOHLBERG, L. Moral stages and moralization: The cognitive developmental approach. In *Moral development and behavior*, ed. T. Lickona. New York: Holt, Rinehart & Winston, 1976.

MILLER, S., W. N. ELANE, D. B. WAEKMEAN and R. BRAZMAN. *The Minnesota Couples Communication Program: Couples Handbook*. Minneapolis: Minnesota Couples Communication Program, 1972.

MONEY, J. and A. A. EHRHARDT. *Man and woman: Boy and girl: The differentiation and dimorphism of gender identity from conception to maturity*. Baltimore: Johns Hopkins University Press, 1972.

PERVIN, L. Personality: *Theory assessment and research.* New York: Wiley, 1975.

ROBINS, L. N. *Deviant children grown up: A sociological and psychiatric study of socio-pathic personality.* Baltimore: Williams and Wilkins, 1966.

SHELDON, W. H. and S. S. STEVENS. *The varieties of temperament: A psychology of constitutional references.* New York: Harper, 1942.

SOLOMON, R. L. et al. *Sensory deprivation.* Cambridge, Mass.: Harvard University Press, 1961.

name index

A

Abelson, R. P., 157
Adams, W. V., 179
Adelson, J., 211
Adinolfi, A. A., 234
Adler, A., 17, 61, 101–11, 328, 329, 348
Adorno, T. W., 156
Agrae, W. S., 358
Ainsworth, M., 123, 127, 181, 182, 184
Alarcon, R. D., 338
Alkire, A. A., 192
Allen, A. 232–33
Allport, 10, 11, 12, 13, 14, 19, 23, 80–83, 89, 166, 197, 304
Alpert, R., 231
Alt, R. L., 179
Alvy, K., 202
Amabile, T., 246
Amsel, A., 259
Angyal, A., 10, 96–101
Ansbacher, H. L., 18
Ansbacher, R., 18
Appelbaum, A. E., 8, 149
Arenbert, D., 296
Argyle, M., 13
Arieti, S., 329
Aristotle, 148, 164
Arndt, W. B., 11, 23, 99
Arnold, M., 187
Aronson, E., 157, 249, 269
Arsenian, J. M., 189
Atkins, A. L., 308

Atkinson, J. W., 239, 240, 243, 294
Atthowe, J. M., 358
Attneave, F., 7
Averill, J. R., 252, 253, 255
Ayllon, T., 48, 358
Azrin, N. H. 48, 358

B

Back, K. L., 225
Bacon, M., 204
Baer, D. M., 189
Bakerman, S., 223
Baldwin, A. L., 146, 147, 192
Bales, R. F., 283–84
Balloun, J. L., 250
Bandura, A., 39, 48–50, 52, 193, 206–8, 266, 267, 275, 276, 297–99, 336, 356, 339–40, 361
Bannister, D., 113, 115, 311
Banquet, J. P., 350
Banta, T. H., 351
Barber, T. X., 353–354
Barclay, A. M., 276
Barker, B. M., 12
Barker, R. G., 237, 259
Baroff, G. S., 358, 359
Baron, A., 297, 298
Barry, H., 204
Bateson, G., 330
Beach, F. A., 272
Beary, J. F., 355

Beck, A. T., 324, 328, 361–62, 368
Becker, W. C., 296
Beckwith, L., 184
Beigel, A., 357
Bell, S. M., 123, 184
Beller, E. K., 232
Bem, D. J., 232–4
Bem, S. L., 205
Benson, H., 350–51, 355
Berenson, B. G., 368
Berkowitz, H., 221
Berkowitz, L., 273
Berlyne, D. E., 140, 244, 256
Bernardin, A. C., 266
Berne, E., 362
Berwick, P. T., 357
Betz, B., 349
Bieri, J., 112, 308–9, 311–12, 314
Bigner, J. J., 192
Bindra, D., 293
Binswanger, L., 84
Birch, H. G., 165
Birdwhistell, R. L., 285
Birren, J. E., 221
Bischof, L., 223, 225
Blake, F., 202
Blanchard, E. G., 360
Bloomfield, H. H., 350–52
Blos, P., 215
Bohmert, T. J., 327
Bohvert, M., 324
Bonarius, J. C. J., 314
Bornstein, R., 192
Borovec, T. D., 337
Boss, M., 84–86
Botwinick, J., 224
Bower, T. G. R., 173, 182
Bowers, K. S., 234
Bowes, W. A., 169
Bowlby, J., 123, 124, 126, 127, 132, 183
Brazelton, T. B., 168
Breger, J., 127, 128, 132, 133, 136, 170
Brehm, J. W., 251
Briar, S., 308
Brock, T. C., 250
Brody, E. G., 327, 328, 333, 338
Brody, N., 141, 244
Brofenbrenner, U., 193
Bronson, W. C., 133, 200
Broverman, D. M., 219
Broverman, I. K., 219
Brown, B., 361

Bruner, J., 8, 115, 178, 179, 180
Bryant, P., 181
Buck, R., 255
Buhler, C., 223, 225
Burdock, E. I., 317
Burgess, M., 275
Buros, O. K., 304
Burton, A., 346
Buss, A. H., 276, 337
Butler, R. A., 134
Butler, R. N., 222–23
Butz, R., 358
Byrne, D., 269

C

Calder, B. J., 246–47
Callahan, E. J., 357
Cameron, R., 367
Campbell, S. B., 179
Campos, J., 133
Campus, N., 237
Carkhuff, R. R., 368
Carlson, R., 211
Carol, M. P., 355
Cartwright, D., 241
Caruso, I., 355
Cattell, R. B., 12, 13, 215, 303–4
Chance, J. E., 50
Chesno, F. A., 336
Chess, S., 16, 165
Child, I., 204
Chodoff, P., 338
Churchill, D. W., 330–31
Clark, R. A., 239, 276
Clarkson, F. E., 219
Cobliner, W. G., 212
Cohen, A. R., 251
Cohen, D., 202, 204
Cohen, L. B., 141
Cohen, M. F., 275
Coleman, J. S., 191, 193, 211
Collins, J. K., 212
Conger, J. J., 120, 133, 207, 214, 215
Coombs, R. A., 199
Coopersmith, S., 198–99
Cornelison, A. R., 330
Coules, J., 353
Cowgill, D. O., 223
Crawford, J. L., 284
Crockett, W. H., 308

Cronbach, L., 293, 294
Crowe, R. R., 327, 336, 337
Cullen, T. O., 260
Cummings, G., 224
Curtis, H. J., 223

D

Dahlstrom, D. E., 303
Dahlstrom, W. G., 303
Dana, R. H., 305
David, K. H., 283
Davis, C., 189
Davis, K. E., 211, 270
Davis, R. C., 353
Deaux, K., 204
Deci, E. L., 246
Degenhardt, A., 210
Dembo, T., 259
Denenberg, V. H., 186, 273, 274
DeWolfe, A. S., 9, 154, 309–10, 327
DiCaprio, N. S., 80, 278
DiCara, V., 296
DiLeo, J. H., 305
Dodson, J. D., 258
Dohrenwend, B. P., 336
Dohrenwend, B. S., 336
Dollard, J., 39–40, 42, 44, 46–48
Domino, G., 293
Douvan, E., 211
Dowds, B. N., 371
Dreikurs, R., 13, 110, 209, 217, 253, 270
Dua, P. S., 371
DuCette, J., 300
Ducharme, R., 258
Duncan, O. D., 285
Dworkiss, B., 296
Dymond, R. R., 368

E

Eber, H. W., 304
Edwards, A. L., 266
Ehrenwald, J., 334
Ehrhardt, A. A., 203
Eibl-Eibesfeldt, I., 126, 127, 129, 146, 209, 215, 217, 218, 285–87
Eisdorfer, C., 224

Ekman, P., 150–51, 285, 290
Elane, W. N., 135
Elkind, D., 202
Elliott, R., 261
Ellis, A., 360, 365–66
Emde, R., 133
Emswiller, T., 204
Endler, N. S., 260
Erdelyi, M. H., 8, 149, 150, 260
Eriksen, C., 150, 255, 260
Erikson, E., 36–39, 134, 202, 210, 216
Eron, L., 305, 306
Eysenck, H., 10, 13, 14

F

Fantz, R., 141, 171–73, 182
Farina, A., 296
Farnsworth, D. L., 211
Faust, M. S., 210
Feather, N. T., 241, 242
Fenz, W. D., 331, 337
Ferguson, P., 351
Fernandez, L. E., 208
Ferster, C. B., 47
Feshbach, N., 202
Feshbach, S., 202, 274
Festinger, L., 157, 250, 259
Fiedler, F. E., 368
Fisher, S., 29, 35, 349
Fiske, D., 190, 294
Fleck, J. R., 179
Fleck, T., 330
Fonda, C. P., 150, 255, 260
Foord, E. N., 155, 177
Forbes, J. D., 203
Ford, C. S., 272
Forgus, R., 9, 136, 140, 149, 151, 154, 171, 180, 190, 214, 309–10, 327
Formica, R., 266
Foulds, M. L., 371
Frank, J. D., 369
Frankie, G., 207
Franks, C. M., 354
Freedman, A. M., 350
Frenkel-Brunswick, E., 156
Freud, S., 8, 25–37, 40, 60, 61
Friedman, M., 326
Friedman, S., 336
Friesen, W. V., 290
Furth, H. G., 181

G

Gaensbauer, T., 133
Gajdos, E., 360
Galanter, 139
Galle, O. R., 237
Gardner, R. W., 155, 177, 178, 247, 249, 257
Gargon, M. A., 158
Garner, W., 148
Gates, D. W., 371
Gecas, V., 200, 209
Geen, R. G., 277
Gerwitz, J. L., 181, 189
Gibson, E. J., 173, 174
Gibson, J. J., 174
Gill, M., 35
Gisvold, D. A., 266
Glick, J., 156
Glickman, S. E., 244
Goffman, E., 13
Gold, M., 211
Goldberg, E. L., 353
Goldberg, P., 307
Goldfarb, W., 124
Goldfried, A. P., 362
Goldfried, M. R., 362
Goldstein, A. P., 369
Goldstein, J. H., 275
Goldstein, K., 92, 94–98, 100, 259, 294
Goodall, J., 285
Goodenough, D. R., 214
Goodenough, F., 305
Goodman, C. C., 178, 179
Gordon, T. F., 275
Gove, W. R., 237
Gough, H., 303
Gowan, C. G., 351
Grams, A., 191
Greenberg, B. S., 275
Greenberg, R. P., 29, 35
Greene, D. M., 240
Greene, M. A., 370
Grossman, S. P., 271
Grusec, J., 207, 261
Gruzelier, J. H., 331
Guerney, G., Jr., 284
Guskin, S. A., 296
Gutmann, D. L., 224
Gynther, M. D., 303
Gynther, R. A., 303

H

Haaland, G. A., 284
Haley, J., 330
Hall, C. S., 9, 74
Hall, E. T., 287, 289
Haller, D. L., 301
Hamburg, D. A., 128, 273
Hanratty, M. A., 276
Hardesty, A. S., 317
Hare, R. D., 336, 337
Harlow, H., 123, 124–26, 127, 128, 134, 183, 184, 244, 269
Harlow, M. K., 269
Harrell, R. F., 168
Harris, B., 249
Harris, N. B., 207
Harrison, R., 115
Hartap, W. W., 204
Hartmann, D., 275
Hartmann, H., 26
Hartshorne, H., 230
Harvey, J. H., 249
Harvey, O. J., 244
Hathaway, S. R., 301
Havighurst, R. J., 224
Havlena, J., 186
Hayes, F., 287
Heath, D. H., 217, 222
Hebb, D. O., 133, 136, 137, 139, 141, 146, 155, 177, 180, 190, 225, 258
Hedvig, E., 9
Heidegger, M., 83–84
Heider, F., 157
Heilbrun, A. B., 369
Heiman, J., 272
Hein, A., 173–74
Held, R., 173–74
Helmreich, R., 199
Helms, D. B., 168
Helweg, G. C., 371
Henderson, C., 133
Henry, W. G., 224, 305
Herbert, M. E., 328
Heron, W., 137
Hersch, P. D., 340
Hertzig, M. E., 165
Heston, I., 330, 336
Hetherington, E. M., 207
Hilton, I., 267
Hippocrates, 14
Hirsch, H. V. B., 139, 140

Hoffman, L. W., 220
Hogg, E., 158
Hokinson, J. E., 275
Hollander, E. P., 200
Holmes, C. S., 260
Holmes, L. D., 223
Holt, R. R., 309
Holton, R. B., 259
Holzman, P. S., 155, 177, 247, 257
Horner, M., 150, 220, 242
Horney, K., 61–5, 70, 86, 89, 280
Horowitz, M., 333, 338
Horrocks, J. E., 196–97, 202, 210
Hosken, B., 204
Houston, B. K., 340
Hubel, D. H., 139, 140
Hull, C. L., 39, 41, 42
Hunt, D. E., 244
Hunt, J. McV., 134, 136, 178, 190, 260
Husserl, E., 83–84
Hustmyer, F. E., 370
Huston, A. C., 207
Hutchings, B., 336

I

Inhelder, B., 190
Irwin, M., 308

J

Jacklin, C. N., 202–3, 267
Jackson, D. D., 330
Jackson, D. W., 196–97, 303
Jacobs, L. J., 199
Jacobson, S., 328
James, W., 355
Jaspers, K., 10, 84
Jefferey, R. W., 360
Jessor, R., 266
Johnson, V. E., 270, 271
Jones, A., 140, 141, 244
Jones, M. C., 210
Jones, S. C., 337
Jung, C. G., 14, 55–61, 68, 89

K

Kaats, G. R., 211
Kagan, J., 120, 133, 141, 174, 179–80,
    204, 207, 214, 257, 266–67
Kahn, M. H., 192

Kalish, R. A., 224
Kallman, F., 329–30
Kamiya, J., 354
Kanfer, F. H., 356
Kantor, J. R., 353
Kaplan, B. J., 168
Kaplan, H. I., 350
Karabenick, S. A., 236
Karp, S. A., 214, 370
Karras, G. G., 186
Karst, T. O., 362
Katz, R., 287
Kauffman, H., 273
Kaufman, A., 297, 298
Kay, D., 328
Kelly, G., 18, 111–15, 149, 250, 278,
    311, 312–14, 323, 326
Keniston, K., 207
Keongh, J., 204
Kerckhoff, A. C., 270
Kilmann, P. R., 336
Kimble, C., 199
Kimmel, D. C., 220, 225
Kissin, B., 370
Klein, G. S., 128, 257
Kleinmentz, B., 303, 327, 335
Kliejunas, P., 157
Kliman, G., 353
Kline, P., 35
Kluckhohn, C., 71
Koch, H. G., 168, 169
Kohlberg, L., 204, 207–8, 213–14, 231
Konečni, V. J., 277
Koriat, A., 252
Kopp, R. E., 297, 298
Korn, S., 165
Korner, A. F., 165, 183
Krasner, L., 45–47, 337, 346, 356–57,
    358
Kretschmer, E., 14, 15
Kringlen, E., 333
Kruglanski, A. W., 246
Kuhlen, R. G., 220
Kuo, Z., 129, 273

L

Laird, J. D., 210
Lakin, M., 167
Landauer, T. J., 131, 186
Landers, N. G., 212
Landers, T. J., 212

Landfield, A. W., 115, 314, 336–38
Lang, P. J., 266
Latané, B., 158–59
Laude, R., 324
Lawick-Goodall, J., 127, 128
Lazarus, A., 52, 297, 346, 356, 360, 362
Lazarus, R. S., 150, 160–61, 252–54, 255, 256, 260, 281
Lazovik, A. D., 266
Leaman, R. L., 308
Lefcourt, H. M., 158, 300, 371
Le Francois, G., 211
Leibniz, G. W., 23
Leitenberg, H., 357, 358, 361
Lepper, M. R., 246
Leskow, S., 210
Levin, J., 141
Levin, H., 189, 191, 204
Levine, J., 209
Levine, S., 130–31, 186
Levinson, D. J., 156
Levis, D. J., 357
Levy, D., 170, 182, 183
Levy, L., 154
Lewinsohn, P. M., 296
Lewis, H. B., 370
Lewis, J. M., 217
Lidz, T. S., 330
Liebermann, M. G., 320
Liebert, R. M., 208, 359
Liem, G. R., 249
Lindner, D., 269
Lindzey, G., 9, 74, 304
Linton, H. B., 257
Lipowski, Z. T., 326
Locke, J., 23
Loeb, R. C., 179
Long, R. I., 155, 178, 249
Lorenz, K., 128, 129, 146, 273
Lovaas, I., 49
Lowell, E. L., 239
Luborsky, L., 368, 369, 372
Luborsky, L. B., 369
Lussier, R. J., 158
Lykken, D. T., 331, 336

M

McCall, R. B., 174
McCandless, B. R., 257
McCarter, R. E., 320

McClelland, D., 154, 192, 238–42, 245, 305
Maccoby, E., 189, 191, 202–3, 204, 205, 211, 267
Maccoby, M., 211
McDill, E. G., 211
McGhie, A., 331
Machotka, P., 287–89
Machover, K., 305
McHugh, P. R., 338
McKeachie, W., 293
McKinley, J. C., 301
McKinney, J. C., 179
Mackinnon, R. A., 314
MacNeill, 139
Maddi, S., 10, 86, 190, 256
Maddox, E. L., 224
Magaro, P. A., 339
Mahoney, M. J., 297, 346, 356, 360, 365–66
Main, M., 127
Mair, J. M. M., 113, 115, 311
Malamed, L., 136, 149, 151, 171, 180, 190, 214
Mallick, S. K., 259
Mancuso, J. C., 115, 149
Mandler, G., 259
Mariotto, M. J., 296
Marks, P. A., 301
Marmor, J., 362, 363
Masling, J., 35
Maslow, A. H., 226, 243
Masserman, J., 349–50
Masters, J. C., 357
Masters, W. H., 270, 271
Matas, L., 133
May, M. A., 230
May, R., 86, 87, 355
Mead, M., 203, 211, 219
Mednick, S. A., 330, 336
Meehl, D. E., 303
Megargee, E. I., 303
Mehrabian, A., 267, 289–90, 346
Meichenbaum, D., 356, 361, 366–67
Melzack, R., 258
Michael, L. B., 158
Michels, R. M., 314
Miller, D. L., 224
Miller, G. A., 139, 283
Miller, H., 308
Miller, I. W., 135, 339
Miller, N. E., 39–40, 42, 44–48, 278
Miller, S., 135

Milewski, A., 141
Mischel, W., 207, 222, 232, 259, 260, 261, 356
Mishler, E. G., 283
Mitchell, K. M., 368
Modiane, H., 211
Money, J., 203
Monson, T. C., 234
Montagu, A., 124, 166, 168, 273
Moore, S., 276
Moos, R. H., 237
Morris, D., 128, 136, 216
Morris, J. D., 225
Mosak, H. H., 103, 109, 256, 319
Moss, H., 257, 267
Mosteller, F., 191
Moyer, K. E., 273, 274
Moynihan, D. P., 191
Mullener, N., 210
Murray, H., 23, 71–77, 89, 143, 266, 305–6
Murstein, B. I., 270, 305–6, 308
Mussen, P. H., 120, 133, 203, 207, 211, 214, 266

N

Naditch, M. P., 158
Nakamura, C. Y., 179
Neale, J. M., 359
Neisser, U., 149, 150
Neugarten, B. L., 220, 221, 224, 225
Newcomb, T., 10
Nicoll, M., 355
Nidich, S., 351
Nisbeth, R. E., 249
Norman, W. T., 11, 12
Notz, W. W., 246
Nowlis, D. P., 354

O

O'Leary, K. D., 296
O'Leary, S. G., 296
Oltman, J., 336
O'Neal, E. C., 277
Opton, E. M., 253, 255
Orme-Johnson, D. W., 350
Owens, W. A., 347

P

Pardes, H., 370
Paschke, R. E., 274

Passini, F. T., 11, 12
Paul, G. L., 296
Pavlov, I., 39, 40
Peck, R. F., 221
Pederson, D. R., 183
Percell, L. P., 357
Perdeck, A. C., 146
Perris, C., 333
Pervin, L. A., 47
Phares, E. J., 50, 158, 300, 340, 341
Piaget, J., 49, 71, 180–81, 182, 190
Pines, H. A., 300
Platz, A., 370
Polster, E., 362
Polster, M., 362
Poorkaj, J., 224
Pratt, C. L., 269
Pribram, K., 35, 139
Prociuk, T. J., 158

Q

Quintard, G. A., 303

R

Radin, N., 192
Rafferty, J. E., 306
Rafman, S., 133
Raimy, V., 368
Raphelson, A. C., 242
Rau, L., 231
Ray, A., 160
Reese, S., 246
Renner, V., 268
Rheingold, H., 126, 184
Rhine, W. R., 192
Ribble, M., 123, 124
Riecken, H., 275
Rimm, D., 357
Ripley, H. S., 314
Ritter, B., 360
Robins, E., 327, 336
Robins, L., 336
Rogers, C., 77–80, 86, 89, 279–80, 368
Rohrberg, R., 371
Rokeach, M., 142, 156, 354–55
Rosen, J. L., 224
Rosenberg, M. J., 157
Rosencrantz, P. S., 219
Rosenthal, R., 292

Ross, D., 207, 266, 275, 276
Ross, S. A., 207, 275, 276
Roth, M., 328, 329
Rotter, J., 39, 49, 50, 51, 157–58, 299, 306–8, 365
Roussel, J. S., 259
Rubin, Z., 270
Ruble, D. N., 179
Russakoff, L. M., 320
Rychlak, J., 18, 25

S

Sackett, G. P., 128, 269
Sadock, B. J., 350
Salmon, D., 113
Sanford, M., 10
Sanford, R. N., 156
Santrock, J. W., 192
Sarason, I. S., 235, 259
Sata, S. L., 327, 328, 333, 338
Schacter, S., 158–59, 192, 249, 256, 266–67, 277, 330
Scheibe, K. E., 340
Scheid, A. B., 368
Scheier, I., 293
Scher, J., 324
Schiff, B. B., 246
Schmauk, F. J., 159
Schranger, J. S., 339
Schroder, H. M., 244
Schroeder, S. R., 244
Schulsinger, F., 330, 336
Schwartz, G. E., 340
Scoggins, W. F., 224
Scott, J. P., 273
Sealey, A. P., 215
Sears, R. R., 35, 189, 191, 199, 204, 231
Sechrest, L., 111
Seeman, W., 301, 351
Seligman, M. E. P., 260
Selman, R. L., 213
Senn, D. J., 269
Sensibar, M. R., 276
Shaffer, M., 296
Shannon, J., 284
Sheldon, W. H., 15
Shulman, B. H., 103, 104, 107, 109, 128, 197, 271, 329, 330
Sigel, I., 257
Sigueland, E. R., 141
Silberman, C. E., 193

Silverman, J., 340
Singer, B., 369
Singer, J. E., 158, 256
Singer, M. T., 330
Skinner, B. F., 39–40, 41, 43, 44
Slater, E., 329
Slavney, P. R., 338
Sloane, R. B., 369
Smith, J. A., 327
Smith, O., 202
Smith, P., 202
Smith, R. E., 371
Smock, C. D., 210
Snow, R. E., 293
Snyder, M., 234
Sokolov, E. W., 139
Solomon H., 296
Solomon, R. L., 138
Sommer, R., 285
Sontag, L., 166, 167
Sordoni, C., 158
Sorrentino, R., 243
Sousa-Poza, J. F., 371
Spence, B. P., 368
Spence, D. P., 257
Spiegel, J., 287–89
Spinelli, D. N., 139, 140
Spitz, R., 123, 124, 126, 183
Sroufe, L. A., 133
Srull, T. K., 236
Stampfl, T. G., 49, 357
Stang, D. J., 257, 283
Staub, E., 275, 340
Staw, B. M., 246–47
Stayton, D. M., 123, 127
Stendler, C., 134, 187–91, 266
Stephen, F. F., 283
Stevens, S., 15
Strang, R., 202
Su, W. H., 370
Sullivan, H. S., 10, 65–71, 89, 314–15, 328, 329
Sundberg, N., 294, 304, 312, 315, 347
Sundstrom, E., 236
Sushinsky, S. W., 246
Swanson, B. W., 327

T

Tate, B. G., 358, 359
Tatsuoka, M. M., 304

Tautermarova, M., 181
Teddlie, C., 236
TerVrugt, D., 183
Thelen, M. H., 208
Thibaut, J., 275
Thomae, H., 225
Thomas, A., 16, 165
Thorndike, E. L., 39–40
Tiger, L., 273
Tinbergen, N., 146
Toman, E. B., 183
Tomkins, S., 285
Tompkins, W. T., 168
Tresemer, D., 220
Trexler, L. D., 362
Tripodi, T., 308
Truax, C. B., 368
Tudor, T. G., 260
Turasky, B., 340
Turiel, E., 213–14
Turner, J. S., 168, 169

U

Ude, L. K., 300
Ullman, L. P., 45–47, 337, 356
Updergraff, R., 276
U'ren, R. C., 199

V

Valins, S., 159–60, 252
Velner, J., 331
Venables, P. H., 331
Verbeck, E., 338
Vernon, P. E., 304
Veroff, J., 243–44, 305
Vogel, S. R., 219
Vogler, R. E., 300

W

Waechter, G. H., 202
Waekmean, D. B., 135
Walk, R. D., 173, 174
Wallace, R. K., 350–51
Walters, E., 133
Walters, R., 49, 193, 207–8, 266, 267
Washburn, S. L., 128
Watson, J. B., 40
Watson, S., 204
Weatherford, M. J., 141
Weil, E., 370

Weiner, B., 52, 241, 285
Weininger, O., 186
Weinstein, J., 255
Weiss, J. M., 296
Welsh, G. S., 303
Wenger, M. A., 260
Werboff, J., 186
Werner, H., 70, 180
Wertheimer, M., 6
White, R., 134, 136, 190, 217, 244, 317–18
Whitehorn, J., 315, 349
Whiting, W. M., 131, 186
Wiens, A. N., 314
Wiesel, T. N., 139, 140
Wiggins, J. S., 13, 207, 268, 271, 312
Wilkins, W., 369
Williams, R. J., 164
Wilkie, F., 224
Windle, W. F., 166
Wine, J., 300
Winokur, G., 327
Winter, D., 240, 243
Winze, J., 358
Witkin, H. A., 156, 178, 180, 214, 249, 257, 267–68, 340, 341, 370
Wolfensberger-Hässig, C., 133
Wolk, S., 300
Wolpe, J., 49, 357, 360
Woodruff, D. S., 221
Worchel, S., 236
Wright, C. L., 360
Wright, F. A., 202
Wright, M. E., 259
Wortman, C. B., 249
Wulf, F., 155, 177
Wynne, L. C., 330

Y

Yalom, I., 273
Yarrow, 184–86
Yates, A. J., 337
Yerkes, R. M., 258

Z

Zarrow, M. X., 273, 274
Ziegler, H. P., 273
Zimbardo, P. G., 266, 275
Zook, E. A., 204
Zubek, J. P., 139

subject index

A

Accomodation and assimilation,
180–81
and development of competence,
190
Achievement motivation, 35, 238–44
sex differences in, 242
social and cultural factors in, 242
Adaptive Behavior, 118–43
motives and, 121–43
perceptual system and, 119–120,
146 ff.
physiological needs in, 120–21
stress adaptation, 130–32, 186
Adler's theory of personality (Individual Psychology), 101–11
assessment technique, early recollection, 319–20
change, 110
development, 103–6
dynamics, 106–8
gemeinschafts gefuhl (social interest), 101
life style, 102–4, 108
life tasks, 106
mistaken attitudes, 109
movement, 106–8
psychopathology, 109–10
striving, 101–3, 106, 108
Adolescence, 208–15
cognitive development and morality, 213–14

differentiation of motives, 208–11
identity, 210, 214–15
peer group and, 210–11
sexuality, 211–12
Adulthood, 215–23
love and family, 215–16
motive differentiation in, 215–21
stability and differentiation of self,
221–23
vocation, 219–20
Affect hunger, 182–83
Affiliation, 127–28, 243, 245
dynamics, 268–73
emotional components of, 272–73
friendship, 269
love and marriage, 269–70
sexuality, 270–72
Aggression, 128–29
according to Kelly, 114
and non-humanistic behavior,
277–78
categories, 274–75
cognitive labeling, 277
dynamics of, 273–78
frustration-aggression hypothesis,
31–32
hostile aggression in Kelly, 114
in psychoanalysis, 31–32
modeling and, 275–76
sexual factors, 276–77
Allport's theory of personality, 80–83
development, 82–83
functional autonomy, 82

Allport's theory (*cont.*)
  proprium, 82
  traits, 81
Androgeny, 205
Anger (see Aggression)
Antisocial personality, 334–38
Anxiety
  and attachment, security, 132–34
  and courage, 187
  and curiosity, 133
  and goal behavior, 259–63
  and unfamiliarity, 133
  basic (Horney), 63
  castration anxiety, 30
  defense against, 260–61
  Dollard and Miller, 44, 46
  existential, 86
  Freud's theory of, 33
  Kelly, 113–15
  reduction of by cognitive interven-
    tion, 160
  separation, 132–34, 187
  stranger and strangeness, 187
  Sullivan, 68–69
Arousal, 257–58
Assertiveness training, 357
Assessment of personality, 292–320
  behavioral methods, 295–97
  cognitive context for behavioral as-
    sessment, 297
  cognitive techniques, 308–14
  early recollection, 319–20
  integrated profile, 311
  interview, 314–17
  life history, 317–19
  measuring person and situation,
    293–94
  objective tests, 300–304
  of locus of control, 299
  projective techniques, 304–8
  social learning theory methods,
    299–300
Attachment motive, 121–29
  aggression, 128–29
  anxiety and security, 132–34
  contact in the development of,
    124–27
  development of, 181–84
  differentiation of, 127
  love, affiliation and sexuality,
    127–28

B

Behavior theories of personality,
    39–52
  abnormal responses according to
    Skinner, 46
  assessment techniques, 295–97
  reinforcement theory (Dollard and
    Miller, Skinner), 39–49
  social learning theories, 49–52
  technique of behavior change, 48,
    356–62
Behavior modification of therapy,
    356–62
  a subset of cognitive therapy,
    360–62
Belief system, altering, 354–55
Biochemical individuality, 164
Birth order
  and dependency, 104–5
  in Adler, 104–5

C

Change of behavior and personality,
    346–73
  altering belief systems, 354–55
  behavior modification, 356–62
  cognitive styles and, 369–73
  cognitive therapy, 346–48, 354,
    360–62, 365–66, 368
  in Adler's theory, 110
  in existential theory, 87, 346
  in Freud, 34, 346
  in Horney, 64–65
  in Kelly, 115
  in reinforcement theory, 45–49, 346
  in Rogers, 79
  in Sullivan, 2
  meditative and hypnotic methods,
    350–54
  psychotherapy, 362–69
  social learning theory of, 346
  somatic methods, 349–50, 354
  trait theories, 346
Character, 16–17
Closed minds (see Open and closed
    minds)
Cognitive assessment techniques,
    308–14
  intelligence testing, 311
Cognitive balance, 137

Cognitive complexity, 308–9
Cognitive consistency, 157, 249–52
Cognitive development, 180–81
  Piaget's stages, 180–82
Cognitive dissonance, 157, 249–52
Cognitive intervention
  in coping with emotions, 253
Cognitive motive, 136–42, 244–52
  and creativity, 141
  and preference for complexity, 141
  curiosity, novelty and, 140
  development of, 180–81
  differentiation of, 142
  intrinsic motivation, 244–47
Cognitive styles, 155–58
  and behavior (personality) change,
    369–73
  and dependency, 267–68
  and emotional arousal, 257
  and goal-directed behavior, 247–49
  and identity, 214–15
  and person, situation interaction,
    236–37
  and psychopathology, 340–42
  cognitive consistency, 157
  development 177–79
  locus of control, 157–58
  psychological differentiation, 156
  scanners, 155–56
  sharpeners and levelers, 155, 178
  tolerance for ambiguity, 156–57
Cognitive theory
  and social learning, 50–52
  assessment techniques of, 308–10
  cognitive neurological model in
    Freud, 35–36
  complexity-simplicity, 112
  in Jung, 61
  in Murray, 76
  interpretation of outcome research
    in psychotherapy, 365–66
  of emotion, 158–61
  of personality, 146–61
  of personality change, 346–48,
    360–62, 365–66
  of personality in Adler, 101–11
  of personality in Kelly, 111–15
  of psychopathology, 323–25
  of somatic meditation and hypnotic
    intervention, 354
  of Sullivan, 65, 71
Cognitive therapy, 346–48, 360, 362,
  365–66

Collective unconscious, 56
Communication, 281–90
  measurement of, 281–90
  non-verbal, 285–90
  personality style, 281–83
  reciprocal effects between commu-
    nicator and receiver, 283
  verbal, 283–85
Competence motive, 134–36
  achievement, 135
  development of, 187–91
  differentiation of, 135
  opportunistic species, 135
  play and, 190
Conflict
  according to Dollard and Miller,
    44–46
  and the basic motives, 280–81
  cognitive perspective, 280–81
  in Adler, 107–8
  in Lewin, 96
  in psychoanalysis, 33
  motivational, 278–81
Consistency in personality, 232–34
  individual differences in, 237
Courage, 187

D

Defense
  cognitive interpretation, 260–61
  mechanisms in psychoanalysis,
    32–33
  perceptual, 8, 9
Dependency, 266–68
  and birth order, 267
  and cognitive style, 267–68
  and competence, 187–90
  and gender, 267
  and modeling, 267
Development of personality, 164–227
Differentiation, 95–96, 97
  in personality development, 170
  of motives, 201–2, 209–11, 215–21
Discrepancy hypothesis, 141

E

Early recollection, 319–20
Effectance motive, 134

Emotion
  and cognitive style, 257
  cognitive aspects of, 252–57
  cognitive theory of, 158–61
  differentiation of, 258–63
  FAP Program (Ekman), 150–51
  in affiliation, 272–273
  in motivated behavior, 252–63
  mediated by perception (Adler),
    107
Erikson's theory of personality, 36–39
  psychosocial stages, 37–38
Existential theories of personality,
    83–89
  behavior change, 87
  Dasein, 84–87
  dynamics, 85–86
  existential anxiety, 86
  phenomenology, 84
  psychopathology, 86
  structure, 85

F

Facial Affect Program (FAP) of emo-
    tions, 150–51, 286–87
Families,
  love and, 215–16
  successful, 217, 219
Family climate
  in motive development, 191–92
Family constellation, 104
Fear (see Anxiety)
Field theory (see Holistic-field theory)
Form perception, development of,
    171–73
Friendship, 209
Frustration, 258
Functional autonomy, 82, 83

G

Gemeinschaftsgefuhl, 101
  in old age, 227
  (see also Social interest)
Gender identification, 203–6
  and vocation, 219
  cognition and learning in, 204
Generativity, 216

Gestalt theory
  applied to personality, 92–101
  law of perceptual organization, 6–7
Goal
  distorted, 106–7
  final or dominant, 106, 152–54
  guiding ideal as goal, 102

H

Hierarchy
  in Angyal's theory, 98
Histrionic personality (see Hysterical
    personality)
Holistic-field theory of personality,
    92–101
  Angyal (Holistic theory), 98–100
  autonomy and homonomy, 98
  conflict, 96
  differentiation, 95–96
  Goldstein (organismic theory),
    92–94
  level of aspiration, 96
  Lewin, 94–98
  life-space, 95–96
  satiation, 96
  valence-vector, 96
Horney's theory of personality, 61–65
  basic anxiety, 63
  compensatory strategies, 63–64
  movement, 62
  neurotic claims, 62–63
  psychopathology, 62–64
  search for glory, 63
  self, real, ideal and actual, 61–62,
    64–65
  self-realization, 62, 65
  structure and dynamics, 61–62
Humanistic behavior, 277–78
Hypnosis, 353–54
Hysteria
  Angyal's view, 99–100
  Sullivan's view, 69
Hysterical personality, 338–40

I

Identification, 202–8
  and observation, 206–8
  cognition and learning in theories,
    207–8

gender, 203–6
self-classification and, 202–5
sex-typing, 205–6
Identity, 210, 214–15
and cognitive style, 214–15
Ideographic laws, 18–19
I-E Scale, 157–58, 249, 299–300
Imitation (see Observational
learning)
Implosion therapy, 49, 357–58
Incomplete Sentence Blank (ISB),
306–8
Independence
care/respect, 189–90
development, 187–90
Infant stimulation, and stress adapta-
tion, 186
Intelligence testing, 310–11
Interview methods of assessment,
314–17
Intrinsic motivation, 244–47

J

Jung's theory of personality, 55–61
constituent parts (ego, personal unconscious, collective unconscious, persona), 56
contents (complexes and archetypes, attitudes, functions),
56–57
equivalence, 58
integration of opposites and harmony, 60
introversion & extraversion, 57
personality types, 57
self-actualization, 58

K

Kantian views, 25
Kelly's theory of personality, 111–15
aggression and hostility in Kelly,
114
assessment techniques of, 308–9
change, 115
construing, 111
dynamics, 113–14
personal construct, 111–15
psychopathology, 114

Role Repertory Construct Test,
112, 113, 311, 314
structure and development, 111–13

L

Learning dilemma, 42, 44
Leibnizian views, 23–25
Levelers and sharpeners, 155, 178,
257
Level of aspiration, 96
Life History assessment, 317–19
Life space, 95–96
Life style, 102–3, 104, 108, 109
and motives, 199–200
stability into old age, 225
Lockeau views, 23–25
Locus of control, 157–58, 249
and psychotherapy, 371–72
assessment of, 299–300
Love, 127–128
and family in adulthood, 215–16
and marriage, dynamics of, 269–70
generativity, 216

M

Maladaptive personality, 323–43
cognitive explanation of, 323–25
motive systems and, 323–26,
340–43
personality disorders, 327–43
person and situation in, 325–30
Masculine protest in Adler, 104
Mastery need, 134–36
Maternal caretaking variables,
184–87
Mate selection, 270
Minnesota Multiphasic Personality
Inventory (MMPI), 301–4
Modeling (see also Observational
learning, 49)
and dependency, 267
assessment of, 297–99
expectancy, 50–51
freedom of movement, 50–51
imitation (see Observational
learning)
observational learning, 49
of aggression, 276–79
Morality
cognitive theory of (Kohlberg, Piaget), 213–14

Motivations, 121–43
  cognitive style in goal behavior,
    247–49
  conflict in, 278–81
  dynamics of goal-behavior, 230–52
  in emotions, 257–63
Motives, 121–43
  and anxiety, 187
  and life style, 199–200
  and psychopathology, 323–26
  as organized by perception, 121,
    148–51
  conflict in, 280–81
  development of, 180–91
  differentiation in adolescence,
    209–11
  differentiation in adulthood,
    215–21
  differentiation in goal behavior,
    239
  differentiation in preadolescence,
    201–2
  four basic systems, 142–43
  hierarchically organized, 152–54,
    306
  measurement of, 240–45
  relation of Murray's needs to, 143
  social influences on, 191–93
Movement (in goal behavior)
  according to Adler, 106–8
  according to Horney, 62
Murray's theory of personality, 71–77
  dynamics, 72–76
  ego ideal, 72
  establishment, proceeding and se-
    rial programs, 71, 72, 75
  need-integrate and press, 72–76
  needs, list of, 73
  psychopathology, 76
  structure and development, 71–72
  thema, 72–76
  Thematic Apperception Test, 76
  themes, 71

N

Need
  definition of, 121
  for contact, 121–29
  for mastery, 134–36
  for safety, 129–34
  for sensory variation, 136–42
  need perception hypothesis, 8, 150
  physiological, 120–21
  potential, 50, 51
Nomothetic laws, 18–20

O

Observational learning, 49–50
  a comparative perspective, 207–8
  and identification, 206–8
Obsessive-compulsive personality,
    324–34
  Angyal's view, 99–100
  in Sullivan, 69
Old age, 223–27
  differentiation of motives in,
    225–26
  preservation and decline of person-
    ality in, 224
  stability and integration of self in,
    225
Open and closed mind, 142, 156,
    354–56
Operant conditioning, 43
  scheduling reinforcement, 43
Operant techniques of behavior mod-
    ification, 358–59

P

Paranoid personality, 327–29
  in Sullivan, 69–70
Perception, 8
  and defense, 8, 9
  chronic sets of, 8, 9
  directing emotions, 107
  form, 171–73
  narrowing of (Kelly), 114
  need and, 8
  private, according to Adler, 107
  selective inattention (Sullivan), 66
  selectivity in, 9; according to Adler,
    107
Perceptual learning in personality
  development, 170–74, 181
Perceptual system, 119–20
  and personality development,
    170–74
  as organizer of personality struc-
    ture, 145–46
Peer relationships
  in adolescence, 210–11
  in motive development, 192–93

Personal constructs (Kelly), 111–15
  and psychotherapy, 366–68
  complexity, 112
  constriction, dilation and imperme-
    ability, 114
  function, 112
  range of, 112, 114
Personality
  adolescence, 208
  adulthood, 215–23
  and cognitive styles, 177–79
  and motives, 180–91
  as hierarchically organized, 98, 151
  as unity (Goldstein), 92–93,
    (Adler), 102
  cognitive differentiation in, 196
  character as a construct of, 16–17
  culture, 3
  definition of, 9–11
  development of, 164–227
  dynamics, 230–90
  importance of study of, 3
  learning, 3
  old age, 223–27
  pattern, 3
  perceptual programs in, 170–74
  postulates for a theory of, 4–9
  preadolescence, 201–8
  prediction of, 3
  prenatal foundation, 164–69
  role as a construct of, 12–13
  selectivity, 3, 66
  structure, 145–61
  style as a construct of, 17–18
  temperament as a construct of,
    14–16
  trait as a construct of, 11–12
  type as a construct of, 13–14
  types (Jung), 57
Personality disorders, 327–43
  antisocial personality, 334–38
  cognitive style and, 340
  hysterical personality, 334–40
  motive systems in, 340–343
  obsessive-compulsive personality,
    332–34
  paranoid personality, 327–29
  schizoid personality, 329–32
Personality inventories, 300–304
Personality style
  and communication, 281–83
  in emotional expression, 255–56

Person and the situation paradigm,
    230–37
  and psychopathology, 325
  assessment of, 293–94
  cognitive style formulation, 236–37
Personology, 23
Phenomenology, 84
Play, 190
  in the growth of competence, 190
Power, 243, 245
Preadolescence, 201–8
  differentiation of motives, 201–2
Primitivation, 97
Private logic according to Adler, 107
Projective techniques, 304–8
  Incomplete Sentence Blank (ISB),
    306–8
  Thematic Apperception Test
    (TAT), 305–6
Proprium, 82
Psychoanalysis, 25–36
  cognitive-neurological model, 35–36
  cognitive translation of defense
    mechanisms, 261
  conflict, 33
  defense mechanisms, 32–33
  dynamics of personality, 31–33
  id, ego, superego, 26–30, 32–33
  libido and aggression, 31–32
  personality structure, 26
  primary and secondary process, 26
  primary or pleasure principle, 26
  psychopathology, 33–34
  psychosexual stages of development
    (oral, anal, phallic, latency,
    genital), 28–31
  secondary or reality principle, 27
Psychological differentiation, 156, 249
  and psychotherapy, 370–71
Psychopathology (see Maladaptive
    personality)
Psychotherapy, 362–69
  behavior of the therapist, 368, 372
  cognitive therapy, 346–48, 354,
    360–62, 365–66
  outcome research in, 365–66
  personal constructs and, 366–68
  social learning approach to, 365
  social learning techniques of behav-
    ior modification, 359–60
  what changes in, 363–65

R

Reinforcement
  theory, 39
  primary and secondary reinforcers,
    42
  operant conditioning, 43
  value, 50
Religious conversion and experience,
    355
Repressors and Sensitizors, 161,
    255–56
Response, 41
  cue, 41; as drive stimulus, 44
  generalization of, 42
  habit family hierarchy, 42
  habit strength, 41
  learning dilemma, 42, 44
  primary and secondary drive stim-
    uli, 44
  stimulus, 41; generalization of, 42
Roger's theory of personality, 77–80
  behavior change, 79
  fully functioning person, 78–79
  phenomenal field, 77–78
  psychopathology, 78–79
  self-concept, 77–78
  structure, development and dynam-
    ics, 77–78
  unconditional positive regard, 79
Role, 12–13
Role Repertory Construct Test, 112,
    113, 308–9
  score on as a guide to psycho-
    therapy, 366–68

S

Satiation, 96, 256–57
Scanners, 155
Schemata, 9
  development of, 174, 177
Schizoid personality, 329–32
School and cultural influences
  on motive development, 193
Security motive, 129–34
  and anxiety, 187
  and courage, 187
  attachment and anxiety, 132–34
  development of, 184

  differentiation of, 132–34
  stress adaptation, 130–32
Selective perception, 3, 8, 9
  according to Adler, 107
  determined by personality, 5
  perceptual defense as selectivity, 9
  selective inattention, 66
  selective processing in personality,
    153
Self
  actual, 64
  actualization (Jung), 58; (Gold-
    stein), 93; in old age, 226–27
  as an organizer of development,
    196–99
  as an integrator of personality
    structure, 154
  classification and identification,
    202–5
  creative self in Adler, 104, 106
  definition, from a cognitive view,
    196–97
  differentiation of, 197–99
  guiding self-ideal, 102–3; in old
    age, 226–27
  ideal (idealized image), 62, 64, 65
  organizer of adolescent motive dif-
    ferentiation, 209–11
  real, 61, 62, 64, 65
  resistant to change, 347–48 (see
    also Proprium, 82)
  self-concept (Rogers); 77–78
    (Adler), 103
  self-system (Sullivan), 66–67
  self-training in Adler, 106
  stability and differentiation in
    adulthood, 221–23
  stability and integration in old age,
    225
Self-esteem, 193–99
  and motives, 199
Self-theorists, 54–89, 196
  comparison of key concepts, 89
Sensitizers and repressors, 161,
    255–56
Sensorimotor integration, 173–74
Sensory deprivation, 137–39
  and preference for complexity,
    141–42
Sensory-variation need, 136–42
  and preference for complexity, 141

Sets
 chronic, 8, 150, 260
 perceptual, 9
Sex-typing, 205–6
 cognitive (self-classification) theory,
 205–6
 observational learning theory, 206
 psychoanalytic theory, 205
Sexuality, 127–28
 and aggression, 276–77
 cognitive factors in, 272
 dynamics of, 270–72
 in adolescence, 211–12
Sharpeners and levelers, 155, 178, 257
Sibling constellation
 in motive development, 192
Situation
 in Murray, 72
 in Rotter, 50
Social interest, 101
Social learning theory of personality,
 49–52
 assessment techniques, 197–300
 cognitive social learning theory of
 Rotter, 50–52
 modeling and observational learning, 49
Somatic methods of behavior change,
 349–50, 354
Stress
 adaptation, 130–32, 186
 and psychopathology, 325–26
 coping and cognitive intervention,
 160–61
Striving
 as a pattern, 103
 as psychopathology, 106
 for significance, 101
 to give meaning to life, 108
Style, 17–18
Sullivan's theory of personality, 65–71
 anxiety, 68
 change, 70
 developmental stages (6), 68
 empathy, 66, 68
 mode of thought (prototaxic, parataxic, syntaxic), 66
 personifications, 67
 psychopathology, 69–70
 selective inattention, 66
 structure and dynamics, 66–69
Systematic desensitization, 49, 357

T

Temperament, 14–16
 and physique, 16
 Hippocrate's theory, 14
 Kretschmer's theory, 14–15
 Sheldon's theory, 15–16
 Thomas and Chess' theory, 16
Thematic Apperception Test (TAT),
 176, 305–6
 cognitive scoring of, 307
Token economy, 358
Tolerance for ambiguity, 156–57
Traits, 11–12
 assessment of, 300–4
 in Allport, 81
 source, 12
 surface, 12
Transcendental Meditation (TM),
 350–52
Type, personality, 13–14
 molar, 14

U

Uniqueness,
 Adler's theory, 110–11
 in personality, 3

V

Valence-vector
 in Lewin, 96–97
 in Murray, 74–75
Visual cliff, 173–76
Vocation, 219–20
 gender identification and, 219–20

Y

Yerkes-Dodson Law, 258